Surviving Sexism in Academia

CW00506760

This edited collection contends that if women are to enter into leadership positions at equal levels with their male colleagues, then sexism in all its forms must be acknowledged, attended to, and actively addressed. This interdisciplinary collection—*Surviving Sexism in Academia: Strategies for Feminist Leadership*—is part storytelling, part autoethnography, part action plan. The chapters document and analyze everyday sexism in the academy and offer up strategies for survival, ultimately "lifting the veil" from the good old boys/business-as-usual culture that continues to pervade academia in both visible and less visible forms, forms that can stifle even the most ambitious women in their careers.

Kirsti Cole is an Associate Professor of Rhetoric, Composition, and Literature at Minnesota State University. She is the faculty chair of the Teaching Writing Graduate Certificate and Masters of Communication and Composition programs. She has published articles in *Feminist Media Studies*, *College English*, *Harlot*, and *thirdspace*, and her collection *Feminist Challenges or Feminist Rhetorics?* was published in 2014. Her work ranges the intersections of writing studies, social media, and gendered rhetorics.

Holly Hassel is a Professor of English and Gender, Sexuality and Women's Studies at the University of Wisconsin–Marathon County. She has co-authored the introductory women's and gender studies textbook *Threshold Concepts in Women's and Gender Studies* with Christie Launius. She is currently editor of the journal *Teaching English in the Two-Year College*.

"Cole and Hassel's book captures in rich dimension that which is often caricatured as 'women agitating'—telling the truths about their lives in the academe, traversing the rocky terrain of sexist, racist, anti-queer, and motherhood-unfriendly institutional structures. It offers cause for celebration, as their resilience and creativity shines through, offering both strategy and sustenance for the hard work of change that faces us all. With wit and bravery, intelligence and insight, the women in this collection resourcefully buck the constrictions of university life, to make it something altogether more feminist, and simultaneously, more human."

—**Susan Marine**, *Associate Professor of Higher Education, Women's and Gender Studies Faculty Affiliate, Merrimack College*

"*Surviving Sexism in Academia* is a powerful—and practical—compilation of research and personal narratives written for and by women in the academy. The chapters cut across academic silos seamlessly. From STEM to Philosophy, from faculty governance to state politics, the chapters offer insights into the world of women academics—be they tenured, tenure track, contingent, or staff. Poignant personal stories are interwoven with engaging empirical analyses and conceptual chapters to show that *surviving sexism* is an act of resistance—and a powerful form of feminist activism within the academy."

—**Ashley E. Nickels**, *Assistant Professor of Political Science at Kent State University, Co-Editor of* Feminist Pedagogy, Practice, and Activism: Improving Lives for Girls and Women

"Becoming clear—and telling the truth—about experiences of gaslighting, marginalization, exclusion, and other forms of direct and structural trickery within the academy are essential elements of healing and undoing their effects. In *Surviving Sexism in Academia: Strategies for Feminist Leadership*, Cole and Hassel hold gracious and courageous space for colleagues to share their nuanced and intersectional lived experiences; all while powerfully imparting enabling strategies for (re)claiming rightful places as practitioners, teachers, and scholars within higher education."

—**Jason Laker**, *Professor in the Department of Counselor Education and Ed.D. Program in Educational Leadership at Lurie College of Education, Salzburg Fellow at San José State University in California*

"This book draws in the reader through the power of stories. The contributors recount their experiences 'surviving sexism in the academy' illuminating the ways in which some dimensions of identity, from race to motherhood, intensifies individual and institutional sexism. They also share insights that serve as points of entry for the empathetic reader who wants to engage reflectively and critically deploy feminist strategies to dismantle persistent sexism and other forms of oppression in the academy. This book will jolt awake anyone who believes gender discrimination is a thing of the past. The authors reveal the many ways gender is (still) employed in the academy to regulate behavior and maintain power; yet they also provide practical examples of how to lead feminist action to produce real structural change in the academy."

—**Susan V. Iverson**, *Professor and Coordinator, Higher Education Leadership, School of Education, Manhattanville College*

"*Surviving Sexism in Academia: Strategies for Feminist Leadership* is a timely compilation of personal experience and empirical research that illuminates the on-going issue of sexism in the academy. Countering the post-feminist narrative that dominates current social discourse, these compelling chapters cover the gamut of higher education contexts, utilizing powerful counterstories to suggest provocative approaches to leading for change."

—**Amy Aldous Bergerson**, *Director of the Student Success and Empowerment Initiative and Professor in the Department of Educational Leadership and Policy, University of Utah*

Surviving Sexism in Academia

Strategies for Feminist Leadership

Edited by Kirsti Cole and Holly Hassel

Routledge
Taylor & Francis Group

NEW YORK AND LONDON

First published 2017
by Routledge
711 Third Avenue, New York, NY 10017

and by Routledge
2 Park Square, Milton Park, Abingdon, Oxon, OX14 4RN

Routledge is an imprint of the Taylor & Francis Group, an informa business

© 2017 Taylor & Francis

The right of Kirsti Cole and Holly Hassel to be identified as the authors of the editorial material, and of the authors for their individual chapters, has been asserted in accordance with sections 77 and 78 of the Copyright, Designs and Patents Act 1988.

All rights reserved. No part of this book may be reprinted or reproduced or utilized in any form or by any electronic, mechanical, or other means, now known or hereafter invented, including photocopying and recording, or in any information storage or retrieval system, without permission in writing from the publishers.

Trademark notice: Product or corporate names may be trademarks or registered trademarks, and are used only for identification and explanation without intent to infringe.

Library of Congress Cataloging-in-Publication Data
Names: Cole, Kirsti, editor. | Hassel, Holly, editor.
Title: Surviving sexism in academia : strategies for feminist leadership / edited by
    Kirsti Cole and Holly Hassel.
Description: New York, NY : Routledge, 2017. | Includes bibliographical references.
Identifiers: LCCN 2016056737 | ISBN 9781138696839 (hardcover : alk. paper) |
    ISBN 9781138696846 (pbk. : alk. paper) | ISBN 9781315523217 (ebook)
Subjects: LCSH: Sexism in higher education. | Sex discrimination in higher
    education. | Women in higher education. | Feminism and education.
Classification: LCC LC197 .S87 2017 | DDC 378.0082—dc23
LC record available at https://lccn.loc.gov/2016056737

ISBN: 978-1-138-69683-9 (hbk)
ISBN: 978-1-138-69684-6 (pbk)
ISBN: 978-1-315-52321-7 (ebk)

Typeset in Goudy
by Apex CoVantage, LLC

We dedicate this volume to the role models, mentors, and allies who have helped initiate difficult but necessary conversations about equity, diversity, and inclusion.

We are inspired by the colleagues whose institutional change work has improved working conditions every day.

We are inspired by the advocates in our academic disciplines.

We are inspired by the grit and courage of the scholars who challenge the academic publishing status quo.

And we are inspired by the friends with whom we drink wine and build community in person and on social media to recharge for the daily social and emotional labor that feminist leadership requires.

We dedicate this book to you all.

Contents

Figures and Tables

Figures

Tables

Introduction

"I'm Afraid This Will Hurt Me": Addressing Sexism in Higher Education

"Feminism is a movement to end sexism, sexist exploitation, and oppression. . . . To end patriarchy (another way of naming the institutionalized sexism) we need to be clear that we are all participants in perpetuating sexism until we change our minds and hearts, until we let go of sexist thought and action and replace it with feminist thought and action."

—bell hooks, *Feminism Is for Everybody: Passionate Politics* (2000, viii–ix)

Kirsti

May 15, 2015, marked the end of my second year in a controversial administrative role. It's with a sense of irony that I use the term "controversial" because I'm the director of writing across the curriculum at my institution. The value of writing for students on a college campus would seem to be the least controversial issue possible, but the politics at play, the egos at work, and the sometimes shocking disregard for my expertise in the face of my mid-30s femaleness made the position one that was at best challenging and at worst abusive. After a particularly rough day in which someone whom I trusted told me that I was too scary to be approachable, I posted the following to Facebook (see Figure 0.1):

Figure 0.1 A Call for Help

My public persona in this post, though casual, was carefully cultivated. I used "thing" a lot. I was a little flippant. But the morning before I posted it, I was sobbing, I was ranting, I was looking for different jobs, any jobs, that were not here and these people. So I reached out for help. Over half of my Facebook friends are colleagues, nationally and internationally, and I wanted to crowdsource the almost irreconcilable divide between being openly bullied by a 60+-year-old man for daring to express my opinion and being asked to take on major leadership and lobbying roles at my institution simultaneously. We know that academic culture notably relies on women to do the bulk of the invisible labor (service work) while at the same time denying them authority, credibility and, in many cases, collegiality (Masse and Hogan 2010). When I became visible, taking on a leadership role on my campus, the abuse that I received correlated directly to skill sets traditionally associated with leaders: decision making, problem solving, initiative. I did what any good leader would do: I asked questions, I organized a team, I got moving. I was immediately characterized as a bitch attempting to thwart the work of the union. I was immediately labeled "not a team player"—which is as good as a death knell in a union environment. Or at least that's what I thought. What happened shocked me: I was offered two more leadership roles IN the union that were even more public. I was so confused and hurt, so unsure of myself, that I need to reach out to my colleagues at other institutions. The response I received was overwhelming and a testament to the power of social media as a networking tool (see Figure 0.2).

Figure 0.2 We Need to Talk about This

As Masse and Hogan (2010) point out in their collection on service work in the academy:

> The invisibility of [service work] is repeatedly reproduced . . . [w]hen viewed from a gender and class perspective, service emerges as the well-trained handmaid of the academy, quietly going about schools' work while other forms of labor call more loudly for attention.
>
> (1, 3)

It was Adrienne Rich who demystified service work as work and made it a feminist issue; however, it is an issue that results in the continued reliance on "the unpaid altruism of women" (1979, 4). And like Masse and Hogan, what I discovered in my brief, informal survey was that many women experience the exact same kind of abuse when the step beyond quiet altruism and move into and call attention to the institutional labor practices (see Figure 0.3).

Holly sent me a private message and we began a conversation which resulted, a mere 10 days later, in a call for papers (CFP) for this collection. We posted the CFP around 10:00 a.m. on May 26th, and by 1:00 p.m. we had a tentative offer from an academic press seeking the opportunity to publish this collection. The response to the CFP was and remains exhilarating, thought provoking, exhausting, and full of anxiety.

Figure 0.3 Apparently This Is Pretty Common

Holly

Kirsti and I had been acquainted in person only relatively briefly—through shared service on a national committee in the U.S. charged with feminist work in the field of writing studies—and only recently had we talked in person, at a professional meeting two months prior to the social media conversation Kirsti cites. Like Kirsti, my own professional pathway has taken me in recent years into leadership roles—six years as chair of a state-wide, 13-campus women's and gender studies program and two years as a department chair's representative to the steering committee of our institution's state-wide governance body, representing academic departmental values and priorities to a governance body concerned with policy and practice within the institution.

Academic trade publications like *Inside Higher Ed* and *The Chronicle of Higher Education* regularly feature news stories documenting how sexism, misogyny, and patriarchal assumptions pervade academia (Jaschik 2014; Baker 2014; Mason 2009) and sexist assumptions in student perceptions of teaching effectiveness and professional participation (Mulhere 2014; Marlowe 2012). My own experience of sexism within academia matches the published documentation on the topic. As a new faculty member and Ph.D. recipient at age 27, tenured at 33, and full professor at 38, a period during which I gave birth to two children, I had taken on increasingly demanding leadership roles over multiple years, and my experiences mirrored Kirsti's: my work in multiple governance committees as the only female member was questioned or silenced; my foray into governance as a faculty representative included multiple experiences where the votes and opinions of my female senator colleagues were questioned, dismissed, or rejected, including a gender-coded and bullying email "rereading" rational objections to a problematic policy change as "ALARMIST" and "unbecoming." Simultaneously, I was appointed to coordinate the reaccreditation process of my 13-campus, state-wide institution and serve on a range of institutional, system-wide, and national professional organizations. Like Kirsti, I struggled to understand the mixed messaging I was experiencing. The messages seemed to read both "take on more" and "keep working harder" while simultaneously saying "don't be so loud" and "don't ask for so much" and "you're not in charge."

Examples abounded in professional and social spaces: a male colleague and Facebook friend repeatedly commented only on images on my Facebook profile of a prominent tattoo and once suggested that an *Inside Higher Ed* story I shared about women executives in higher ed being made uncomfortable by "boys' club activities" like hot tubbing invited him to imagine me in a hot tub with the chancellor. Simply my presence as a female body (see Cohen et al. 2011 on the concept of identity threat), junior by a decade or more to the male-dominated demographic at "leadership meeting seemed to destabilize 'business as usual' (e.g. at a faculty representative meeting lunch with ten men at a table and me, plus a male Regent member of our system's governing body). An informal dinner meeting with colleagues from another campus included a confession about how one colleague was familiar with my work from comments by colleagues on his campus—and I'm not a "bitch like he had heard." I was painfully aware of a dozen subtle verbal and non-verbal communications of the sexual politics of interpersonal behavior (see Henley and Freeman 2011)[1]: inappropriate physical familiarities, invitations to share (literally) alcoholic beverages ["oh, this {*stronger, higher alcohol concentration*} one is good—here, share mine!"].

On the department level, I was publicly accused of "hostility" from a male colleague merely after questioning an unsupported assertion in a department meeting. The department election results in which our executive committee (the group who evaluates tenure, promotion, and retention files) resulted in a female-dominated committee caused an outraged male faculty colleague to email the entire department, complaining, "Academic feminists, like other power-hungry groups I could name, use the language of fairness and inclusion when they are in a subordinate position. When they are in a dominant position, they drop such language, never to pick it up again." Though this volley resulted in an ongoing and vituperative email discussion that involved the Office of Equity, Diversity, and Inclusion as well as two subsequent grievances, the critiques (and subsequent wounds) linger in the department culture and the words have power to undermine the authority, credibility, and effectiveness of the elected women voted in by the nearly 140 voting members of the department.

Like Kirsti, I have turned to social media to express my frustrations—venting with colleagues and friends in private groups and, in particular, funneling the experiences I've had in navigating academic leadership into social media satire. In particular, Rebecca Solnit's concept of "mansplaining" so suffused my workplace environment that it became part of the social media presence of a rotating group of female colleagues as "Allow Me To Mansplain This To You," with "ripped from the headlines" status updates, which has accumulated over 1,700 followers since its inception (see Figure 0.4–Figure 0.8).

Figure 0.4 Ripped from the Headlines of an Email Thread on a Faculty Governance Issue

Figure 0.5 Selective Apologizing

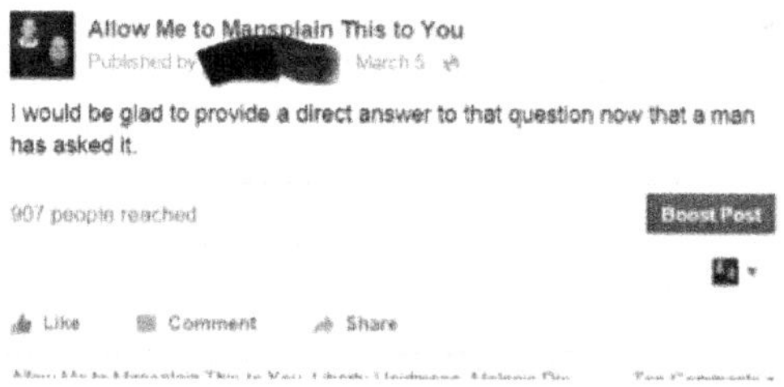

Figure 0.6 Now that a Man Has Asked

Figure 0.7 Why Are You Ladies So Paranoid?

Figure 0.8 #leadership

These "subversive" social media strategies are satisfying and, for better or worse, can become a substitute for directly calling out or identifying sexism, microaggressions, or even clear misogyny. Besides the all-too-frequent result of "gaslighting," ["Wait? What problem? What do you mean? Oh, I didn't take it that way!"], sometimes the effort simply to demonstrate the problem *exists* is as exhausting as seeking to ameliorate it. For women of color, this work is even more labor intensive. As a result, women in leadership roles find themselves belittled, demeaned, and exhausted. In the end, moving from indirect resistance to tackling the issues in a formal way—through scholarship and research—seemed a natural next step.

The Current Context(s)

Like the broader framework that hooks first provided in 1990 and again in 2000, academic culture reflects institutional and patriarchal sexism. Sociologist Allan Johnson, in his now-classic definition, more specifically describes patriarchal society as one that is "male dominated," male centered, and male identified, and it is within these definitions that we situate this project, an effort to unpack how patriarchal and masculinist values are replicated within academia, how these values shape the environment and the outcomes of the work that takes place within it, and how, as importantly, collective action is needed to transform it. And it seems that now, more than ever, questions about gender, sexuality, and power are at the forefront of our national consciousness.

Though we were working on this project prior to the November 2016 U.S. presidential election, we can't help but reflect on how the dynamics of identity have been an intense part of the pre- and post-election public discourse. Pre-election, national media coverage focused on Donald Trump's disposition and character, his disrespect of women, racial minorities, and people with disabilities; and his xenophobia; Hillary Clinton was examined and scrutinized for her health, her ability to lead, her credibility, and her social class. Post-election, news story after opinion column attempt to dissect what has been called the biggest "upset" in presidential election history—with special attention paid to gender, race, social class, and region as factors that explain the electorate and, for some pundits, its apparently inexplicable voting patterns. Politics as a rough game—and thinkpieces have abounded in efforts to "autopsy" and understand the hows and whys of Donald Trump's election—with theories about White supremacy, socioeconomic status and class resentment, and misogyny chief among the explanations. For us, the election sits at the intersections of the pain and fear that moved us to put out a call for this collection. A startling uptick in bullying and harassment incidents have been reported across the nation in elementary schools, junior high schools, and high schools (SPLC 2016), the Southern Poverty Law Center is tracking over 500 reported hate crimes (SPLC 2016), and a surge of misogynist hatred is being tracked across social media outlets. Women and girls are experiencing fear and strong negative emotions about their self-worth based solely on the results of the Electoral College. We have yet to understand fully what the election of an openly misogynist candidate means, but the devastating loss of our potential first female president[2] has had a measurable impact on the perceived acceptability of sexism both inside and outside the academy.

In the context of this national dialogue, then, we find it helpful to theorize about the intersections of gender, power, and labor. As Michael Kimmel argues,

> When we say that we live in a gendered society we imply that the organizations of our society have evolved in ways that reproduce both the differences between women and men and the domination of men over women. Institutionally, we can see how the structure of the workplace is organized around demonstrating and reproducing masculinity.
>
> (2016, 16)

This is signaled most strongly by the *values* that are associated with femininity and masculinity and those that are privileged within larger society. Allan Johnson explains how

> cultural descriptions of masculinity and the ideal man [are stated] in terms that closely resemble the core values of society as a whole. These include qualities such as control, strength, competitiveness, toughness, coolness under pressure, logic, forcefulness, decisiveness, rationality, autonomy, self-sufficiency, and control over any emotion that interferes with other core values (such as invulnerability). . . . In contrast, qualities such as cooperation, mutuality, equality, sharing, compassion, caring, vulnerability, a readiness to negotiate and compromise, emotional expressiveness, and intuitive and other nonlinear ways of thinking are all devalued and culturally associated with femininity and femaleness.
>
> (2005, 7)

More specifically, academia, as a particular type of workplace, reproduces a wide range of patriarchal values—such that the values described by hooks are especially influential.

Johnson's definition is particularly resonant when aligned with an examination of academia and the academic hierarchy more broadly. High status is assigned to jobs that are research intensive, and we can see that those jobs simultaneously have low contact with students (particularly undergraduates) and are privileged for their association with rank, status, funding, and high publication output. The peer-review process is by necessity a zero-sum game, competitive, and available to those who have low teaching loads and high resources as well as mentorship and networking with those faculty at research-intensive institutions (see Hassel and Giordano 2013). Further, peer review is ostensibly part of the academic hazing process of withstanding often-withering criticism and rejection, while single authorship/lead authorship is the default assumption in the publishing game, and collaborative work is viewed with skepticism. Service is characterized by the collaborative, team-based workflow that Johnson indicates is associated with femininity while it is simultaneously low in the currency of the tenure and promotion economy (see Misra 2011). To choose the life of an academic is to enter into an institutional "game" that has been structured to value masculine "ways of doing"—and remodeling that structure requires specific, deliberate, and often exhausting institutional change work.

The "slow professor" movement complements our current project because it provides principles and strategies for a potentially repurposed feminist framework for academic governance. This edited collection aims to provide resources and strategies for doing that institutional change work. In a way, *Surviving Sexism in Academia* also supports some of the recently published texts that attempt to push back against the patriarchal hierarchies integral to academic life. Maggie Berg and Barbara K. Seeber, in their 2016 book *The Slow Professor: Challenging the Culture of Speed in the Academy*, target the corporatization of the contemporary university and argue that by emulating the values of the Slow Movement, academics can push back against the "erosion of humanistic education" (Preface). While the three main activities of the academy are research, teaching, and service, Berg and Seeber focus on teaching, research, and collegiality. Collegiality has been critically analyzed by professional organizations such as the American Association of University Professors (see "On Collegiality as a Criterion for Faculty Evaluation") as an invalid criterion for tenure (partly *because* it was typically a code for "old boys' club" decision making). Berg and Seeber repurpose collegiality, along with the rhetoric of the "slow food" movement to invite readers to reimagine collegiality as collaboration and intentional relationship building, essentially applying feminist values to a previously sexist practice.

The focus on collegiality is a subtle but effective way to begin unpacking the implicit sexism of the academic working life. Berg and Seeber argue that "corporatization has imposed an instrumental view of not only time but also each other" (1214). Citing Jane Tomkins, who argues,

> You can't put a good conversation on your vita [and as a result] there's no intellectual life left in universities, or precious little, because people are too busy getting ahead professionally . . . to stop and talk to each other.
>
> (2001, 21)

Isolation is a clear component of the corporate university, which works directly against a collegial, intellectual environment. Berg and Seeber argue that "in the 'new regime' of connectivity, we are losing our place" (1252). They encourage, instead, an immersion in local cultures, in our home departments; a pushback against the "ghost places" of our department hallways (1252). They recognize that we "are losing a sense of collegiality but [are uncertain] about how to bring it back" (1278). Any attempt to overcome the problems with collegiality must focus beyond the individual to avoid discrimination and instead take into account the social and political context of the workplace. As such, Berg and Seeber suggest a shift in how we perceive collegiality in higher education: "Collegiality needs to be seen as 'an ongoing social accomplishment'" (1365) that "acknowledge[s] that workplace loneliness is real . . . that loneliness is not the result of [individual] deficiency in social intelligence . . . [that] a fractured climate is not the result of individuals failing their responsibilities" (1380–1382). Human relationships that acknowledge emotion, need, and vulnerability, and that create spaces in our professional lives for such human traits, are necessary for a collegial, non-discriminatory, and non-sexist environment.

Academic work structures and timelines not only match up with the values of a neoliberal economy but also are often *exacerbated* by the timelines of an academic career, based on the traditional assumption about doctoral study and tenure line work. With high status assigned to tenured versus contingent employment, Ph.D. holders are encouraged to move quickly and in lockstep through undergraduate and graduate education, entering directly into the most demanding period of academic careers, the pre-tenure years (see Hewlett 2007). As graduate education and early employment align most directly with the most fertile reproductive years for women (the average age of Ph.D. graduation is 34; see Mason 2012), the expectations of this lockstep timeline is predicated on the "unencumbered workers" model, one in which reproductive labor is handled by a partner who concentrates largely on the domestic realm while the primary wage earner concentrates on "his" professional aspirations: as Ann Crittenden observes,

> The ideal worker is "unencumbered," that is, free of all ties other than those to his job. Anyone who can't devote all his or her energies to paid work is barred from the best jobs and has a permanently lower lifetime income.
>
> (2001, 87–99)

Responsibilities for reproductive labor place additional demands on, in particular, women with children. With many fields remaining largely male dominated (such as philosophy, engineering, and others), stereotype threat perpetuates this low rate of participation of women (see "What Is Stereotype Threat" 2015; Steele 2010) while identity threat (see Cohen et al. 2011) creates a sometimes hostile environment that deters women (and men of color) from participation.

Finally, non-physical forms of what bell hooks calls "patriarchal violence" prop up a system based on adversarial forms of communication and "logic" divorced from ethics or nuance. As hooks (2000) notes, "Patriarchal violence . . . is based on the belief that it is acceptable for a more powerful individual to control others through various forms of coercive force" (61). Fields that reward combative communication styles and an academic environment that privileges assertive and critically oriented approaches to getting work done are deterrents to participation from all but the most privileged few.

As feminist academics, then, we are aware of the scholarship on sexism and academia: in higher education leadership, women are making substantial inroads occupying about a quarter of university presidencies (Moltz 2011). However, women remain underrepresented in critical leadership roles (Dominici, Fried, and Zeger 2009). Simultaneously, the mere presence of recognizable "female" bodies can result in a dismissal of the need to attend to or even acknowledge sexism whether overt, covert, or through microaggressions. As a result, sexism in the academy can lead women to question the contentious discourse that surrounds them: they may be attacked personally for leading from one direction while simultaneously recognized and awarded for their leadership from another, resulting in a dissonance that discourages them from further participation in leadership positions. They may experience a kind of "culture switching" between feminist communities that are safe spaces and the broader academic communities—or male-dominated organizational bodies, units, or departments—which employ hostile, dismissive, or sometimes bullying and harassing strategies to resist change, silence dissent, or reinforce traditions and conformities that reward the usual patriarchal values.

Scholars inside and outside academia have sought to identify as well as strategize for these barriers (Williams and Dempsey 2014; Solnit 2014; Ward and Wolf-Wendel 2012; Connelly and Ghodsee 2011). We hope this collection adds to feminist change work to build on the strengths of academia's function as an institution—while making it a more hospitable site for all.

Our Shared Perspective

We can think of no better way to highlight the issues surrounding the rampant sexism in academia than an email we received from a potential contributor (see Figure 0.9):

Figure 0.9 Of Course [I Am] Afraid

Fear, danger, damage, backfiring. Academic culture produces and sanctions experiences that cause tears, anger, stomachaches, sleepless nights, or nightmares. Further, pushing back against sexism in any setting can result in a feeling that the sexism may be institutionally sanctioned (which was Kirsti's experience in the WAC Director position). What do you say about something you also fear? What will coming out against sexism in your workplace mean for you? How will people react? There aren't good answers to these questions, but we hope that this collection will lay the groundwork for strategic and plausible responses. Perhaps the simple acknowledgment of the pervasiveness of sexism across disciplines, from contingent labor to the highest levels of administration, will help. How will it affect one's credibility?

Holly's answer to our potential contributor was framed within the arguments from *Presumed Incompetent: The Intersections of Race and Class for Women in Academia* (2012), edited by Gabriella Gutiérrez y Muhs, Yolanda Flores Niemann, Carmen G. González, and Angela P. Harris. Based on their work, Holly's recommendation was methodological:

> I'm not sure whether there is a completely risk-free way to undertake discussion of these issues, but my initial thinking is that pieces that blend personal experience with empirical data and theory can mitigate some of the claims of observations being anecdotal.
>
> (Hassel 2015)

Like many of the researchers in humanities and social sciences fields, we rely on the feminist tradition valuing personal experience grounded in data and theory. The responsibility does not lie with the author alone, however:

> In terms of professional implications, we're committed to a rigorous review process with a high quality university press, so we hope that the final product is well-received and reviewed so it will serve contributors well on the job market or in the tenure and promotion process.
>
> (Hassel 2015)

The peer-review process marks the high standards to which we hold our publications, and as editors of a collection with such a sensitive and potentially problematic subject, our commitment to our authors is to subject our text to rigorous scrutiny.

Ultimately, this collection contends that if women are to enter into leadership positions at equal levels with their male colleagues, then sexism in all its forms must be acknowledged, attended to, and actively addressed. To achieve this goal, we have assembled an interdisciplinary collection which we imagine as part storytelling, part autoethnography, part action plan. A necessary element for us in the initial stages of our discussion about this collection was that it be as diverse as possible—diverse in perspectives, in methods, in voices; in types of institutions; in contributor backgrounds. We chose to include chapters that tackle sexism in the academy from not only a range of intellectual, disciplinary, and methodological approaches but also a diversity of tone, style, genre, and conventions. Though we are acutely aware that there are a number of perspectives, experiences, and disciplines missing from our chapters, we believe that as an entry point into this conversation our authors are representative of a rich diversity: they come from countries around the world, they come from a broad range of different disciplines, they are administrators, graduate students, and faculty at every rank. Though they predominantly self-identify as women, their experiences as researchers, teachers, students, mothers, friends, mentors, writers, scientists, and artists reach across spectrums of identity to provide what we believe to be an accessible tool for understanding and confronting sexism in higher education. The authors in this collection negotiate everyday sexism in the academy and offer up strategies for survival. The collection will "lift the veil" from the good old boys/business-as-usual culture that, we contend, continues to pervade academia in both visible and less visible forms, forms that can stifle even the most ambitious women in their careers. We address the following questions:

- What does sexism in the academy look like? What forms does it take? How does it oppress (or inspire, or invigorate, women?)
- How best do we address sexism in the academy?
- What communication strategies challenge or reinforce sexist cultures in academia?
- How do we work to dismantle the politics of dress, from too "mannish" to too "sexy"?
- What is the role of survival strategies such as male identification and co-optation (in which women who advance to leadership roles in the field sometimes adapt by physically altering their bodies or conduct?
- How have women contributed to sexism by perpetuating the exact same aggressive identity policing that they may have bemoaned in their early careers on junior colleagues?
- What feminist leadership strategies are supported by evidence?
- How does overt or coded misogynist language such as "bossy," "loud," "hysterical," "histrionic," "noisy," "nosy," "bitchy," "uncivil," and "uncollegial" get deployed to "put girls in their places"?
- How do gender non-conforming academics participate in binary cultures that privilege masculinized/male-coded way of leading and trivialize or dismiss feminized/feminine/female-coded approaches?
- How might race, ability, class, or sexuality shape experiences of sexism in the academy?

Answering the Questions

In Section 1: **Mapping the Challenges**, we begin by defining what sexism is in the academic context. We give an overview of the ongoing challenges faced by women in academia, identifying the far-ranging, institutional, structural, and ideological barriers that shape women's experience as academics and as they move into leadership positions. In Part 1, "**Dis/Locations**," our authors chart the physical spaces of sexism. Heather Maldonado and John Draeger open the section and draw on work from several distinct literatures to develop a taxonomy of sexism in the academy. They illustrate with examples and discuss why each form of sexism in higher education is wrong. They offer strategies for addressing sexism in its many forms at both the personal and institutional levels. In Chapter 2, Kirsti Cole, Holly Hassel, and Eileen Schell discuss shared governance in its many forms and the ways in which women in governance positions can negotiate the confounding and difficult gender dynamics of these historically male spaces. In Chapter 3, Shelly Schaefer Hinck, Salma Ghanem, Ashley Hinck, and Sara Kitsch state that examining reasons why current and past female administrators have chosen to serve in leadership roles and how they make decisions concerning leadership style as well as understanding more fully what concerns that female faculty have in moving to administrative roles is necessary if changes in gendered academic leadership roles are to occur. In Chapter 4, Heather Hill-Vásquez and Laurie Ann Britt-Smith explore how contemporary female-authored self-help books and advice pieces for would-be women leaders ignore, obscure, and leave unvoiced the sexist constructions and systems of power which they ostensibly set out to address. In Chapter 5, Hawa Ghaus-Kelley and Nathan Durdella track the meanings that community college women executive leaders ascribe to critical learning moments in their educational leadership practices. In the final chapter of "Dis/Locations," E-K. Daufin provides a critical discourse that calls out how pervasive, usually unconscious White supremacist (racist) and patriarchal (sexist) assumptions in academia oppress Black women in the United States Professoriate.

Part 2, "**Disciplinary Contexts**," showcases scholarship from not only a wide range of academic disciplines including the hard and social sciences, the arts, and the humanities, but also an international context, extending the locations of our study outside the United States. In Chapter 7, Diane Rodriguez-Kiino, Yuko Itatsu, and Yuko Takahashi shine a bright light on women and gender bias in Japanese higher education. In Chapter 8, Melissa Kozma and Jeanine Weekes Schroer unpack Philosophy's White male problem and the discourse that sustains it. They articulate why the common mainstream solutions tend to fail or falter: A masculinist line of thinking not only controls the narratives around sexism in Philosophy but also determines the criteria by which we judge what kinds of narratives, strategies, and understandings are legitimate. In Chapter 9, Susan Diab draws from her work in the visual arts, asking if writing about the attempt to make the work and tackling the difficulties that gives rise to can make it easier to get on and make the piece? In other words, if finding a voice for those aspects of internalized sexism which hold us back gives rise to a new space—or a clearing in the thicket of problems—in which creative responses to sexism can be born. Returning to the sciences, in Chapter 10, Kathryn Northcut tells not just her story but also the story of so many women academics in humanities departments who started out in STEM fields one or more decades ago. Far too many of us accepted harassment and discrimination as "signs" that we would fare better on other parts of campus. In Chapter 11, Heather Rosenfeld gives us an exciting play on traditional academic genre by writing and drawing a critical ethnography on feminism and sexism in the field of geography in zine (comic) form. The last two chapters tackle questions of labor and the profession within the field of writing studies. In Chapter 12, Jennifer Heinert and Cassandra Phillips describe specific strategies designed to move feminized labor toward feminist working conditions. These strategies begin with broad feminist practices but develop into deliberate and specific actions that can challenge and destabilize traditional academic value systems. In the final chapter of "Disciplinary Contexts," Krystia Nora, Rochelle Gregory, Ann-Marie Lopez, and Nicole Williams give an overview of several Rhetoric and Composition scholars who have published about how family-rearing is an enriching and rewarding part of their academic success. They report on the findings from anonymized surveys and select interviews with more than 200 Rhet/Comp tenure track mothers.

Part 3, "**Embodied Gender**," focuses on the critical role of the body in discourses of sexism. Chapter 14, by Saba Fatima, explores epistemic insecurity experienced by young women of color in not having their lived reality validated by colleagues and the academia at-large. In Chapter 15, Mary Louise Gomez addresses two key questions: How do ethnicity and social class shape the experiences of sexism faced by Latina staff members of color at a large, Midwestern university? What might be done to address the sexism and accompanying racism and classism experienced by these individuals? In Chapter 16, Yvette Lapayese presents the narratives of mother-scholars in higher education to illuminate what the relationship between maternal and academic identity implies for those of us in it. How do we survive? How can maternal identity be a source of empowerment in intellectual spaces? In Chapter 17, Carol Glasser discusses her experience managing and reacting to sexism from students in her first year as an assistant professor at a medium-sized state university. She ties these experiences to the patterns of patriarchy in the academy and society more broadly and discusses how such situations might be parlayed into teaching moments that can help students unlearn their sexist behavior. Finally, in Chapter 18, Katie Manthey concludes by focusing on the implications of adhering to "professional" dress codes, which are especially complex for people who exist outside of the White, male, able-bodied, young, cisgender, thin mold and reflects on what this means to the larger academic community, specifically in the context of feminist microaggressions that police bodies.

Section 2: **Feminist Strategies for Action** is an action plan that focuses on changes to the material conditions (Part 1) and on the ideological conditions (Part 2) that promote and support sexism in the academy. In Chapter 19, the first chapter under "**Changing Material Conditions**," Laura Jennings and Lizabeth Zack draw on social movements literature to describe their work mobilizing for change around sexist campus decision making disproportionately affecting women faculty, staff, and students. In Chapter 20, Molly Niesen, Safiya Umoja Noble, Christine Quail, and Michelle Rodino-Colocino discuss how the maternal wall constitutes a significant barrier for women faculty. In Chapter 21, Diane Hodge situates an autoethnographic example of transforming personal experience into action, taking the form of real structural change in the academy.

Three subsequent chapters unpack the role of mentoring as a strategy for material support and advocacy. In Chapter 22, Jen Almjeld, Meg McGuire, and Kristine Blair discuss a three-generation mentoring lineage spanning nearly ten years and serving women at various stages in their careers. They explain how these unofficial mentoring relationships grew out of relaxed conversations outside the institution walls and are rooted co-equally in academic and personal concerns. Further elaborating on the importance of mentorship, in Chapter 23, Missy Skurzewski-Servant and Marilyn Bugenhagen offer an exploration of the lived career journey of women in upper administrative positions (i.e., dean level or higher) in higher education. Through semi-structured interviews, the women expressed the barriers they encountered along their career path, their involvement in mentoring relationships, and the meaning of these relationships. In Chapter 24, Kristen Moore, Lisa Meloncon, and Patricia Sullivan begin with a brief overview of the Women in Technical Communication's history, structure, and projects, highlighting its cross-institutional, cross-platform design. They then provide an overview of mentoring as it has traditionally been theorized and implemented and illustrate how our model differs from existing models and, specifically, the ways that it addresses institutional structures that perpetuate sexism.

Part 2, "**Changing Ideologies**," begins with Chapter 25, by Anna Grigoryan—part storytelling and part autoethnography—that reflects on current literature in sociology and psychology and reveals the various forms of gender bias and sexism that pervade the workplace and hinder women's rise to leadership positions. Chapter 26 by Jessica Moriarty critically examines through lyrical reflection her autobiographical and researched experiences with academic life, specifically completing an autoethnographic doctorate. She identifies autoethnography as an empirical methodology that synthesizes autobiography and social critique in order to resist, and also change, dominant academic discourse. In Chapter 27, Elise Verzosa Hurley, Amanda Wray, and Erica Cirillo-McCarthy seek to make the discursive power of interruption as rhetorical tactic visible and aim to give voice to the diverse ways in which feminist academics choose to use interruption in order to navigate and negotiate sexist, misogynist, patriarchal, and exclusionary practices in various academic contexts. Other ideological tactics are emphasized in Chapter 28, where Karla McCain examines three lessons she learned from overcoming the harassment and bullying rooted in explicit sexism she experienced from a senior male colleague as a new tenure track faculty member through the lens of the accumulation of advantage and disadvantage.

Closing the final section, chapter contributors unpack rhetorical and collective strategies for feminist leadership. In Chapter 29, Bre Garrett, Aurora Matzke, and Sherry Rankins-Robertson, through feminist and embodiment theories, offer brief labor narratives of three female administrators in order to examine the following questions: How does history, experience, theory, and pedagogy influence and inform women's ways of "making it" in administration (Ballif, Davis, and Mountford 2008)? How might collective action across institutions influence and inform women as administrators? In Chapter 30, Sara Hillin argues that the feminist academic leader can make use of the techniques of rhetorical listening and invitational rhetoric, as articulated by scholars Krista Ratcliffe and Sonja and Karen Foss, to make inroads that build trust and encourage initiatives that foster students' and colleagues' success. In the final chapter, Fran Sepler discusses the surprising prevalence of "quiet" woman-on-woman bullying and suggests adaptive strategies for individuals and institutions. We close the book with an Infographic intended to synthesize the collection into "takeaways" that are distilled for easy discussion and consideration by readers.

Notes

1 For example, "In observations of incidents of touch in public urban places, higher-status persons did touch lower-status persons significantly more. In particular, men touched women more, even when all other variables were held constant. Not only behaviors, but also social interpretations of behavior associate power/dominance with touch; as Hall noted, "People's beliefs, anecdote, self-report, [and] observational studies of socioeconomic status and age, and one true experiment favor either the power-privilege idea or the idea that relative dominance increases as a consequence of touch initiation."

2 Hillary Rodham Clinton won the popular vote by over 2.5 million votes as of December, 1, 2016 (Cook Political).

References

Crittenden, Ann. (2001). *The Price of Motherhood: Why the Most Important Job in the World is Still the Least Valued.* New York: Henry Holt and Company.

Johnson, Allan G. (2005). *The Gender Knot: Unraveling Our Patriarchal Legacy.* Philadelphia: Temple University Press.

Kimmel, Michael. *The Gendered Society.* Oxford: Oxford University Press, 2016.

Masse, Michelle, and Katie Hogan. (2010). *Over Ten Million Served: Gendered Service in Language and Literature Workplaces.* Albany: SUNY Press.

Moltz, David. (2011). "What Women (Presidents) Want: Four female academic leaders use panel to call for more representation at the top of academe." Inside Higher Ed. 25 March 2011. https://www.insidehighered.com/news/2011/03/25/presidents_discuss_changing_roles_of_women_in_academic_leadership

Rich, Adrienne. (1979). "Toward a Woman-Centered University." In *On Lies, Secrets, and Silence: Selected Prose 1966–1978,* 125–155. New York: Norton.

Tompkins, Jane and Gerald Graff. (2001). "Can we talk?" In *Professions: Conversations on the Future of Literary and Cultural Studies,* edited by Donald Eugene Hall, 21. Chicago: University of Illinois Press.

Acknowledgments

We are grateful to all of those who have made this work possible. We thank our editor at Routledge, Samantha Barbaro, and editorial assistant, Athena Bryan, for their confidence in and commitment to this project. We are grateful to the authors who contributed their time, research, and expertise to this project, collecting our stories, our arguments, or data, and our theories to create a book that will be a resource both inside and outside the classroom.

We intend this book to be a tool for activism—and we want to acknowledge the real human suffering that is reflected in these pages and in the academy. Discrimination, bias, and exclusion are a daily reality for many teacher-scholars, and they leave us wounded. We hope that this book will be a source that sustains readers in their quest for stability and security in their academic vocations.

As such, we also acknowledge those who have sustained us, and those whose actions galvanized our work on this collection.

Section I

Mapping the Challenges

Dis/Locations

Surviving Sexism in Academia

Identifying, Understanding, and Responding to Sexism in Academia

Heather Maldonado and John Draeger

Introduction

The existence of sexism in academia is well-documented (Basford, Offermann, and Behrend 2014; Stainback, Ratliff, and Roscigno 2011). Students, faculty, and staff report that sexist interactions on campus impact their psychological well-being, interpersonal relationships, and career trajectories (Berg 2006; Fields, Swan, and Kloos 2010; Goh and Hall 2015; Risman 2004). Sexism manifests itself in academia through the underrepresentation of females in STEM disciplines, overrepresentation of women in contingent faculty, and pay inequities (Hanappi-Egger 2013; Lerner 2000; Robbins and Robbins 2006; Roos and Gatta 2009). It also contributes to the underrepresentation of women in senior leadership roles (Fitzgerald 2014; Monroe, Chiu & Comm Status Women Profession 2010).

Conventional wisdom, especially in the often progressive world of higher education, holds that "sexism is bad." While we believe that sexism is bad, we also believe that the "badness" is related to a wide range of behaviors, attitudes, and institutional arrangements. We contend that formulating an effective response to sexism requires understanding the precise nature of the harm. The purpose of this chapter is to heighten awareness of sexism in its many forms and effectively challenge sexism when it occurs.

It is important to note that this chapter does not provide a comprehensive study of the problem. The complex issues of intersectionality (Harris 2012) and masculinity (Connell 1995) require separate treatments. We do note, however, that women outside of their campus's majority group will likely experience sexism in ways complicated by other elements of their identity such as race, ethnicity, religion, ability, gender identity, or sexual orientation. Further, we must acknowledge that parity among women on college campuses is as important an issue as women's parity with men, and we must work to improve the representation and the experiences of women from minority groups. Finally, we recognize that the performance and policing of masculinity impact men's behaviors in multifaceted ways and, thus, play a role in the sexism occurring in academia.

Unpacking "Sexism Is Bad"

This section unpacks some of the complexity surrounding the claim that "sexism is bad." Sexism is perpetuated by both individual "bad actors" and institutional "bad structures." Giddens (1984), for one, argues that understanding structure and agency cannot be established separately from each other. Structures, such as institutions of higher education, cannot be analyzed without recognizing that the academic structure is (re)produced by the actions of the people in those structures. Family medical leave policies, for instance, are part of an institution's operational framework. Those same policies are also the products of the agency of those working within the academy. Differences in family medical leave policies can be used to show how the personal agency of higher education administrators, faculty, and staff can be used to influence the structure of the academy in ways that may either enable or constrain gender equity. This chapter focuses on the actions of individuals within larger structures.

Individual sexist behaviors can range from blatant to more subtle violations. We recognize, for example, that women in academia are victims of sexual assaults, sexual harassment, and other forms of blatant hostility. While we would not want to dismiss the seriousness of these behaviors, we are as concerned about subtle behaviors that might not even seem worthy of notice to many. Sue et al. (2007) explore microaggressions that are "often unconsciously delivered in subtle snubs or dismissive looks, gestures, and tones. These exchanges are so pervasive and automatic in daily conversations and interactions that they are often dismissed and glossed over as being innocent and innocuous" (273). Sue et al. further subdivide microaggressions into microassaults (e.g., hurtful name calling), microinsults (e.g., insensitive comments), and microinvalidations (e.g., dismissing a woman's lived experience). We will discuss each in relation to higher education in the next section.

Both overt and subtle forms of sexism can be either hostile or benevolent (e.g., protective paternalism) although both can be traced back to attitudes about power, gender differentiation, and sexual intimacy (Glick and Fiske 1996). Examining hostile sexism (e.g., antagonistic attitudes and acts that subjugate women), benevolent sexism (e.g., a subjectively positive orientation toward women that adopts chivalrous or paternalistic lens), and microaggression (e.g., small—often seemingly unintentional—verbal and non-verbal acts that target and demean a group) allows for a deep analysis of gender oppression in the academy. While sexism in all its forms is "bad," it is bad in different ways. Surviving sexism in the academy requires appreciating these differences.

Our brief discussion of sexism has uncovered four dimensions of analysis. First, sexism can be the result of large-scale structural forces and individual actions. Second, sexist behaviors can be more or less overt with the consequences being more or less severe. Third, sexist behaviors can be more or less intentional (e.g., harms are intentionally inflicted or inadvertently insensitive). Especially at the microaggression end of the spectrum, men (and women) might be unaware of the fact that they are dismissing and thereby invalidating women's experiences. Fourth, sexist behavior can be hostile, benevolent, or somewhere in between.

The academy has procedures in place to deal with blatant cases of sexism. Men who violently assault women on campus, for example, would likely face legal action and termination of employment. However, given formal policies and the "politically correct" nature of the academy, there are many things that most academics have the good sense not to do or say in public. For example, female campus leaders who vigorously argue for their views or assert their authority might be considered as "bitchy," but it is more likely that she will be publically referred to as "bossy" or "pushy." It might be hard for men to believe that they have engaged in sexist behavior because they do not interpret their actions in those ways. Because a man may not have intended to give offense, it may be difficult for him to recognize that his actions were even inadvertently harmful. In contrast, women who have been on the receiving end of such dismissals are likely to take it as obviously true that sexism has occurred. Indeed, questioning whether sexism has actually occurred or asking for a justification of her view is often taken to be a denial of her lived experience and itself a microaggression. Yet it may still be the case that sexism has not, in fact, occurred, or at least that the case is open to reasonably different interpretations. Unlike blatant violations, the consequences of microassaults tend to be less severe and vary by degree. They are far less likely to result in legal action or even a call to human resources. However, like environmental pollution where the acts of individuals might seem trivial and the effects might seem minimal, the accumulation of seemingly small harms contributes to widespread gender pollution that should not be ignored (Draeger, 2016).

Our overarching view is that formulating an effective response to sexism requires understanding the precise nature of the harm. The next section considers some of these ambiguities and interpretive issues in more detail.

Cases of Sexism in the Academy

This section locates examples of sexism in the academy within our proposed taxonomy. We identify four subtypes of individual behavior ranging from blatant discrimination to microaggression. Each subtype will have an example, description of institutionalized responses, and the general climate in higher education toward the subtype. We will also attempt to classify each example as either cases of hostile or benevolent sexism. Many of the examples, however, resist easy classification. We believe this tells us something important about the nature of sexism and the challenges facing strategies to confront it. Even in seemingly clear cases, for example, there is room for interpretation. Individuals may disagree, for example, about standards of "unacceptability" and their application in particular cases. On the one hand, it is clear that women should not be fondled in the workplace. On the other hand, interpretations of what constitutes inappropriate touching is likely to vary (e.g., shoulder, arm, small of the back, breast). This sort of complexity is worth remembering as we consider strategies for surviving sexism. If it is not clear to all concerned that sexism has even occurred, then it becomes even more difficult to address the behavior. If even blatant cases of sexism, including those clearly covered by institutional policies, can be difficult to address then this underscores the difficulty as we consider more subtle forms.

The following examples are meant to be illustrative rather than exhaustive.

Example A: A search committee discusses not hiring a female candidate for an Associate Director of Student Life position because she mentioned her small children during the interview and the committee is concerned that she will not be able do the job during the late hours sometimes required of the position.

Example A represents acts that are blatant forms of sexism, which have become increasingly infrequent in higher education due to legislation such as Title VII of the 1964 Civil Rights Act and Title IX of the Educational Amendments of 1972 which provided legal standing to contest sex-based discrimination, increased policy education on campuses, and improved reporting procedures and complaint handling due to recent court verdicts and Department of Education investigations. The current climate of the academe openly discourages and responds to these subtypes of sexist acts, and most people are aware that such behaviors are unacceptable. While the existence of a legal remedy has not eliminated their occurrence, blatantly illegal sexist acts represent one end of the continuum we are considering here.

Example B: A male faculty member from another department comments, "Of course she'd get tenure with an ass like that" about a female faculty member's promotion to associate professor.

Talking about a female colleague's anatomy (Example B) is arguably less egregious than the blatant denial of employment (Example A). While many women in the academy will be annoyed by such comments, they might simply shrug off comments with a disgusted "Men!" with no further informal confrontation or formal complaint. Or they might respond by saying, "What do you expect from the old boys' network?" More troubling, some women might even launch into a critique of the female faculty member's attire and her tendency to flirt with men. While not saying that she is "asking for" such comments, these women might conclude that the female candidate could have done more to shore up her scholarly seriousness, especially given a world in which female scholars have to fight for recognition. Many men might remain unaware of the harm done by comments about a female faculty member's appearance. They might respond by saying, "Well, I didn't really mean it like that" or "I was just kidding; she really is good at her job." In their minds, comments about her appearance are ultimately unrelated to her workplace performance.

Context is important to consider in such cases. The "direct attack" may seem more confrontational, but it may be that comments about a female colleague's anatomy are easier to address because they can be immediately confronted, reported by a primary agent in the situation, and addressed accordingly. Sexist comments that are reported back to an individual are more problematic due to the secondary nature of the report creating space for deniability which creates difficulty in responding (either as an individual or as an institution) and has the added negative consequence of expressing a sexist norm in the work environment. Microassaults are likely more frequent on college campuses than acts of hostile blatant sexism given their more subtle nature and the fact that they are open to interpretation. Depending on the egregiousness of the act, protections under sexual harassment policy should be provided (wherever possible) to those subjected to microassaults—including investigations of secondhand reports of microassaults—and the campus climate should be such that it condemns such acts when they occur.

Example C: Faculty senators (male and female) critique their president's appearance after she gives her report at a university senate meeting. The senators note the cut of her shirt's neckline, the color of her suit, the length of her skirt, the style of her stockings, and the height of her heels; they do not comment on the content of her report.

Unlike microassaults (Example B), microinsults tend to be insensitive rather than conscious attempts to wound. The microinsult Example C is likely to resonate with many readers but is unlikely to be found in many Title IX compliance officer complaint logs. They represent the lived experiences of many women in academia and yet they are the sort of experience that often fail to rise to the level formal complaint. Depending on how college sexual harassment policies are written, these types of sexist acts may not even qualify for investigation. However, microinsults in the academy perpetuate the policing of women and their bodies while positioning appearance over intelligence, competence, and contribution—which all contribute to a climate wherein women are not perceived as worthy leaders. The situation is more difficult for those not conforming to traditional gender stereotypes.

Example D: A new female faculty member has been scheduled to teach all evening classes at her suburban institution. There has been a recent spike in violence on campus and she is concerned about walking on campus alone at night, but others on campus tell her not to worry.

Like microinsults (Example C), microinvalidations are subtle and leave plenty of room for interpretation. The microinvalidation Example D may appear to be casual conversation between colleagues; however, it is much more problematic because it nullifies the female faculty member's fears, or data about safety and crime. These fears may be based on past acts of violence the woman has experienced or the result of gendered socialization. In either case, invalidating women's concern for their safety on campus a sexist act. Varieties of microinvalidations often happen on campus, but they are not the sort of sexist behavior that are rarely addressed by policy. Rather, microinvalidations require intervention at the relational level (either through personal conversations or departmental professional development sessions) to help raise awareness about the inappropriateness of these types of comments.

Example E: The advising and mentoring load in academic department has gradually shifted to become the disproportionate responsibility of the female faculty, given how compassionate and intuitive the female faculty seem to be toward the students and their needs, and the female faculty find themselves with less time to do research than their male colleagues.

Example E differs from the preceding cases because it is more clearly an example of benevolent rather than hostile sexism. Benevolent sexism highlights the fact behavior can be sexist without seeing women in a negative light. Indeed, the benevolent sexist views women as more nurturing, more virtuous, and more refined than men (Glick and Fiske 2001). Example E illustrates how the stereotypical use of "good feminine qualities"—such as compassion, intuition, and nurturing—can be used in the workplace to enforce traditional gender norms and derail women from being able to fully dedicate themselves to primary job responsibilities that will best position them for advancement in the academy. Women may be caught in a double bind in cases of benevolent sexism. If they question these types of assignments that are based on positive stereotypes, then they may receive hostile microassaults or microinsults in return for their resistance (e.g., "Don't be bitchy about this," "Why are you being so sensitive?", "But you're so good at this type of thing," "I'm just trying to look out for you, don't get angry").

Gender Asymmetries and Implications for Sexism in the Academy

This section considers the importance of gender asymmetries. Consider, for example, an analogy between racial and gender identities. In the case of race, some racial insults are more hurtful than others, and it seems unlikely that there is any insult hurled at White people that rises to the level of a racial epithet (Blum 1999). Because the history of racial discrimination is asymmetrical, it should come as no surprise that racial identity matters to the analysis of the case. Likewise, the long history of gender discrimination has had unequal effects on men and women. Men and women occupy asymmetrical positions and, thus, analysis depends on appreciating these asymmetries (Draeger 2011). We will explore gender asymmetries by attempting to "flip" the gender of the examples offered in the previous section to examine the implications of gender reversal in these situations to assess the impact of the acts.

Flip A: A search committee discusses not hiring a male candidate for an Associate Director of Student Life position because he mentioned his small children during the interview and the committee is concerned that he will not be able do the job during the late hours sometimes required of the position.

Some readers might find this example implausible. In Flip A, they might doubt the possibility of a search committee questioning a male applicant's commitment to a position given the social assumptions and gendered norms related to childcare provision. While male faculty members often have young children at home, it is not typically assumed that they will be primary caregivers. As a result, the late hours are not likely to be seen as an impediment to his successful performance in the job. These assumptions speak to the gendered landscape against which higher education is set.

Flip B: A female faculty member from another department comments, "Of course he'd get tenure when he's built like that" about a male faculty member's promotion to associate professor.

Much like in the flipped examples from the prior subtype, some might find the flipped examples implausible. In Flip B, there is reason to doubt that a woman would ever comment publicly about a man's body and, if she did, that the comment would be taken as an offense. One reason might be that a man's worth is not usually equated with his physical appearance. Consequently, it is unlikely that his case for promotion will seem related to his physical appearance at all. The asymmetrical response, therefore, is directly related to the asymmetrical history.

Flip C: Faculty senators (male and female) critique their president's appearance after he gives his report at a senate meeting. The senators note the cut of his suit, the color of his tie, and his shoe choice; they do not comment on the content of his report.

Deconstructing the flipped examples for hostile microinsults leads to discussion the question at issue. While it may appear that, when comparing Example C with Flip C, the question at issue is fashion choices, a deeper investigation may reveal that fashion choice may be at play in both the example and the flip—but the example also exposes the regulation of the female body (note the additional items critiqued and the implied judgment related to necklines, skirt lengths, and heel heights). Although neither the example nor the flipped example addressed the content of the presidents' reports, an evaluation of the senators' differing perceptions of their presidents' competency may be made based on the amount and type of energy spent on presidential wardrobe critique. Here again, like in the case of hostile microassaults, it may be quite difficult to address microinsults through campus policy or legislative regulations due to the interpretation involved in such cases.

Flip D: *A new male faculty member has been scheduled to teach all evening classes at his suburban institution. There has been a recent spike in violence on campus and he is concerned about walking on campus alone at night, but others on campus tell him not to worry.*

   The flipped example of hostile microinvalidation provides interesting insight. Flip D presents a glimpse into masculinity studies, in that if a man were to express these concerns he may likely be the subject of blatant hostile sexism where he would be told to "man up and get to class, because he would be fine and could protect himself." What the flipped example of our cases expose is the many ways gender is employed in the academe to regulate behavior and maintain power.

Strategies

Our discussion details some ways in which "sexism is bad" in academia. It highlights the nuance in identifying and complexity in confronting sexism. Acknowledging the interplay of factors (e.g., who is involved, what is occurring, where/when/how it is happening, why it is happening) allows us to respond effectively to cases of sexism in higher education. Challenging sexism may be harder than it seems. As Sue (2010) notes, members of marginalized groups and victims of sexist microaggressions often do not respond at all when they experience oppressive acts for five key reasons: attributional ambiguity, response indecision, time-limited nature of responding, denying experiential reality, and impotency of actions. We now suggest feminist strategies to assist with confronting sexism in the academy by adapting lessons from themes found in feminist pedagogy (Kahn and Ferguson 2009)—since eliminating sexism in higher education should be considered, at its root, a (re)education project of social justice.

Strategy 1 *(Addressing Systemic Power): In order to confront sexism within the existing institutional power structures, we should (a) acknowledge that change in higher education is (at best) evolutionary, (b) work within existing policies and procedure, and (c) work to improve campus policy and culture.*

   When search committees do not hire candidates because of their small children (Example A), campus policy can be used for formal complaints. However, campus culture may also need to be changed which will require additional steps, such as enlarging policy to cover additional gender issues and providing search committee education about appropriate practice. Depending on the level of seriousness in the case of sexist comments during tenure discussions (Example B), campus policy might apply or it might require changing campus culture to discourage commentary unrelated to academic performance.

Strategy 2 *(Raising Consciousness): In order to confront more subtle cases of sexism and support resistance of blatant cases of sexism, we should (a) reflect upon workplace interactions—who is involved, what occurred, when/where/when/how/why it happened—in which you are a primary actor and (b) reflect on workplace interactions in which you are a bystander in order to support colleagues both "in the moment" and after witnessing sexist behaviors by naming the offense, interrupting the behavior, supporting/confronting those involved, and (possibly) reporting the act.*

As noted earlier, comments about a colleague's appearance (Example C) might not be covered by formal campus policy. The tendency will be to dismiss such comments, unless the concern is raised by a thoughtful colleague. However, we should recognize that who does the confronting often matters. Men, for example, can confront the comments of other men in ways that women cannot. Understanding that comments may be unintentional may help craft the response most likely to resonate with the offender. Likewise, the perception of danger (Example D) will depend on a variety of factors, and it is important to understand these factors to best address a situation or support a colleague in a given circumstance.

Strategy 3 *(Emphasizing Diversity): In order to confront monolithic representations of gender in academia, it is essential to (a) ensure representative voices are included in institutional decision making and (b) conduct periodic institutional reviews that include assessments of diversity, marginalization, and privilege to continually move toward equity.*

Assigning advising tasks to women (Example E) on the basis of stereotypical gender strengths (e.g., women as nurturing) is problematic. Rather than making stereotypical assumptions, it is important to have varied representation on campus decision-making bodies (e.g., shared governance, personnel committees). Further, larger institutional review committees (e.g., strategic planning, accreditation) should include diverse voices in a meaningful way.

Each of these strategies are interrelated. Sexist institutional power structures cannot be transformed without raising consciousness and emphasizing diversity. Merely raising consciousness or emphasizing diversity will be insufficient. Even if there are policies on campus capable of addressing inappropriate comments about a woman's anatomy, these policies will not be utilized unless individuals are aware of the inappropriate nature of such remarks and know about the existence of procedural remedies. Listening to the voices of others and seeking to understand their experience can help raise awareness. Male faculty who believe that such comments are "no big deal" would benefit from conversations with women about how their appearance in general and their anatomy in particular is always under scrutiny. Men and women could talk about the various gender asymmetries found in their experience. Likewise, a conversation about a female faculty member's genuine interest in her scholarship could help dispel the notion that she should take the bulk of the advising responsibilities because "she is good at it." While such conversations will not immediately solve the problem, they point to a healthier gender environment.

Surviving sexism in academia requires appreciating the wide variety of ways that sexism can be "bad." Sexism can take the form of acts, attitudes, and institutional structures. Sexism can be blatant and subtle. It can be hostile and benevolent. It can also be clear and open to a range of interpretations. Given this complexity, individuals should modulate their responses accordingly. We must guard against the paralyzing belief that challenging sexists acts will not yield change because it is only through past challenges that a heightened awareness of sexism in the academy and positive strides toward gender equality have been made. We must seek to reshape institutional culture through individuals' actions in response to sexism in the academy in order to bring about an equitable higher education structure.

References

Basford, T. E., L. R. Offermann, and T. S. Behrend. (2014). "Do You See What I See? Perceptions of Gender Microaggressions in the Workplace." *Psychology of Women Quarterly*, 38 (3): 340–349.

Berg, S. H. (2006). "Everyday Sexism and Posttraumatic Stress Disorder in Women: A Correlational Study." *Violence Against Women*, 12 (10): 970–988.

Blum, L. (1999). "Moral Asymmetries in Racism." In *Racism and Philosophy*, edited by S. E. Babbitt and S. Campbell, 79–97. Ithaca, NY: Cornell University Press.

Connell, R. W. (1995). *Masculinities*. Berkeley, CA: University of California Press.

Draeger, J. (2016). "Every Sexism: What's the Harm in Looking?" *International Journal of Applied Philosophy*, 30 (1): 163–174.

———. (2011). "What Peeping Tom Did Wrong." *Ethical Theory and Moral Practice*, 14 (1): 41–49.

Fields, A. M., S. Swan, and B. Kloos. (2010). "What It Means to Be a Woman: Ambivalent Sexism in Female College Students' Experiences and Attitudes." *Sex Roles*, 62 (7): 554–567.

Fitzgerald, T. (2014). *Women Leaders in Higher Education*. New York: Routledge.

Giddens, A. (1984). *The Constitution of Society: Outline of the Theory of Structuration*. Cambridge: Polity Press.

Glick, P., and S. T. Fiske. (1996). "The Ambivalent Sexism Inventory: Differentiating Hostile and Benevolent Sexism." *Journal of Personality and Social Psychology*, 70 (3): 491–512.

———. (2001). "An Ambivalent Alliance: Hostile and Benevolent Sexism as Complementary Justifications for Gender Inequality." *American Psychologist*, 52 (2): 109–118.

Goh, J. X., and J. A. Hall. (2015). "Nonverbal and Verbal Expressions of Men's Sexism in Mixed-Gender Interactions." *Sex Roles*, 72 (5–6): 252.

Hanappi-Egger, E. (2013). "Backstage: The Organizational Gendered Agenda in Science, Engineering and Technology Professions." *European Journal of Women's Studies*, 20 (3): 279–294.

Harris, T. M. (2012). "Flying Solo: Negotiating the Matrix of Racism and Sexism in Higher Education." *Women and Language*, 35 (2): 103.

Kahn, J. S., and K. Ferguson. (2009). "Men as Allies in Feminist Pedagogy in the Undergraduate Psychology Curriculum." *Women & Therapy*, 33 (1–2): 121–139.

Lerner, P. (2000). "Harassment: A Symptom of Sexism." *Equity & Excellence in Education*, 33 (1): 84–86.

Monroe, K. R, and W. F. Chiu. (2010). "Gender Equality in the Academy: The Pipeline Problem." *The Profession*. https://www.cambridge.org/core/services/aop-cambridge-core/content/view/S104909651000017X

Risman, B. J. (2004). "Gender as Social Structure: Theory Wrestling With Activism." *Gender & Society*, 18: 429–450.

Robbins, E., and L. Robbins. (2006). "Reflections on the Current Status of Women in American Higher Education." *Forum on Public Policy: A Journal of the Oxford Round Table*, Fall: 1–11.

Roos, P. A., and M. L. Gatta. (2009). "Gender (in)Equity in the Academy: Subtle Mechanisms and the Production of Inequality." *Research in Social Stratification and Mobility*, 27 (3): 177–200.

Stainback, K., T. N. Ratliff, and V. J. Roscigno. (2011). "The Context of Workplace Sex Discrimination: Sex Composition, Workplace Culture and Relative Power." *Social Forces*, 89 (4): 1165–1188.

Sue, D. W. (2010). *Microaggressions and Marginality: Manifestation, Dynamics, and Impact*. Hoboken, NJ: John Wiley & Sons.

Sue, D. W., C. M. Capodilupo, G. C. Torino, J. M. Bucceri, A. M. B. Holder, K. L. Nadal, and M. Esquilin. (2007). "Racial Microaggressions in Everyday Life: Implications for Clinical Practice." *American Psychologist*, 62 (4): 271–286.

2 Remodeling Shared Governance

Feminist Decision Making and Resistance to Academic Neoliberalism

Kirsti Cole, Holly Hassel, and Eileen E. Schell

Shared governance is considered by many (American Federation of Teachers [AFT] Position on Shared Governance and 2002 Resolution, American Association of University Professors [AAUP] 1966) in higher education to be foundational to higher education. The "shared governance" model was conceived to attempt to respect the interests of external and internal groups, even when criticism flows at a constant rate (Kerr 2001). Recently, however, in the higher education trade dailies, dissatisfaction about the state of shared—or what used to be called "faculty governance"—has increased. Brian Rosenberg, in his 2014 article for *Inside Higher Ed*, laments,

> Faculty members complain that they are being disempowered by administrators and trustees who are creating an increasingly "corporatized" academic environment and who are more concerned with budgets than with quality. Administrators lament the extent to which faculties seem oblivious to the fiscal realities threatening the status quo and to the need for significant or even radical change. . . . And legislators seem baffled by the whole system.
>
> (para. 1)

Gary Olson claims,

> The phrase shared governance is so hackneyed that it is becoming what some linguists call an "empty" or "floating" signifier, a term so devoid of determinate meaning that it takes on whatever significance a particular speaker gives it at the moment.
>
> (para. 5)

We highlight, briefly, the differences between faculty governance and administrative leadership because in the faculty context, credibility must be earned. Instead of being attributed the role of leader by virtue of title, faculty involved in governance must work to build authority among peers and are elected to represent. This kind of leadership work is complicated by gender because the behaviors and activities associated with leadership tend to read as negative when displayed by women (see Williams and Dempsey 2014; Huston 2016).

The economies of engagement that circulate in higher education leadership shift depending on the power structure in which the engagement occurs. In the contemporary, neoliberal university, leadership in administration and leadership in faculty governance bank on entirely different models of engagement. For administrators, particularly the increasingly large class of mobile administrators who spend no more than two to four years in their role, mobility is a method for advancement, a way to increase power, but also a way to avoid being fired and maintain a reputation. For faculty, contingency undercuts power, not only in teaching and research roles, but also in faculty governance because of the voluntary engagement (time, money, ethos) through which faculty members must train to become active in unions, senates, or in governance bodies. Instead of leadership being an access point for money, faculty leadership opens access to constituents, who are also peers.

In this chapter, three faculty members from differing campus environments who are union or faculty governance leaders share our experiences. Our intention was, at the outset, to trace access points through which women can navigate the overlapping circles of governance work. Though we do this, we found that our narratives led us to a broader understanding of the possibilities, challenges and, quite frankly, the failure of shared governance in many situations. We discuss ways to navigate governance systems, including methods for identifying access points written into the existing structures of governance, as well as ways in which we might coalition-build outside of the given institutional structures. More significantly, we make a series of proposals for navigating governance structures that have largely failed as a way of resisting the neoliberal, corporatist model of higher education management that looms large at the current moment. The institutions included in this chapter are a flagship master's granting state school in Minnesota, a public two-year college part of a larger University System in Wisconsin, and a private university ranked in the top 100 universities in the United States. We argue that, like any other organization, issues of gender cut across the academic culture of shared governance. We know that women's past participation in labor unions has amounted to secretarial work (Dickason 1947; Dewey 1971), or the women in the organization felt as though the union didn't represent their unique concerns (Roth 2007). According to a 1996 study from the AAUP, women, particularly non-tenure track women, are more likely to be shut out of faculty governance processes by the institutions that employ them. And with the latest data from the TIAA Institute released in April 2016, we know that though colleges are hiring more minority and female professors, most of the jobs filled are adjunct positions, not tenure track—and in many governance models, non-tenure line instructors have minimal roles for participation or feel no incentive to or reward for participation. This convergence of labor exploitation and diminishing participation in shared governance affects the whole higher education enterprise.

A study from 2001 confirms these trends as long standing. Author Elizabeth Harper and her colleagues confirm that women are overrepresented and in the majority of full-time, non-tenure track faculty members. According to the TIAA study, "The proportion of all women faculty who are tenured or on the tenure track has actually declined from 20 percent to 16 percent and 13 percent to 8 percent, respectively" (Finkelstein 5). How, then, do women lead without being co-opted or ineffective in this changing era of institutional structures that seem increasingly built to work against governance by the governed? In old models, there can be a cult of personality around university leadership to which faculty responds. If university leaders and leaders in faculty governance have a relationship that makes it easier to negotiate on the basis of this cult of personality (part of a system built on "boys' club" values), the negotiation takes place behind the scenes and is dependent on only the individuals involved. This method relies on getting limited access to power rather than keeping the balance of power between administration and faculty. So are there productive ways to think about how the outsider status could work? To leverage our strengths as leaders outside of more traditional, masculinist networks? Perhaps our strength lies in our own coalitions, our connections to other bodies and to other agents and in using, disrupting, and renegotiating the economy of engagement that governance provides.

As we began discussing this project, we realized that aspect that we all have in common is how we understand our own identities in the context of faculty governance. We regard ourselves as activists and feminists—not just union members or faculty senate leaders—which means that part of what we think about as we engage in governance in our different environments is our sense of strategy, tactics, context, and intersectional gender justice. We also think about our rhetorical training—our language, our stance, and our agency—in order to strategically engage our activist identities in governance spaces. Within this activist identity, we also realized that we have shared experiences in terms of how we are perceived in often sexist ways. As women in leadership roles we have all been told that we are mouthy or loud—that we are bossy, pushy, or bitchy—that we are inappropriately "loud" women. This means that there is a contrast between expectations of gender conduct, that there is also value in our violations of gendered norms (we have all been elected, multiple times, to positions of power at our institutions) but that it carries a love/hate relationship. We are valuable but resented or objects of concern for our intensity and powerful advocacy.

We know from experience that shared governance has the potential to be a feminist space and also an exploitative space, partially because of the history of women's work in academy. A lot of the labor-intensive service, or housekeeping, goes to women faculty members, while the service that is male dominated is more public and less active (see Masse and Hogan 2010). With a growing and increasingly powerful administrative class, state disinvestment in public funding, a growing and increasingly disenfranchised contingent class, and students being squeezed financially to make up the difference, there has been an alarming erosion of faculty governance and academic freedom. Administrators are making more top-down decisions, especially as states continue to defund higher education. Among those recent top-down decisions are administrators at LIU Brooklyn locking out unionized faculty and staffing classes with underqualified or unqualified scabs, unilateral wage cuts, furloughs, layoffs, program eliminations, and other cost-reducing measures that have a major impact on students' learning conditions, teaching conditions, and the quality in general of American higher education. Shared governance, then, is one of the most significant sites through which faculty can become and remain active in shaping and pushing back against the power structures and inequities that are currently shaping higher education.

In the face of such barriers, *what, then, is a feminist shared governance model?* How might it serve to reverse trends toward neoliberal corporate discourses and practices in higher education? We argue that a feminist shared governance model often looks radically different on each campus and radically different from existing governance structures. We argue that fundamental values of shared governance—which are dialogic, negotiated, deliberate, contemplative, and consensus building—are productively aligned with feminist values. Applying the feminist label to the space of shared governance operates in the context of opening access, including diverse voices, building relationships, sharing knowledge, and achieving goals collectively. We can derive these feminist principles by beginning with questions like the following:

- How can we make the existing structures work?
- How can we transform them to make them better, more inclusive, and accessible for all stakeholders?
- How can we reach outside the structure/system and leverage other actors/agents to make it effective?
- What coalitions can we build and enact?
- What happens when the ideal of and goals for engagement in faculty governance fails? What happens when shared governance doesn't work, and when our feminist ideals cannot be realized? How do we maintain hope and carry on?

Eileen: Playing by the Rules, Silenced by the Rules? University Senates and the Quandary of Access

Given the conditions of the neoliberal university, many of us are struggling to steer the budgetary and intellectual futures of our colleges and universities. We are fighting to maintain our right to design and influence curricula, to exercise academic freedom, and to guarantee access to higher education for students of all incomes and backgrounds. Many of us have learned the hard way that our university leaders are more interested in top-down decision making than shared governance processes.

As a feminist scholar who has held a variety of administrative positions, as a writing program administrator (WPA), department chair, chair of a humanities council, and a university senator, I am a believer in the power that might be gained from shared governance as exercised through established bodies such as university or faculty senates; however, I am aware that senates on college campuses can be spaces that are exclusionary and that shut out particular voices and bodies. On my campus, a private university in upstate New York, our main university-wide faculty governance structure is a university senate. On our campus, the university senate offers a broad representation of elected faculty representatives from nine colleges and professional schools plus appointed representatives from the staff, elected student representatives, and the chief administrative officers who are ex officio non-voting members but, nevertheless, carry major weight in steering decisions. A university senate, thus, can be a space with broad and diverse constituencies, where faculty staff, students, and administrators are all at the table; however, a University Senate can also be an exclusionary space, as noted in the introduction to this chapter. If a faculty member is not elected or appointed to serve, he or she must rely on elected colleagues to represent his or her concerns. If the constituency one is representing is so clearly outnumbered, as in the case of the two senate representatives who are part-time faculty members on my campus, then one risks being tokenized or rendered ineffective through lacking sufficient numbers to truly influence voting.

In my capacity as a longtime elected senator, a former senate agenda committee chair (the main organizing committee of the senate), and a member of many senate committees, I am often asked how one gets elected to the senate.

"Put your name in and run for election when the cycle comes around," I tell these colleagues. "Let others know you are interested and would like to serve."

Some then remark that they worry that they will not be elected. They are concerned that their views are not popular or that they are not well-known or regarded by others in their colleges or professional schools. Often these remarks are made by White women colleagues and faculty of color. Some note, too, that the university senate is a White male space, where they believe their styles of participation will not be valued or will be talked over as White male senators command the floor through speaking privilege and a superior grasp of Robert's Rules. These conversations have given me pause because they represent a gap between the desire to serve and take part in shared governance and questions of the gendered and raced politics of accessibility, recognition, and voice.

These questions raise more questions: who gets to serve? Who does not, and why? And once elected, will specific bodies be heard, listened to, and respected? Already we know that department chairs, deans, and chief academic officers, all the way from provosts to vice presidents, presidents/chancellors, are overwhelmingly White males. It stands to reason that many university or faculty senates would also look the same way and be overwhelmingly full of tenured White male colleagues with the time, space, privilege, and inclination to speak up and expect to be heard. How then to explain women senators like me who consistently get elected?

Two of my other longtime senate colleagues, both White female tenured academics like me, and I have agreed that we are elected to serve as senators because we are viewed as "big mouths" (something we've been told at different points and in different ways in our tenure in the senate). In a variety of both flattering and unflattering ways, we've been told that we are consistently nominated and elected as senators because we will speak out for those afraid to do so. We will ask tough questions, and we won't mince words. We are thought to be "fearless" because we seemingly speak out without fear of repercussions. As one colleague asked me recently, "Who and what are you protesting now?", implying that I am in a constant search for a cause to fight. The apparent sexism is that other senators aren't "big mouths" or seemingly more reasonable in their approach and delivery than me and my fellow female senators. "Senior statesmen," as one colleague once said of many of the White men serving in the senate. The "men" in "statesmen" made it clear who was being referred to—the actual men stating their views while the women like me were erupting or "going off" on our views or somehow pursuing the political cause du jour. Also, the keepers of the flame of Robert's Rules tend to be men—the ones to whom points of order and procedure are referred, making such some senate meetings take on the overtones of "Boys' State" or the yearly finals of the Debate Club.

Finally, another challenge with shared governance in university senates is quite simply the question of timing. Monthly full senate meetings of an hour or an hour and a half with committee meetings timed in-between may mean that a senate cannot respond swiftly enough to pending issues and concerns. The decisions may be made before the senate can react.

Where university senates fail to achieve proportional representation of all university stakeholders, ignore or pass over women and minority faculty members' arguments, and cannot respond swiftly enough to pending issues, organizing outside formal governance structures is an option for action. Even as we need to fight to shift the structures of power that exclude the bodies and voices of women and colleagues from underrepresented racial groups, interdisciplinary coalitions working toward labor solidarity and action can be particularly helpful modes of organizing, especially on private university campuses or in "right-to-work" states where tenure line faculty do not have the ability yet to collectively bargain and where administrators are busy ignoring shared governance principles and going on their merry way.

Organizing for Equity: Material Concerns, Rhetorical Outcomes

When shared governance has broken down and failed or when the slow timing of the university senate proves to be a challenge for effective action, one model for organizing that we have turned to historically on the Syracuse University campus centers on coalition building and direct action. This organizing is often guided by a labor consciousness and is also informed, often, by feminist coalition building and Marxist principles of labor solidarity. Faculty members, graduate students, staff members, union leaders, and undergraduate students have historically joined together to organize protests and direct actions around issues of campus-wide concern. For instance, early in my career at Syracuse in 1998, faculty and students organized a support group with the Service Employee's International Union strike of physical plant and cafeteria workers on campus, helping to successfully end the strike and pressure the university to offer a fair contract. The faculty support group was led by feminist scholar Linda Martin Alcoff, who brought her training as a feminist philosopher and activist to the endeavor, guiding the efforts of a faculty support group, which offered a teach-in, rallies, petitions, letter writing campaigns, and picket line support.

The labor consciousness and organizing sparked by the strike did not cease once the contract was settled, but it seeped into other actions and groups for some time. One solidarity group that has sprung up in recent years is the Syracuse University Labor Studies Working Group, an interdisciplinary group based out of Maxwell's Program for the Advancement of Research on Conflict and Collaboration (PARCC). The Labor Studies Working Group is an interdisciplinary group of Syracuse University faculty members from the Departments/programs of African-American Studies, Anthropology, Geography, Religion, Sociology, and Writing and Rhetoric. Convened by two Associate Professors, one in the Department of Geography and the other in Sociology, the primary goal of the group is to "institutionalize Labor Studies at SU and to elevate labor as a topic of intellectual inquiry and social and political importance on campus" ("Labor Studies Working Group" 2014).[1] This group sponsors frequent lectures and panels by labor scholars and labor activists. Members of this group along with members of the local AAUP chapter and other stakeholders have also co-sponsored direct action and protest events to advocate for labor justice and shared governance. This loosely affiliated and shifting faculty coalition has co-sponsored and taken part in rallies, protests, and petitions to organize around specific labor issues and protest decisions around budgetary and governance matters. These actions, steeped in social protest traditions such as confrontational rhetoric and non-violent direct action, have been essential to shaping a different discourse of the future for the university from the one imagined by institutional leaders with short-term timelines and different educational metrics. Sometimes these actions have taken place in vain, not achieving the exact outcomes desired. At the same time, these actions have been central to a culture of both resistance and advocacy that is intertwined with the values of shared governance.

Working toward shared governance in the senate auditorium and also on the campus sidewalks or the steps of the campus chapel, carrying protest signs, many of us, nevertheless, fight on for what we believe in even as other faculty members might be indifferent, unmoved, or simply preoccupied with other matters. Indifference and learned inaction regarding shared governance is a key challenge, raising the question of how faculty can learn and actively pursue the skill sets that ensure successful shared governance, a topic for the conclusion of this essay. As writing faculty members, feminist scholars, and activists, as those who believe that words and deeds matter, we must continue to develop a model of leadership that contributes to shared governance and critical leadership skills. WPAs and faculty who embrace a critical rhetoric are well-positioned to engage in this struggle for shared governance. Our rhetorical training means we have good ideas about how to address questions of audience, purpose, and communication as we debate the futures of our institutions. As many of our field call for public engagement and community literacy as sites of work and scholarship, let us not forget how much we need to apply our communication skills and advocacy work on our own campuses.

Finally, the organizing we have done to stem the breach in shared governance has demonstrated to many of us on our campus it that if we do not act now to preserve the opportunity to voice our opinions and visions about the future of our institutions, we miss the opportunity to preserve what most of believe in despite rank and position: the right of faculty of all ranks to shape higher education curricula and innovative pedagogies and research, the right for higher education instructors to be adequately compensated and fairly treated, and the right for our students to access a quality and affordable education. Without these rights, there is no university.

In the next section, Holly will outline the state of higher education and shared governance in Wisconsin, where Governor Scott Walker has worked to elide and destroy the rights of faculty and teachers across the state, changing permanently the university system that was heralded for decades as a "world class" institution (a refrain circulated repeatedly in state public discourse) and a progressive voice for public outreach and workplace quality.

Holly: Masculinist Values, Feminist Strategies: Shared Governance under Assault

In the UW System, the bedrock principle of tenure and shared governance has been embedded into the fabric of the state-wide system since its inception, emerging from the flagship University of Wisconsin–Madison. Defined in the earliest days as "faculty governance," the central pillar of shared governance is the active participation of faculty and staff in the shaping institutional decision making. Defining features of the UW System have been the Wisconsin Idea, rooted in UW President Charles Van Hise's 1904 speech declaration that "I shall never be content until the beneficent influence of the University reaches every home in the state" (University of Wisconsin 2016). Over time, this reach became a balance of public service and faculty participation in legislative innovation, including "the nation's first workers' compensation legislation, tax reforms and the public regulation of utilities" and "university's commitment to public service—a mission that substantially predates the progressive political era" (University of Wisconsin 2016). However, in 2010 with the election of Governor Scott Walker, a stark reversal of these principles was initiated, starting with the passing of Act 10—legislation severely curtailing the powers and the formation and recognition of public unions (overturning a decades-long tradition in Wisconsin, which was the first state to authorize public unions); what later was called the "Wisconsin uprising" resulted—with 80,000 protesters converging at the State Capitol in Madison over multiple days to protest that gutting of this foundational tradition.

As a faculty member transplant to Wisconsin from the neighboring state of Minnesota, these changes to the traditions of the system that I had come to love pressed me to become involved in the governance bodies that were being eroded. Here, I contend that the masculinist traditions of the governance system—and the accompanying hollow yet powerful masculinist power structures and values of the state legislature—eventually converged to subvert the authority of faculty expertise and role in shaping the System; and that without a decisive commitment to dismantling these masculine traditions, faculty involvement in the progressive values of the system and the state will ultimately be substantially undermined.

Governance Conditions

My own intervention into the faculty governance structure[2] began in earnest serving as a department chair's representative to the faculty and staff senate governing committee, Senate Steering. In the course of this work, the material realities of this service emerged more clearly to me, including the underrepresentation of women in the governance body and the near non-existence of women at the executive leadership levels. As a geographically decentralized institution, the material makeup of the senate body is not always apparent nor controllable, as the system elects faculty senators on 13 individual campuses who convene four times during the year. In one year (2009–2010), just one woman faculty senator was elected to the 17-member Faculty Council. This challenges of a minority membership makeup of women senators is best illustrated during particularly challenging academic year in which the public, united traditions of the UW System were under assault by a neoliberal legislature and a corporate values-minded system president who sought to spin off the flagship university from the rest of the system, a potentiality that exacerbated existing tensions between the well-resourced Research 1 institution and the struggling regional and rural comprehensive campus.

The material division of gendered leadership in the middle of the tumultuous institutional history seems reflective of what Jay Newton-Small observes in her book *Broad Influence: How Women Are Changing the Way America Works* (2016), noting,

> So, somewhere between 20 percent and 30 percent, women really begin to change an institution, whether it's a legislature or a corporate board, a Navy ship or an appellate court. And then I started looking at all those corners and finding other areas where women had reached this sort of tipping point, and they were really beginning to change the way we govern, change the way we manage, change the way we command.
>
> (2016, X)

In these early debates during the high-intensity work of faculty senate after Act 10, the small percentage of women did not have sufficient sway—through the election of a female faculty senate chair for the first time in a decade (the author) and additional senators—for the upcoming 2016–2017 academic year, it has reached 64%—has substantially changed the tone and timbre of the governance body.

Ideologically, faculty governance in the UW Colleges under a masculinist tradition has operated heavily on the principles of Robert's Rules of Order and meetings have been largely transactional, with the male-dominated leadership transmitting information and shaping the tone of the gathering (rather than a dialogic and cooperative model of governance); this emphasis on hierarchical authority, coupled with the "male bodies" occupying those spaces of power across all levels had the effect of creating an "old boys" club that operated on hoarding of information and shoulder-tapping to install faculty in committee and leadership positions rather than transparent invitations for participation. Governance of the boys' club model has the effect of excluding those who exist outside of the group and who do not have access to the information.

Some material and ideological shifts that promoted a more transparent governance process included regular clear and specific updates about governance work (rather than pro forma circulation of dense, hundred-page minutes from senate meetings), creation of a blog, transparent calls for committee and leadership positions, increase in dialogic meeting time, and open access to information. Rather than "closed circle maintenance," support feminist principles like those outlined in Carolyn Shrewsbury's "What Is Feminist Pedagogy?" (1997). Though geared largely at the classroom, her values of community, leadership, and empowerment translate well to the governance process. Shrewsbury's philosophy emphasizes a vision of knowledge making and knowledge building that is "concerned with gender justice and overcoming oppressions" (167). Redefining power as "empowerment," in Shrewsbury's view, power is "creative community energy," suggesting that "strategies be developed to counteract unequal power arrangements" (168). In shared governance, this means collaborative conversation and consultation; it means sharing access to information so knowledgeable participation is possible by all involved. Shrewsbury's vision of community—that this shared space is a "re-imaging" from individual learning to "both autonomy of self and mutuality with others" (170)—supports shared governance that is collectively concerned with the institutional values and mission and that emphasizes the representative role played by each in the body (not speaking just for oneself but as a representative for constituents who themselves have diverse interests, needs, and values). This philosophy speaks to Shrewsbury's third pillar—leadership—defined not as a role of dominance but rather "an embodiment of our ability and our willingness to act on our beliefs" (171). Though governance structures rely on defined roles—chairs, committees, elected representation—all of these roles can be invited and encouraged to share ownership of the work of the deliberative body and contribute meaningfully according to their priorities as a group or individual in ways that are compliant with the larger community.

State-wide, however, the legislative changes—largely because of the culture of hierarchy that masculinist values and traditions fostered, contributed to the changes at the legislative level that were mirrored by values accepted by the dominant leadership within the UW System. Debates over defining the role of faculty within the system structures ultimately led to the imposition from high-level legislative bodies—the Wisconsin Joint Finance Committee—fundamentally redefining the role of faculty within shared governance. Initially defined in policy language as having "primary responsibility" for academic and educational activities and personnel matter, it was redefined through legislative language as "subordinate to," enshrining in policy language a hierarchical relationship that had previously been more loosely defined. Further, the revised language specifies insists on the inclusion of STEM faculty. It is certainly no coincidence that all of these fields are highly male dominated and that demanding participation from fields with heavily masculinist traditions and claims to objective epistemological methods is an attempt to maintain traditional claims to power.

Rhetorical Strategies for Narrative Control

Last, at all levels of academic governance, control of the narrative—and control of the discourse—shapes material and ideological dimensions. A specific outcome of the legislative, state-level, and system-level reshaping emerged—efforts to fundamentally change the definition of tenure and shared governance were launched, culminating in a highly public debate between UW Faculty, the Board of Regents, the System President Ray Cross, and the state legislature. The rhetorical framing of these debates reveals the way that feminized language and values are demonized, deployed as strategies to tap into cultural misogyny in order to undercut faculty objections to these substantial changes to their working conditions. In this way, cultural sexism became a weapon of credibility erosion, calling upon both internalized sexism and broad-scale patriarchal values to undermine objections from faculty leadership.

On an interpersonal level, certainly women in leadership positions experience this rhetorical assault, for example, finding themselves in the position of balancing assertive behavior with greater social consequences for doing so. Women are 2.87 times as likely as men to be referred to as "pushy," for example (Khazan 2014), or may find themselves, like those in Kieran Snyder's analysis of gender bias in performance reviews, more likely (87.9% of women) to receive critical feedback versus men (58.9%). Tone policing was evident with personality criticism appearing in 71 of 94 reviews received by women compared with 2 of the 83 reviews received by men. More specifically, as Snyder (2014) observes, "words like *bossy*, *abrasive*, *strident*, and *aggressive* are used to describe women's behaviors when they lead; words like *emotional* and *irrational* describe their behaviors when they object," with women in particular (used 17 times to describe 13 women—and never to describe men who were similarly evaluated) evaluated with this language. During the Wisconsin Tenure battle—where faculty first resisted the changes that would weaken tenure protections and enhance unilateral chancellor's powers to make decisions about laying off faculty and closing programs—such language was routinely used by system and state leaders to diminish the faculty objections.

Shared governance and faculty senates who proposed alternative policy language found themselves repeatedly being characterized with language culturally coded as feminized. In a March 2, 2016, interview with UW System President Ray Cross for the *Chronicle of Higher Education*, the *Chronicle* headline labeled faculty as "nervous professors" while Cross responded to queries about faculty objections highlighting faculty as "emotional" and policy language as "rational": "It's difficult to separate the emotional distrust that the faculty have of the governor, of the legislature, from what I would call a rational language in the policies" (Schmidt 2013). Just a week later, Cross again called on the rhetorical power of sexism to diminish faculty objections and reframe them around neoliberal and capitalist rhetoric, stating in a news story:

> Faculty are indeed leaving, he said. But that's largely because the system doesn't pay its faculty enough, not because of changes to tenure. "Those things are causes to make faculty nervous. I understand that," Cross said. "And much of that is the result of political distrust that exists. I got that. But the real reason I think faculty are being lured away is compensation packages. That concerns me a lot. That really does."
>
> (Rocha 2016)

This reframing of faculty objection about working conditions into both an emotional response and "really" about something else—financial concerns—serves to gaslight faculty, to minimize the concerns expressed, and to redirect the public narrative. In a further effort to delegitimize faculty resistance, Cross reframed the objections from academic workers as an issue of "low morale" and patronizingly reassured them: "This is not a personal attack on faculty and it's really important for them to understand that it's not" (Martens 2016). By skillfully repositioning the objections as simply hurt feelings—a personal attack—Cross sidestepped real engagement with the substance of the objections.

After a series of no confidence votes from multiple UW campuses in May 2016, President Cross again called faculty out for "emotional" responses: "We all are worried about the future," he said. "That's a concern and an anxiety. But no one is going to make an arbitrary decision to just close a program . . . I sympathize with faculty and I understand their concerns, but much of that is predicated on their fears, not on substance" (Milewski 2016). The emphasis on fear, nervousness, and anxiety has particular resonance in the academic environment which historically has allied itself with rational inquiry and logic—and, thus, rings strongly as an accusation of "weakness" for faculty expressing careful and measured objection. The rhetorical framing of faculty—male or female—as feminized serves as a tool to control the discourse around the issue.

What became increasingly apparent is that even in an environment with a strong union presence, unlike the UW System, the problems and erosions of higher education are still present. An article published in the 2008 issue of the *Labor Studies Journal* confirms our discussion: the authors found "to our surprise and disappointment" that unionization doesn't seem to protect the tenure track (Dobbie and Robinson 2008, 119), finding "no correlation between high union representation levels and lower than average reliance on part-timers." At least part of the explanation, they write, may be that "tenure-track faculty members were focused on their own economic well being, rather than the changing shape of the professoriate" (Jaschik 2008).

However, community college unions tell a different tale. There is more protection of tenure at community colleges with unions:

> Since many of these union locals included tenure-track and (full-time) non-tenure-track faculty in the same bargaining unit from the outset, we might expect successive rounds of collective bargaining to reduce substantially the compensation differential between the two faculty statuses. In addition, virtually all two-year faculty focus primarily on teaching, avoiding the potential research/teaching division that often maps onto the tenure-track/non-tenure track division at four-year schools.
>
> (Dobbie and Robinson 2008, 113)

In Kirsti's case, the trends hold: a historically strong union has not been able to prevent the changing material conditions from impacting students and faculty regardless of the nature of our contract.

Kirsti: Participation and Demand: Young Women's Leadership in Shared Governance

In 1938, a group of loosely connected campus organizations from the five existing state colleges in Minnesota joined forces to form the Inter-Faculty Organization (IFO). The Minnesota legislature enacted the Public Employee Labor Relations Act (PELRA) in 1971, enabling the IFO to become the official bargaining agent for state-wide State University faculty. From 1975 to 1980, the IFO worked to establish faculty rights under a collective contract. The contract was drafted to protect and regularize decisions governing tenure, promotion, and economic benefits, including evaluation and retention. The IFO was and is largely run by men. The first female state-wide IFO president was elected in 2012, and the first president of our Mankato campus union was elected in 2014. Because of the demographics of age (50+) and gender (majority male) in our union, many of the contract negotiations centered on retirement and healthcare planning. Our contract included no language on family leave, for example, until the 2013–2015 contract was ratified. However, the earliest versions of the contract put into place one of the most humane and transparent tenure systems I have ever seen.

Ratified in the 1986–1987 contract, Article 22 determines the criteria through which faculty members are evaluated for tenure. Article 22 is, ultimately, the reason that I chose to accept a tenure track position at Minnesota State University, Mankato—the flagship institution in the system. The evaluation of faculty for tenure is not dictated arbitrarily by administrators, and in an era in which the tenure of an average dean at a U.S. institution is just three years, this hard-won bargaining right is crucial. Article 22 lays out five criteria[3] through which a faculty member is judged each year he or she is on the tenure clock. In order to evaluate how well the faculty member is meeting the criteria, faculty members write a professional development plan in fall and a professional development report at the end of the year. Both documents are circulated through the department, to the chair and to the dean, and written feedback is provided. The annual administrative evaluations, as well as the plans and reports, all go into the faculty member's tenure file at the end of a five-year probationary period which means that faculty know exactly where they stand when they go up for tenure. Instead of a one-time, third-year review, faculty in the MnSCU (Minnesota State Colleges and Universities) system get a review each year based on their own goals. In a nutshell, what this means is that the IFO has created an environment in which faculty are safe. We are not hired and fired at the whim of administrative turnover or because our work might be controversial. We are protected, and our intellectual freedom is sacrosanct. Or, at least, that is the myth of tenure—that it affords faculty protection to do the hard, and sometimes confrontational, work that faculty members must do.

Faculty representatives in our union, those who serve on the IFO faculty association (our faculty senate, elected positions), and on our IFO Board (a state-wide group of faculty representatives from each university, elected positions) do not have to fight to protect what many in academia consider to be basic faculty rights: intellectual freedom, tenure and promotion, healthcare, family leave rights, and decision making in areas such as curriculum, evaluation of students, admissions policies, budget planning and allocation, long-range planning, selection of personnel—in short, faculty are guaranteed in our system the right to as much participation as they demand. I sketch out this brief history in order to provide context for what follows: the complications with faculty governance in a system that has had official and state-supported faculty governance for nearly eight decades.

Because of the protections of Article 22, and because I had gone to graduate school in a right-to-work state, I became involved in the union immediately as a first-year faculty member. When I was hired, I read my faculty contract carefully. I took my time and pored over the structures of faculty governance, our rights and responsibilities, the protections of the contract. I talked to colleagues, my chair, and my dean about their experiences in the union, their experiences on the tenure track, and solicited advice from anyone who would give it. I showed up to our first faculty association meeting of the year, looked at the empty committee seats, and signed up for one of them. No one else ran against me; thus, I was elected as a member of the Assessment and Evaluation Meet and Confer committee, one of the standing union committees that has monthly meetings with the administration. After two years serving on the committee, I ran for and was elected to chair it for another two years, becoming, at age 28, the youngest faculty member in the system to chair a standing union committee. On the basis of my involvement in our assessment committee, I also became involved with our campus reaccreditation team for five years. In the following three years, I was hired by the provost to serve as the first director of Writing Across the Curriculum; I was elected, on the recommendation of the union president, to head the President's Committee on the Status of Women; and I was elected to serve as one of our campus representatives to the state-wide faculty association leadership group.

This list in no way accounts for the massive amount of work that all of this involvement and leadership demanded—the massive amount of work demanded of *all faculty who participate in shared governance*. Just as women's labor is frequently invisible, so too is the labor of faculty members outside of more traditional conceptions of our work (research and teaching). Upcoming faculty members and graduate students frequently see themselves as researchers first, teachers second, and as having to do maybe a little service. This supposition, and the way that we train graduate students into this supposition, is deeply problematic, as it does not give an accurate picture of academic labor. I understood myself not just as an academic but as a citizen of my university, and as someone passionate about faculty and student rights. I could not have done it without a network of like-minded faculty activists. That network, particularly of senior women, was a lifeline for trying to navigate the politics of the institution, the system, and the state. My work gave me access to the people in power. I am recognized across campus as a faculty leader. However, because my work was visible, it was assumed that I was in it for some kind of power. My labor was not invisible, and though I was effective within the structure of our union, I was not quiet. As I worked to coordinate with administrators and faculty outside of single commit- tee channels, I was judged as a problem. One faculty member tried to get me removed from the WAC Director position and started a gossip campaign that took a massive emotional toll. Even when the bullying I experienced was at its worst, I felt and feel passionately committed to faculty shaping their university contexts—environments, conditions of labor, and public and private discursive networks.

Looking back, I realize I was encouraged in my involvement because I was such a young faculty woman: "We just haven't had someone like you before." My work across my union, and sometimes my arguing face to face with our president, CFO, and provost had no negative impact on my job security. Academic freedom and security are the mightiest tools in our arsenal; they are also the reasons that tenure is under attack throughout higher education systems in the United States. My union work did impact the ways in which other faculty, usually older White men, viewed me. I no longer keep track of how often people say things like, "I was a little scared to talk to you at first, but you're not a bitch at all!" I developed a reputation for getting things done. As a woman, that meant that I was intimidating, that people talked about me, made assumptions about me, and spread those assumptions to other faculty members. "Maybe you're not a team player, maybe you're just in it for yourself"—that was after I disagreed about a new assessment initiative for our general education curriculum with the retirement-age man who wrote the curriculum 25 years ago.

Like Eileen and Holly, I repeatedly heard from people that I was "actually willing to speak out." I was told on one particularly memorable occasion that since I'm not from Minnesota, my willingness to be blunt makes me "exactly the kind of bulldog this union needs." In an environ- ment, and state, in which passive aggressiveness reigns supreme, the fact that I spoke my mind made me an anomaly. And since I present as a young (read feminine and soft-spoken) female, the fact that when I open my mouth I'm neither soft spoken nor traditionally feminine is exactly the kind of "shock this union needs." The repetitiveness of the phrase needs struck me as peculiar at the time—particularly since most of the elected leadership roles in the union that carried course release time were filled by men. Was I being mentored into one of those roles? No. Was I being used as a mouthpiece after which union leadership could smooth things over and look like "good guys"? Absolutely. The fact that I present according to traditional gender roles, but do not function in accordance with them, makes me a kind of tool to shake up a complacent administration—but it also shook up the power dynamic within our union leadership. This has made me popular with the older women who have long been participants in our union and had to use other strategies to survive which did not include being vocal or challenging. It made me unpopular with the older men who like to talk over the women. I do not use the phrase "talk over" lightly. Upon discov- ering the existence of the Gender Timer app,[4] I used it in five consecutive faculty association meetings: two with administration and three without. In the two meetings that included adminis- tration, men composed 72% of the group and spoke 68% of the time.[5] In the three meetings with just faculty association members, men composed 55% of the group and spoke 48% of the time. Though this is a small sample, it is indicative of common communication trends that take up a great deal of space in self-help books for women leaders. The idea that a woman speaks her mind seems to be antithetical, so improbable that it demands attention—either as a recruiting tool, or as a tool to silence, or both.

Our ability to speak up, regardless of gender dynamics, however, has been overshadowed by the constant rhetoric of crisis dominating the discourse of the neoliberal university. Though my campus is the most financially stable in the system, the one with the fewest retention issues, the one whose incoming population of students is growing, we are told in every meeting that we have with administration that unless we adopt increasingly severe austerity measures, the administration will have to start laying off faculty. While the ranks of our administration swell with only White men (six new positions in four years, all middle-aged, straight, White men, four of whom have no experience or credentials in higher education), our tenure track faculty lines are increasingly non-renewable after retirements, and our general education curriculum, including first-year writing, is taught almost exclusively by non-tenure track faculty and graduate students. Fortunately, at least so far, Minnesota and the Minnesota State university system faculty remain committed to our union status and, therefore, we remain able to fight and to push back against misdirected austerity measures that include keeping up-and-coming women faculty in non-tenure line, temporary jobs. Our commitment, however, may benefit from a new direction, one that does not work within the confines of traditional shared governance. Though it is true that we have protected our academic freedom, our tenure lines are shrinking, and our administration is constantly attempting to work around the shared governance structures. Our values as faculty members are at odds with the values of corporatist administrators, and an understanding of how to position ourselves within the rhetoric of their values while simultaneously working against them is something to which faculty must turn their attention. We believe that feminist principles can support us in this work.

Conclusion

In exploring what has happened nationally and historically with shared governance, we identified both the affordances and the constraints of faculty leadership on campus, particularly for women. Part of why faculty organize so often and so much is because on many campuses in the contemporary university, shared governance does not work. Our narratives illustrate, in part, the ways in which faculty governance fails. Many administrators and faculty in leadership roles that are appointed, but not elected, establish an economy of information that shifts the ways in which academic economies of engagement can occur. There are structures, traditions, and principles that form expectations around shared governance, but those differ broadly in the real and daily actions of union and/or shared governance environments. While we believe that shared governance can be an inherently feminist space around which to coalesce, one thing that we discovered in writing this chapter is that much of the feminist work takes place outside of the expected structures.

A feminist shared governance model may mean importing and reimagining traditional labor practices in ways that preserve the traditional principles of dialogue, engagement, governance by expertise rather than position, and collaboration of equals. However, they may also incorporate the feminist materialist principles that draw from labor studies and Marxist traditions in order to position university faculty first and foremost as workers, rather than as occupying a sort of middle-space between (or outside of) labor and management. The practices and ideologies of the neoliberal university (and the increasingly the corporatist leadership models) suggest that university governance is rigged. Part of the backlash against shared governance from administrators across the United States is that they cannot carry out the corporate mandates of the new university because faculty structures and activities get in the way; we work at cross purposes. The labor conditions of higher education have changed so much that a lot of the models faculty value are no longer privileged—they're not driving the decision making any longer, and we have to think and work beyond our ideals.

Those of us who have participated in shared governance have struggled within the material and ideological conditions. Recognizing its imperfections, we seek to preserve and refashion rather than abandon the investment and engagement that faculty have held responsibility for over curriculum, evaluation, and programs. However, we know there are a lot of faculty who have simply "opted out," believing shared governance to be impotent or co-opted. A significant aspect of the failure of shared governance, however, is the failure of those in leadership roles to mentor in the next generation. Even the idea of who the next generation is has changed. Graduate students face careers that are primarily in non-tenure track jobs. Contingent and contractual faculty positions are now dominant in the academic job market. The old discourse—not doing anything until you are on the tenure track, or protected by tenure—no longer applies. Faculty cannot wait for safety to speak out. Faculty cannot rely upon tenure as protection if it does not exist. But faculty cannot passively take what they are given by administrators more interested in profit than education. Faculty, however, are not implicated alone in the failure of shared governance. It is, after all, shared.

No-confidence votes are taking place at a number of institutions across the United States (UW System campuses, Long Island University, University of Iowa, among many). Faculty are taking action in voicing the ways in which corporate values are not faculty values—and do not serve students, faculty, staff, or the mission of educational institutions. However, in the majority of cases such as the faculty lock out at LIU Brooklyn, "value-led" rhetoric falls on deaf ears. In this way, faculty do not seem to understand our audience. Blame is placed on administrators, particularly those who become administrators. A commonplace description of these individuals is that they have drunk the administrative Kool-Aid. They may have, but being drugged is far too simple an answer. Administrators and faculty think about information differently, they do different work and, in an ideal world, they do that work, differently, in order to support the education of students from widely diverse backgrounds. Just as the administration need faculty to do the work of educating, faculty need administrators who understand numbers, enrollment dynamics, diversity trends—people who think like administrators. Because neoliberalism, and austerity, dictate market-led values for the individuals running the organization, there is an impasse across which we must learn to speak and be understood. It is not just economic factors that divide us, however; in some cases, it is the very lore of the academy that does that work.

One of the predominant myths of higher education is the myth of mobility. That as an academic, or as an administrator, individuals are mobile—can shift jobs, climb in rank, can move to new places. This is not reality for the contemporary academy. Yes, some individuals do move. A chair might become a dean at a different institution, a faculty member on the tenure track might make a lateral move to a different institution for a better "fit." We see this as a bygone myth, however, because the changing demographics of the faculty population and the changing nature of the job market increasingly make this an anachronism; more tenure line faculty are not "unencumbered" workers who can simply pick up and leave for greener pastures—because this is based on an assumption that no other worker with similarly demanding work obligations has to be taken into account. The tenure line job market has also been shrinking for decades; thus, there is no longer (if there ever was) a bounty of well-compensated senior faculty positions or named chairs to jump up to. More likely, today's faculty will spend their careers either on limited contract or, if they have tenure, they will remain where they are or give it up for a new institution. In many cases, faculty may not invest in shared governance because they believe their fate lies elsewhere. They do not believe that their current workplace is theirs. And in some cases, they do not even see themselves as a worker—they do not participate in a labor mentality, in a labor consciousness model. Our understanding of labor consciousness is feminist.

Part of what feminist shared governance means is changing how women are represented in governance, getting them to the table, mentoring them, encouraging them to be leaders who believe in and value shared governance. The labor consciousness model is part of feminist consciousness at the intersections of race and class. What feminists, critical race theorists, and Marxists have long recognized is that faculty life is not now, nor has it really ever been, a life of the mind. Being a faculty person is a job. It is work. It is a field in which people labor. We must acknowledge the embodied experiences of faculty life as a part of the value of shared governance in which we build coalitions. We must climb out of the towers that never existed in the first place. It is a necessity that we retrain away from the traditional academic mind-set and reorient toward an embodied understanding of labor. In order to do so, one place to start is with the people who will run higher education. We must make sure that graduate education includes a feminist labor perspective when we discuss what higher education is, where education is happening, and we must include in those discussions an understanding of the different models of governance, and what the roles and responsibilities of faculty are in relation to it.

We also need to prepare and join a new generation of institutional leaders who are interested in leading institutions where faculty have a voice and weigh in on decisions affecting the institutions in which they work. Ethical leaders who believe in shared governance are needed to unite all campus constituencies, not just answer to governing boards or Trustees or donors. Any conversation of shared governance must attend to the need to build a better generation of university leadership—one that represents the student bodies and faculty bodies of an increasingly diverse higher education landscape.

In addition to rethinking graduate education, and the material conditions in which we labor, we propose the following strategies for cultivating an effective, feminist governance environment:

- Understand shared governance work as activism.
- Find, build, and cultivate allies.
- Work both inside and outside the system (reach out to other groups, including non-academic unions).
- Check in with yourself and each other—acknowledge the emotional and embodied aspects of governance.
- Communicate with frequency and transparency, solicit feedback.
- Work out a defined strategy for action in advance.
- Actively engage board members, administrators, and **elected** faculty leaders in a serious discussion of what shared governance is and is not.
- Provide as many opportunities as possible for faculty members who are interested in governance to learn about all aspects of their institution. Seek out, actively recruit, and mentor young, diverse faculty members at the contingent and tenure track levels.
- Provide faculty equitable conditions in which they can do the work of shared governance.

The time is now for faculty of all ranks and stripes to reengage with shared governance as part of a larger strategy to retain and enrich the academic mission of higher education. Not doing so risks eroding the very fiber of post-secondary education in the U.S.

Notes

1   https://www.maxwell.syr.edu/parcc/Research/advocacy/Labor_Studies_Working_Group/.
2   The UW System has never had a union but rather relied on the strong Wisconsin State Statutes–granted authorities of a bedrock tenure system and firm shared governance structure.
3   1. Demonstrated ability to teach effectively and/or perform effectively in other current assignments.
    2. Scholarly or creative achievement or research.
    3. Evidence of continuing preparation and study.
    4. Contribution to student growth and development.
    5. Service to the university and community.

4   https://itunes.apple.com/us/app/gendertimer/id926041160?mt=8.
5   One clear reason for this is that the President and his officers all give reports in joint meetings, and there is only one woman among the administrative officers.

References

Baldridge, Victor J. (1978). *Policy Making and Effective Leadership: A National Study of Academic Management*. Los Angeles, CA: Higher Education Research Inst., Inc.

Dewey, Lucretia. (February 1971). "Women in Labor Unions." *Monthly Labor Rev*, 94: 42–48.

Dickason, Gladys. (May 1947). "Women in Labor Unions." The Annals of the American Academy of Political and Social Science, 251.

Dobbie, David, and Ian Robinson. (June 2016). "Assessing the Potential Impact of Labor Law Reforms on University Faculty: Findings from a Midsized Public University in Ontario." *Labor Studies Journal*, 41: 204–219.

Dobbie, David, and Ian Robinson. "Reorganizing Higher Education in the United States and Canada: The Erosion of Tenure and the Unionization of Contingent Faculty." *Labor Studies Journal*, vol 33, no 117, 2008. 117–140. DOI: 10.1177/0160449X07301241.

Finkelstein, Martin J. (2016). "Taking the measure of faculty diversity." Advancing Higher Education. TIAA Institute, April 2016. pp. 1–18. http://www.chronicle.com/blogs/ticker/files/2016/08/taking_the_measure_of_faculty_diversity2.pdf.

Harper, Elizabeth, Roger G. Baldwin, Bruce G. Gansneder, and Jay L. Chronister. (Spring 2001). "Full-Time Women Faculty Off the Tenure Track: Profile and Practice." *The Review of Higher Education*, 24 (3): 237–257.

Huston, Therese. (2016). *How Women Decide: What's True, What's Not, and What Strategies Spark the Best Choices*. New York: Houghton-Mifflin Harcourt.

Jaschik, Scott. (June 3, 2008). "The Union Impact and Non-Impact." *Inside Higher Ed*. Web.

Jaschik, Scott. (February 3, 2014). "Philosophy of Sexism?" *Inside Higher Ed*. Web.

Khazan, Olga. (May 23, 2014). "Pushy Is Used to Describe Women Twice as Often as Men." *The Atlantic*. Web.

Kerr, Clark. (2001). *The Gold and the Blue, v. 1*. Berkeley: University of California Press.

Martens, Bill. (March 15, 2016). "Tenure Changes 'Not a Personal Attack' on Faculty, UW System President Says." *The Joy Cardin Show*. Wisconsin Public Radio. Web.

Masse, Michelle, and Katie Hogan. (2010). *Over Ten Million Served: Gendered Service in Language and Literature Workplaces*. Albany: SUNY Press.

Newton-Small, Jay. (2016). *Broad Influence: How Women are Changing the Way America Works*. New York: Time.

Rocha, Polo. (March 9, 2016). "Amid Tenure Debate, UW System Campuses Say Faculty Departures Rise." *WisBusiness.com*. Web.

Roth, Silke. (2007). "Sisterhood and Solidarity? Women's Organizations in the Expanded European Union." *Soc Polit*, 14 (4): 460–487. doi: 10.1093/sp/jxm019.

Schmidt, Peter. (March 2, 2013). "Heading a University System with Nervous Professors." *Chronicle of Higher Education*. Web.

Shrewsbury, Carolyn. (1997). "What Is Feminist Pedagogy?" *Women's Studies Quarterly*, 1/2: 166–173.

Snyder, Kieryn. (August 26, 2014). "The Abrasiveness Trap: High-Achieving Men and Women Are Described Differently in Reviews." *Fortune*. Web.

University of Wisconsin–Madison. (2016). "The Wisconsin Idea." UW Madison. Web. www.wisc.edu/wisconsin-idea/.

Williams, Joan, and Rachel Dempsey. (2014). *What Works for Women at Work: Four Patterns Working Women Need to Know*. New York: New York University Press. Print.

3 Exploring the Decision to Pursue a Career in Higher Education Administration

An Analysis of Gendered Constraints and Opportunities

Shelly Schaefer Hinck, Salma Ghanem, Ashley Hinck, and Sara Kitsch

The environment surrounding higher education is challenging: concerns involving affordability and access to college, demands for innovative instructional delivery systems, financial constraints due to changes in state funding, and calls for increased regulatory requirements are just a few of the issues that university administrators are facing (Thelen 2011). If colleges and universities are to successfully negotiate current and future issues, talented individuals are needed to serve in academic leadership roles. However, research suggests that universities are facing a shortage of qualified and capable academic administrators. Many faculty are "reluctant to fill these important positions, concerned that academic leadership is incompatible with work–life balance, that it detracts from their commitments to research and teaching, and that it is tantamount to 'going to the dark side'" (DeZure, Shaw, and Rojewski 2014, 7). Compounding the problem, statistics concerning current gender representation in administrative ranks indicate that women are less likely to be in leadership roles than men, suggesting women are not making the move to administration. Utilizing information from the 2006 *AAUP Faculty Gender Equity Report* of 221 doctoral-granting institutions in the U.S., Bilen-Green, Froellich, and Jacobson (2008) found that only 13.5% of doctoral institutions are led by women presidents and just 23.5% have women provosts. A 2012 study by the American Council of Education shows 26% of presidents across institutions types are women (Cook 2012).

Given the need to attract capable and talented applicants to academic leadership positions coupled with the evidence that women are underrepresented in current administrative ranks, this study explores the perceptions of internal and external barriers and motivators experienced by faculty and current/former academic leaders in pursuit of higher education administration roles. Attention was focused on whether gender influenced university faculty and administrators' career trajectory, opportunities, and aspirations. Faculty and administrators at three universities spanning multiple institution types (religious/public/private) were asked to complete a survey addressing administrative interests, perception of concerns (barriers) involving moving into administrative roles and, if applicable, reasons for moving into leadership positions (motivators).

Institutional Culture and Faculty Leadership

As the literature demonstrates, both institutional and personal concerns impact an individual's choice to pursue a position in academic administration. DeZure, Shaw, and Rojewski (2014) suggest that "many mid-career faculty are reluctant to fill these important positions" (7), citing reasons that range from systemic issues inherent in the university itself to individual concerns involving work–life balance and demands on time (7). Institutionally, faculty are experiencing greater demands and expectations concerning research, publication, and grant writing. At many universities/colleges, current research requirements for tenure are more than triple what they were in the 1970s (Kezar et al. 2007). In order to meet the higher research and publication standards, faculty members are directing more and more of their time to research activities and less time to service and/or leadership opportunities. Many perceive administrative opportunities as a barrier to future promotions. Currently, faculty members are strongly encouraged to write, receive, and participate in outside contracts. This growing trend, often referred to as "academic capitalism," requires individual faculty members to write grants in order to secure supplementary income and is particularly common in the sciences. This university expectation rewards faculty autonomy, reinforcing the perception that involvement in external research activities is more important than campus leadership and committee membership, negatively impacting faculty members' interest in participating in important administrative and leadership roles (Kezar et al. 2007).

A second institutional change that seems to be affecting the number of faculty interested in and actively moving into administrative positions is the rise of part-time and non-tenure faculty appointments. In 2009, approximately 33% of faculty held tenure track positions and 67% of faculty were not eligible for tenure, holding either part-time or full-time positions, many of whom are women (Kezar and Maxey 2014). Underscoring this change, data from the National Center for Education statistics indicate that "from fall 1993 to fall 2013, the number of full-time faculty in degree granting postsecondary institutions increased by 45 percent, while the number of part time faculty increased by 104 percent" (Kezar and Maxey 2014, 2). Non-tenure track faculty members are not expected to undertake leadership roles, requiring the smaller percentage of tenured/tenure track faculty to fill the gap.

Gender and Academic Leadership

Research continues to identify gender as an issue that negatively impacts interest in academic leadership roles. Issues surrounding gender, race, ethnicity, and and/or sexual orientation have been found to influence participants' perception of leadership readiness, capability, and willingness to serve, noting that academic leadership ranks have fewer women and people of color (DeZure, Shaw, and Rojewski 2014). Limited mentoring, increased teaching loads, greater service expectations, family responsibilities, and gendered stereotypes involving leadership styles and communication have been identified as factors that impede women's advancement, often creating a chilly academic climate experienced by female graduate students, faculty members, and administrators.

For women, mentoring, "the process whereby a more experienced individual provides counsel, guidance, and assistance to another person" was identified as a key factor in a woman's career success, in a woman's development of leadership characteristics, and in the creation of higher levels of confidence in a woman's leadership abilities (Dunbar and Kinnersley 2011, 17). It appears that women who are interested in administrative roles would do well to have a mentor to help them navigate the often complex university leadership context. There is support for the idea that mentoring works best when the mentor and the mentee share similarities—similar gender and ethnicity in particular (Dunbar and Kinnersley 2011). However, finding a mentor for women and women of color may be very difficult given the small number of females in administrative roles and the even smaller number of minority women.

Lack of mentoring is one factor that may explain why women's paths to academic leadership positions may be different from men's—another possible reason why fewer women seem to find themselves in leadership roles. As Dominici, Fried, and Zeger (2009) share, "Administrative positions in academia have a well-defined hierarchy, with progressive ranks that are fairly uniform nationwide, from division director to department chair, dean, and then university leadership positions" (1). Academic administrators usually move through these positions linearly. Women, however, navigate the leadership context differently, often drawing experience from directing academic programs, chairing committees, or leading research centers or institutes, often serving on more time intensive but less powerful committees (Dominici, Fried, and Zeger 2009). Juggling home and professional responsibilities, greater service roles, and gender stereotypes continue to disadvantage women as they seek to participate in administrative leadership roles (Bilen-Green, Froelich, and Jacobson 2008).

Research has also noted gendered expectations concerning how leaders are viewed, discouraging many women from participating in administrative leadership roles. Agentic leadership attributes, more closely aligned with a masculine approach, include assertiveness, control, ambition, independence, and competitiveness and are often equated with effectiveness and success. Communal leadership attributes, more closely aligned with a feminine approach, include creativity, innovativeness, sensitivity, cohesiveness, and an "other" orientation. In many institutions and universities, masculine, transactional, and hierarchical models of leadership are valued over more feminine, transformative, and relational-driven leadership perspectives, often creating leadership traps and/or double binds for women. Despite women's willingness to negotiate gender boundaries, women have often found that their leadership choices and actions were restricted by others' expectations based upon stereotypes of their sex (Christman and McClellan 2012).

While the current academic climate is not conducive to women interested in pursuing academic leadership, it is hoped that as more women take on leadership roles within universities (e.g., department chair, associate dean, dean, provost, president), the climate will change. Bilen-Green, Froellich, and Jacobson (2008) offer that "having more women in formal leadership positions actually models the desired culture change in a conspicuous and powerful way, while opening valuable networking opportunities for both women and time to experience a new outlook" (4). Noting how current female administrators successfully negotiate leadership double binds and manage the dialectal tensions involving normally mutually exclusive leadership strategies of rationality, control, and objectivity with qualities of compassion, co-orientation, and subjectivity will potentially create a climate of possibility for other women (Christman and McClellan 2012).

Examining reasons why current and past female administrators have chosen to serve in leadership roles as well as understanding more fully what concerns current female faculty have in moving to administrative roles is necessary if changes in gendered academic leadership roles are to occur. Additionally, investigating how men are also making decisions concerning administrative opportunities will yield data that enable universities to understand more fully what is needed to attract both talented and qualified men and women in key administrative positions. Toward that end, the following research questions are posed:

1. What were the reasons that current and former administrators pursue(d) an administrative path? Are there differences between males and females?
2. When did current and former administrators become interested in pursuing an administrative path? What is their level of satisfaction with administration? And are there differences between males and females?
3. What were the concerns that current and former administrators had prior to assuming their administrative roles? Are there differences between males and females?
4. What are the reasons that faculty members did not pursue an administrative path, and what are the concerns that faculty members have about administration? Are there differences between males and females?

Method

Tenure track faculty, academic administrators, and former academic administrators were recruited from three institutions spanning various institution types (public/private/religious). All eligible faculty/administrators received an invitation through each institution's email to participate; the email included a short description of the study and a link to the survey (housed in SurveyMonkey). Two hundred and fifty-four individuals participated in the study; 40.5% of the responses were from individuals working at a public institution, and 59.5%of responses were from individuals working at private institutions. Within the sample, 74 are current administrators (30.8%); 123 have never been administrators (51.2%); 43 are former administrators and are currently not serving in an administrative capacity (17.9%); and 14 individuals did not identify their status. Regarding gender, 134 respondents identified as male (55.6%), and 105 respondents identified as female (44.4%). The majority (203) of the respondents identified as White (84.%), while 14 (5.8%) identified as Black, 13 (5.39%) as Asian, 3 as multiracial (1.24%), and 10 individuals did not identify their ethnicity.

All participants completed an informed consent form and a demographic questionnaire (gender, ethnicity, marital status, children, etc.). Subjects who identified as current administrators also completed a Likert scale questionnaire (10 questions) indicating reasons for becoming an administrator (5-*strongly agree* and 1-*strongly disagree*), a Likert scale questionnaire (10 questions) indicating concerns for becoming an administrator (5-*strongly agree* and 1-*strongly disagree*), and answered a question concerning satisfaction with the administrative experience (How satisfied are you with being an administrator; 5-*very satisfied* and 1-*very dissatisfied*). Subjects who identified as never serving as administrators completed a Likert scale questionnaire (14 questions) indicating reasons why the respondent has not served as an administrator (5-*strongly agree* and 1-*strongly disagree*). Finally, subjects who identified as former administrators completed a Likert scale questionnaire (9 questions) indicating reasons for becoming an administrator (5-*strongly agree* and 1-*strongly disagree*), a Likert scale questionnaire (10 questions) indicating concerns for becoming an administrator (5-*strongly agree* and 1-*strongly disagree*), and answered a question concerning satisfaction with experience (Please rate your experience with being an administrator; 5-*very satisfied* and 1-*very dissatisfied*). Questions for the survey were derived from the literature concerning administrative interest and non-interest.

Results

RQ1: What were the reasons that current and former administrators pursue(d) an administrative path? Are there differences between males and females?

The strongest reason for pursuing an administrative path by current and former administrators was to make positive changes (M = 4.38), followed by being encouraged by others (M = 4.11). Table 3.1 presents the reasons from highest to lowest.

The only significant difference between males and females in terms of reasons for pursuing academic administration was for the increase in salary with males (M = 3.25), indicating that a salary enhancement was more of a motivator for males than females (M = 2.67) ($t = 2.29, p < .05$).

RQ2: When did current and former administrators become interested in pursuing an administrative path? What is their level of satisfaction with administration? And are there differences between males and females?

Of the current and former administrators, 8.5%of respondents indicated that they were interested in administration from the beginning of their academic careers while 19.7%indicated that

Table 3.1 Reasons for Pursuing an Administrative Path by Current and Former Administrators (all survey respondents)

Reason	Mean
To make positive changes	4.38
Individuals encouraged me	4.11
For career challenge	3.68
A mentor encouraged me	3.36
I had good role models	3.19
For an increase in salary	3.14
Because it was my turn	2.63
To satisfy my ego	2.40
Because of the power that comes with the position	2.32
To move to another institution	2.30
To leave my current department	1.69

Table 3.2 Concerns of Current and Former Administration about Pursuing a Career in Administration (all survey respondents)

Concern	Mean
Giving up or reducing research	3.91
Time involved	3.72
Headaches involved	3.60
Work–life balance	3.52
Reducing or giving up teaching	3.25
Impact on family	3.23
The value of administration	2.99
Going to the dark side	2.50

their interest developed several years into their career. The largest percentage of respondents (30.8%) indicated that they became interested after someone indicated to them that that they would be good at administration. Open-ended responses also indicated that many current and former administrators became administrators by happenstance, because no one else was there to do it, were talked into it, or as a result of a natural evolution. No significant differences were found between males and females. The level of satisfaction with the administrative role was relatively high (M = 3.57), with no significant differences between males (M = 3.64) and females (M = 3.47).

RQ3: What were the concerns that current and former administrators had prior to assuming their administrative roles? Are there differences between males and females?

The strongest concerns about pursuing an administrative path mentioned by current and former administrators was reducing or giving up research (M = 3.91) followed by the time involved in administration (M = 3.72). Table 3.2 identifies the concerns from highest to lowest. No differences were found between males and females.

Table 3.3 Reasons Why Faculty Did Not Pursue an Administrative Path (all survey respondents)

Reason	Mean
Not appealing	3.33
No opportunity	3.02
Not encouraged	2.90
No mentor	2.63
No role model	2.63
Lacking organizational skills	1.90

Table 3.4 The Concerns that Faculty Have Regarding Administration (all survey respondents)

Concerns	Mean
Impact on research	3.70
Headaches involved	3.54
Impact on teaching	3.54
Time involved	3.10
Impact on family	2.87
Not sharing the same values as administrators	2.76
Going to the dark side	2.42

RQ4: What are the reasons that faculty members did not pursue an administrative path, and what are the concerns that faculty members have about administration? Are there differences between males and females?

Faculty members who have never served as administrators responded to several Likert scales to determine the reason for not pursuing an administrative path. The reason indicated by most faculty was that administration is not appealing to them followed by not having an opportunity to do so. Table 3.3 provides the reasons why faculty did not pursue an administrative path from highest to lowest.

The only significant difference between female and male faculty members was in "Not encouraged" with females (M = 3.16), indicating that not being encouraged was more of a reason for females than for males for not pursuing an administrative path (M = 2.66) ($t = -2.35, p < .05$).

Giving up research was the highest concern that faculty have regarding moving into an administrative position, followed by the headaches, and the impact on teaching. Table 3.4 provides the concerns that faculty have regarding administration from highest to lowest.

The only difference between males and females was the concern of time, with females (M = 3.44) being more concerned than males (M = 2.82) ($t = -2.65, p < .05$).

Discussion

Several interesting conclusions can be drawn from the data. First, faculty reasons for not transitioning into administration are more centered on maintaining an active research agenda and teaching interests than in the perception that moving to administration is the equivalent of "going to the dark side." From this data, it appears that male and female faculty members simply find the current way that administration exists unappealing and full of headaches. A lack of interest concerning the role of administrative leadership may reflect the growing trend of increased research expectations, greater emphasis on grant writing, and the emergence of a climate of academic capitalism. This trend, while more prevalent at research institutions and within the sciences (Kezar et al. 2007), reinforces the idea that a university values research productivity more than service or leadership; hence, faculty may be afraid to leave their active research programs for fear that they will not be able to reengage their research when their administrative term has been completed. This supports previous research where the most frequently identified concerns about moving into administrative and leadership roles focused on less involvement with teaching, research, and student activities that faculty enjoyed and that time away from current research programs would have a negative impact on future promotions.

A lack of interest concerning the role of administration may also reflect a faculty member's unfamiliarity with administration. Strained faculty-administration relationships coupled with little opportunity for interaction between faculty and university leaders may perpetuate feelings of disinterest. Limited presence on key committees that address critical issues concerning policy, tenure/promotion, and budgetary decision making and planning may also explain female faculty members' disinterest in administrative leadership. Activities that allow for faculty and administrators to gather and talk about topics of common interest may serve as encouragement for faculty to "try" serving on important governance committees and in administrative roles. Using their institution as an example, Esterberg and Wooding (2013) share that a series of conversation dinners created "the space for discussion involving faculty, administrators and staff around topics such as pedagogical innovation, retention problems, curriculum changes, and budgetary issues, for both discussion and getting to know each other" (78). Programs such as this may appeal to and encourage female faculty, as the conversations promote a climate that is more egalitarian and less power oriented or hierarchical.

Second, encouragement from others played an important role in an individual's decision to move into an administrative role. The data indicate that former and current administrators rated the reason "others encouraged me to apply for an administrative position" as more important than "career challenge," "a mentor encouraged me," and "I had good role models." Faculty responded in a similar way to current/former administrators in that a critical factor for not pursuing an administrative position was that "no one encouraged me." Interestingly, there was a significant difference between male and female faculty in how important encouragement was in a faculty member's decision to pursue administration; female faculty members rated "no one encouraged me" as more important in their decision not to pursue an administrative role than male faculty members. The findings of the current study reinforce the importance of affirmation, mentoring, and support in regards to women and administrative positions. With fewer women in administrative positions and a gendered organization climate that has favored the advancement of men, the importance of encouragement and mentoring cannot be underestimated. Giddis (as cited in Dunbar and Kinnersley 2011) found that mentoring was an important and critical determinant in the career success of female administrators. Research has found that encouragement and mentoring served as an important stimulus to a faculty member's interest in academic leadership and as a confidence boost in regards to being successful in the position (DeZure, Shaw, and Rojewski 2014; Kezar et al. 2007). This may be especially true for female faculty who may enact a communication style that is different from the male-oriented leadership approach or have served as leaders for committees perceived as less powerful and important.

Finally, there are still concerns about the amount of time required for administrative positions. Both male and female faculty are concerned about maintaining an appropriate work–life balance while pursuing an academic leadership position; however, women perceive the issue of time to be more of a concern than male faculty. This may suggest that women pay significant attention to issues involving the tensions surrounding family and work responsibilities. Research has addressed the issue of a "second shift" where women "juggle" home and professional responsibilities and the impact this has on administrative advancement, career success, and feelings of stress, fatigue, and resentment (Bilen-Green, Froelich, and Jacobson 2008; Wood and Fixmer-Oraiz 2016). Finding ways to address issues of time and to ensure a sense of work–life balance are needed if universities want to entice female faculty to fulfill administrative positions. In a study examining work–life culture at two universities, Lester (2015) found that a symbol of cultural value of work life involved the behaviors and discourses of academic leaders (department chairs, deans, and presidents) on the college campuses. One leader who participated in the study offered, "Everybody on my staff sees my calendar and it says pick up Lily. So because the dialogue is there and because it is modeled at the highest level of leadership to me that facilitates work–life balance" (148). Seeing academic leaders successfully struggle with the tensions of family/illness/children and work may serve as a sense of possibility for female faculty interested in higher education administration.

Summary

This study sought to explore the perceptions of internal and external barriers and motivators experienced by faculty and current/former academic leaders in pursuit of higher education administration roles. Attention was focused on whether gender influenced university faculty and current/former administrators' career trajectory, opportunities, and aspirations. The data include signs of hope in that administrators and the idea of administrative work are not perceived negatively, that the value of administration is not the key reason for not pursuing a leadership position, and that moving into administration is not tantamount to "going to the dark side." Additionally, it appears that male and female faculty members are concerned about many of the same issues involving pursuing administration in regards to issues of research, teaching, and work–life balance. However, there are still critical issues that need to be addressed if we hope to attract capable faculty to administrative roles. This study demonstrates the importance of encouragement and mentorship of women if they are to take on leadership roles at a rate equal to men. Research has found that "workplaces with at least 35% women are better working environments for women," further noting that "attaining a critical mass of women in the leadership structure is especially important to position an institution for change" (Bilen-Green, Froelich, and Jacobson 2008, 3–4). As more women serve in higher positions, the more likely it is that a climate that promotes and values the advancement of women will be created. At the three universities where data were collected, a movement toward a more positive representation of women in the academic dean role is noted with 33%–50% of the dean positions held by women and approximately 40%–45% of women holding department chair positions. However, it should also be noted that all of the institutions had a president and a provost that was male. Indeed, our universities still have more work to do. As universities (hopefully) continue to work to address gender disparities in women's salaries and organizational policies that disadvantage women and families, our findings demonstrate that universities must also turn their attention to ways in which they can more fully value transformative, relational, and collaborative leadership and communicative styles of women while creating a university culture that encourages, supports, and welcomes women in administrative roles.

Bibliography

Bilen-Green, Canan, Karen A. Froelich, and Sarah W. Jacobson. (2008). "The Prevalence of Women in Academic Leadership Positions, and Potential Impact on Prevalence of Women in the Professorial Ranks." *Women in Engineering ProActive Network.* http://journals.psu.edu/index.php/wepan/article/viewFile/58533/58221.

Christman, Dana, and Rhonda McClellan. (2012). "Discovering Middle Space: Distinctions of Sex and Gender in Resilient Leadership." *Journal of Higher Education*, 83 (5): 648–670.

Cook, Bryan. (Spring 2012). "The American College President Study: Key Findings and Takeaways." *American Council on Education*. Web.

DeZure, Deborah, Allyn Shaw, and Julie Rojewski. (January/February 2014). "Cultivating the Next Generation of Academic Leaders: Implications for Administrators and Faculty." *Change*, 7–12.

Dominici, Francesca, Linda P. Fried, and Scott Zeger. (July/August 2009). "So Few Women Leaders: It Is No Longer a Pipeline Problem So What Are the Root Causes." *Academe*. http://aaup.org/article/so-few-women-leaders#.VqfvXPF-g1F.

Dunbar, Denise, and Ruth Kinnersley. (2011). "Mentoring Female Administrators Toward Leadership Success." *Delta Kappa Gamma Bulletin*, 77 (3): 17.

Esterberg, Kristin, and John Wooding. (2013). *Divided Conversations: Identities, Leadership, and Change in Public Higher Education*. Nashville, TN: Vanderbilt University Press.

Kezar, Adrianna, Jaime Lester, Rozana Carducci, Tricia Bertram Gallant, and Melissa Contreras McGavin. (2007). "Where Are the Faculty Leaders? Strategies and Advice for Reversing Current Trends." *Liberal Education*, 93 (4): 14.

Kezar, Adrianna, and Dan Maxey. (2014). "Faculty Matter: So Why Doesn't Everyone Think So?" *Thought & Action*, Fall: 29.

Lester, Jamie. (2015). "Cultures of Work-Life Balance in Higher Education: A Case of Fragmentation." *Journal of Diversity in Higher Education*, 8: 139–156.

Thelen, John. (2011). *A History of American Higher Education*. Baltimore, MD: Johns Hopkins University Press.

Wood, Julia T., and Fixmer-Oraiz. (2016). *Gendered Lives*. Boston: Cengage Learning.

4 Do We Really Want the Flies that We Might Catch?

Interrogating "Post-Feminist" Lessons for "Success"

Heather Hill-Vásquez and Laurie Ann Britt-Smith

Many of our female colleagues who have served in academic leadership positions have responded to Sheryl Sandberg's *Lean In: Women, Work, and the Will to Lead* (2013) with a sense of defeat and emptiness despite the hopeful and energetic call to action which it trumpets. Seeking the source of our colleagues' responses, we decided to read *Lean In* for ourselves and, unfortunately, felt similarly disheartened. Despite its inspirational tone, *Lean In* is an experience in advice-giving that often ignores, obscures, or just leaves unvoiced the sexist constructions, restrictions, and systems of power which we thought Sandberg had set out to address.

And, unfortunately, as female leaders in the academy, we have experienced similar situations which may account for the unhappy responses of our sister colleagues to *Lean In*. Like ourselves, these are women who have tried to lead while resisting the sexist stereotypes and backlash that women in authority positions—even those in academia—continue to experience. Thus, despite (or in spite of) the claims of our institutions that they believe in and advocate for equality and pro-feminist policies, women leaders in higher education are still living and working within an oppressive system built upon biased and unjust attitudes. And, as we will argue is the case for *Lean In* and other similar contemporary self-help books, those assumptive and unexamined claims to equality and equal treatment are a main reason for why the oppressive system continues to exist.

Operating under the guise of "this is for women so it must be about equality and justice for all women," *Lean In* and our own institutions present a post-feminist mentality and rhetoric that works to silence much of what still needs to be asserted, analyzed, and overcome while simultaneously endorsing sexist stereotypes of those women who risk resisting that silence. For women trying to lead effectively and ethically at our universities and colleges, *Lean In*, while it focuses on the business world, nonetheless reflects their own experiences in the academy. Sandberg perkily encourages her female readers to engage in the very types of attitudes and behaviors which feminism and female academic leaders have, for decades, worked to confront and combat. We assert that a similar situation exists in the academy.

The disheartening parallels that emerge between the situation of women in the corporate world and the reality of life for contemporary feminist women in the academy are not, necessarily, so hard to explain. As our institutions move more and more to corporate models—money, power, the bottom line—we see a corresponding definition of success taken up not only by our students and our CFOs, but also by our faculty. As the life of the mind, of self-reflection, of ethical citizenship, of social justice are given lip service, so too is gender equality. What these things mean, why they are important, how we must continue to work with and for these concepts are questions that become obscured by tokenism. We let the words stand in for the goals; we let the mere fact that we have women leaders at our institutions stand in for feminism. We corporatize rather than examine and happily accept the trending urge to, like our institutions, do what we have to do in order to "succeed."

The rhetoric of *Lean In*, then, also operates in the academy—a rhetoric which purports to be feminist while restating institutionalized beliefs rather than change and revolution. This rhetoric is a function of a mentality that has superimposed corporate thinking and values onto the feminist cause and the academy's value. Reflected in *Lean In* and in similar leadership books for women is the corporate world's refashioning of a reflective, interrogating, assertive feminism to feminism *lite*—a more palatable version that doesn't threaten the established system and which incongruously suggests "chang[ing] the world by adhering to biased rules and expectations" (48). Unfortunately, in its increasing attention to the bottom line as the main definition of success for itself and for its students, the academy, too, has adopted this "faux feminism"—depleted, self-defeating, fakely performative, and driven by a rhetoric that encourages women to deceive themselves as well as others.

Feminine—Not Feminist—Rhetoric

Lean In spent numerous weeks as a bestseller and spawned several follow-up books that do little to nothing to update Sandberg's basic message—more women need to "lean in" to the world of business. Yet "women" as addressed in the book is a false monolithic "she"—one that really doesn't exist other than as a limited version of the author's own identity. Thus, this "she" is not reflexive or reflective of the broader audience the book attracts or of the broader contexts, including the academic world, in which we see its misguided, and unvoiced, principles reflected and applied. What, then, accounts for the appeal of this book?

The chapters of *Lean In* are episodic, moving from topic to topic with little tying them together thematically. In this way, Sandberg casts herself as just "one of the girls" sharing advice while trying to erase the rather obvious cultural barriers that exist between herself and the monolithic "she" community of her imagination, a perspective that erases race, gender identity, or other intersecting identities. She begins with stories about her pregnancy and attempts to reassure the reader that she is not "a scholar, journalist, or sociologist" but rather a woman who decided to speak out about the "complex challenges" that all women face (9). She even makes a move toward community building stating that *Lean In* "is not a feminist manifesto—okay, it is a sort of a feminist manifesto, but one that I hope inspires men as much as it inspires women" (9).

Ironically, these stylistic choices strongly evoke what has been identified as the feminine style of rhetoric and connects Sandberg to the long history of women protest writers who employed that style. In her text *Man Cannot Speak for Her* (1989), Karlyn Kohrs Campbell defines the feminine style of rhetoric by examining the oratory of women who fought for abolition and suffrage. Challenged first as speakers attempting to persuade their audiences—both male and female—that they had a right to speak at all, these women achieved an ethos through developing a style that relied on relational strategies. Campbell thus identifies the feminine style as the process of craft learning as applied to the rhetorical situation, but always with the intention of improving the situation of women by enabling them to critique effectively the systemic injustices in which they lived. Based on a long tradition of the passing on of life skills, of keeping traditions alive, and of sharing advice, the rhetorical voice of the feminine model is personal in tone and relies heavily on individual experience and anecdotes. Employing a voice that urges the audience to test their experiences against those of the speaker in order to achieve agreement through identification with that speaker, the goal of feminine rhetoric is to empower the audience: to inspire them to believe that they have a credible voice and, thus, negate the personal insecurity that allows the status quo to operate unchallenged (12–15).

That Sandberg follows this pattern is undeniable, but there are some vital differences between her project and other women, historical and contemporary, who write toward the goal of cultural change. Sandberg may be writing in the feminine style, but her claim to Feminism, in the way that feminist scholars and activists define the word, is tenuous. As defined by Foss, Foss and Griffin (1999), "Feminism" is always most concerned with offering alternate models of communication and living in the world that do not oppress or exploit individuals, regardless of gender. Allowing individuals to make choices based on their experience while, most importantly, validating and affirming those choices, feminism "establishes and legitimates a value system that privileges mutuality, respect, caring, power-with, interconnections, and immanent value" (5)—values which are in direct opposition to those in the dominant culture which Sandberg and other self-help success gurus expound. Moreover, the terms "feminine" and "feminist" have become confused in popular culture, as well as in the academy—and that confusion serves the purpose of Sandberg's argument—to convince her readers that she is writing for progress and change even as she is not. Instead, she claims it is enough of a goal for her to be writing simply to increase the role and presence of the feminine in the business world because somehow this will change everything: "[i]f we can succeed in adding more female voices at the highest levels, we will expand opportunities and extend fairer treatment to all" (10). Unlike the much more expansive goals of those women who developed the feminine style she is using, Sandberg's motivating purpose is limited to "there aren't enough women here."

Feminist theorist and activist bell hooks takes Sandberg to task for promoting, in *Lean In*, simplistic "faux feminism" that begins and ends with the idea that equal rights for women is based solely on gender representation in existing modes of corporate power. As hooks (2013) passionately argues,

> The work [of feminism] does not end with the fight for equality of opportunity within the existing patriarchal structure. We must understand that challenging and dismantling patriarchy is at the core of contemporary feminist struggle—this is essential and necessary if women and men are to be truly liberated from outmoded sexist thinking and actions.
>
> (para. 5)

Why then is this narrative of equality based upon mere gender representation so entrenched in the cultural mind-set? Moreover, why does the academic world, where what hooks calls the "academic sub-set of feminism" exists, increasingly seem willing to embrace this narrative and to resist the call to reimagine and accept alternative visions of success—for men and women—within its own walls?

At one point in *Lean In*, Sandberg mentions attending a Women's Studies course, but then confesses—almost cheerfully—that she didn't pay too much attention. Perhaps this accounts for why she believes that her project is somewhat vaguely related to feminism. Any Women's Studies course would likely have included the essential point that just increasing the women's numbers is far from enough. In fact, suggesting this as a *main* or *central* goal of her book and accompanying projects indicates a dangerous inattention to what would also have been emphasized in that Women's Studies course as vitally important: the need for critical, reflective analysis of the status quo and its standard operations. Similarly, while it is worth applauding the fact that there are more women in academic leadership roles than ever before, and that a Women's Studies/Gender Studies (WS/GS) program is de rigueur at most accredited colleges and universities, the mere existence of such women and programs has come to be considered sufficient. In reality, women leaders and women's programs do not, in and of themselves, enable progress just as the mere presence of women—or more women—at "the highest levels" of the business world does not naturally ensure more equitable work, opportunity, or pay. Existence cannot stand in for discussion, action, and change as the university continues its standard operations. There must be an interrogation of the sexist ideologies that may drive and sustain those operations.

Yet another misuse of the feminine style that also curtails inquiry and, therefore, true progress, is Sandberg's assertion—and she dedicates a whole chapter to it—that one of the largest threats to women's progress is when women "attack" other women (especially because the media is quick to report any perceived hint of a "catfight"). Ostensibly a nod to the feminist tenet of communal ties between and among women, the result is yet another form of silencing. Not only is this seemingly gentle reminder that "When arguments turn into 'she said/she said,' we all lose" (162) a preemptive attempt to silence Sandberg's own critics, it is also a subtle but effective assertion that any questioning or examination of other women—simply because they are women—is unjust. Thus, the historical example from over 40 years ago of Betty Friedan refusing to shake hands with Gloria Steinem becomes, in Sandberg's estimation, an example of what's wrong with the current struggle for women's rights. Calling for "us" not to make this mistake and to stay focused on "shared goals," she claims this is not a "plea for less debate, but for a more constructive debate" (162). Unfortunately, both those shared goals and what would make a more constructive debate remain undefined. Instead she conveniently maintains a focus on blaming women who critique other women's achievements or life choices, no matter how questionable these might be. This apparent feminist call to and defense of female community serves, instead, to maintain the status quo as any examination or questioning of any other woman's choices or situation is, itself, mislabeled as anti-woman.

Evoking another unfortunate trend in the academy, this mind-set uses the tools of the feminist movement to forestall that movement and the reflection and revelation for self and society that such a female sense of community was intended to encourage and inspire. Such effective rhetorical silencing techniques accounts as well for WS/GS programs being asked to support any event, course, speaker, and so forth merely because they involve women in some way—with little to no expectation that the nature or message of the event might actually conflict with the goals of gender equality. Even asking for time to examine an event is seen as "anti-woman" because doing so might actually reveal the emptiness of the premise that the mere presence of women is the solution to all issues of gender oppression. The assumption that it is enough to have women in leadership positions, enough for universities to have WS/GS programs negates true critique, true questioning of the systems that continue to control and oppress. Being a woman, being a female, being feminine—tokenism without interrogation of what these mean—has dangerously replaced feminist.

Assertively Feminine—Not Feminist

Without the element of attention and inquiry to systemic injustices and to self, so central to feminism, Sandberg's use of a feminine style of rhetoric that has previously enabled women to expose and challenge such injustices only suggests the language of change and amounts to little more than suggestions for coping with a profit-driven, male-dominated, winner-take-all system. While *Lean In* ostensibly supports a more assertive style for women, urging women to ask for what they need and want, it also advises giving the current biased system what *it wants*. Women, Sandberg says "need to combine niceness with insistence," need to "smile frequently" and practice being "relentlessly pleasant" (a term she borrows from another woman leader) (48). While she admits "the paradox of advising women to change the world by adhering to biased rules and expectations," she says that women must, of necessity, do these things "as a means to a desirable end" (48).

Similarly, under the guise of empowering women, other contemporary advice books for women leaders—such as Katty Kay and Claire Shipman's *The Confidence Code: The Science and Art of Self-Assurance—What Women Should Know* (2014)—likewise insist upon women being more confident and assertive, but yet paradoxically concede that women "have to deal with the world as it is" because "ignoring centuries of tradition would be shortsighted to say the least" (99). While the title of Lois Frankel's *Nice Girls (Still) Don't Get the Corner Office: Unconscious Mistakes Women Make that Sabotage Their Careers* (2014) directly declares that women need to stop acting like little girls, the book is full of advice that also demurs to long-standing conventions regarding women's behaviors, clothes, hairstyles, and physical appearance. Ironically, in a dangerously inverted use of feminist thinking, conceding to such sexist traditions is portrayed as assertive and realistic while contesting them is weak, inefficient, even self-destructive. Even Emily Toth in *Ms. Mentor's New and Ever More Impeccable Advice for Women (and Men) in Academia* (2009) asserts that the smart girl knows how to act like the "big boys" (29) but also knows how to attend to the words and needs of others: "Smiling is always welcome" (20). The so-called empowerment offered to women, then, amounts to a self-interested coping mechanism that endorses a "winner-take-all" (and male-coded) mentality *and* the disingenuous (and female-coded) advice to smile and connive. Because of a lack of interrogation of the worthwhile nature of the systems Sandberg and these other self-help authors are promoting, the use of a feminine style of rhetoric that in the past enabled women to expose and challenge such systems, becomes a trick, a shell game that speaks the language of change and feminist principles, while actually promoting and protecting the status quo.

While *Lean In* and similar books urge women to adopt certain masculine styles of leadership and success—often while praising these styles by contrasting what men do right with what women do wrong—they also advocate for an equally troubling readoption of stereotypical feminine behaviors in order to "succeed" in a "man's world." Such advice to women allows for a bizarre and dangerous reintroduction of gendered stereotyping and biology as destiny. Frankel, for example, asserts that "[m]en are simply not wired to take things as personally as women do. To them, work is just business, it's not personal" (80) while Kay and Shipman present the approaches of male executives as exemplary of what men do that women don't—or can't (18). Are women just naturally prone to the *101 Unconscious Mistakes* (or more) that Frankel says *Sabotage Their Careers* or the *Mistakes . . . Made at Work* by women described by Jessica Bacal? Like *Lean In*, the conversational and practical tone of these books obscures the assumptions that drive them: that gender binaries are simply inescapable, that women "naturally" act one way and men another, and that sexism is just an everyday reality in which *women* must learn to live.

Since traits traditionally associated with men are applauded, those things that distinguish women become indicators of failure in the working world: "They [men] project a level of comfort with themselves that gets them noticed and rewarded" while women have too much "female self-doubt" and "lack" not only "self-belief," but also "a certain boldness, a firm faith in [our] abilities" (Kay and Shipman 2014, xiii). In camouflaging a reassertion of gendered stereotypes as practical advice, these writers stifle what could be valuable opportunities to truly compare experiences or advance visions of success that run counter to the status quo. "Self-doubt," might actually be self-reflection; "lacking faith in one's abilities" might actually be an indicator of thoughtfulness, a resistance to attention and reward, a lack of arrogance. Might not some self-reflection, some advanced thought, some humility and attention to others serve us all well, and better, than the limited characterization of success that these writers associate with what men have and what women don't? In other words, might we do well to ask what is Sandberg's "desirable end"? Is the meaning of success—wealth, power, status—that primarily drives these books left unvoiced in order to detract from the fact what is presented as a way for women to create a more equitable society actually serves to undermine that objective: instead, just play the game, go ahead and use those sexist stereotypes to your own advantage (Evans 2001), get what you want *and deserve* in this world even as you compromise self, being, and existence in order to do so.

Years ago, an acquaintance boldly announced at a department dinner that she did and would use her sexuality and physical appearance to get what she wanted and that she saw nothing wrong with doing this. There is a flaw in this argument—not her attention to her sexuality or physicality but, rather, her intent to use it to get want she wants. We all know and recognize this tactical behavior—in ourselves, in other women, in committee meetings, in classrooms, at donor events. These tactics—smile, be pleasant, congenial, don't push too hard, flatter, focus on others instead of yourself (or at least pretend to) and so on—are softening agents meant to make the audacity of the idea of female leadership and authority more palatable. What remains a controlling instrument of sexism in our culture—our bodies, our clothes, our external appearance—is presented both directly and indirectly as a more dressed up version of "you'll catch more flies with honey than with vinegar"—that is, if you are female. But *do we really want the flies that we might catch?* Do we really want women who conform—who display the attributes and behaviors which Sandberg and others say are required—portrayed as true leaders when they are performing and modeling stereotypes and biases and, thus, practicing a form of self-deception and self-denial? There is nothing wrong with being nice, with practicing good manners, with supporting others and putting the "we" before the "I"—indeed, all humanity should be practicing this, but practicing it as a matter of course, as a value, and not for money and power because then it becomes a form of deceit, a masking of our truest selves in order to participate in the long-running masquerade our society entices everyone to join. Perhaps this explains the sense of defeat that many colleagues feel in response to *Lean In.* They know that universities shouldn't operate like businesses, but they also know that corporatization has arrived and will continue—and, with the definition of individualistic success that accompanies this, comes the expectation (if not the requirement) that women will act like female stereotypes of themselves, that they will have and make use of "a full arsenal of tactics and techniques . . . that are consistent with being a woman [and] not acting like a man" (Frankel 2014, 48). Perhaps, and with great sadness, they have seen that women, in order "to get ahead," will perform the very subjugated roles which their own scholarly and pedagogical work has striven to combat.

Decorporatizing Feminism, Decorporatizing the Academy

While we are not necessarily surprised to find a gender-based definition of success and "looking out for number one" operating in the corporate and business worlds, its growing presence in academia is disturbing and destructive, not only because so many of our universities and colleges claim a dedication to social justice, as well as gender equality, but also because such a definition may encourage academic women to accept the incongruous idea of "chang[ing] the world by adhering to biased rules and expectations." There is a revealing intersection between the corporatization of the academic world and female faculty and administrators accepting, performing, and perpetuating their subjugated positions "as a means to a desirable end." Just as women are told that they need to start living in the "real" world at work, so too are universities being forced to come into the "real" world of business and corporations; however, there have been and continue to be those in the academy who refuse to silently accept the "faux feminism" of advice that focuses on navigating (thus accepting) the institution as it exists. These academics understand and apply the ideologies of feminist critique in their work, challenging the status quo, and motivating their readers to do likewise toward sustainable change that validates the entire community.

As discussed by Foss, Foss and Griffin (1999) feminist—and particularly, feminist rhetorical—critique, functions to discover how individuals construct and make meaning of the world around them and then reimagine and redirect that world (7). They point to the work of Cheris Kramarae, who calls for the creation of "woman's world" where "interconnection, safety, holism, trust, mutuality, adaptability, and equal access to information" are achievable (48). Kramarae insists that the only way to enable her vision is the de- and reconstruction of our current linguistic and narrative structures that distort or omit the lived experience of being a woman. "I'm interested," she says, "in pushing on words and their definitions, questioning and often mocking traditional practices in order to make possible new meaning and practices" (55). A similar project is taken up in the writing of sociocultural linguist Deborah Tannen, whose texts *You Just Don't Understand: Men and Women in Conversation* (1991) and *Talking from 9 to 5: Women and Men at Work* (1995) explore how the culturally coded differences in male/female conversation styles affect their ability to communicate and work together. By identifying and questioning the status quo, her work creates a space for "woman's world" to be envisioned, challenging the reader to not just agree that these things are but to pursue what could be—to change the rhetorical principles by which we communicate and persuade each other.

Laura R. Micciche (2010), too, focuses on the particular power the act of writing has in disturbing the status quo and in reimagining and revisioning reality because it "establishes links between language, action, and consequences" (176). Micciche speaks of the importance of caring for language as we promote a vision of what could be instead of what is. She quotes Toni Morrison, who writes, "Word-work is sublime . . . because it is generative; it makes meaning that secures our difference, our human difference" and Trinh T. Minh-ha, who claims that all women must be "language stealers" as they create their own agency: "Shake syntax, smash the myths, and if you lose, slide on, *unearth* some new linguistic paths" (179). (Italics in original) Micciche adds, "Writing documents and makes visible those experiences and ways of knowing that require unearthing because they have been buried in the shit of oppressive discourses" (179). In contrast, urging empowerment for women yet simultaneously accepting the system as the authors of popular advice texts for women do, works against such empowerment, works against the excavation of the foundation that can disable the reconstruction of old ideologies into newly imagined realities. Unfortunately, as they are not invested in the deeper work of feminist rhetorical critique, these contemporary female role models waste a powerful opportunity to engage in truly challenging the narratives that continue to perpetuate the patriarchal underpinnings of the corporate structures that exist in the worlds of work and the academy.

Thankfully, newly imagined narratives that do critique these underpinnings and structures continue to appear. In *The Slow Professor: Challenging the Culture of Speed in the Academy* (2016), Professors Maggie Berg and Barbara K. Seeber invoke the slow food model in order to reject the "corporate university" where "power is transferred from faculty to managers, economic justifications dominate, and the familiar 'bottom line' eclipses pedagogical and intellectual concerns" (x). Not simply complaining about a well-documented crisis in education, they offer a model which runs counter to the long-standing history and mythology of "self sufficient individualism and rationalism that sustained the old narrative" of what the academy was, and continue to "prop-up the new." They claim these old, patriarchal values, which run counter to the relationship-based, communal activities of women, "actually opened the door to corporatization" of the university (12). Believing that power still remains with the people who create and disperse knowledge—not administrators and especially not politicians—Berg and Seeber's new narrative runs an intentionally brief, but powerful, 90 pages. Engaging in this type of writing situates them, then, squarely in the camp of feminist rhetorical critique. They are questioning and ultimately recreating the spoken and unspoken, written and unwritten, narratives that define and control women's work in the academy.

As women in the academy, our role should be to engage in this type of questioning and reenvisioning of our own workplace practices instead of performing the same old script. Why, for example, do we continue to play a game with ancient and arcane rules of advancement that are so counter to the values of those women and men who want to balance their research with family or who are more engaged with pedagogy than theory? Why do we continue to sacrifice ourselves on the altar of the tenure system, even as that model becomes increasingly susceptible to abuse, including sexist exclusion based on the desire to have a child; dated, yet stubborn, stereotypes about the intellectual capacity of women; and sexist characterizations of what makes a woman a valuable colleague? We must allow ourselves to reimagine the work we do in the academy so that we can encourage and promote alternate visions of what it means to be successful.

We believe that many academic women are looking for an alternative attention to the self and to society—one that is not primarily defined by hairstyles or facial expressions or feminine pleasantness, and one whose goal is not primarily self-promotion and advancement. Indeed, this attention is a foundational part of a true, contemporary feminist manifesto rather than Sandberg's "sort of feminist manifesto" (9). This kind of attention to self and society neither blames ourselves for not leaning in enough nor is about accepting society and participating in a system from which, patently, women have been and continue to be excluded. Rather, this attention to self and society is a call to engage in a form of self-examination that allows us to identify our own practices, actions, and ways of being that do and do not help to perpetuate and sustain systems of power which we say we want to change. It is a call to be brutally honest with ourselves about the fears, the dangers, and the selfishness which those systems encourage in us and to which they hold us—as women—hostage. As women invested in more than simply paying lip service to feminist ideology, we desire the further creation and implementation modes of communication that are true alternatives to the status quo, that offer more than just means to survive sexism in the world of work and the academy, but instead to change it, to thrive in it.

References

Bacal, Jessica. (2014). *Mistakes I Made at Work: 25 Influential Women Reflect on What They Got Out of Getting It Wrong*. New York: Penguin.

Berg, Maggie, and Barbara K. Seeber. (2016) *The Slow Professor: Challenging the Culture of Speed in the Academy*. Toronto: University of Toronto Press.

Campbell, Karlyn Kohrs. (1989). *Man Cannot Speak for Her*. New York: Preager.

Evans, Gail. (2001). *Play Like a Man, Win Like a Woman: What Men Know About Success that Women Need to Learn*. New York: Random House.

Foss, Karen A., Sonja K. Foss, and Cindy L. Griffin. (1999). *Feminist Rhetorical Theories*. Thousand Oaks, CA: Sage Publications.

Frankel, Lois. (2004). *Nice Girls Don't Get the Corner Office: 101 Unconscious Mistakes Women Make that Sabotage Their Careers*. New York: Warner Business Books.

———. (2014). *Nice Girls Still Don't Get the Corner Office: Unconscious Mistakes Women Make that Sabotage Their Careers*. New York: Business Plus.

hooks, bell. (October 28, 2013). "Dig Deep: Beyond Lean In." *The Feminist Wire*. www.thefeministwire.com/2013/10/17973/.

Kay, Katty, and Claire Shipman. (2014). *The Confidence Code: The Science and Art of Self-Assurance—What Women Should Know*. New York: HarperCollins.

Micciche, Laura R. (2010). "Writing as Feminist Rhetorical Theory." In *Rhetoric in Motion: Feminist Rhetorical Methods & Methodologies*, edited by Eileen E. Schell and K. J. Rawson, 173–188. Pittsburgh: University of Pittsburgh Press.

Sandberg, Sheryl with Nell Scovell. (2013). *Lean In: Women, Work and the Will to Lead*. New York: Knopf.

Tannen, Deborah. (1991). *You Just Don't Understand: Women and Men in Conversation*. New York: Balantine Books.

———. (1995). *Talking from 9 to 5: Women and Men at Work*. (Reprint 2001). New York: William Morrow Paperbacks.

Toth, Emily. (2009). *Ms. Mentor's New and Ever More Impeccable Advice for Women and Men in Academia*. Philadelphia: University of Pennsylvania Press.

5 Understanding Leadership with Women Community College Executives

Hawa Ghaus-Kelley and Nathan R. Durdella

"I'm not afraid to try new things or take risks. . . . Bureaucracy impedes creativity. . . . I'm always trying to figure out my way around a rule . . . people are naturally resistant to change . . . but we facilitate change all day . . . all year long . . . THAT'S the key. And when people develop a plan, they want to move that plan . . . so then, THEY become part of the change movement—they are the change agents."
—Superintendent-President Darlene Huntersail

Within the context of strategies for feminist leadership, critical learning moments are self-reflective opportunities of the significant occasions when overall lived histories of leadership experiences intersect with organizational knowledge and educational practice that lead to systemic reform for their campuses, with the potential to convey meaningful and insightful perspectives for women executive leaders. The need to explore the meaning of what we call the critical learning moments (CLM) phenomena led to our conversations with women executive leaders of two-year public colleges and districts in California who had demonstrated transformative leadership practices. Given our purpose to explore the *meaning* community college women executive leaders ascribe to CLM in their educational leadership practices, two research questions guided our inquiry: (1) What is essential for women executive leaders at California community colleges to describe CLMs as meaningful in their leadership practice, and (2) What transformative leadership practices have women leaders utilized to lead their campuses to systemic reform? By understanding how they manage their colleges and adapt their leadership style to meet the needs of their institutions and stakeholders, we hoped to shape how practitioners and policy makers will be able to better understand current female experiences and leadership strategies of women executives.

Using a multitheoretical lens, we framed our work in the study through adaptive and emergent female leadership styles and theories related to transformative change with critical feminism to better understand and explore CLM and, in particular, what meaning female executive leaders ascribe to CLM from their overall leadership practice toward transformative systemic change. These learning moments are crucial to better understand practical approaches in the field which can lead to transformational and systemic institutional reform. This understanding will, in turn, benefit a larger circle of stakeholders, including practitioners, policy makers, academics, and future researchers in the field of educational leadership. Indeed, how women executive leader change agents make meaning of their experiences can help link practical approaches in the field of leadership in higher education institutions (AACC 2012; ACE 2012).

Women in Leadership Positions in Community Colleges

Even though there has been an increase of women in leadership positions in community colleges, recent trends still show that there are fewer women leaders than men (ACE 2012; Eddy 2010; USDE 2013). Although women earn the majority of post-secondary degrees in undergraduate and graduate schools, with 61% of community college students enrolled nationally being female and 56% in California, they are still underrepresented in the field of leadership and executive positions. Indeed, women occupy just 26% of all college presidency positions according to recent data from AACC (2012) and ACE (2012). According to AACC's (2012) statistics, 28% of current CEO leaders of community colleges are women. Thus, despite demographic trends of a leadership vacuum, with 84% of current presidents expecting to retire by 2016, the increased routes to executive leadership positions, and women's significant presence at community colleges, the leaders of these institutions are still mostly White men. Not only are women and minorities still underrepresented as presidents, but also, according to the report by The American College President (ACE 2012), the rate at which these two groups are rising to the presidency is beginning to slow. Women hold 26% of all college presidencies, according to recent data from AACC (2012) and ACE (2012). While women have increased their representation (26% in 2011, up from 23% in 2006), the proportion of presidents who are racial and ethnic minorities declined slightly, from 14% in 2006 to 13% in 2011.

Community colleges are known for their open-door mission and have provided many women students with access to higher education (Cohen and Brawer 2008; Eddy 2010). Community colleges have been noted to be good places for women to work (Townsend and Twombly 2007). Eddy's (2010) study confirms that more community college presidencies may be awarded to women in the future, especially if they are "mentored and supported as they move along their career pathway" (120). Moreover, with a mission to serve all underrepresented groups, community colleges and their executive leaders are in a position to promote, through their leadership practices, ethnic, racial, and gender equity at their institutions. Yet, despite being inclusive and supportive of women, stereotypes and mobility challenges exist that may impede the success of female leaders and the advancement of women to upper leadership positions (Eagly 2007; Townsend and Twombly 2007). Other researchers agree that there are stereotypes and mobility challenges, such as Leatherwood and Williams (2008), who assert that women make up the majority of students enrolled in colleges and universities, yet leadership positions in higher education have not been a strong area for women.

Critical and Feminist Paradigm

The critical theory paradigm, also known as advocacy or participatory framework, focuses on social justice to address inequality (Creswell, as cited in Bloomberg and Volpe 2012). Perspectives within the paradigm include research strategies "such as narrative analysis that are openly ideological and have empowering and democratizing goals" (Bloomberg and Volpe 2012, 29). In reconceptualizing this study through this framework, the focus was to provide a platform for community college women executives to voice their experiences and CLM in their leadership practice.

Critical and feminist research perspectives are increasingly influencing qualitative research; further evidence that even though the leadership norm continues to be male oriented, more women are occupying positions of leadership in our society and the need to explore how effectively they lead reform in their institutions. Consequently, feminists believe that organizational change is central to improving the condition of women and that without change, women's social, political, and economic conditions will continue to be unequal to men's and women will not have a significant voice in the power structures that drive society; therefore, "the kind of change that feminists envision is not mere tinkering but requires a paradigmatic shift, a breaking out of the mold of patriarchal thinking" (Townsend and Twombly 1998, 78).

Community colleges are highly patriarchal, traditional institutions, yet they are loosely coupled, extremely team- and collaboratively oriented organizations (Eddy 2010; Kezar 2001; Townsend and Twombly 1998). Thus, successful reform initiatives must involve leadership practices involving all stakeholders in a shared governance process characterized by whole-systems change (Burns 2005; Malm 2008; Northouse 2012). Full systemic reform improvements—characterized by long-term, second-tiered, whole-systems change—must engage a transformative practice approach by leaders attempting paradigmatic shifts toward successful reform initiatives in traditional male-dominated organizations (Kezar 2001; Wheatley 2006).

Methodological Approach

A scaled, multicase study approach and design within the phenomenological research tradition informed our exploratory work with women executive leaders. In-depth interviewing technique by use of open-ended, semi-structured questions provided data during two iterative, sequenced sessions with each woman executive leader and assisted in providing a better understanding of the meaning and fundamental nature of CLM phenomena in each participant's leadership practice (Seidman 2006). Evidence from phenomenological research is derived from first-person reports of life experiences (Moustakas 1994), which allowed us to better understand the essential structures of women leader experiences (Bloomberg and Volpe 2012; Creswell 2012; Miles and Huberman 1994; Rossman and Rallis 2003). Consequently, we based research site and participant selection on how we could best learn from women executives in their real-life work contexts. Using a mixed sampling strategy of criterion and network techniques, we used interviews with a district chancellor, college superintendent-president, college president, and vice president in community colleges and districts in California. With transcribed personal interviews of firsthand narrative accounts of their experiences, we analyzed data in iterative stages using analytical techniques guided by the phenomenological research tradition: coding, clustering, and thematizing (Bloomberg and Volpe 2012).

Leadership's Pathways and Difficult Choices for Women

Although participants came from diverse backgrounds, they shared strong influences and structures that supported future executive leadership roles: supportive familial upbringing where education was valued, having supervising male mentors in the workplace and female role models, and the support of encouraging partners. Participants' lived histories and leadership paths to becoming CEOs were difficult. With much hard work and sacrifice in their educational and professional career paths, they navigated to become CEOs. The women executive leaders sacrificed much in their personal lives, limiting interactions with friends and family due to busy work schedules, and expressed nostalgia from missing quality time and having to uproot and move multiple times. Four of the five chose their leadership careers over having children due to the strains of their chosen field. Study findings supported previous empirical research showing few women leaders in higher education executive leadership (Cook 2012; Krause 2009; Townsend and Twombly 2007). Findings proposed connections among social forces and gender roles in women CEOs' leadership pathways. Male CEOs on the same track typically do not face such difficult decisions in choosing their career trajectories, given their gender and larger societal expectations of male CEOs.

Leadership Themes and Critical Learning Moments

From thematic data analysis of participant profiles, three leadership profile themes emerged from the results:

1. Internal and external motivation, perseverance, optimism and willingness to volunteer beyond their call of duty;
2. Gender issues and leadership style differences experienced in previous leadership positions;
3. Gender as individually and organizationally significant. In addition, a second category of results emerged: focusing on the leadership experiences and practices of women executive participants.

These critical learning moments in leadership emerged as follows:

1. Realization and reconciliation moments: challenges of leadership in struggles, disappointments, and compromises;
2. Impactful moments: leadership is a lifestyle, a commitment, and a calling in shaping daily lives of constituents;
3. Relational moments: egalitarian leadership behavioral styles of change agents;
4. Pioneering moments: emergent, interactive organizational processes in systemic reform;
5. Empowerment moments: countering obstacles to innovate and sustain;
6. Capacity-building moments: mentoring and paying it forward.

We discuss these themes and learning moments in turn in this section.

Internal and External Motivating Forces

Perhaps because of influences and supportive structures, an unwavering drive and commitment to contribute to the field of education, and optimistic outlooks, women executive leaders expressed the need to prove themselves and persevered through difficult personal and professional episodes, driven to succeed in their roles as executive leaders and agents of change for their colleges. Because internal motivation was a large factor in participants' sense of purpose—personal belief in their ability to contribute to and positively impact their field, the community college mission, and their leadership profession—they exhibited strong willingness to go beyond their call of duty. For example, President Sara Schenectady articulated, "I also want to continually stretch my own world—my own aspirations even at this stage in my career because that makes me better, and that also enables me to make a better and a bigger contribution." Having positive predispositions, women executive leaders continually challenged themselves professionally—meeting external challenges in times of crisis and maintaining a strong belief that they had power to change the future. For example, when faced with major obstacles to campus construction projects, President Schenectady framed perseverance this way: "Being the kind of person who is incredibly tenacious—I don't give up easily."

Gender Issues and Leadership Style Differences

All participants expressed the need to be strategic in seeking and advancing to higher positions of leadership. They actively accessed career-growth opportunities but felt the lack of opportunity for advancement. Extant empirical research findings give evidence that organizational barriers limit women's mobility in higher learning institutions, restricting their ability to access executive leadership positions (Cook 2012; Eagly 2012; Eddy 2010; Krause 2009; Townsend and Twombly 2007; Weisman and Vaughan 2007). Links between hierarchical structures of community college organizations may impede women's direct path to executive roles within their colleges; women leaders needed to be strategic, leaving their current colleges and districts to advance to their next leadership positions. On this point, Superintendent-President Darlene Huntersail illustrated this point best when she shared,

> I realized that if I could compete in that arena . . . I want to be a president. . . . I had to leave, so I was very strategic . . . and went somewhere to give me the experience that I could get in a condensed fashion.

Gender as Individually and Organizationally Significant

Participants experienced sexism in the workplace and perceived gender differences in leadership style in past leadership positions. Community colleges have hierarchical structures, and studies point to issues of gender and sexism facing women leaders (Cook 2012; Eddy 2010; Leatherwood and Williams 2008). For example, before Superintendent-President Darlene Huntersail became a CEO, women middle management leaders had to deal with male administrators who "would make passes . . . and it just was another target toward whom to be assertive." In this vein, gender remains significant; perhaps even a cultural force—filtering problems of sexism in their leadership roles, in opportunities for internal advancement to becoming a CEO, and leadership style differences in their organizational contexts. Specific examples that illustrate how they experienced these events included stories like Vice President Anne Reina's, where she conveyed that she used her "charm as a woman"—because she knew there would be times that allowed her to "make a little bit more headway" in getting the agenda she needed. Similarly, here, President Sara Schenectady expressed her experience with male members of the board of trustees: "I think that stakeholders often—especially male stakeholders—don't accept women as readily on face value."

Critical Learning Moments in Leadership Practice: Six Thematic Patterns

We developed the term "CLM" as self-reflective opportunities wherein lived histories of leadership experiences intersected with organizational knowledge and educational practice that led to systemic reform for colleges and districts. This study's findings related to the first research question: "What is essential for women executive leaders at California community colleges to describe CLMs as meaningful in their leadership practice?" confirmed that CLM conveyed significant and insightful perspectives for women executive leader participants, including reconciliatory moments when facing major challenges and struggles, realizing the necessity to compromise. Participants described their leadership practice as impactful and empowering: not only a lifestyle and a calling but also requiring total commitment. Sharing their leadership experiences and stories during the interview process reinforced their self-worth and belief in a higher cause.

The challenges of their positions, struggles, disappointments, and compromises were essential when describing meaningful CLMs in their leadership practices with regard to this study's first research question. Learning as they led, they had a strong inclination to continually try new avenues and take substantial risks, and they were aware enough to be able to know when to step back, reassess, listen, and pool information when leading small or large-scale organizational change. Superintendent-President Darlene Huntersail articulated these shared perceptions:

> You have to have a vision . . . you have to believe you can [transform] it and you have to be willing to work hard enough to do it. . . . You can't be a good leader if you're not committed to constantly learning and changing . . . picking large battles but being flexible all at the same time.

Supported by literature on organizational change (Burns 2005; Kezar 2001; Kotter 1995; Northouse 2012; Senge 1990; Wheatley 2006), participants experienced various obstacles and resistance to change when introducing, implementing, or instituting reform initiatives or processes in their colleges and districts.

Realizing Moments of Struggles and Compromises

The challenges of their positions, struggles, disappointments, and compromises were essential when describing meaningful CLMs in their leadership practices with regard to this study's first research question. As individuals and as female executive leaders who transformed two-year public higher education institutions, they needed to express practicality and flexibility in their leadership approach. Learning as they led, they had a strong inclination to continually try new avenues, take substantial risks, and were aware enough to be able to know when to step back, reassess, listen, and pool information when leading small or large-scale organizational change. Consistent with what we know, participants experienced various obstacles and resistance to change when introducing, implementing, or instituting reform initiatives or processes in their colleges and districts. Women executive leaders at the college level each expressed very strong feelings regarding their struggles with districts' lack of support for their leadership authority, the politically driven environment of community colleges, and the lack of commitment of members of the board of trustees. For example, President Sara Schenectady shared feelings on the lack of support from superiors:

> I didn't feel like I had support from higher ups . . . our organization . . . it's not supportive of leadership. We're always criticized . . . always asked to explain and justify everything . . . rarely complimented . . . there's a significant . . . almost . . . schizophrenic mentality, with holding the presidents responsible for everything, but . . . telling them, no, they can't make those decisions. And that is really hard. It's really hard to be a leader in that environment. If it weren't for the fact that I absolutely am totally committed to what Basin College does and is about, and this community that we serve, I would have probably resigned a long time ago, because it's really an untenable situation.

Here, President Schenectady illustrates how institutional resistance to change forced many of these women executives to be challenged in their leadership.

Leadership as an Empowering Lifestyle

When we asked about CLM in their lives more globally, we learned how these opportunities conveyed significant and insightful perspectives for women executive leaders, as they overwhelmingly expressed the impact they believed their leadership made on the daily lives of constituents. Women leaders viewed their leadership practice as impactful and expressed an unwavering dedication and commitment to making a difference in the lives of students and a wide range of constituents. Further, they viewed leadership as an all-encompassing lifestyle, a worthy and righteous cause, and perceived their lifetime commitment as a higher calling. Women CEOs attached considerable meaning to the impact of their leadership, as the true test of their leadership ability, as an individual, as a leader, and as a female executive. The women participant CEOs perceived leadership not only as impacting others but also empowering in their own lives as well.

Here Superintendent-President Darlene Huntersail described how she sees leadership informing the person she is:

> The memories of the people and the moments that occurred around which I tell the stories are forever motivating. . . . They have informed the person that I am . . . I don't see my job as a job . . . it's who I am and . . . how I share or articulate my leadership experiences . . . and giving good guidance . . . that empowers me.

Similarly, in sharing and reflecting on her experiences, Vice President Anne Reina surprised herself with the realization of the contribution of leadership to her confidence and overall self-worth:

> I look at leadership as something that gives me . . . self-worth . . . my ability to feel like I'm doing something right for the world . . . because . . . I'm able to have some good results that came out of those

leadership experiences. . . . It allows me to feel more self-aware . . . self-confident in terms of making other decisions that impact other areas of my life . . . I guess looking back and reflecting I'm a little surprised by that. I do feel that it empowers me and that . . . by hearing my experiences, it empowers other people to know that they're not alone and that they can go on the same pathway.

Relational and Egalitarian Leadership Styles as Change Agents

We also discovered female leaders had highly relational, people-oriented communicative behaviors and egalitarian leadership styles as change agents. Research shows that women tend to lead using more participative and collaborative styles than men, more likely to use transformational-leadership behaviors associated with contemporary notions of effective leadership (Eagly 2007; Eddy 2010; Northouse 2012).

Moreover, the greater use of egalitarian and democratic style tended to not simply be adaptive in that they used only the style that produced the most favorable evaluations for their colleges. In fact, as relational leaders, this study's participants expressed how and when they used particular leadership behaviors and explained their leadership styles in enacting and sustaining reform initiatives in their institutions during crisis and even when their colleges did not "meet numbers" during assessment cycles. As relational executives, participants tended to exhibit leadership techniques that were profoundly people oriented, instructive and direct, compassionate, and considerate communicators.

Women Leaders' Pioneering Moments in Organizational Processes

Due to their democratic leadership styles, relation-driven leadership behaviors in forging and maintaining relationships, cultivation of collaborative responsibility, and transparent communication in shared decision making, participants experienced great success as change agents. Their leadership qualities of commitment to constituents and themselves, motivation, and perseverance contributed to pioneering moments of initiating, implementing, and maintaining interactive, flexible forms of organizational change.

What we found was that women CEOs tended to leverage emergent, interactive, cyclical change processes on their campuses by being instructive, directive, and persistent in their management practices. By adapting the entrepreneurial techniques of risk taking and building and sustaining partnerships, foundations, external advisory committees, and networks, they created a sense of urgency, accountability, and shared ownership through high-performance teaming. They fostered capacity building by mentoring other women leaders in their institutions and districts. As a result, participants seemed to believe that generally, effective leadership can be learned and taught to other women by modeling and mentoring. Superintendent-President Darlene Huntersail expressed leadership development, mentorship, and support of women in her college:

> I've mentored about 20 people through . . . the administrator's association mentor program [I helped establish]. . . . Four of my vice presidents have become college presidents. . . . When I came here, there were eight of us administrators . . . [was] . . . one other woman. . . . This semester, I'm mentoring four people I think most of our division deans . . . three VPs, our head of security . . . [are] all women, so I think it's about a belief and a loyalty to the profession that you mentor."

Superintendent-President Huntersail's comments here illustrate the scope of mentoring in community college contexts.

We observed another shared pattern related to the need for future leadership development in community colleges and participants' own support of leaders, specifically women, by modeling, mentoring, and providing leadership guidance. Interim Chancellor Selma Flores shared the importance of empowering mentees in making hard choices in their careers and leadership pathways by providing guidance, given her own personal experience in making such a difficult decision herself:

> I try to be supportive of . . . women leaders, [by] . . . modeling. . . . I mentor now. . . . I have the experiences that I can . . . relate to them when they have to make a choice between climbing the career ladder and staying home . . . [like] when I made a decision. . . . Everything was really . . . stressful, I couldn't afford to quit my job, . . . I couldn't afford to stay home, I had to take care of the parents, and I couldn't afford to be a full-time mom to my kids . . . I think my life stories are such that I can relate what I've done . . . why I've done things and how . . . what my thought processes were so that I can help other young women as they're making similar choices.

Here, we see how guiding the leadership development of upcoming women leaders supports future capacity building in community colleges. Indeed, Interim Chancellor Flores shared her perception of the importance of providing leadership guidance for potential leaders. Vice President Anne Reina summed it up like this: "I mentor several young women who are in their late 30s, early 40s and they're still climbing the career ladder . . . to get them to think about [options], that there's a whole life ahead."

Clear Expectations, Accountability, and Priority Goal Setting

What we discovered tended to confirm managerial change (Burns 2005; Kotter 1995; Malm 2008) and educational leadership literature (AACC 2012; Kezar 2001; Northouse 2012; Wheatley 2006) but specifically to women's ability to create a sense of urgency in a shared ownership culture. Participants articulated clear and high expectations on accountability, goal setting, planning, and transparency to their leadership team and college constituents when initiating a change, continually transmitting priorities to the campus at large with regard to the first research question on what is essential in describing CLMs in their leadership practice toward reform. Through communication and collaboration, participants spoke openly about the state of events on their campuses and districts, explaining urgent needs during crises and their aftermath.

These discoveries seemed to corroborate previous research showing community colleges are highly patriarchal, traditional institutions, yet loosely coupled, highly team and collaboration-oriented organizations as well, involving all stakeholders in a shared governance process (Eddy 2010; Wheelan 2010). With regard to the second research question on transformative leadership practices, participants encouraged high-performance teaming during leadership meetings and professional training, creating and encouraging collaborative structures by modeling and negotiating a committed culture in their institutions. In cultivating collaborative work and collective commitment, executive women leaders expressed these concepts as complementary, sharing why consensus building creates accountability and ownership, confirming studies showing successful reform initiatives must involve all stakeholders in a shared governance process characterized by whole-systems change (Wheatley 2006; Wheelan 2010).

Countering Obstacles to Innovate and Sustain Systemic Reform

With transformation come obstacles: individual resistance, group opposition, and bureaucratic roadblocks. In explaining CLM in their leadership practice, change-agent CEOs expressed cyclical reassessment in planning, decision-making, and problem-solving environments was essential when they encountered obstacles. Critical feminist literature strongly sustains the belief that organizational change is central to improving the condition of women; the criticality lies in a dialogue of change in institutional organizational structures among the leadership team (Cook 2012; Eddy 2010; Milligan 2010). Findings substantiate empirical literature on systemic improvements characterized by long-term, second-tiered, whole-systems change that must engage transformative practices by leaders attempting paradigmatic shifts toward successful reform initiatives in traditional male-dominated organizations (Burns 2005; Kezar 2001; Malm 2008; Wheatley 2006).

When we consider how women leaders have used transformative leadership practices to guide their campuses to change, we confirmed that change agents participants developed and evolved methods such as interest-based problem solving, cyclic-reassessment measures, and a continual revamping in strategic planning, essential to counter obstacles to innovation and sustain transformative change toward systemic reform. They adapted and adjusted leadership practices to the situation at hand, continually developing and evolving mechanisms and methods, and involving large parts of constituents in an interactive, whole-systems approach to transform organizational processes. Participants' commitment, perseverance, and entrepreneurial skills were pivotal in gathering data and soliciting expertise.

Leadership Development of Women CEOs: Mentoring as Capacity Building

We can report that all participants had male mentors and female role models in their career paths who were instrumental in influencing and challenging them, modeling, teaching leadership skills, and encouraging them to seek higher positions. Participants shared a CLM in their reform practice was the need to develop future leaders in community colleges and supported women and men leaders by modeling, mentoring, and providing guidance as transformative practices they've used. Participants specifically sought leaders with qualities of commitment, motivation, and confidence (but not necessarily formative skills) when assisting in women's leadership capacity building. They believed that effective leadership can be learned and taught to others by modeling and mentoring.

Participants generally seemed optimistic about the future of women in community college executive leadership, but not as hopeful about the future of leadership and training in general in community colleges and districts; they noted the lack of preparedness and the failure of educational institutions to train future leaders and found state policy to unnecessarily deter people from pursuing leadership positions. They considered modeling, mentoring, and providing leadership guidance for future women leaders significant and, therefore, findings support previous research (Green 2011; Krause 2009; Milligan 2010) on succession pathways for leadership development and for community colleges to meet the needs of future leadership development in California in response to unprecedented retirement and vacancies in the executive leadership level.

Transforming Policy and Informing Practice

We discovered a multitude of challenges and complexities of contemporary female executive leaders' experiences from firsthand accounts, sharing the CLM in their practices toward systemic reform. On the basis of what we learned, we recommend specific actions for district and community college administrators, team leaders, and policy makers to advance educational leaders' best processes and procedures, practiced by change-agent leaders to generate and maintain long-term institutional change. The following topics may guide closer examination of ways to improve educational policy and practice at the local, state, and federal levels, using action planning to advance systemic reform in the underrepresented and underfunded community college system of higher education:

- Advance college and district institutional action to improve the planning, developing, implementing, and evaluating of organizational and interinstitutional processes.
- Use neutral third parties to assess communication channels, structural forces, interactions, and organizational processes between districts and college campuses.
- Increase community college districts' budgetary, line-item resources and provide female executive leaders more authority to pilot, initiate, and implement change initiatives.
- Evaluate state policy to determine factors that deter leaders, especially underrepresented women, from pursuing executive leadership positions toward social justice.
- Evaluate community college hierarchical structures to analyze issues preventing the internal advancement of women toward executive leadership positions in academia.
- Use mentorship programs to prepare future CEOs in community colleges.
- Actively recruit and support new and current middle-tier women leaders, specifically minority women of color and ethnicity.
- Continue funding of state and university-level leadership development programs.
- Examine organizational forces and observe interactions between district managers, boards of trustees, and college leaders.
- Examine more closely internal social, gender, and organizational interactions during transformational stages in academic settings.

These specific steps and action plans will improve processes for colleges to plan, pilot, and implement institutional change, thereby advancing women's leadership development and best practices toward systemic reform in academia.

Appreciating Women Executive Leaders Work in Community Colleges

Our use of in-depth interviewing led to a deeper appreciation and comprehension of the challenges and experiences of change-agent women leaders in times of crisis and growth and a more conscious awareness of the power of the social and organizational context of executive leadership experiences of women in academia. With a fuller appreciation of the complexities and difficulties of organizational change and transformative leadership practices in higher education today, findings break new ground in illuminating the previous gap in empirical knowledge surrounding critical learning moments phenomena in the leadership experiences and leadership practices of women executive change agents in two-year community colleges and districts in California. In informing educational policy and leadership practice, outcomes revealed the challenges women leaders face with economic, political, and budgetary issues in leading their colleges, and social issues with regard to district and college CEO leaders' interactions, and gender issues with regard to sexism and bigotry encountered in their organizations. These discoveries contribute to building transformative-change theory, providing a better understanding of how, why, and when women change-agent leaders use reform practices in leading systemic change in their organizations.

Bibliography

American Association of Community Colleges. (2012). *Reclaiming the American Dream: A Report from the 21st-Century Commission on the Future of Community Colleges*. www.aacc.nche.edu/aboutcc/21stcenturyreport/21stCenturyReport.pdf.

American Council on Education. (2012). *ACE Convenes Discussion on Women in Higher Education Leadership*. www.acenet.edu/newsroom/Pages/Discussion-Women-Leadership.aspx.

Bloomberg, Linda D., and Marie F. Volpe. (2012). *Completing Your Qualitative Dissertation: A Roadmap from Beginning to End*, 2nd ed. Thousand Oaks, CA: Sage Publications.

Burns, Bernard. (2005). "Complexity Theories and Organizational Change." *International Journal of Management Reviews*, 7 (2): 73–90.

Carli, L., and A. Eagly. (2011). "Gender and leadership." In *The Sage Handbook of Leadership*, ed. A. Bryman, D. Collinson, K. Grint, B. Jackson, and M. Uhl Bien, 269–285. London: Sage Publications.

Cohen, Arthur M., and Florence B. Brawer. (2008). *The American Community College*, 5th ed. San Francisco: Jossey-Bass.

Cook, Sarah G. (2012). "Women Presidents: Now 26.4% but Still Underrepresented." *Women in Higher Education*, 21 (5): 1–3.

Creswell, John W. (2012). *Educational Research: Planning, Conducting, and Evaluating Quantitative and Qualitative Research*, 4th ed. Boston: MA: Pearson Education, Inc.

Eagly, Alice H. (2007). "Female Leadership Advantage and Disadvantage: Resolving the Contradictions." *Psychology of Women Quarterly*, 31 (1): 1–12.

Eddy, Pamela L. (2010). *Community College Leadership: A Multidimensional Model for Leading Change*. Sterling, VA: Stylus Publication.

Green, Dolly M. (2011). "Succession Pathways for Leader Development in California Community Colleges: A Phenomenological Study." Doctoral dissertation, Capella University.

Kezar, Adrianna J. (2001). "Understanding and Facilitating Organizational Change in the 21st Century: Recent Research and Conceptualizations." *ASHE-ERIC Higher Education Reports*, 28 (4): 1–184. San Francisco: Jossey-Bass.

Kotter, John P. (1995). "Leading Change: Why Transformation Efforts Fail." *Harvard Business Review*, 73 (2): 59–67.

Krause, Ann M. (2009). *Leadership Development and Mentoring that Matters: Insights from the Career Trajectories of Women Community College Presidents and Chief Academic Officers*. ProQuest LLC. n. p., Retrieved from ERIC database.

Leatherwood, Laura, and Mitch Williams. (2008). "Gender and Career Paths." *Journal of Women in Educational Leadership*, 6 (4): 261–273.

Malm, James R. (2008). "Six Community College Presidents: Organizational Pressures, Change Processes and Approaches to Leadership." *Community College Journal of Research and Practice*, 32 (8): 614–628.

Miles, Matthew B., and Michael Huberman. (1994). *Qualitative Data Analysis: An Expanded Sourcebook*, 2nd ed. Thousand Oaks, CA: Sage Publications.

Milligan, Michelle L. (2010). "Access Granted: First Female Presidents, Leadership Style, and Institutional Culture." Doctoral dissertation, University of Pennsylvania.

Moustakas, Clark E. (1994). *Phenomenological Research Methods*. Thousand Oaks, CA: Sage Publications.

Northouse, Peter. (2012). *Introduction to Leadership Concepts and Practice*, 2nd ed. Thousand Oaks, CA: Sage Publications.

Rossman, Gretchen B., and Sharon F. Rallis. (2003). *Learning in the Field: An Introduction to Qualitative Research*, 2nd ed. Thousand Oaks, CA: Sage Publications.

Seidman, Irving A. (2006). *Interviewing as Qualitative Research: A Guide for Researchers*, 3rd ed. New York: Teachers College Press.

Senge, Peter. (2006). *The Fifth Discipline*, revised ed. Crown Business.

Townsend, Barbara K., and Susan Twombly. (1998). "A Feminist Critique of Organizational Change in the Community College." *New Directions for Community Colleges*, 102: 77–85.

———. (2007). "Accidental Equity: The Status of Women in the Community College." *Equity and Excellence in Education*, 40 (3): 208–217.

U.S. Department of Education. (2013). *National Center on Educational Statistics: Digest of Education Statistics*. Washington, DC: Author.

Weisman, Iris M., and George B. Vaughan. (2007). "The Community College Presidency: 2006." *American Association of Community Colleges*. www.aacc.nche.edu/Publications/Briefs/Documents/09142007presidentbrief.pdf.

Wheatley, Margaret J. (2006). *Leadership and the New Science: Discovering Order in a Chaotic World*, 3rd ed. San Francisco: Berrett-Koehler Publishers, Inc.

Wheelan, Susan A. (2010). *Creating Effective Teams: A Guide for Members and Leaders*. Thousand Oaks, CA: Sage Publications.

6 The Problem with the Phrase "Women and Minorities"

Racism and Sexism Intersectionality for Black Women Faculty

E-K. Daufin

There is a notion in U.S. culture that Black women are androgynous work horses, with no needs of their own, who live only to happily serve others as a stereotypical "Mammy." Professional status and education cannot protect Black women from the Mammy image.[1] A disturbingly frequent number of times many Black women faculty members, including the author, have been mistaken for clerical staff, maids, even prostitutes.[2] "Ironically, African American women faculty are not only the 'maids of academe' but the work mules (i.e., carrying a heavy load) as well."[3]

This chapter is a narrative discourse analysis exploring the intersectional White supremacist *and* patriarchal obstacles to success for Black women faculty at PWIs (Predominantly White Institutions) and HBCUs (Historically Black Colleges and Universities). The author proposes that a primary strategy to overcome *both* White supremacy and patriarchy in academia is to both conceptually and linguistically correct our discourse by ceasing to use the term "women and minorities." Instead, we should use the more accurate and intersectional "*White* women and minority *people/people* of color," or "women of all ethnicities/races and men of color," depending on which is accurate. The chapter is written from the perspective of an African American woman from a working-class, abusive family who became the second college graduate in her direct family line, a faculty member at public and private PWIs and HBCUs, and a full professor at a public HBCU.

The narrative discourse approach is especially appropriate for studying African American women in academia because it allows those "who have been traditionally underrepresented, marginalized and disenfranchised in higher education an opportunity to tell their stories in formal scholarly writing (to) thus challenge and question the dominant white, male, Western research ethos in the university."[4] The problematic political position of Black women in the academy has been, in a word, embattled.[5] In exploring surviving sexism in academia, we must understand the potentially antagonistic conditions under which Black women work that are intersectional, not entirely like the experience of Black and other men of color, or White women and other women of color.

Research on African American women faculty finds that "individually and collectively, African American women suffer from a form of race fatigue as a result of being over extended and undervalued."[6] African American female faculty experience institutional and personal racism and sexism; racial and sexual harassment; salary inequity; inordinate psychological stress; extreme professional and personal isolation; hyper-visibility and resulting double standards; bias in student evaluation, tenure, and promotion process; homophobia (whether lesbian or straight, as Black straight women are often masculinized and/or assumed lesbian[7]); service and teaching load inequities; and gender and racially motivated direct and veiled threat and even battery.[8]

At HBCUs, most African American women faculty experience much of the same including sexism and a subtler form of racism, as well as common HBCU institutional challenges including:

1. Teaching four or more classes per semester and spending additional time outside of the classroom mentoring their majority low-income, first-generation college students who are often underprepared.
2. At the highest level, earning a little more than half of what their counterparts earn at the national level.
3. "(A) lack of respect for faculty governance."[9]

To define central terms of this study: I use "White supremacy" rather than "racism."[10] White supremacy here doesn't refer to the extremist, blatant racism of "White supremacist" groups but rather to the often unconscious, pervasive belief that characteristics and behaviors identified as belonging *to* White people are the wholesome norm/right/best. Also the term "White supremacy" allows for the internalized racism that people of color have acquired from living in a White supremacist society. Similarly, I use "patriarchy," rather than "sexism," to account for beliefs that all things male identified are the norm/better than those female identified and allowing for women's internalized sexism.[11] Some people object to using the term "minorities" to describe people of color (AHANA people, an acronym meaning African American/Black (*excluding* Black Hispanics/Latinos), Hispanic/Latino (*including* Black Hispanics/Latinos), Asian, and Native American[12]) because "minority" often means lower in status. Another objection is that, globally, White people are the smallest (in number) "race." The author capitulates to the use of "minorities" for AHANA people and "Blacks" for non-Hispanic/Latino Blacks in North America for this chapter.[13]

Using the term "women and minorities" is damaging to women of color because rather than *counting* women of color twice (its own kind of inaccuracy), typically it *excludes* women of color . . . twice. In addition to being vague, "the term *minority* used with *women* obscures the existence of multiple intersecting categories."[14] Using that vague, misleading term makes it difficult, if not impossible, to decipher what studies may actually show regarding women of color, much less Black women:

> For example when we use "women and minorities" to describe pay inequities) . . . the unique experience of Black women is impossible to detect. The higher pay of White women masks the lower pay of Black women relative to White women; the lower pay of Blacks masks the lower pay of Black women relative to Black men despite Black women's greater education.[15]

The usage contributes to the damaging myth that Black woman have gender *privilege* rather than the truth that patriarchy is alive and well in the mainstream *and* Black communities, at PWIs *and* HBCUs.

Black women suffer more inequity than most White women *and* Black men in many ways. For example, the *2015 Black Women in the United States* report says the economic recovery has left Black women behind in terms of (1) higher unemployment, (2) lack of pay equity even when they are highly educated, (3) more likely to be poor than any other race women even though Black women are more likely to work outside the home, (4) underrepresentation in politics, (5) lack of healthcare coverage, especially in states that have rejected Medicaid expansion, (6) increasing infant mortality, and (7) most likely of all race women to be the victim of murder and other violent crimes.[16]

Jennifer Mabry says in "Your Blues Ain't Like Mine: America's War Against Black Women,"

> The mythical, long-held rationale for ignoring the plight of (B)lack women and girls has been that we are better off and more resilient than (B)lack men and boys; and that somehow, magically, the

implementation of programs for one group will trickle down and eventually benefit the other group. Statistical and empirical evidence, however, show this is not true.[17]

This double exclusion is made clear in the title of the iconic Black feminist text *All the Women Are White, All the Blacks Are Men, But Some of Us Are Brave: Black Women's Studies*.[18] Kimberlé Crenshaw mentions in a 2015 *Washington Post* editorial that nearly three decades after she first coined the term "intersectionality" (to communicate how Black women's experience of race and gender discrimination is compounded, rather than the same as White women or Black men), "women and girls of color continue to be left in the shadows, something vital to the understanding of intersectionality has been lost."[19] Lisa Bowleg says in "The Problem With the Phrase *Women and Minorities*," that there is an "implied mutual exclusivity of these populations. Missing is the notion that these 2 categories could intersect, as they do in the lives of racial/ethnic minority women."[20]

As a result of this exclusionary rhetoric, many Black women see that they suffer from White supremacy AND patriarchy.[21] However, too many who aren't Black women (including Black men) believe that Black women aren't penalized for being Black *or* for being female.[22] This causes many Black men to feel much undeserved resentment toward Black women.[23] Both HBCUs and PWIs often use studies with the term "women and minorities" as justification to focus on helping Black males rather than Black men *and* women. For example, the Penn Graduate School of Education Center for Minority Serving Institutions recommends in their guidelines for HBCU success, *no* gender-specific support for Black women. However, they say that HBCUs must act "today to empower Black *men*."[24]

On most indices of oppression, Black men and women may be a little ahead or behind each other as a group, but rarely by much. Usually Black women and men are equally disadvantaged when compared with White people *of their own gender*. Even among Black, Latina, Asian, and American Indian women, there are also sometimes broad differences between those groups of women, with Black women remaining disproportionately near, or on, the bottom (see data from AAUW for examples).[25] At the upper echelons of success in and out of the academy, Black women tend to be behind Black men but not *by as much* as White women are behind White men. This is patriarchy in action when one looks at the relatively equal lower status of Black women and men on many indices, as a travesty for Black *men* alone. It's as if the culture were saying, "Men must always do much better than women or patriarchy is not properly being enforced."

For example, the latest TIAA-CREF Institute report on recruiting and retaining "female and minority faculty" makes this common mistake.[26] The report says that "the reasons for the underrepresentation of female and minority faculty are different,"[27] again negating Black women and other women of color. It posits that the main reason *women* in academia are underrepresented is a recruitment issue surrounding the difficulty of combining family and career. If "family" here means being a mother also working outside the home, that is problematic for Black women. If "family" includes extended family, then Black women, indeed, are going to be affected because we are the most likely to be single heads of households, supporting our own children and other family, as illustrated by the U.S. Department of Health Resources and Services Administration.[28] Most of the African American women faculty I know and I have survived *extreme* financial hardship to complete our terminal degrees and survive on very low beginning faculty salaries, virtually without family support—financial, in-kind, or even moral. Research indicates that African American women rely on their own finances and very likely will finish graduate school with *even greater debt* than other races/gender identity intersections.[29]

That TIAA-CREF report also says that the biggest problem for recruiting *minority* faculty is a problem in the pipeline. However, since 2003, women of all ethnicities, at all levels of education, earn more degrees than men of the same ethnicity.[30] Here, "minority *men*" would have been the accurate term.

Further, using the term "women and minorities" distorts the measurement of even the presence of Black women in the academy. In 2015, the National Center for Education Statistics (NCES) reported that among full-time academicians, 58% are White men (compared with 39% of the total U.S. population[31]) and 25% are White women (also 39% of the total population). *Condition of Education*[32] reports have shown that since 2000, typically Black faculty compose about 6% of total full timers but show no breakdown according to gender. One may calculate, using NCES data for 2011 and 2013, that Black people represented about 5.5% of the full-time faculty at degree-granting institutions (compared with 13% of the population).[33] Though the difference is not statistically significant, Black women represented a little over 3% (compared with nearly 7% of the total population).[34]

So when compared with the percentage of the total U.S. population, White men are over-represented in the academy and the rest of us are underrepresented. Black women are *far more* underrepresented than White women and *slightly more* underrepresented than Black men. Black men historically far outnumbered Black women in the academy.[35] However, a *Journal of Blacks in Higher Education* article bemoaned that 2003–2007, 51% of Black academicians were women.[36] Still, Black women have not won parity, even compared with Black men in academia. There are almost *twice* as many Black male faculty than Black women at the typically tenured, better paid, and with better working conditions, *upper* ranks.[37] At the full professor level, Black women make up .003%of the total full-time faculty.[38]

Black women faculty are more likely to experience greater social isolation and loneliness in academia than other race/gender identity intersections. In 1950, roughly the same percentage of White and Black women were married. Since then, more Black women than any other race women, of all socioeconomic brackets, have found the prospect of marrying a man of their own or any race "more or less hopeless."[39] Though full-time faculty women of all races are less likely to be married than men in academia and women in the general population,[40] White supremacy and the academy place extra burdens upon the Black woman in this area. Black women are the least likely of all women to ever marry in the first place and the most likely to be divorced of all other race/gender identity intersection categories.[41] The situation only gets worse once becoming a faculty member where a much larger percentage of male faculty is married than are the women.[42] Online dating services offer little hope to most Black women because as Mendelsohn et al. document, too many men there want to date any woman *except* a Black woman.[43]

Also, Black women faculty may have fewer options for non-romantic relationships than do their peers. A 2014 survey of undergraduate teaching faculty reports that Black women were even more likely to experience stressors associated with *alienation, isolation,* and systematic oppression.[44] As a graduate student and early on as an assistant professor, my colleagues invited me to their homes to share many holidays, but no longer. Perhaps for those Black women academicians with intact, functional local families and other connections, the need for community may not be as acute.

Though the 3% of the full-time instructional faculty in degree-granting institutions that African American female faculty compose is concentrated at HBCUs and *not* PWIs, there are many widespread, erroneous assumptions about HBCUs in general and the circumstances of the African American women faculty teaching there in particular. For example, contrary to popular belief, at over 25% of all public HBCUs, Black faculty are in the *minority*[45] but not *as much* of a minority as they are at PWIs. Though the U.S. Department of Education compiles some statistics on HBCUs, the "women and minorities" problem creates "missing institutional data and irreconcilable sums based on gender and race/ethnicity"[46], making it impossible to statistically support much information about Black women faculty at HBCUs. Yet available statistical findings suggest that as HBCUs move toward a focus on the male-dominated fields of mathematics, science, and technology, HBCUs may be hiring more males at the expense of female faculty.[47]

A rare review of Black faculty working at HBCUs compared with those working at PWIs found that Black faculty were clustered at the entry (assistant professor) level at both types of institutions.[48] Though a higher percentage of Black faculty at HBCUs are tenured than Black faculty at PWIs, Black faculty make the same lower (than their White counterparts') salary *at both*.[49]

For faculty of any color, in addition to the financial and workplace struggles mentioned earlier,

> The critical areas of shared governance in which HBCUs come up short include: (a) faculty representation on policy and decision-making bodies; (b) searches and hiring of academic personnel; (c) faculty grievances; (d) promotion, tenure, and post-tenure hearings and procedures; (e) evaluations of peers and administrators; (f) salary determination and other budgetary matters; (g) program development, review, and revision; (h) development and revision of faculty handbooks; (i) access to information needed for decision making; and (j) the status of the faculty senate as a decision—and policy-making unit.[50]

Many HBCUs require faculty to put in ten weekly office hours when most PWI faculty do four.[51] NCES 2011 statistics show all race faculty at public HBCUs earn less than the national average at all ranks, and even less at private HBCUs.[52]

Yet African American women faculty at HBCUs face many of the same or worse problems than we do at PWIs. High HBCU workloads, lack of facilities and accommodations taken for granted at most PWIs, the gender- and race-based higher workloads for African American women in these institutions, *and* the political struggles one is likely to find in any institution of higher learning[53] still make HBCUs a more tenable, if not wonderful, work environment for many African American women. At least at HBCUs, we are more likely to be tenured rather than fired after seven years.

This narrative discourse illuminates the problematic use of the term "women and minorities" in developing equity for those with the intersectional identity of Black and female, as well as the challenges Black women in academia are likely to face at PWIs and HBCUs. **The following are strategies** I have used with partial, if sometimes fleeting, success to help survive these challenge:

- Keep asking others to use, and yourself use, clear, accurate language regarding the intersectional identities of Black women: NOT "women and minorities."
- Negotiate the highest incoming salary possible and get all promises in writing.
- Identify as best you can what are the important criteria for tenure. Only allow yourself to be obligated to doing those *extra* duties that will actually be counted at tenure time.
- Join and build support in the faculty union with the best free legal support.
- Take courses on how to manage difficult people and apply them.
- Drop hints that you don't have anything planned when peers talk about gatherings you may want to join.
- Join and regularly attend (more than) Sunday service at a Black, or other potentially compatible, church if there is one available.
- If you are a member of a Black sorority or other national organization and there is a chapter near you, seek it out and see if there are friends there for you.
- Using proper precautions, try free online dating sites. Costly sites don't work any better for Black women.
- While being careful about campus politics, join and attend all the meetings of a single campus faculty extracurricular organization for a year.
- Seek out online communities that may be supportive and do more than lurk.
- Try MeetUp.com for possible local interest groups.

- Volunteer on a weekly basis for an organization where you will come in contact with the public. Every week, eat a meal at the same place and sit where people will see your face and have to pass you.
- And, finally, as hard as it may be, others have made the way a little easier for you. The work you do "for the cause" may not feel good or create tangible results for you, but it will help those who come after you . . . a little. And after all . . . It's good karma.

Notes

1 Carolyn M. West, "Mammy, Jeszebel, Sapphire, and Their Homegirls: Developing an Oppositional Gaze Toward the Images of Black Women," in *Lectures in the Psychology of Women*, eds. Joan C. Chrisler, Carla Golden and Patricia Rozee (New York: McGraw-Hill, 2008), 289.
2 West, "Mammy," 287.
3 Debra A. Harley, "Maids of Academe: African American Women Faculty at Predominately White Institutions," *Journal of African American Studies* 12, no. 1 (2008): 20.
4 Carol Logan Patitu and Kandace G. Hinton, "The Experiences of African American Women Faculty and Administrators in Higher Education: Has Anything Changed?" *New Directions for Student Services*, 104 (Winter 2003): 79 and on background both, Corrine Glesne, *Becoming Qualitative Researchers: An Introduction*, 5th ed. (Boston: Pearson, 2015), 86 and Cynthia Gordon, "Analysis of Narrative in Interaction," *The Encyclopedia of Applied Linguistics* (Hoboken, NJ: Wiley-Blackwell, 2012), http://onlineli brary.wiley.com/doi/10.1002/9781405198431.wbeal0025/pdf.
5 Akasha (Gloria T.) Hull, Patricia Bell Scott and Barbara Smith, eds., *All the Women Are White, All the Blacks Are Men, But Some of Us Are Brave: Black Women's Studies* (New York: The Feminist Press, 1982), i.
6 Debra Harley, "Maids of Academe: African American Women Faculty at Predominantly White Institutions," *Journal of African American Studies* (March 2008): 19.
7 Dani McClain, "Black Women Vilified as a 'Lesbian Wolf Pack' Speak for Themselves in a New Film," *The Nation*, July 2, 2015, www.thenation.com/article/black-women-vilified-as-a-lesbian-wolf-pack-speak-for-themselves-in-a-new-film/.
8 E-K. Daufin, "Ending Racism in Durango," *Durango Herald*, November 12, 1993, 3A; Daufin, "Minority Faculty Retention: What It Takes: The Hire Is Only the Beginning," *Black Issues in Higher Education*, (October 21, 1993): 43–44; Daufin, "Living With Racism in Durango," *Durango Herald*, (November 11, 1993): 3; Daufin, "Drying up in Durango: A Case Study in the Hypervisibility and Emotional Isolation of African American Women in Higher Education," Paper presented at the Seventh International Conference on Women in Higher Education, Orlando, Florida, November 11, 1993; Daufin, "Confessions of a Womanist Professor," *Black Issues in Higher Education* (1995): 34–35; Daufin, "How to Thrive as a Wild Woman in the Professorate," *Commission on the Status of Women, Association for Education in Journalism and Mass Communication National Conference*, Washington, DC., August 10, 1995; Daufin, "Response From E-K. Daufin," *Journalism & Communication Monographs: Junior Scholars in Search of Equity for Women and Minorities* (Columbia, South Carolina: Association for Education in Journalism and Mass Communication, 2005), 193–196; Joyce Coleman Nichols, and Carole B. Tanksley, "Revelations of African-American Women With Terminal Degrees: Overcoming Obstacles to Success," *Negro Educational Review* 55, no. 4 (October 2004): 175–185; Deborah Olsen and Sue A. Maple, "Women and Minority Faculty Job Satisfaction: Professional Role Interests, Professional Satisfactions, and Institutional Fit," *Journal of Higher Education* 66, no. 3 (May-June 1995): 6. and; Carol Logan Patitu and Kandace G. Hinton, "The Experiences of African American Women Faculty and Administrators in Higher Education: Has Anything Changed?" *New Directions for Student Services* 104 (Winter 2003): 79–83.
9 Marybeth Gasman, *The Changing Face of Historically Black Colleges and Universities*, (Philadelphia: Penn Graduate School of Education Center for Minority Serving Institutions, 2013), 13.
10 For further explanation of the term "White supremacy," please see both: Tim Wise. "Frequently Asked Questions—And Their Answers (Updated December 2014)," http://timewise.org/f-a-q-s/ and from Dr. bell hooks in *bell hooks: Cultural Criticism & Transformation*, Directed by Sut Jhally (Boston: Media Education Foundation, 1997). Also see the latter regarding using "White supremacy/patriarchy," versus "racism/sexism."
11 Lori L. Tharps, "The Case for Black With A Capital B," *New York Times*, November 19, 2014, A25.
12 Boston College, "We Are More Than Just an Acronym," Updated May 4, 2014, www.bc.edu/offices/ahana/about/history/def.html.

13 I capitalize both "White" and "Black" when those words are used to represent people's ethnicity/race as we do with African Americans, Asians, Latinos, and so forth.

14 Lisa Bowleg, "The Problem With the Phrase *Women and Minorities*: Intersectionality—an Important Theoretical Framework for Public Health," *American Journal of Public Health* 102, no. 7 (2012): 1268.

15 Janis V. Sanchez-Hucles and Donald D. Davis, "Women and Women of Color in Leadership: Complexity, Identity, and Intersectionality," *American Psychologist* 65, no. 3 (2010): 176.

16 Avis Jones DeWeever, ed., *2015 Black Women in the United States* (Washington, DC: National Coalition on Black Civic Participation, 2015), iii–4.

17 Jennifer E. Mabry, "Your Blues Ain't Like Mine: America's War Against Black Women," *Observer*, February 19, 2015, http://observer.com/2015/02/your-blues-aint-like-mine/.

18 Akasha (Gloria T.) Hull, and Patricia Bell Scott, eds. *All the Women Are White, All the Blacks Are Men, But Some of Us Are Brave: Black Women's Studies* (New York: The Feminist Press, 1982).

19 Kimberlé Crenshaw, "Why Intersectionality Can't Wait," *The Washington Post*, September 24, 2015, https://www.washingtonpost.com/news/in-theory/wp/2015/09/24/why-intersectionality-cant-wait/.

20 Lisa Bowleg, "The Problem With the Phrase *Women and Minorities*: Intersectionality—an Important Theoretical Framework for Public Health," *American Journal of Public Health* 102, no. 7 (2012): 1267.

21 Shirley A. Hill, *African American Children: Socialization and Development in Families*, (New York: Sage Publications, 2012), 118.

22 Bakar Kitwana, "Where Did Our Love Go? The New Battle of the Sexes," in *The Hip Hop Generations: Young Blacks and the Crisis in African American Culture* (New York: Basic Civitas Books, 2002), 85–120.

23 Brande Victorian, "#Ask a Black Man: Have Black Women Surpassed Black Men?" End of first season evaluation episode, *MadameNoire*, May 21, 2015, http://madamenoire.com/534176/black-men-and-women/.

24 Marybeth Gasman, *The Changing Face of Historically Black Colleges and Universities*, (Philadelphia: Penn GSE Center for MSIs, 2011), 15.

25 American Association of University Women, "How Does Race Affect the Gender Wage Gap?" April 3, 2014, www.aauw.org/2014/04/03/race-and-the-gender-wage-gap/.

26 Jennifer Ma, *Trends and Issues: Recruiting and Retaining Female and Minority Faculty* (Charlotte, North Carolina: TIAA-CREF Institute, July 2005), 10.

27 Ibid.

28 U.S. Department of Health Resources and Services Administration, Maternal and Child Health Bureau, *Women's Health USA 2011* (Rockville, MD: Health and Human Services, 2011), www.mchb.hrsa.gov/whusall/popchar/pages/104c.html.

29 Kendra Hamilton, "Doctoral Dilemma," *Black Issues in Higher Education* 18, no. 11 (July 19, 2001): 34–37 and Caroline Radcliffe and Signe-Mary McKernan, "Forever in Your Debt: Who Has Student Loan Debt, and Who's Worried?" *Urban Institute*, June 2013, www.urban.org/sites/default/file/alfresco/publication-pdfs/412849-forever-in-your-debt.

30 National Center for Education Statistics, "Fast Facts: Degrees Conferred by Sex and Race," 1999–2010, http://nces.ed.gov/fastfacts/display.asp?id=72.

31 U.S. population percentages are calculated from the: U.S. Census Bureau, Population Division, *Annual Estimates of the Resident Population by Sex, Race, and Hispanic Origin for the United States, States, and Counties: April 1, 2010 to July 1, 2014*, http://factfinder.census.gov/faces/tableservices/jsf/pages/product view.xhtml?src=bkmk.

32 Annually, the Institute of Educational Services National Center for Education publishes a *Condition of Education* report using the latest available data. Each report presents a varying number of indicators on the status and condition of education for which accurate data are available. Searchable by year at https://nces.ed.gov/pubsearch.

33 Calculations for 2011 and 2013 percentages rendered using the National Center for Educational Statistics, "Table 315.20 Full-Time Faculty in Degree-Granting Postsecondary Institutions, by Race/Ethnicity, Sex, and Academic Rank: Fall 2009, Fall 2011, and Fall 2013, *Digest of Education Statistics*, Washington, DC: U.S. Department of Education, 2014. http://nces.ed.gov/program/digest/d14/table/dt14_315.20.asp.

34 Ibid.

35 "The Snail-Like Progress of Blacks in to Faculty Ranks of Higher Education," *The Journal of Blacks in Higher Education* (2007), www.jbhe.com/news_views/54_black-faculty-progress.html.

36 Ibid.

37 Calculations, *Digest of Education Statistics*.

38 Ibid.

39 Kate Bolick, "All the Single Ladies," *The Atlantic*, November 2011, www.theatlantic.com/magazine/archive/archive/2011/11/all-the-single-ladies/308654.

40 Alexis Coe, "Being Married Helps Professors Get Ahead, But Only If They're Male," *The Atlantic*, January 17, 2013, www.theatlantic.com/sexes/archive/2013/01/being-married-helps-professors-get-ahead-but-only-if-theyre-male/.

41 America's Families and Living Arrangements: 2010, U.S. Census Bureau, 2010, www.census.gov/population/www/socdemo/hh-fam/cps2010.html.

42 Stefan Michael Geiger, *Understanding Gender at Public Historically Black Colleges and Universities*, (New York: Thurgood Marshal Scholarship Fund, 2006), 46.

43 Gerald A. Mendelsohn, Lindsay S. Taylor and others, "Black/White Dating Online: Interracial Courtship in the 21st Century," *Psychology of Popular Media Culture* 3, no. 1 (2014): 2–18.

44 Sylvia Hurtado, Kevin Eagan, John H. Pryor, Hannah Whang, and Serge Tran, *Undergraduate Teaching Faculty: The 2010–2011 HERI Faculty Survey*, (Los Angeles: Higher Education Research Institute University of California, Los Angeles, 2012), 12–16 and Jamaal Abdul-Alim, "Survey: Minority Faculty Feel More Stress," *Diverse Issues in Higher Education*, October 26, 2012, http://diverseeducation.com/article/49072/. Though both these studies suffer from the "women and minorities" problem, they seem to support that Black women are more affected.

45 Geiger, *Understanding Gender*, 8.

46 Marybeth Gasman, *The Changing Face of Historically Black Colleges and Universities*, (Philadelphia: Penn Graduate School of Education Center for Minority Serving Institutions, 2013), 16.

47 Ibid.

48 Carol Patitu and Martha W. Tack, "Job Satisfaction of African American Faculty in Higher Education in the South," Annual Meeting of the Association for the Study of Higher Education, Boston, Massachusetts, ERIC Document 339 318, 1991.

49 Ibid.

50 Ivory Paul Phillips, "Shared Governance on Black College Campuses," *Academe*, 88, no. 4 (January 2002): 50–55, www.aaup.org/AAUP/pubsres/academe/2002/JA/Feat/Phil.htm.

51 Scott Jaschik, "Teaching, Stress, Adjuncts," *Inside Higher Education*, October 24, 2012, www.insidehighered.com/news/2012/10/24/new-survey-faculty-activities-and-attitudes.

52 Marybeth Gasman, *The Changing Face of Historically Black Colleges and Universities*, (Philadelphia: Penn Graduate School of Education Center for MSIs, 2013), 13.

53 Geiger, *Understanding Gender*, 29.

Bibliography

Abdul-Alim, Jamaal. (October 26, 2012). "Survey: Minority Faculty Feel More Stress." *Diverse Issues in Higher Education*. http://diverseeducation.com/article/49072/.

American Association of University Women. (April 3, 2014). "How Does Race Affect the Gender Wage Gap?" www.aauw.org/2014/04/03/race-and-the-gender-wage-gap/.

Bolick, Kate. (November 2011). "All the Single Ladies." *The Atlantic*. www.theatlantic.com/magazine/archive/archive/2011/11/all-the-single-ladies/308654.

Boston College. (May 4, 2014). "We Are More than Just an Acronym." www.bc.edu/offices/ahana/about/history/def.html.

Bowleg, Lisa. (2012). "The Problem with the Phrase *Women and Minorities*: Intersectionality—An Important Theoretical Framework for Public Health." *American Journal of Public Health*, 102 (7): 1267–1273.

Coe, Alexis. (January 17, 2013). "Being Married Helps Professors Get Ahead, But Only If They're Male." *The Atlantic*. www.theatlantic.com/sexes/archive/2013/01/being-married-helps-professors-get-ahead-but-only-if-theyre-male/.

Crenshaw, Kimberlé. (September 24, 2015). "Why Intersectionality Can't Wait." *The Washington Post*. www.washingtonpost.com/news/in-theory/wp/2015/09/24/why-intersectionality-cant-wait/.

Daufin, E-K. (October 21, 1993). "Minority Faculty Retention: What It Takes: The Hire Is Only the Beginning." *Black Issues in Higher Education*, 43–44.

———. (November 11, 1993). "Drying Up in Durango: A Case Study in the Hypervisibility and Emotional Isolation of African American Women in Higher Education." Paper presented at the Seventh International Conference on Women in Higher Education, Orlando, Florida.

———. (1995). "Confessions of a Womanist Professor." *Black Issues in Higher Education*, 12: 34–35.

———. (2005). "Response from E-K. Daufin." In *Journalism & Communication Monographs: Junior Scholars in Search of Equity for Women and Minorities*, edited by Ruth Rush, Carol Oukrop and Others, 193–196. Columbia, South Carolina: Association for Education in Journalism and Mass Communication.

DeWeever, Avis Jones, ed. (2015). *2015 Black Women in the United States*. Washington, DC: National Coalition on Black Civic Participation.

Gasman, Marybeth. (2013). *The Changing Face of Historically Black Colleges and Universities*. Philadelphia: Pennsylvania Graduate School of Education Center for Minority Serving Institutions.

Geiger, Stefan Michael. (2006). *Understanding Gender at Public Historically Black Colleges and Universities*. New York: Thurgood Marshal Scholarship Fund.

Hamilton, Kendra. (July 19, 2001). "Doctoral Dilemma." *Black Issues in Higher Education*, 18 (11): 34–37.

Harley, Debra A. (March 2008). "Maids of Academe: African American Women Faculty at Predominantly White Institutions." *Journal of African American Studies*, 19–36.

Hill, Shirley A. (2012). *African American Children: Socialization and Development in Families*. Thousand Oaks, CA: Sage Publications.

Hull, Akasha (Gloria T.) and Patricia Bell Scott, eds. (1982). *All the Women Are White, All the Blacks Are Men, But Some of Us Are Brave: Black Women's Studies*. New York: The Feminist Press.

Hurtado, Sylvia, Kevin Eagan, John H. Pryor, Hannah Whang, and Tran Serge. (2012). *Undergraduate Teaching Faculty: The 2010–2011 HERI Faculty Survey*. Los Angeles: Higher Education Research Institute University of California, Los Angeles.

Jaschik, Scott. (October 24, 2012). "Teaching, Stress, Adjuncts." *Inside Higher Education*. www.insidehighered.com/news/2012/10/24/new-survey-faculty-activities-and-attitudes.

The Journal of Blacks in Higher Education. (2007). "The Snail-Like Progress of Blacks Into Faculty Ranks of Higher Education." www.jbhe.com/news_views/54_black-faculty-progress.html.

Kitwana, Bakar. (2002). "Chapter 4: Where Did Our Love Go, the New Battle of the Sexes." In *The Hip Hop Generations: Young Blacks and the Crisis in African American Culture*, 85–120. New York: Basic Civitas Books.

Ma, Jennifer. (July 2005). *Trends and Issues: Recruiting and Retaining Female and Minority Faculty*. Charlotte, NC: TIAA-CREF Institute.

Mabry, Jennifer M. (February 19, 2015). "Your Blues Ain't Like Mine: America's War Against Black Women." *Observer*. http://observer.com/2015/02/your-blues-aint-like-mine/.

McClain, Dani. (July 2, 2015). "Black Women Vilified as a 'Lesbian Wolf Pack' Speak for Themselves in a New Film." *The Nation*. www.thenation.com/article/black-women-vilified-as-a-lesbian-wolf-pack-speak-for-themselves-in-a-new-film/.

Mendelsohn, Gerald A., Lindsay Shaw, Andrew T. Fiore, and Cheshire, Coye. (2014). "Black/White Dating Online: Interracial Courtship in the 21st Century." *Psychology of Popular Media Culture*, 3 (1): 2–18.

National Center for Educational Statistics. (1999–2010). "Fast Facts: Degrees Conferred by Sex and Race." http://nces.ed.gov/fastfacts/display.asp?id=72.

———. (2014). "Table 315.20 Full-Time Faculty in Degree-Granting Postsecondary Institutions, by Race/Ethnicity, Sex, and Academic Rank: Fall 2009, Fall 2011, and Fall 2013." *Digest of Education Statistics*. Washington, DC: U.S. Department of Education. http://nces.ed.gov/program/digest/d14_315.20.asp.

Nichols, Joyce Coleman, and Carole B. Tanksley. (October 2004). "Revelations of African-American Women with Terminal Degrees: Overcoming Obstacles to Success." *Negro Educational Review*, 55 (4): 175–185.

Olsen, Deborah, and Sue A. Maple. (May-June 1995). "Women and Minority Faculty Job Satisfaction: Professional Role Interests, Professional Satisfactions, and Institutional Fit." *Journal of Higher Education*, 66 (3). www.questia.com/read/1G1-17039360/women-and-minority-faculty-job-satisfaction/.

Patitu, Carol L., and Kandace G. Hinton. (Winter 2003). "The Experiences of African American Women Faculty and Administrators in Higher Education: Has Anything Changed?" *New Directions for Student Services*, 104: 79–83.

Patitu, Carol L., and Martha W. Tack. (1991). "Job Satisfaction of African American Faculty in Higher Education in the South." Annual Meeting of the Association for the Study of Higher Education, Boston, MA, ERIC Document 339 318.

Phillips, I. P. (January 4, 2002). "Shared Governance on Black College Campuses." *Academe*, 88: 50–55. www.aaup.org/AAUP/pubsres/academe/2002/JA/Feat/Phil.htm.

Radcliffe, Caroline R., and Signe-Mary McKernan. (June 2013). "Forever in Your Debt: Who Has Student Loan Debt, Who's Worried?" *Urban Institute*. www.urban.org/sites/default/file/alfresco/publication-pdfs/412849-forever-in-your-debt.

Sanchez-Hucles, Janis V., and Donald D. Davis. (2010). "Women and Women of Color in Leadership Complexity, Identity, and Intersectionality." *American Psychologist*, 65 (3): 171–181.

Tharps, Lori L. (November 19, 2014). "The Case for Black with A Capital B." *New York Times*, A25.

U.S. Census Bureau, Population Division. (June 2015). *Annual Estimates of the Resident Population by Sex, Race, and Hispanic Origin for the United States, States, and Counties: April 1, 2010 to July 1, 2014*. http://factfinder.census.gov/faces/tableservices/jsf/pages/productview.xhtml?src=bkmk.

U.S. Department of Health Resources and Services Administration, Maternal and Child Health Bureau. (2011). *Women's Health USA 2011*. Rockville, MD: Health and Human Services. www.mchb.hrsa.gov/whusall/popchar/pages/104c.html.

Victorian, Brande. (May 21, 2015). "#Ask a Black Man: Have Black Women Surpassed Black Men?" End of first season evaluation episode. *MadameNoire*. http://madamenoire.com/534176/black-men-and-women/.

West, Carolyn M. (2008). "Mammy, Jeszebel, Sapphire, and Their Homegirls: Developing an Oppositional Gaze Toward the Images of Black Women." In *Lectures in the Psychology of Women*, edited by Joan C. Chrisler, Carla Golden and Patricia Rozee, 287–299. New York: McGraw-Hill.

Disciplinary Contexts

7 STEM Education in Japan

Examining the Pipeline for Female Leadership

Diane Rodriguez-Kiino, Yuko Itatsu, and Yuko Takahashi

Post-secondary systems in Asia are on the brink of global triumph with outstanding students, preeminent leaders, and unprecedented monetary investments (Mahbubani and Chye 2015). It should come as no surprise that many Japanese universities are Ivy League competitors, offering equally reputable programs in science, technology, engineering, and math (herein "STEM") (Ni 2014). As the top producer of Nobel Prize winners in science in East Asia—hailing from such campuses as Nagoya University, Osaka University, and the University of Tokyo—Japan's long-standing nation-wide dedication to rigor and excellence in STEM is world renowned (Yang 2016).

Accolades in STEM notwithstanding, Japan faces a conundrum that will impact its position as a global powerhouse in higher education. Eclipsed by their male counterparts, women remain an untapped source of knowledge and power across important sectors of Japanese society. The most recent Global Gender Gap report by the World Economic Forum ranked Japan 102 out of 142 countries on the economic participation and opportunity scale (Bekhouche et al. 2014, 9). Though Japanese women in their 20s and 30s are more educated than their male counterparts, a bamboo ceiling (Hyun 2005) continues to present seemingly insurmountable barriers for women (Holding Back Half 2014). Several workforce examples highlight these inequitable outcomes. Female labor force participation rates hover at a low 60%, females represent only 10% of all corporate leaders nation-wide, and women earn 71% compared with men (Matsui et al. 2014). In 2015, Prime Minister Shinzo Abe lowered an important national goal promoting women—to achieve 30% female managers by 2020—to more realistic and achievable targets; namely, 7% at the federal level and 15% in the corporate sector (Aoki 2015). This drastic policy setback warrants an examination of the lack of females in the STEM leadership pipeline.

Deconstructing the organizational biases that women face in higher education, particularly those in STEM, contributes to the broader conversation that aims to support women's leadership. Vongalis-Macrow (2012) argues that it is critical to examine gendered barriers across higher education, to include the professoriate, observing that "In order to further explain the lack of women in the top leadership positions, understanding the barriers that create obstacles for women's progression necessitates investigating the earlier stages of the leadership progress from which the movement toward leadership originates" (2). Applying similar methods to uncover the systemic barriers that become obstacles for female students and faculty in STEM may lead to clues for advancing female leadership in Japan.

The Purpose of This Chapter

The purpose of this chapter is to examine the leadership pipeline for women faculty in the STEM disciplines. The chapter will (1) provide a brief depiction of gender inequity in STEM education, (2) introduce contemporary realities related to women's enrollment patterns in STEM, and

(3) illuminate the hiring patterns and workplace satisfaction of women faculty in STEM. In conclusion, we will spotlight one country-wide leadership strategy to increase the professional status of women, *Josei Kenkyusha Shien Modelu Ikusei* (Support for Best Practice for the Promotion of Female Researchers). With the singular objective to advance women in STEM, this targeted program integrates government, industry, and higher education partners. In this section, we use Tsuda College in Tokyo as a case study that exemplifies the concerted efforts needed to facilitate women's active and meaningful leadership roles in higher education. Recommendations to activate systemic change in Japan will conclude the chapter.

Gender Inequity in STEM Education

Understanding gender bias in the STEM fields in modern day Japanese higher education requires canvassing policies and practices that have contributed to the gender gap in women entering STEM. It should be noted, though, that the snapshot we provide here only partially represents the deeply rich and complex history of women in STEM education in Japan. We respectfully acknowledge this as a limitation of this chapter.

The onset of the Meiji Era in 1868 gave rise to a sharpened focus on the role of women in Japanese society. With an emphasis on loyalty and harmony during this profound cultural shift, *ryosai kenbo* or "good wife, wise mother" became the quintessence of womanhood (Sekiguchi 2010, 106). Providing women and girls education was central to inculcating this philosophy (Kodate and Kodate 2015). So, while the principle narrowly defined women, the axiom (1) served as a gateway for girls to access K-12 education (Sekiguchi 2010) and (2) extended women's authority and leadership in the home (Kodate, Kodate, and Kodate 2010). That said, Kodate, Kodate, and Kodate (2010, 317) intimate the ideology curbed women's advancement in higher education "with a few exceptions being made for the women intellectuals who went on to study at the leading research universities in both Japan and abroad in the early 1920s." Despite female renegades who prevailed in collegiate STEM programs in Japan in the early twentieth century (e.g., Drs. Sada Orihara, Katsuko Saruhashi, and Chika Kuroda), the pervasive cultural image of women as homemakers constrained their full participation in society (Kodate and Kodate 2015; Tokyo Institute of Technology 2015; Yount 1999).

In 1958, the Japanese government segregated high school courses in an effort to reinforce a societal structure in which women's primary duties were domestic: "The general tone of the national curriculum meant that sex discrimination was the norm, and single-sex education at the secondary and tertiary levels was widely accepted until the 1990s" (Kodate and Kodate 2015, 317). Though aiming to uphold a nationalistic and community ethos, this governmental approach—to offer technology to boys and home economics to girls—served to undermine the advancement of females in STEM in K-12 education.

Between 1965 and 2007, Japan experienced a surge in the attendance rates of women in higher education (Huang 2012). Women's enrollment in four-year universities rose from 16% in 1965 to 40% in 2007 (Huang 2012). Today, nearly half of all university freshmen in Japan are women (Inuzuka 2014). Factors kindling this dramatic escalation have included (1) the burgeoning independence and professional aspirations of women (Tachibanki 2010), (2) shifting gender norms (Huang 2012), and (3) increased access to higher education (Kodate and Kodate 2015).

Female Enrollment Patterns in STEM

Despite overall increased matriculation, gendered inequities in post-secondary education remain, thwarting women's progress and leadership in STEM. For the purpose of this chapter, we will discuss two present-day realities related to women's academic pursuits in STEM. First, women continue to be significantly overenrolled in junior colleges (herein "two-year colleges"). Second, females are underrepresented in STEM, particularly at the graduate level.

Persistence in Junior College

The preponderance of women in two-year institutions is salient to understanding gender bias in higher education. In 2013, the number of females entering two-year colleges was 56,990, compared with that of males at 7,073 (MEXT 2012a). Though two-year institutes serve a critical purpose in Japanese society, they are perceived as a less prestigious option for collegiate learners, 90% of whom happen to be women (The Ministry of Education, Culture, Sports, Science, and Technology [MEXT] 2012a). In 1985, Fujimura-Fenselow opined, "The curriculum at the majority of these schools is oriented toward preparing women for marriage and homemaking, and for this reason they have earned the nickname *hanayome gakko* or bridetraining schools" (476).

Stereotype or not, both gender and departmental enrollment patterns corroborate these perspectives. Data show that two-year college women are overwhelmingly drawn to degrees in home economics and education/teacher training, as opposed to social sciences and humanities. Further, there persists a serious lack of enrollment in engineering. In 2012, the total number of engineering majors across the two-year system was 137,282 (MEXT 2012b). Of these, women represented less than 1%. Table 7.1 offers a sample of two-year college enrollment in 2012 by selected fields of study and gender; it does not represent all academic majors in the two-year system.

The absence of women in STEM in two-year colleges provides a backdrop for examining women's academic choices more broadly. Table 7.1 proves that very few women select engineering as an academic major. The fact that women constitute the majority of two-year college students makes engineering a gendered field at this level of the higher education pipeline. Said another way, because male and female college enrollment rates are balanced across higher education and presumably gender restrictions in academia do not exist (save for women's colleges), men and women are *theoretically* on an equal playing field to pursue STEM degrees. Yet gender parity in engineering is not the reality. The next section aims to extend the conversation, delving into the skewed enrollment patterns of women in graduate school.

Persistence in Graduate School

Though men continue to dominate in STEM, the number of female students majoring in the STEM fields has grown. Statistical data show that between 1980 and 2010, women in the natural sciences steadily increased their degree attainment rates at the bachelors, masters, and doctoral levels (Kato, Chayama, and Hoshikoshi 2012). Further, the ratio of female students receiving degrees in physical sciences and engineering increased substantially (see Table 7.2).

However, a closer look at the various subdisciplines of STEM shows that there is a noticeable difference in the engagement of women in engineering. Figure 7.1 shows the gender ratio of students who completed Ph.D. programs (Kato, Chayama, and Hoshikoshi 2012). Across all

Table 7.1 Junior College Enrollment by Major and Gender

	Humanities	Social Science	Engineering	Home Economics	Education/Teacher Training
Female	12,406	10,634	548	24,814	46,134
Male	1,430	3,148	3,210	1,170	2,752

Source: Adapted from MEXT 2012a

Table 7.2 Percentage of Female Students Receiving Degrees in Physical Sciences (PS) and Engineering (ENG)

	1980		1990		2000		2010	
	PS	ENG	PS	ENG	PS	ENG	PS	ENG
Bachelor	17.2	1.2	20.0	3.3	27.7	10.3	26.9	11.3
Masters	8.6	1.2	10.2	2.6	19.7	7.8	22.5	10.3
Doctoral	4.6	0.8	7.6	4.4	13.0	7.7	18.5	12.5

Source: Adapted from Kato, Chayama, and Hoshikoshi 2012

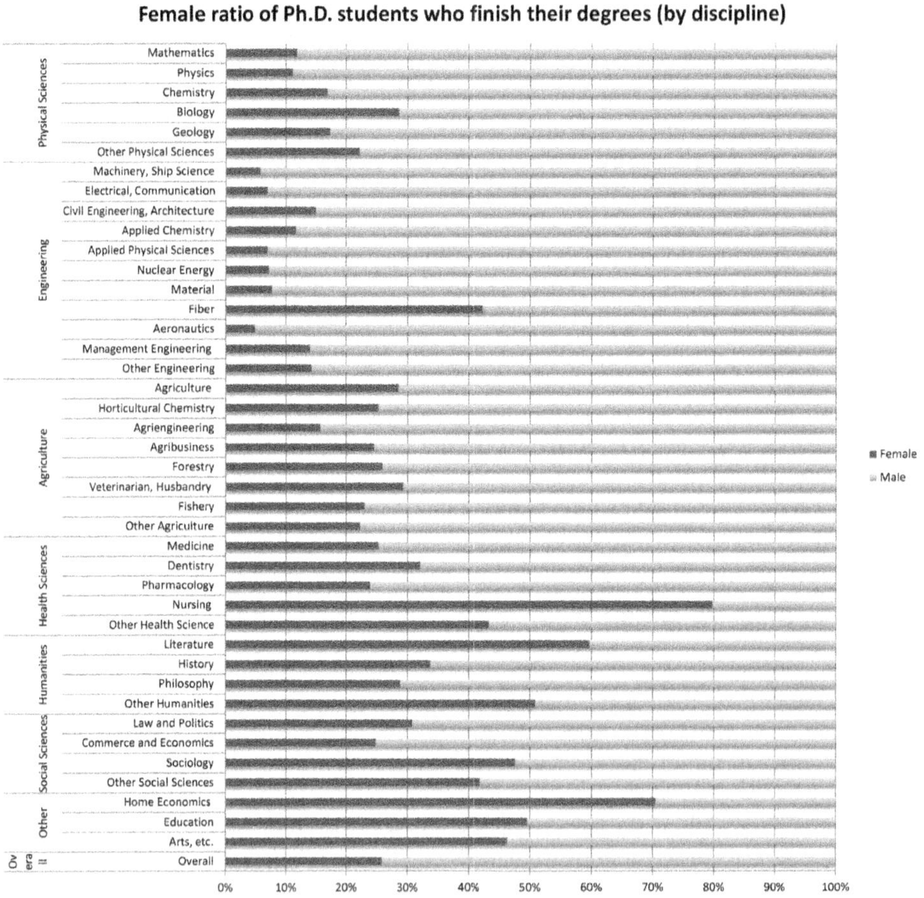

Figure 7.1 Female Ratio of Ph.D. Students Who Finish Their Degrees (by Discipline)

Source: Adapted from Figure 11, "Gender breakdown by discipline and midcategory (of students who finished their Ph.D.'s)." Kato, M., Chayama, H., and Hoshikoshi, A. Analysis on Ratio of Women in Science in Japan. Ministry of Education, Culture, Sports, Science and Technology (MEXT), May 2012. pp. 10–11.

academic disciplines, females compose 25% of doctoral students, representing a higher ratio in social science and humanities students. Disaggregated by individual discipline, women occupy the majority of nursing and home economics majors, a pattern consistent at the two-year college level. On the contrary, men vastly outnumber women in physical science and engineering.

Drilling down in engineering, the female ratio hovers around 10% in most subdisciplines (e.g., nuclear energy, ship science, aeronautics), yet in fiber science (or textile technology) women represent an impressive 42% of doctoral program completers (Kato, Chayama, and Hoshikoshi 2012).

As academia moves to recruit and retain more women in STEM, it will be critical to use fiber science as a model for increasing women's enrollment in the sciences. In other words, what is fiber science doing differently to attract more women? Furthermore, it will be prudent to unpack the legacy of home economics in Japan. Historically speaking, departments of home economics served as an academic entry point for women in the sciences (Kodate and Kodate 2015). Similar to understanding pathways in fiber science, it is important for higher education stakeholders focused on women's leadership to examine the access, recruitment, and retention strategies of women in home economics who were, indeed, pursuing natural and physical sciences.

The Female Faculty Leadership Pipeline

Despite the demonstrated incremental progress, *access* to STEM in higher education does not translate to women's leadership. Evidence of this includes a persistent gender gap in faculty hiring and promotion within the Japanese academy. Across disciplines, women occupy approximately 17% of the professoriate (Inuzuka 2014; Kimoto 2015; McNeill 2007). For the purpose of this chapter, the academic trajectory for a STEM scholar consists of the following leadership track: research associate, assistant professor, associate professor, and full professor (Shima 2012). Described in this section are two chief areas that cripple the university career ladder for women in STEM: (1) hiring practices and (2) academic quality of life.

Hiring Women Faculty

The incongruent reality between who qualifies for STEM and who pursues the STEM professoriate has gained the attention of Prime Minister Shinzo Abe. The 2011–2015 Science and Technology Master Plan published by the Prime Minister's Cabinet included a series of aggressive objectives in higher education, ranging from reserving up to 30% of research positions in the sciences for women (Inuzuka 2014). Such quotas were lofty considering the percentage of female Japanese researchers hovers around 14%, one of the lowest among all OECD countries (Inuzuka 2014; Kimoto 2015). Among this select group of women, 25% work in universities, making it the largest source of employment ahead of governmental and non-profit institutions (15.4%) and corporations (8%) (Ministry of Internal Affairs 2014). Research shows universities are considered more stable places of employment and, therefore, are more appealing despite salaries being less competitive than the other sectors (Kato, Chayama, and Hoshikoshi 2012). Female academics in Japan earn roughly $5,000 per month, a 14% divergence from their male counterparts earning on average over $5,700 (Shima 2012).

Figure 7.2 juxtaposes the ratio of women appointed to full-time research positions against governmental hiring goals and the percentage of females who complete their Ph.D.'s (Kato, Chayama, and Hoshikoshi 2012). Overall, data show university hiring committees are demonstrating efforts to ameliorate the status quo in STEM by hiring more female researchers than the field is producing (Kato, Chayama, and Hoshikoshi 2012). Yet with the exception of health sciences, significant gaps remain between the percentage of female new hires and Ph.D. completers. For example, in the physical sciences, less than 60% of all female Ph.D. recipients were hired into full-time faculty positions. Even still, once women are hired, studies show they tend to be more frustrated than their male counterparts, suggesting that the statistics mask the deeper realities for women related to quality of life in higher education.

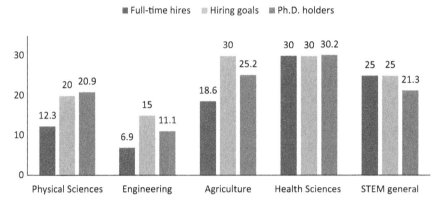

Ratio of female full-time hires and Ph.D. Holders

■ Full-time hires   ▨ Hiring goals   ■ Ph.D. holders

Numbers indicate percentage in each discipline.

Figure 7.2 Ratio of Female Full-Time Hires and Ph.D. Holders

Source: Adapted from Figure 33, "Breakdown of reasons for leaving position among Japanese faculty according to gender and academic rank." Kato, M., Chayama, H., and Hoshikoshi, A. Analysis on Ratio of Women in Science in Japan. Ministry of Education, Culture, Sports, Science and Technology (MEXT), May 2012. p. 30.

Academic Quality of Life

Researchers of Japanese higher education have contributed important interpretations of the International Survey of the Academic Profession conducted in 1992 and 2007 by the Carnegie Foundation for the Advancement of Teaching (Altbach and Lewis 1995; Arimoto 2007; Kimoto 2015). One such understanding is that faculty life in Japan is significantly more stressful than in other countries when it comes to balancing the trifecta of academia: teaching, research, and service (Altbach and Lewis 1995; Arimoto 2007).

A second critical insight is that too many female professors are dissatisfied in and with the profession (Altbach and Lewis 1995; Kimoto 2015). Several realities provide clues as to why. First, the gender gap widens with increased leadership and academic rank. For example, women compose roughly 20% of assistant professors in engineering yet only 3% of full professors (Inuzuka 2014). Second, female faculty occupied more part-time positions or when hired for full-time slots, assumed less prestigious positions than their male counterparts (Kimoto 2015). Third, diminishing the status of women on campus impacts their academic engagement. For instance, Kimoto (2015) found that while male faculty members spend an equal amount of time devoted to teaching and research, female professors spend double the amount of time teaching when, in fact, they would prefer to conduct research. Workload assignments invariably impact the capacity and speed with which faculty can generate and produce research, leaving women trailing behind men in number of publications (Kimoto 2015).

In the classroom, female professors have a heavier undergraduate course load than their male counterparts, who teach more graduate courses (Kimoto 2015). The significance of this nuance in workload distribution is that undergraduate courses tend to constitute larger class sizes and generalized curricula, compared with the specialized and more advanced themes present at the graduate level. At the graduate level, faculty members have more opportunities to pursue focused research agendas with their students (Kimoto 2015). These examples of gender bias have conceivably deteriorated the morale of women faculty, leading to stronger workplace dissatisfaction. In fact, Japanese women faculty members have shown a dissatisfaction rate 1.6 times higher than that of their male colleagues (Fujimura 2005; Kimoto 2011).

Greater displeasure with their work has led more female faculty to leave their academic positions, exacerbating the leakage of the STEM leadership pipeline. This should come as no surprise, considering women's overall sense of academic belonging and community declined on the Carnegie survey between 1992 and 2007 (Kimoto 2015). When female faculty members are pushed out of STEM, colleges and universities forfeit invaluable mentors for underrepresented female college students. As Figures 7.3a and 7.b show, more women leave their positions for reasons other than job transfer or retirement, particularly in the first three phases of an academic career in Japan—as a research associate, assistant professor, and associate professor (Kato, Chayama, and Hoshikoshi 2012). Disaggregating "other" is of critical importance since nearly 55% of all research associates

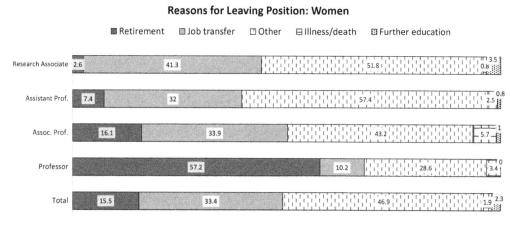

Figure 7.3a Reasons for Leaving Position: Women

Source: Adapted from Figure 48, "Breakdown of reasons for leaving position among Japanese faculty according to gender and academic rank." Kato, M., Chayama, H., and Hoshikoshi, A. *Analysis on Ratio of Women in Science in Japan.* Ministry of Education, Culture, Sports, Science and Technology (MEXT), May 2012. p. 43.

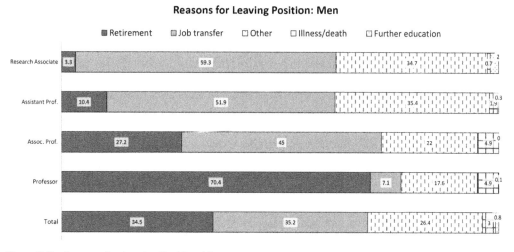

Figure 7.3b Reasons for Leaving Position: Men

Source: Adapted from Figure 48, "Breakdown of reasons for leaving position among Japanese faculty according to gender and academic rank." Kato, M., Chayama, H., and Hoshikoshi, A. *Analysis on Ratio of Women in Science in Japan.* Ministry of Education, Culture, Sports, Science and Technology (MEXT), May 2012. p. 43.

and assistant professors claim to have left the faculty due to the nebulous "other." Though further research is warranted, one explanation may be that 65% of female researchers have spouses who are fellow researchers, and in these dual-income households, the male's occupation is prioritized (Japan Inter-Society Liaison Association Committee for Promoting Equal Participation of Men and Women in Science and Engineering 2008).

As evidenced, the number and ratio of female students who receive their degrees in STEM has slowly but steadily increased since the 1970s. However, the STEM pipeline remains leaky in Japan for three prominent reasons: (1) compared with males, fewer female students pursue higher degrees in STEM; (2) the number of women researchers hired in Japanese universities is not proportionately equal to men who earn Ph.D.'s; and (3) the promotion of females in academia comes less frequently than that of their male counterparts. While efforts to increase female students in STEM have yielded some progress, the incongruity between education and employment opportunities of female researchers is emblematic of continual gender injustice in STEM. The next section aims to describe one nation-wide initiative to address this powerful disparity and promote women's advancement in higher education.

Building Women's Leadership Capacity in STEM

In 2006, MEXT took aim to increase the number of women researchers in the sciences, bolster egalitarian scientific communities, and develop women's full potential in research, particularly during their childbearing years. Today, nearly 100 institutions across Japan have been awarded MEXT funding under Support for Best Practice for the Promotion of Female Researchers (Japan Science and Technology Agency [JST] 2013a) to specifically accomplish these goals.

Supporting women's leadership, funded institutions received up to $450K to implement purposeful activities (Kodate and Kodate 2015) such as holding seminars to discuss scientific grant opportunities and application procedures, establishing job-sharing systems and part-time professional arrangements, and offering childcare for working mothers (JST 2013b). Additionally, core collegiate spaces were created for women. For example, the Support Office for Female Researchers at Hokkaido University was designed specifically to bolster the number of women in science and foster a female-friendly research climate (Kodate and Kodate 2015).

Drawing largely from Tsuda College President Dr. Yuko Takahashi's keen insight as director of the MEXT-funded Center for Women in Research from 2008 to 2011, this section employs Tsuda as a model in three areas: (1) childcare availability, (2) K-12 modeling in STEM, and (3) partnerships with government and industry. It is important to note that as one of the oldest and most time-honored women's colleges in Japan, Tsuda added a Science Department in 1943, which evolved into a Mathematics Department in 1949, and currently houses the Departments of Mathematics and Computer Science.

Several institutional award recipients implemented plans to establish and/or expand their daycare centers for children, so that researcher moms could maintain their professional cadence. The need for childcare options for female academics had been duly noted in Japan as earlier published studies "identified the discontinuity, and break from their research activities as the major obstacle to female researchers in science and engineering" (Kodate and Kodate 2015). At Tsuda College, *Sakuranbo Nursery* (Cherry Nursery) is an affordable childcare option open five days a week throughout the calendar year, serving faculty, staff, and students' young children. Since its inception in the late 1970s, Sakuranbo's early childhood educators have offered distinguished age-appropriate curricula and provided reliable and consistent communication with working parents. The child-teacher ratio is typically 2:1.

Institutional award recipients aimed to reach younger generations of female students within the formative K-12 pipeline, hoping to spark a passion for STEM. Efforts to change STEM stereotypes required college campuses to showcase successful female scientists. In 2009 and 2010, Tsuda College offered a three-day summer technology camp for 40 female high school students, focusing on robotics and mathematics. As a programmatic feature, high school students met for mentoring sessions with computer science graduate students and young women professionals in information and telecommunications. A modified version of the technology camp continues today.

Finally, universities have collaborated with each other as well as industry and government partners to share ideas and model best practices. Coordinated symposiums unite university presidents committed to women in research for the purpose of sharing best practices in gender equity, promoting women scientists and researchers, and issuing joint statements to pursue gender equality. In 2009, ten private universities including Tsuda College issued a "Joint Statement for Promoting Gender Equality," which gave immediate rise to the pressing needs of women across higher education and spurred work–life balance policy development and implementation.

Though success under the MEXT initiative is protracted and, thus, drawing continued criticism, participating female scientists made strides that should not be overlooked. Kodate and Kodate (2015) outline these achievements. Here we will cite just a few national successes. Within the life of the grant, more women researchers in their childbearing years maintained their professional status; thus, resignations dropped significantly. On average, women beneficiaries published over two scholarly papers per year compared with their non-participating counterparts, who published fewer than one. Finally, more women in participating institutions received research funding compared with women at non-participating institutions.

Bolstering the STEM Leadership Pipeline for Women

Strengthening the STEM leadership pipeline for women in higher education requires continued country-wide dedication and commitment. In turn, bolstering women's achievement in the sciences will serve as a vehicle for stimulating a national economy with inadequately low female workforce participation rates. What follows are four recommendations to facilitate the growth and development of women leaders in STEM.

First, though national comprehensive efforts are underway, the federal government must continue to shore up resources that advance women scholars in the sciences. With annual numeric targets and leadership development programs expressly for women, the success of the MEXT-funded initiative can serve as a blueprint for other nationally scaled programs that aim to put women in STEM leadership positions. Second, institutions of higher learning are responsible for strengthening new and existing K-12 STEM partnerships as a method to instill scientific curiosity in school classrooms. Ideally, as Dr. Takahashi described, professional female scientists and collegiate women in STEM can serve as role models for young girls. Third, the role and function of the two-year college cannot be overstated in the national STEM landscape (Rodriguez-Kiino 2014). The possibilities are endless with 2+2 transfer and pathway programs that bridge prestigious research universities with women's two-year colleges. It is imperative that two-year colleges be viewed as catalysts for women's advancement. Fourth, the myths and realities that plague women in STEM must be overturned. In order to increase the number of females in the STEM leadership pipeline, higher education, government, and industry must offer and mandate women-friendly research communities. Women in STEM cannot reach their full potential if they are consistently and systemically trampled in higher education because of their gender.

References

Altbach, Philip G., and Lionel S. Lewis. (1995). "Professorial Attitudes—An International Survey." *Change: The Magazine of Higher Learning*, 27 (6): 50–57.

Aoki, Mizuho. (December 25, 2015). "Japan Drastically Lowers Its Goal for Female Managers in Government and Private Sector." *Japan Times*. www.japantimes.co.jp/news/2015/12/25/national/japan-drastically-lowers-its-goal-for-female-managers-in-government-and-private-sector/#.VpFt71KVtSk.

Arimoto, Akira. (2007). "Reflections on the Changing Relevance of the Academic Profession in Japan." In *Key Challenges to the Academic Profession*, edited by Maurice Kogan and Ulrich Teichler, 29–47. Germany: UNESCO Forum on Higher Education Research and Knowledge/International Centre for Higher Education Research Kassel.

Bekhouche, Yasmina, Ricardo Hausmann, Laura D'Andrea Tyson, Saadia Zahidi and Pearl Samandari Massoudi. (2014). *The Global Gender Gap Index*. Geneva: World Economic Forum.

Fujimura, Masashi. (2005). "Dare ga daigaku wo ido surunoka: Idoseiko to manzokudo" [Who Moves Between Universities: Mobility and Satisfaction]. In *Nihon no daigaku kyoin shijo saiko: Kako, genzai, mirai [Reexamination of the University Faculty Market in Japan: Past, Present and Future]*, edited by Hiroshima University Research Institute for Higher Education, 97–110.

Fujimura-Fanselow, Kumiko. (1985). "Women's Participation in Higher Education in Japan." *Comparative Education Review*, 29: 471–489. https://www.hiroshima-u.ac.jp/en/centers/gakunai/rihe.

"Holding Back Half the Nation: Japanese Women and Work." (March 29, 2014). *The Economist*. www.economist.com/news/briefing/21599763-womens-lowly-status-japanese-workplace-has-barely-improved-decades-and-country.

Huang, Futao. (2012). "Higher Education from Massification to Universal Access: A Perspective from Japan." *Higher Education*, 63 (2): 257–270.

Hyun, Jane. (2005). *Breaking the Bamboo Ceiling: Career Strategies for Asians*. New York: HarperCollins.

Inuzuka, Noriko. (2014). *Women in University Research: Strengthening Japan's Research Capacity* (White paper). Tokyo, Japan: Gender Equality Bureau Cabinet Office, Ministry of Internal Affaire and Communication.

Japan Inter-Society Liaison Association Committee for Promoting Equal Participation of Men and Women in Science and Engineering. (2008). "Large Scale Survey of Actual Conditions of Gender Equality in Scientific and Technological Professions." Accessed December 15, 2015. www.djrenrakukai.org/english.html.

Japan Science and Technology Agency. (2013a). "Program to Supporting Research Activities of Female Researchers: Selected Organizations." Accessed January 1, 2016. www.jst.go.jp/shincho/josei_shien/en/kikan/index.html.

———. (2013b). "Program to Supporting Research Activities of Female Researchers: Program Overview." Accessed January 1, 2016. www.jst.go.jp/shincho/josei_shien/en/program/index.html.

Kato, Maki, Hidekazu Chayama, and Asuka Hoshikoshi. (2012). *Nihon no daigaku kyoin No josei hiritsu ni kansuru Bunseki [Analysis on Ratio of Women in Science in Japan]*. Tokyo, Japan: National Institute of Science and Technology Policy and Ministry of Education, Culture, Sports, Science and Technology.

Kimoto, Naomi. (2011). "Jenda baiasu: kyoin no raifu sutairu" [Gender Bias: Faculty Life Style]. In *Henbo suru sekai no daigaku kyojushoku [The Transformation of University Professor Jobs Around the World]*, edited by Akira Arimoto, 89–102. Tokyo, Japan: Tamagawa University Press.

———. (2015). "Gender Bias: What Has Changed for Female Academics?" In *The Changing Academic Profession in Japan*, edited by Akira Arimoto, William K. Cummings, Futao Huang, and Jung Cheol Shin. Kindle ed., Chapter 6. Switzerland: Springer International Publishing.

Kodate, Naonori, and Kashiko Kodate. (2015). *Japanese Women in Science and Engineering: History and Policy Change*. New York: Routledge.

Kodate, Naonori, Kashiko Kodate, and Takako Kodate. (2010). "Mission Completed? Changing Visibility of Women's Colleges in England and Japan and Their Roles in Promoting Gender Equality in Science." *Minerva*, 48: 309–330. Dordrecht: Springer.

McNeil, David. (November 9, 2007). "Few Women Reach the Top in Japan's Universities." *The Chronicle of Higher Education*. http://chronicle.com/article/Few-Women-Reach-the-Top-in/29651.

Mahbubani, Kishore, and Tan Eng Chye. (2015). "Is Asia the Next Superpower?" In *Asia: The Next Higher Education Superpower*, edited by Rajika Bhandari and Alessia Lefebure, 1–22. New York: Institute of International Education.

Matsui, Kathy, Hiromi Suzuki, Kazunori Tatebe, and Akiba Tsumugi. (2014). *Womenomics 4.0: Time to Walk the Talk*. New York: Goldman Sachs.

Ministry of Education Culture, Sports, Science, and Technology. (2012a). *Statistical Abstract*. Edition 1.9 Universities and Junior Colleges. New Entrants (Junior Colleges). www.mext.go.jp/english/statistics/1302965.htm.

———. (2012b). *Statistical Abstract*. Edition 1.9 Universities and Junior Colleges. Students by Field of Study (Junior Colleges). www.mext.go.jp/english/statistics/1302965.htm.

Ministry of Internal Affairs and Communications Press Release. (April 14, 2014). Female Researchers Who Contribute to Our Country's Science Technology. Accessed Dec 30, 2015. www.stat.go.jp/data/kagaku/kekka/topics/pdf/tp80.pdf.

Ni, Zheyan. (June 11, 2014). "Why Go to Harvard When You Can Opt for an Asian Ivy League?" *Forbes*. Accessed December 10, 2015. www.forbes.com/sites/zheyanni/2014/06/11/why-go-to-harvard-when-you-can-opt-for-an-asian-ivy-league/.

Rodriguez-Kiino, D. (2014). "Community Colleges Leveling the Playing Field: Underrepresented Racial and Ethnic Minorities in Science, Technology, Engineering, and Mathematics." In *STEM Models of Success: Programs, Policies, and Practices*, edited by J. Luke Wood and Robert T. Palmer, 1–26. New York: Information Age Press.

Sekiguchi, Sumiko. (2010). "Confucian Morals and the Making of a 'Good Wife and Wise Mother': From 'Between Husband and Wife There Is Distinction to 'As Husbands and Wives Be Harmonious.'" *Social Science Japan Journal*, 13: 95–113.

Shima, Kazunori. (2012). "Working Conditions and Salaries of the Academic Profession in Japan." In *Paying the Professoriate*, edited by Philip Altbach, Liz Reisberg, Maria Yudkevich, Gregory Androushchak and Ivan F. Pacheco, Kindle ed., Chapter 17. New York: Routledge.

Tachibanaki, Toshiaki. (2010). *The New Paradox for Japanese Women: Greater Choice, Greater Inequality*. Tokyo, Japan: International House of Japan.

Tokyo Institute of Technology. (2015). "Rikejo: Japan's Pioneering Women in Science." Accessed January 1, 2016. www.titech.ac.jp/english/about/stories/research_pioneer_rikejo.html.

Tsuda College. (April 1, 2011). "Center for Women in Research." Accessed January 1, 2016. http://cwr.tsuda.ac.jp/english/index.html.

Vongalis-Macrow, Athena. (2012). "'Monkey in a Cage': The Complicated Loyalties of Mid-Level Academic Women Working in Higher Education." *Forum on Public Policy Online*, 1: 1–12. IL: Forum on Public Policy.

Yang, Rui. (2016). "Toxic Academic Culture in East Asia." *International Higher Education*, 84: 15–16.

Yount, Lisa. (1999). *A to Z of Women in Science and Math*. New York: Facts on File.

8 For the Love of the Feminist Killjoy

Solving Philosophy's ~~Woman~~ White Male Problem

Melissa M. Kozma and Jeanine Weekes Schroer

> "When sexual harassment becomes embedded in or as academic culture, then we are talking about how some women do not have access to universities even after they have applied and been admitted. Sexual harassment is an access issue. Sexual harassment is an equality issue. Sexual harassment is a social justice issue. We are talking about women who have to exit the institution to survive the institution. We are talking about **missing women**."
>
> —Sarah Ahmed, "Against Students"

Within the humanities, no discipline is more White and more male than Philosophy (Healy 2011). Data show that women philosophers are far less likely to be published, and their publications are *far* less frequently cited (Healy 2013a). Growing bodies of research both track Philosophy's indifference to women and people of color at all stages in the discipline and investigate the marginalization and oppression of women and people of color (Patel 2016). Although the discipline has been aware of these disproportions for more than 20 years, recent data suggest that Philosophy's "woman problem" is getting *worse*, not better (Norlock 2011).

When mainstream Philosophy[1] engages with its problem, the results are frequently a symphony of stereotype threats, microaggressions, and just-so stories that favor the status quo. After unpacking Philosophy's White male problem and the discourse that sustains it, we will articulate why the common solutions tend to fail or falter: a masculinist[2] line of thinking not only controls the narratives around sexism in Philosophy but also determines the criterion by which we judge what kinds of narratives, strategies, and understandings are legitimate.

We will then discuss the strategies that have been successful in combating the "woman problem" in Philosophy, strategies widely criticized by mainstream philosophers. Public campaigns that embrace and indulge the role of the feminist killjoy, often decried as "finger-pointing," "gossip," "social justice bullying," "partiality," and "coddling," have *worked*. We argue that these campaigns of feminist joy killing are key to solving Philosophy's White male problem. We must reject the typical narratives and embrace the thorny, antagonistic relationship between feminist critique and Philosophy.

Philosophy's Missing Women

Discussions about the women missing from the discipline of Philosophy began as early as the 1980s. The maleness (and Whiteness) of Philosophy put it in league with Physics, Engineering, and Mathematics; in the humanities, only History and Religious Studies were even close to being as homogeneous (Healy 2011). In the last 15 years, approximately 27% of philosophy Ph.D.'s were earned by women, with only 22.2% earned at top 50 doctoral programs (Van Camp 2014). Women represent up to 21% of the paid professoriate (Norlock 2011), but these numbers can be misleading. Breaking down the numbers of employed female philosophers, however, reveals that women are actually doing much better in the "non-regular" job market—women are 26% of those in part-time positions, but only 16.6% of those in full-time positions (Norlock 2011). As women ascend the ranks—associate and full professors—they are represented even less. Women are also underrepresented at conferences and in journals and are less likely to be cited (cf. Healy 2013a; Healy 2013b). Of the top 500 most cited items from 1993–2013 in the four most influential Philosophy journals,[3] 19 were by women; that's 3.6%. As a point of comparison, 6.3% of that same set were authored by philosopher David Lewis. This rate of absence far outstrips women's disproportionate representation in the discipline as a whole. Of course, numbers alone tell only part of the story; as Sally Haslanger says, "With these numbers, you don't need sexual harassment or racial harassment to prevent women and minorities from succeeding, for alienation, loneliness, implicit bias, stereotype threat, microaggression, and outright discrimination will do the job" (Haslanger 2013, para. 7). The persistent disproportionate representation of women in Philosophy can be traced in part to the practice of Philosophy itself. There is growing documentation of how Philosophy has created a climate that is anathema to women (cf. Patel 2016; Langton 2013; Lombrozo 2013; Paxton, Figdor, and Tiberius 2012).

We focus on three categories of "climate" concerns in Philosophy: *hostile climate*, *uncontroversial harassment*, and *sexual assault*. These things combine to create a culture and climate in Philosophy that is unfathomably difficult to navigate. Sexual harassment law makes a distinction between hostile environment and *quid pro quo* harassment and to some degree our distinction follows those contours, but the nature of sexual harassment law—combined with universities' unapologetic, overly simplistic allegiance to the letter of said law (cf. Schroer 2012)—ignores much of the hostility relevant to women's experiences in Philosophy. The alienation, loneliness, implicit bias, stereotype threats, and microaggressions Haslanger mentions are unlikely to be successful as grounds for an actionable sexual harassment case but are often central features of the environment in which women philosophers find themselves (cf. Saul 2013, 2015; Austin 2015; "What is It" 2015; Wylie 2011).[4]

In addition to the more subtle phenomena that compose hostile climate—discussed in detail in the next section—Philosophy has in recent years become infamous for its outrageous instances of sexual harassment and sexual assault. Women philosophers have long had their own version of "The Talk"[5]: warning what departments and which philosophers to avoid and advising how to navigate those that cannot be avoided. Blogs like "What It's Like to Be a Woman in Philosophy" are merely a Web 2.0 version. Recently there has been a shift so that Philosophy (and the rest of academia) is finally talking more about prominent philosophers and their (allegedly) predatory behavior. What is remarkable about two of the most recent and well-known instances—the charges against Colin McGinn, formerly of University of Miami, and those against Peter Ludlow, formerly of Northwestern University—is that the narratives provided by the accused philosophers read as though they followed a predator's playbook (cf. Roiphe 2013 and Wilson 2015 to Johnson 2014). However, the way that Philosophy talks about its hostile environment—the grooming, the sexual harassment, and the sexual assault—you'd think these phenomena were fantastic figments of feminist nightmares, not actual issues that require address (Johnson 2011; Basu 2012; Kuta 2015).

In "Against Students," Sarah Ahmed captures something poignant about the experience of being a successful woman Ph.D.: beyond the subtly and overtly hostile climate for women, beyond the sexual harassment and assault, there is the felt loss. There is a *present absence*. Women are missing, and those who remain are haunted. When you are a "successful" woman in Philosophy—you get a Ph.D.; you get a job—you discover more haunted spaces. The specters become hazier, more faint, but you can sense the absence as you look around departments and conferences. For women, Philosophy becomes a place of mourning.

Getting the Story Right

Philosophy's standard responses to its "woman problem" often turn on assumptions about (or insistence upon) the moral innocence of Philosophy, what women are like, what philosophers are like, and what the world is like. These responses are offered as objective or disinterested, and *presuppose gender equality*. We will look at two narrative structures: one describes the innocence of Philosophy, and the second characterizes the guilt of Philosophy's detractors.

The Clean Hands Strategy

This first set of strategies attempts to minimize the concerns about representation or climate (or both) through comparisons to other equally bad or worse disciplines, by appeal to abstract mathematical inevitabilities, by insisting that the problem is just with the rare individual philosopher and not Philosophy as a whole, or by claiming a personality mismatch between women and Philosophy. While it may be true that the numbers of women are low, this is not due to something *inherent* in the discipline of Philosophy, they claim. There are many versions of this assertion: from pointing out other disciplines with low numbers of women—"What about Physics?!" "Look at Astronomy!"—to admitting defeat to a mathematical inevitability—a pipeline problem, the absence of women in Ph.D. programs and in high-profile jobs, ensures their absence in full professorships and high-impact journals. Further evidence of Philosophy's innocence comes in the form of the *few bad apples* and the *personality mismatch*. According to the few bad apples narrative, in Philosophy, as well as in many other disciplines and the working world at large, there are *individuals* who do harmful things: harassers, assaulters, and others who make workplaces inhospitable to women. Otherwise, the problem is a personality mismatch: Philosophy is based upon argumentation and critique. Conference presentations and graduate seminars can be combative, purportedly because of Philosophy's relentless commitment to discovering truth. Philosophy is the "hard" humanities: it's not for everyone—including many *men*—and women may not be well suited to it, or at the very least, they tend not to like it. In short, Philosophy isn't actively driving women away; the women excluded from it are merely victims of circumstance.

The Feminist Killjoys

At the other end of the spectrum are narratives that identify Philosophy's detractors as the real culprits in its woman problem. They respond to claims of deep-rooted sexism within Philosophy by defending the status quo—again under the guise of rational, objective considerations regarding fairness, freedom, or reasonableness. This recalls Sarah Ahmed's *feminist killjoy*—a figure often seen as exaggerating or even creating the problems she purports to draw attention to (Ahmed 2010). Calling attention to Philosophy's climate issues will only drive *more* women away from Philosophy; isolated incidents will be taken as indicative of a larger, more pervasive problem. Reasonable women will not want to enter a profession with such a bad reputation. Philosophy has also invoked the fashionable dismissal of the so-called feminist *outrage machine*: the recent movement to alter the climate of Philosophy, so the claim goes, is really just the overreaction of a tiny faction of the disgruntled. Fomenting this outrage is unhealthy and, worse, irrational.

The feminist killjoy, somewhat curiously, is also seen as having incredible power, used to smother self-expression, creativity, free speech, and natural human behavior. This worry is especially evident in the discourse around the assessment of the climate in the Philosophy Department at the University of Colorado, Boulder (Hardcastle, DesAutels, and Fehr 2014). Although the department requested the assessment *and* was found lacking in several areas *and* was offered meaningful strategies to correct their climate problems, much of Philosophy's response was that the report was an overreaction by a bunch of overwrought feminists who think they can solve the harassment problem by *outlawing* people hanging out together and shaming grown professionals into not talking shop at pubs. The APA Committee on the Status of Women's report on Boulder's climate noted,

> *The Department uses pseudo-philosophical analyses to avoid directly addressing the situation.* Their faculty discussions revolve around the letter rather than the spirit of proposed regulations and standards. They spend too much time articulating (or trying to articulate) the line between acceptable and unacceptable behavior instead of instilling higher expectations for professional behavior. They spend significant time debating footnotes and "what if" scenarios instead of discussing what they want their department to look and feel like.
>
> (Hardcastle, DesAutels, and Fehr 2014, 7). [emphasis original and author's]

Finally, as the implied argument goes, these feminist critics of Philosophy culture simply fail to grasp the complexity of the world and prefer sterile, pale imitations of the richness of academic life. Such conventional and anti-sex attitudes run counter to a sophisticated philosophical take on the world and even run counter to some feminist concerns and commitments. Love is complex and can blossom in unusual ways; relationships and sex and life are messy. In any case, we should respect the personal autonomy of graduate students. How can feminists ignore feminine agency? The feminist philosopher killjoy is painted as both naïve *and* outraged, both marginal *and* powerful. Finally, the defenders of Philosophy assert, we must be vigilant in remembering that any accusations, particularly of sexual harassment or assault, may be false. The real facts are uncertain and even a *discredited* false accusation could ruin someone's career. Again, this point is offered as objective, disinterested, and fair—especially so if a White male is making it.

The feminist philosopher's inclination is to address these claims as earnest engagements with the serious issues plaguing Philosophy. We spend energy responding to and refuting these dominant narratives. Some of them are fallacies—the comparison to worse disciplines is the two wrongs fallacy, the reference to the pipeline problem is a bit of a red herring, the "bad apples" response is also a *non sequitur*. Others misrepresent the facts—the feminist isn't responsible for the problem she reports, and both the degree of feminist "outrage" and the power of the feminist philosophy cabal are greatly overestimated; finally, some seem to move standard philosophical goalposts or willfully ignore clear-minded analysis. One task of the philosopher is to unveil what is not apparent, to reframe questions in ways that are revelatory. What if seemingly neutral traditions really do contribute to the exclusion and disenfranchisement of a vibrant philosophical community? What if petulantly clinging to these traditions when confronted with their effects gives the lie to Philosophy's commitment to a purely merit-driven discipline? What if Philosophy's stalwart insistence on giving accused parties the benefit of the doubt while denying it to the wronged reflects a willful ignorance about the sexist ideological structures that best explain Philosophy's missing women? These efforts to counteract Philosophy's standard responses, however, are not the best strategies for combating this discourse or for reversing Philosophy's White male problem. In the next section, we discuss the strategies that do work and explain why they do.

The System Is Not Broken: Demon World Philosophy

There are a number of effective strategies that have been used to address the climate in Philosophy; our focus, however, will be on those strategies that function by rejecting the narratives described in the previous section. These strategies function unimpeded by the critiques offered in those narratives, function as if those narratives simply didn't exist, or effectively disprove or nullify those narratives. To explain the way these strategies function and why we extol them, we are going to follow a strategy borrowed from one of our philosophical forefathers: we are going to posit an *evil demon* (Descartes 1993).

Suppose, for the sake of argument, that the system is *not* broken. It is not a misstep or a few bad apples that have created Philosophy as an environment that many women reject outright, some women withdraw from, and few manage to survive. Let's imagine that the toxic climate of Philosophy is a result of structures within it that serve a White male population with and without their intention for it to do so. Let's imagine that many philosophers (men and women) earnestly embrace the values of objectivity and charitableness but don't see how conceiving of one's self as objective when that objectivity is imperfect *at best* will facilitate charitable attitudes toward some views, while blocking that same extension to others. They don't see that this error will make them believe they are empathetic when, in fact, they are not. Let's imagine that some Philosophers may wish to see their discipline unchanged by the impositions made by post-modern theory, feminist theory, critical race theory, or the philosophers invested in those theoretical constructs. They wish to sustain the traditions including the way those practices distribute power to some and not to others. Let's imagine that these folks are very clever and have the capacity to occupy roles as gatekeepers or to endorse structures of gatekeeping that will inherently devalue arguments and efforts that are critical of the status quo that they value and/or function to preserve.

In this imagined world, arguments against those who view themselves as charitable and objective will be useless (after all, they will view the critic as uncharitable, possibly recklessly so, and definitely biased). They will feel it is their duty, possibly the satisfaction of a special function, to unflinchingly denounce and reject such criticisms and possibly those who offer them. They will entrench narratives and values that seem neutral but which instead serve an unjust status quo. When they neutrally seek evidence for their position, they will find it. When they neutrally seek evidence against their interlocutors, they will find that as well. When confronted with countervailing evidence, they will deny it is evidence and double down on their commitments to their traditions.

What would be the best practices for changing the climate in this *demon world*? How would those strategies be described and critiqued? How would one respond to those criticisms? For clarity, we will focus our analysis on three strategies and a few specific examples of feminist attempts to slay Philosophy's evil demon. The strategies include embracing the feminist killjoy, rejecting the culture of justification, and focusing effort and resources on problem-solving action (instead of on discourse and defense). Demon world feminists are licensed to be uncharitable to "earnest" but self-serving responses, to reclaim labels that are meant to demonize them, and to take action toward the goal of social justice (instead of just debating which policies could work in *any* possible world). To a certain degree, these actions employ counternarratives, but key to their success is the way they dismiss, reject, ignore, or even partly embrace the subverting narratives they encounter through Philosophy.

Embrace the Feminist Killjoy

The blog "What It's Like to Be a Woman in Philosophy" is brimming with demoralizing accounts of microaggressions, macroaggressions, sexual predation, sexual assault, and disenfranchisement. It has even confronted those of us who identify as feminists with our worst nightmare: the male colleague unabashedly invested in a compendium of cruel stereotypes about feminists (cf. "What We're Up Against" 2010).[6] It's bad news. How it is often received makes it an exemplar of the feminist killjoy. It's construed as invalid, as propaganda, but also as dangerous and destructive: from this perspective, it both threatens the careers of important philosophers and discourages women who might otherwise join the profession. The blog posts are anonymous and, thus, impossible to verify; they are hearsay, and even the whiff of impropriety is dangerous and can destroy the well-being of the accused, say the Philosophy apologists. Outside the evil demon world, the inclination might be to concede to what Dotson calls a "culture of justification" and presume that the norms by which strategies like this blog will be criticized are legitimate (Dotson 2012, 6–7). We might worry that the blog is rightly criticized as "gossip-y", that it makes dangerous insinuations, that it fails to give the accused the right to defend themselves against their accusers. However, positing the evil demon allows us to ignore these criticisms without justification. We cannot assume that all philosophers share a common set of univocal justificatory norms, so we should resist engagement in justificatory projects that presuppose them (Dotson 2012, 12–16). Failing to justify reframes the critic as the *unrepentant* feminist killjoy. She gleefully tells tales, throws shade, creates chaos, and gets the job done.

The climate review of Colorado provides an even clearer example of embracing the role of the feminist killjoy. Philosophy did not take the report well; its methods, the members of the reviewing committee, and their recommendations were all subjected to more and less explicit demands for justification, including explicit attacks on the philosophical bonafides of the committee members. Our contention isn't that no one tried to justify the review, the committee members, or the committee's recommendations; rather, we're interested in the clear attitude of the committee executing the project. Even convening a committee that would specialize in this sort of climate review—that would engage with the way the sexual harassment thrives in dark corners and is managed only through word of mouth (if it is managed at all)—embraced being flagged as a feminist killjoy who is basically "inventing" the problem rather than discovering it. Both of these efforts—the climate review of University of Colorado and the "What It's Like" blog—revel in voicing Philosophy's problems.

Don't Ask for Forgiveness or Permission[7]

A tremendous amount of feminist energy is directed toward explaining feminist critiques and justifying feminist strategies and principles. Much of the time, these explanations are directed at interlocutors whose arguments are at best inept and at worst simply uninterested in the truth-seeking principles that form the groundwork of philosophy.[8] The culture of justification, however, places a tremendous burden on feminists to indulge these inquiries. Again, looking at the Climate Report on the University of Colorado and the responses to it is helpful here. Among the recommendations made in the report were suggestions that departmental activities no longer occur after business hours and no longer include alcohol. Philosophy's response to these suggestions were flagrantly defensive of a status quo that favored young men and excluded both parents and women. Feminist concerns about systematic sexual harassment and discrimination were weighed against the pleasures of having the opportunity to chat with professors over a beer. *The feminist concerns were found wanting.* Philosophy's disgust with the conclusions of the climate report opened the door to demands for a top-down defense; it became popular again to make the "brave" choice to deny the legitimacy of *all* feminist philosophy (Case 2014). In the aftermath of the critique, however, these feminist philosophers didn't go on the defensive; they just went on with their work.

Perhaps the most crucial strategy is a sharp focus on the tasks at hand—the concrete, practical changes that will allow women (and minorities) to flourish in Philosophy. The discipline of Philosophy may not be for everyone, but it should be truly open to anyone. While embracing the role of the feminist killjoy and rejecting the discipline's standard modes of justification are essential to mitigating the rhetoric that supports the status quo, we must at the same time create and employ the new policies, standards, and modes of interaction that support diverse philosophers. "Diverse" here means anyone straying significantly from the assumed ideal or model philosopher: White, male, pedigreed, "brilliant," unencumbered, with interests in a rather narrow range of philosophical topics (Weinberg 2015).

This demands the initiation of policies that accommodate caregivers, such as home institutions that have parental leave, that stop or lengthen tenure clocks to accommodate those who are the primary caregivers of elderly parents, and conferences that don't occur immediately adjacent to major holidays. It requires supporting strategies that foreground access by actually gathering data about gender, race, and ethnic representation in the undergraduate and graduate student populations and then recruiting students and revising curriculum as needed on the basis of that data. It necessitates providing professional development that focuses on how ableist language or innovative but inaccessible tools might disenfranchise students and faculty with disabilities. It calls for addressing problems using both large-scale approaches—for example, streamlining procedures for reporting sexual harassment and assault on college campuses *and* making those procedures more prominent—and localized ones—making those policies reflect the rights of victims of sexual harassment and assault to seek support without being forced (by reporting requirements) to subject themselves to university bureaucracies. In short, *do something* because to paraphrase feminist philosopher Sally Haslanger, "We are the winning side now. We [must] not relent" (Haslanger 2013).

Notes

1   To highlight the fact that this discussion is focused not on philosophy as method of intellectual inquiry but instead as an ornate bureaucratic professional practice, we will use capitalization to mark this distinction. We will refer to the practice, the main site of our criticism, as "Philosophy." While we will engage with some literature that comes dangerously close to implicating philosophy as a method in the gender and race problem faced by Philosophy (the academic practice), we will table this question. (1) There isn't sufficient space for that inquiry in this essay, and (2) We worry that focusing on philosophical inquiry reframes the problem away from the actions, strategies, and ideologies that function to maintain Philosophy as a discipline that is missing women.

2   Our contention is not that men are the only source or propagators of these narratives but rather that these narratives especially serve the interests of people who benefit from male privilege.

3   More precisely, they are described as "four high-impact, highly-selective, general-interest philosophy journals: *Nous*, the *Journal of Philosophy*, the *Philosophical Review*, and *Mind*" (Healy 2013a).

4   Our view isn't necessarily that we need better or different laws, although we probably do. Equally concerning is the overreliance on legalistic models to respond to these challenges. Schroer suggests that thinking of universities and departments as communities—as opposed to systems of individuals engaged in purely self-interested exchange—is a better model for responding to problems like sexual harassment at universities, especially hostile environment.

5   Cf. Dell'Antonia 2012, Amber 2013, and Gandbhir and Foster 2015.

6   https://beingawomaninphilosophy.wordpress.com/2010/11/10/one-mans-view-of-women-who-do-feminist-philosophy/.

7   Cf. Grace Hopper "It's easier to ask forgiveness than it is to get permission." *Chips Ahoy* magazine, 1986.

8   This practice is shared with a significant segment of contemporary political discourse, cf. Kozma and Schroer 2014.

References

Ahmed, Sara. (2010). *The Promise of Happiness*. Durham, NC: Duke University Press Books.

———. (June 29, 2015). "Against Students." *The New Inquiry*. Accessed September 6, 2015. http://thenewinquiry.com/essays/against-students/.

Amber, Jeannine. (July 29, 2013). "The Talk." *Time*. Accessed September 6, 2015. http://content.time.com/time/magazine/article/0,9171,2147710,00.html.

Basu, Kaustuv. (December 12, 2011). "Women Job Candidates in Philosophy Appalled by the 'Smoker'." *Inside Higher Ed*. Accessed September 6, 2015. www.insidehighered.com/news/2011/12/12/women-job-candidates-philosophy-appalled-smoker.

Case, Spencer. (July 5, 2014). "The Gender Academy." *The National Review*. Accessed September 6, 2015. www.nationalreview.com/article/380716/gender-academy-spencer-case.

Dell'Antonia, K. J. (March 26, 2012). "Trayvon Martin and 'the Talk' Black Parents Have with Their Teenage Sons." *New York Times Online*, sec. Motherlode: Living the Family Dynamic. Accessed September 6, 2015. http://parenting.blogs.nytimes.com/2012/03/26/trayvon-martin-and-the-talk-black-parents-have-with-their-teenage-sons/.

Descartes, René. (1993). *Meditations on First Philosophy*, 3rd ed. Indianapolis: Hackett Publishing Company.

Dotson, Kristie. (May 2011). "Concrete Flowers: Contemplating the Profession of Philosophy." *Hypatia*, 26 (2): 403–409.

———. (May 2011)."Tracking Epistemic Violence, Tracking Practices of Silencing." *Hypatia*, 26 (2): 236–257.

———. (2012). "How Is This Paper Philosophy?" *Comparative Philosophy*, 3 (1): 3–29.

Gandbhir, Geeta, and Blair Foster. (March 17, 2015). "'A Conversation with My Black Son'." *The New York Times*. Accessed September 6, 2015. www.nytimes.com/2015/03/17/opinion/a-conversation-with-my-black-son.html.

Hardcastle, Valerie, Peggy DesAutels, and Carla Fehr. (January 31, 2014). "Climate Review: Summary of Report by the American Philosophical Association to the University of Colorado." *Climate Review. American Philosophical Association*. Accessed September 6, 2015. http://spot.colorado.edu/~tooley/The_Site_Visit_Report_and_Administration_Summary.pdf.

Haslanger, Sally. (May 1, 2008). "Changing the Ideology and Culture of Philosophy: Not by Reason (Alone)." *Hypatia*, 23 (2): 210–223.

_____. (September 2, 2013). "Women in Philosophy? Do the Math." *The New York Times*, sec. The Philosopher's Stone. Accessed September 6, 2015. http://opinionator.blogs.nytimes.com/2013/09/02/women-in-philosophy-do-the-math/.

Healy, Kieran. (February 4, 2011). "Gender Divides in Philosophy and Other Disciplines." *KieranHealy.org*. Accessed September 6, 2015. http://kieranhealy.org/blog/archives/2011/02/04/gender-divides-in-philosophy-and-other-disciplines/.

———. (June 18, 2013a). "A Co-Citation Network for Philosophy." *KieranHealy.org*. http://kieranhealy.org/blog/archives/2013/06/18/a-co-citation-network-for-philosophy/.

———. (June 19, 2013b). "Lewis and the Women." *KieranHealy.org*. Accessed September 6, 2015. http://kieranhealy.org/blog/archives/2013/06/19/lewis-and-the-women/.

Johnson, John. (May 14, 2014). "Women in Astronomy: Fed Up with Sexual Harassment: The Serial Harasser's Playbook." *Women in Astronomy*. Accessed September 6, 2015. http://womeninastronomy.blogspot.com/2014/05/fed-up-with-sexual-harassment-serialhtml.

Johnson, Leigh. (December 4, 2011). "The Philosophy Smoker Controversy." *ReadMoreWriteMoreThinkMore BeMore.com*. Accessed September 6, 2015. www.readmorewritemorethinkmorebemore.com/2011/12/philosophy-smoker-controversy.html.

Justin, W. (January 15, 2015). "'Raw Intellectual Talent' and Academia's Gender and Race Gaps." *Daily Nous*. Accessed September 6, 2015. http://dailynous.com/2015/01/15/raw-intellectual-talent-and-academias-gender-gaps/.

Kozma, Melissa M., and Jeanine Weekes Schroer. (2014). "Purposeful Nonsense, Intersectionality, and the Mission to Save Black Babies." In *Why Race and Gender Still Matter: An Intersectional Approach*, edited by Namita Goswami, Maeve O'Donavan, and Lisa Yount, 101–117. Brookfield, VT: Pickering & Chatto Publishers Limited.

Kuta, Sarah. (January 3, 2015). "After Year of Scandal, CU-Boulder Philosophy Department Sees Latest Departure." *Daily Camera*. Accessed September 6, 2015. sec. CU News. www.dailycamera.com/cu-news/ci_27248228/after-year-scandal-cu-boulder-philosophy-department-sees.

Langton, Rae. (September 4, 2013). "The Disappearing Women." *The New York Times*, sec. The Philosopher's Stone. Accessed September 6, 2015. http://opinionator.blogs.nytimes.com/2013/09/04/the-disappearing-women/.

Lombrozo, Tania. (June 17, 2013). "Name Five Women in Philosophy: Bet You Can't." *NPR.org— Cosmos & Culture: Commentary on Science and Society*. Accessed September 6, 2015. www.npr.org/sections/13.7/2013/06/17/192523112/name-ten-women-in-philosophy-bet-you-can-t.

Norlock, Kathryn. (2011). "Women in the Profession: A Report to the CSW." *American Philosophical Association*. Accessed September 6, 2015. https://docs.google.com/viewer?a=v&pid=sites&srcid=ZGVmYXVsdGRvbWFpbnxhcGGFjb21taXR0ZWVvbnRoZXN0YXR1c29md29tZW58Z3g6NTlmYTExZDBiY2U1MDliYw.

Patel, Vimal. (April 1, 2016). "Diversifying a Discipline." *The Chronicle of Higher Education*, 62 (29): A28–33.

Paxton, Molly, Carrie Figdor, and Valerie Tiberius. (November 1, 2012). "Quantifying the Gender Gap: An Empirical Study of the Underrepresentation of Women in Philosophy." *Hypatia*, 27 (4): 949–957.

Roiphe, Katie. (October 8, 2013). "The Philosopher and the Student." *Slate*. Accessed September 6, 2015. www.slate.com/articles/double_x/roiphe/2013/10/colin_mcginn_sexual_harassment_case_was_the_philosophy_prof_s_story_that.html.

Saul, Jennifer. (2013). "Implicit Bias, Stereotype Threat, and Women in Philosophy." In *Women in Philosophy: What Needs to Change?* edited by Katrina Hutchison and Fiona Jenkins, 39–61. New York: Oxford University Press.

————. (January 23, 2015). "Women in Philosophy." *The Philosophers' Magazine Online*. Accessed September 6, 2015. www.philosophersmag.com/index.php/reflections/9-women-in-philosophy.

Schroer, Jeanine Weekes. (Spring 2012). "Campus as Community: A Better Approach to Sexual Harassment Policy." *APA Newsletter on Feminism and Philosophy*, 11 (2): 20–24.

Van Camp, Julie. (2014). "Tenured/Tenure-Track Faculty Women at U.S. Doctoral Programs in Philosophy." Accessed September 6, 2015. http://web.csulb.edu/~jvancamp/doctoral_2004.html.

Weinberg, Steven. (2015). *To Explain the World: the Discovery of Modern Science*. London: Allen Lane.

"What we're up against: One man's view of women who do feminist philosophy." (November 10, 2010). *What Is It Like to Be a Woman in Philosophy?* Accessed September 6, 2015. https://beingawomaninphilosophy.wordpress.com/2010/11/10/one-mans-view-of-women-who-do-feminist-philosophy/.

Wilson, Robin. (October 24, 2014)."A Test Case for Sexual Harassment." *Chronicle of Higher Education*, 61 (8): 15.

————. (June 19, 2015). "A Professor, a Graduate Student, and 2 Careers Derailed." *The Chronicle of Higher Education*. Accessed September 6, 2015. http://chronicle.com/article/A-Professor-a-Graduate/231007/.

Wylie, Alison. (Springer 2011). "What Knowers Know Well: Women, Work and the Academy." In *Feminist Epistemology and Philosophy of Science—Power in Knowledge*, edited by Heidi E. Grasswick, 157–179. www.springer.com/philosophy/book/978-1-4020-6834-8.

9 Writing Gown

The Challenges of Making a New Artwork about Sexism in Academia

Susan Diab

First, a Story

Purchasing an Academic Gown on Her First Day at University

She went together with her Mom to the university outfitters to buy an academic gown. At the college where she was enrolled as a student, ownership of a gown was required for everyday use to be worn at dinner, not just twice annually for the taking of examinations. They entered the shop and felt the stuffy heaviness of tradition close down around them in contrast to the crisp autumnal air of outside. As was so often occasioned by sudden changes of temperature, her spectacles steamed up instantly so that she was plunged into a fog and walked blindly across the shop guided by her Mother. The mist cleared as she grew aware of a balding, middle-aged man with a tape measure around his neck standing upright behind a long, dark, wooden counter.

"We'd like to buy an academic gown," she said to him. "Are you a Scholar or an Exhibitioner?" he asked, his voice rising on the first and dropping on the second.

She had no idea what he meant, not being familiar with these terms for honors awarded for achievement in the University's entrance exams, so she just looked at him blankly. There was a short pause before he stared down his long, straight nose at her and, raising his voice for all to hear, exclaimed, "You're a Commoner then!" not so much saying the "C" word as coughing it out like something unpleasant that had got stuck in the back of his throat. Then he whipped his body round a half turn and disappeared into the back of the shop to look for the offensive item.

She was at once diminished, put in her place and told of her lowliest of positions in the ranks of University accomplishments. They accepted the black scrap with various lengths of fluttering fabric that he proffered to them, nodded, paid, and exited the shop as quickly as they could back out into the air, to breathe again.

My aim with this piece of writing is to bring into being an understanding of an as-yet, non-existent artwork. Devising, making, and then exhibiting an artwork are powerful acts. As the work is shown and interplays with audiences so also does its author enter into engagement with public life. If the work's content seeks to change the world by challenging prevailing assumptions, then the potential power of the act of making could be said to have multiplied infinitely. An artwork, conceived but not realized, is the equivalent of the artist remaining silent because the work is nothing more than a specter, and is kept back from its participation as agent. I am deciding to write about the project of needing to make "Gown" before I am ready to embark upon its making so as to evoke the work into the world as it would be as a physical, material object. This is a strategy called into force by the urgency of the need for action, not waiting for the right set of emotional, social, or political circumstances for the work to be made, but riding an act of will harnessed to the act of writing into the arena . . . just to see what will happen.

My project as it has developed coincides with Laurel Richardson's ideas about autoethnographic processes of writing bringing worlds into being, "writing is a method of discovery, a way of finding out about yourself and your world."[1] It was only in the research stages that I "discovered" autoethnography for myself and so have been able to locate first-person experience within an academically recognized set of practices. In addition to my own discoveries, I must acknowledge the support and enlightening advice of my University of Brighton colleague Alec Grant, whose own texts on autoethnography as risk taking have empowered me to see the merits and relevance of such an approach to my aims for this chapter.[2]

Alongside my academic activities, my artist self thinks up and mentally develops artworks and brings them into being. I always was an artist but got diverted along the way into more academic pursuits and then began a study of sculpture at the age of 26. Now in my early 50s, I have enjoyed a varied career as an exhibiting artist as well as earning my living teaching Fine Art. For the past three years, this imagined artwork complete with its title "Gown," has lived inside me, coming in and out of vision according to some logic or inner emotional rhythms. I have not logged its movements at all over this period but if I had, I might see some correlation between its strength of presence and the social vicissitudes I have experienced: a correlation which I would be able to use as critical evidence for connections between the personal and the cultural. As it is, all I have is this phantom-gown, still not born but nevertheless insistent, and I am now writing it into being.

In my mind's eye: a black academic gown, hip-length, simply cut, no sleeves, the only adornment being a black strip of fabric sewn into each shoulder that gets caught by the wind or streams out behind the wearer as she hurries down a drafty cloister, late for a tutorial.[3]

Tuesday 27 October 2015

I could write this piece in fragments, construct paragraphs in isolation and then assemble them. Such an experimental approach appeals because it feels quite like making a piece of work, where you try something out, allow yourself to be led by pleasure and follow the drift of what is occurring. It is less head-driven and more ludic, which, to my mind, makes it more creative.

The idea is to embroider an academic gown with a motif consisting of words or images or a combination of these. Embroidery is suggestive of beauty, richness of texture and finish, and of loving care in its making. The motifs could be repeated across the whole garment with space around each one so that they stand out and are legible.

A stumbling block of the work, which has stopped me more than anything else in making it, is not knowing what the motif is. I have carried out research to assist my imagination to "see" what it looks like and what it should "say": I visited the embroidery displays at the Victoria and Albert museum in London and read through a book about heraldry.

I could vary the motif to include hidden messages, slight differences, across the spread of the whole gown, which would come to light only if someone were to study it really carefully. I like this possibility, which allows for a few safe hiding places, from which to speak about what is best said from the sidelines, some "home truths." I know that the motif is in cream-colored thread on black. Some decisions about work are already made, already clear, and it would not do to go questioning them.

I am writing "in the dark" as if in a pitch-black room, an unlit space with no light coming in at all, not so much as a chink. I am entering that room with a small torch, which I use to cast a beam of limited range around the space as I grope about. In each new place where the light falls, a small detail of the whole appears, comes to mind, becomes visible. I am discovering more about the work as I write about it, by writing about it.

My primary aim is to unpick this unmade "Gown" for any understanding it might yield of my own psychosocial makeup within and through academic contexts. I recognize the particular difficulties of making "Gown" the artwork and acknowledge that I have not even got moving on making it, despite the idea refusing to leave my mind. I have come to understand that the ethical issues as they affect me, as artist, author, academic, and woman are centrally placed in the knot of threads that this writing seeks to unpick. I wish to expose ways in which I have been affected by derogatory messages about my intellectual abilities via institutionalized sexism, internalized and manifesting as symptoms of what has been identified as Imposter Syndrome: a feeling of being a fraud despite actual achievements.[4] I will be shining a light on vulnerabilities, which in the course of a working life usually remain hidden or which I do my best to keep covered up.

Making a visual artwork about this subject matter and exhibiting it within academic settings where I am employed would be a making-visual, a making-evident, of those issues. To take the matter one stage further into the public realm by writing about them for publication would be to consign the problematic to a longevity which the working through of such issues (in the making, in the writing) might mitigate against. So it is that this research toward a piece of writing and the publication of that research constitute alternative, perhaps less visible, forms for the ideas which at the same time allow for a more personal, more *confessional* aspect of the work to come about than "Gown" the artwork would be able to demonstrate.

A concern is, therefore, how voluntary exposure of my vulnerabilities—even if experienced as empowering to me—could be construed as weakness in the increasingly highly competitive setting of contemporary academia and whether such weakness could be used against me? I am willing to take that risk because I recognize the potential value of being honest about the personal cost of managing a career to those who are younger and just starting out on theirs. I hope that the insights this writing yields will give others courage and make them feel less alone in those difficult moments of work that they are bound to encounter. Naming and articulating a set of difficulties can illuminate as well as diminish those obstacles and might move myself and readers of this on to the next stage. This makes of my writing an emancipatory act of resistance, a feminist strategy where I am in charge.

* * *

Excerpts from an email exchange with Rosalind Gill (2012)[5]:

SD: *I am currently holding off making a piece of artwork about the internalized feelings of inferiority felt by academics within the university . . . One reason I have held back is a fear that if I am honest about the levels of my own internalized oppression then I will be, in effect, showing myself in a 'weak' light and this will not do anything to improve the situation. But I am experienced enough as an artist, actually, to let the work play its part to convince and separate an issue from my personal experience into an expression of broader, more humanly shared, concerns.*

RG: *Your experience really struck a chord with me . . . . It sounds a great idea to make an artwork 'about' this—I'd love to see it. Please do let me know what you do or create around these ideas—maybe we could offer you a space to exhibit it or something like that in the future?*

SD: *The offer of perhaps exhibiting the work at a future date not quite so close to home seems really appealing, easier somehow, depersonalizing it and opening up the subject to a broader context. I am going through a long, slow process with this piece of grounding it properly, creating a safe and good place in which it can exist. And that feels right.*

* * *

When internalized sexism and institutionalized sexism work together they can keep you down.[6]

Time to Indulge the Self

As of 2016, I will have been teaching in Higher Education for 30 years. Always part time contrac-tually but by no means always part time if you add up all the hours spent on the job. And in those

30 years, which see me only a decade and a half away from retirement age, I have climbed to the glorious heights of Senior Lecturer on a fractional contract. For much of that time I have been forging a moderately successful career as a visual artist alongside teaching in higher education so I have not totally devoted myself to the academic cause, have not been "single"-minded in that respect. However, despite this reasonable explanation for the lack in advancement, inside me a voice cries out, "What happened?"

It is the voice of someone who looks back at her schoolgirl self, whom a Headmaster once described as "the cleverest girl he had ever taught."

> If cleverness doesn't lead to success, then what goes wrong?
> Why does my salary run out two thirds of the way through the month?

Why am I teaching more hours than the growing coterie of male professors appointed for the REF,[7] who earn at least four times as much as me?[8]

> This kind of silent howl I carry around inside me most days.

20/10/15

Reading Bearman, Korobov, and Thorne on internalized sexism who speak of the "threads out of which conversations are woven."[9] I imagine reversing the weave of the gown until it is entirely gone, creating a mass of tangled undoneness. That way madness lies.

Does madness lie even as it points toward the truth?

* * *

I did think about creating anagrams from the word "imposter" and designing the motif from them. In fact, I am still fond of that idea. I ran "imposter" through an online anagram generator, and it came up with a very long list, some of which were most evocative and surprisingly revealing of my situation (boldfaced and italicized are those options which I could possibly consider using):

> merits op, smite pro, emits pro, *ripe mots*, *ire stomp*, me ripost, *poem stir*, moper sit, more tips, *more spit*, some trip, tomes RIP, smote rip, *trope ism*, store imp, ire ms top, ire ms pot, tie ms pro, *me I strop*, me sir top, me sit pro, me tis pro, *me its pro*, met I pros, rope it ms, pose it mr, *poet I mrs*, poet is mr, re I stomp, re mi post, *erst I mop*, rest I mop, set mi pro.

I have been revisiting Nancy K Miller's "Getting Personal" about allowing the personal and the academic to co-exist. Studying my annotations of 20 years ago, I am reminded of the pleasure of reading her book for the first time and wonder about the "identity politics" of it and whether those ideas are all very dated now? Blowing the dust off Naomi Schor's "Aesthetics and the Feminine," I search the index for "embroidery" but it is absent. I borrow Rosie Parker's "The Subversive Stitch" from the library and reread its introduction and note her refusal to allow Tracey Emin to be considered a feminist. These works themselves do not exactly inform the development of ideas for "Gown," but rather, in reconnecting with them, they perform the function of touchstones, which I use to ground myself in the feminisms of my youth. From their source I draw strength and encouragement.

Friday 23 October (Mom's Birthday)

The gown is a sort of "Tarnkappe," a "cloak of invisibility" which gives me the omnipotence of the invisible.[10] At the same time as it pushes me up there, visible, seen as a clever woman.

Saturday 7 November

An idea for a performance: I am in a small office in the building where I teach and I am putting on and taking off an academic gown. Putting it on and taking it off, in a cycle that repeats, just like that and nothing else. There is a chair in the room and I am sitting down on it and then standing up, just these simple actions: sitting down and standing up, putting on and taking off. The chair represents a professorship, an ambition. So here I am in this room, sitting down, standing up, sitting down, standing up, putting on the gown and taking it off, putting on and taking off because that is what you do with an academic gown, like all clothes, you put it on and take it off. These actions allow into this whole exercise that most abject and real—as in actually lived—aspect of my experience, the menopausal woman's body with its temperature fluctuations and accompanying rock-bottom feelings of despair.[11] As I sit here and research and imagine I put on and take off my cardigan, one minute cold to the core, the next hot and bothered. I am blowing hot and cold about this whole topic, and I am really not sure at all about telling you any of this. Never mind for publication.

Three Allies and Encounters with Their Works

I invoke the three-legged sturdy support of a tripod of other works of fabric and stitching by female artists ("support" as in the foundational material upon which the artwork is created, that is, canvas in painting and also to denote allied encouragement, a "support group" of my own devising). The first (in chronological order of their making) is the hand-embroidered jacket of Agnes Richter.[12] The second is the short text "The Chest of Drawers" by Marguerite Duras[13] to which I return frequently for nourishment and encouragement. The third is "Avid Metamorphosis 1," a work by Rona Lee.[14] The dates of my first encounters with these works take me back to my younger self, and it is in this encounter between my present and my younger self that the unpicking of "Gown" takes place.

Agnes Richter embroidered a woman's jacket with tiny handwriting with the right side of the sewing on the inside of the jacket and the outside of the sleeves. Agnes was an inpatient at the Hubertsburg asylum, case no. 52 with a diagnosis of schizophrenia. I first saw the jacket at the Prinzhorn exhibition at the Hayward gallery and was struck by how compelling it is. The script draws you in, wanting to read, to understand, but its overlayering keeps you out. As such, it simultaneously speaks and withholds what it is saying. Undoubtedly an object of great beauty in its meticulousness of manufacture, one imagines Agnes working away at it for hours, telling it all to an item of clothing, her thoughts and feelings worn on the sleeve as it were. Looking at it now, I feel a sense of constriction, the holding in of women's clothing of the time, yet simultaneously of release, in her getting the words out. So the jacket has a "push-me pull-you" quality, speaking and withholding, drawing in and letting go. The accompanying text on the Prinzhorn website speculates on processes of writing within a psychiatric institution as ways of creating and affirming the self in an environment which is dehumanizing and which invades and colonizes the intimate space of the human lives existing within it.[15] This customized garment gives up subjective experience as outerwear and makes private the social being.

If Agnes Richter's jacket provides a point of reference for identity created and maintained by inscribing the self into clothing in the face of institutional incarceration, then Marguerite Duras's short text "The Chest of Drawers" represents another life history reimagined into existence. It is an anecdote about Duras finding a woman's underblouse scrunched up in a seventeenth century chest of drawers she had bought as an antique. Somehow the garment had got gathered up by the drawer above, pushed to the back and forgotten about for a couple of centuries until Duras reencounters it. With no information about its owner and giving only scant details about the blouse—it is made of lawn, it bears some light menstrual blood stains, and it has been repeatedly darned—Duras creates a connection across time between herself and the unknown woman taking us right into her mind so that the passage ends with her imagining how the owner must have searched for it for days and days, not knowing where it could possibly have gone. A chance find is transformed into a calling up of someone else, of another woman in another time in this conflation of the imagined woman's response and Duras's evocation of her thoughts. "It was covered with months and years of darns—with darns which had been darned themselves, as beautiful as embroidery."[16] The undergarment is elevated out of its mundanity by the carefulness of the repairs which the text recreates as an image in the reader's mind.

Perpetually fascinated by it, I return to this text regularly, revisiting it for what it offers. I am drawn in by Duras's writing of it as an everyday event, the tidying of a drawer, which leads to an extraordinary discovery. It is as if the search for her blouse the woman began in the 1720s continued beyond her death and across two centuries to be taken up by Duras, unwittingly, and the search has been transferred to me so that I return to the book and flick to those pages to look again for something—even though I do not know what exactly I am searching for. The underblouse is a "timeshare" garment that does not really belong to anyone and transcends time, place, and context, very like "Gown" itself. The academic gown I once possessed and wore and the archetypal gown worn by graduating students to this day are connected by the imaginary embroidered gown I intend to make as an artwork and which I am evoking through this text. Making manifest the significance of the garment, real and imagined, enables me to take my power on my terms in my own way.

Demonstrating a taking-apart of male power, Rona Lee's performance "Avid Metamorphosis 1" consists of the artist patiently unpicking a man's suit. Wearing a mask of a bird's beak, she stands impassively and cuts every stitch that has held the suit together up to that time. She lays each loosened piece of fabric on the floor beyond the outer edge of the suit and the action of unpicking. The work enacts an undoing of patriarchy, a deconstructive act demanding time and care. It marks a moment of clarity of visualization of the task of dismantling patriarchy; a tough job to take apart an institution which has been so firmly stitched together but bit by bit, the task can be attempted without losing courage or faith that one day it will be entirely undone.

The three garments: woman's jacket, underblouse, man's suit; the three artists: Richter, Duras, Lee; the three activities: embroidering, darning, unpicking. Language worn on the body. Three institutions: psychiatry, domesticity patriarchy. These activities have meticulousness, dexterity, and care in common. In each case, there is a lot left unknown: the character of Agnes Richter, the majority of the meaning of her embroidered writings, the identity of the owner of the underblouse, the owner of the man's suit. They are partial evocations of experience just as "Gown" is only part formed; I do not know everything about it, it has not yet revealed its full face to me, the specifics of what its motif says or shows, the story has not ended yet, it remains open-ended—perhaps this is the point?

Sunday 22 November

A Memory from Camford Days

I had to give a paper at a post-grad seminar about the Romantic poet I was researching toward a Ph.D. The forum was a showing-off place of one-upmanship among the fellows, and my 23-year-old self experienced it as wholly intimidating. I used to come home from those meetings and weep, distressed by how knowledge was abused by them as a self-aggrandizing tool. All my academic career, it felt like I yearned for a place where knowledge was shared, where people wanted to talk to each other in order to allow what they knew to complement and expand thinking rather than using the sum of their knowledge to prove how little the next fellow had. The days leading up to giving my paper, I grew increasingly ill with worry and could not sleep, and this made my anxiety greater. I took myself off to the doctor. It was relief to speak openly to someone about how terrified I was to open my mouth and talk about my subject of research, a female poet, in front of all those men and one other woman, who on the whole was keen to dissociate herself from feminist ideas. I managed to give my paper without resorting to any calming medication. To my surprise, it went down well among some of the forum. One of the academics I was most keen to impress because of his radical, forward-thinking approach was quite complimentary, praising my work to me in front of the others without his words being in any way condescending. I was caught in the middle of a web of power dynamics as a female post-grad. One fellow was fond of telling me how the female poet and subject of my dissertation, was second rate. He made that remark to me on more than one occasion, usually when I had refused to let him fuck me. The power dynamics of which I speak I cannot spell out because those involved are still alive, are still exerting power, might recognize themselves. Also, I was complicit in my caughtness in that web of power. The more I struggled against it, the more it stuck to me like glue and kept me tethered.

Friday 20 November 2015

Invoke: the word which came to mind on my run today. Also, avoid self-pity and self-indulgence above all else. This is my mantra and I learn, in reading about autoethnography what I have always suspected, that concern with the personal extends beyond the limits of the self:

> Subjectivism should not be confused with solipsism or self-indulgence. The subjectivist stance in autoethnography is predicated on quite the opposite: that culture flows through self and vice versa (Ellis and Bochner 1996), and that people are inscribed within dialogic, socially shared, linguistic and representational practices (Bakhtin 1984; Frank 2005) and through their daily occupations. The self is therefore understood as a social and relational rather than an autonomous phenomenon.[17]

I have got to do it, I have got to write it down because to do so will be to plant a signpost for others who come along this same or a similar path to assist them in their own self-interrogations and provide all-important companionship in their questioning. Apart from anything else I need to plant a waymarker for myself, to acknowledge that this interrelationship of feelings and reality exists.

* * *

My niece is moving out of the family home to share a flat with her boyfriend. She has told me the color scheme of the flat is gray so I have gathered together a few oddments of wool and am knitting them into a piece as a cushion for her new place. I like knitting like this: rows, back and forth, making up patterns as I go, intuitively. I have done some diamond shapes knitted into the texture, which turned out well. I think of her, my first niece, of her life, its present and its future, of how she will fare with this young man of hers, how they will get on, how it will be, how they will organize their domestic surroundings. I imagine her laying her head on the pillow, letting her thoughts, her imagination wanders: a place to rest her head and dream and wake up with the pattern of the stitches imprinted on the skin of her cheek where her head has grown heavy. I am writing this like knitting, I realize, with little rhyme but with a reason, an evolving process, which makes some sense. In bringing her in, I am creating a connection with a younger female of my family, acknowledging how important I want her to be to herself. I can see how she is already socialized and I want her to know her freedom, to explore and expand it as much as she can beyond the limits of what life's social roles offer.

Notes

1   Laurel Richardson, "Getting Personal: Writing-Stories," *International Journal of Qualitative Studies in Education* 14, no. 1 (2001): 35. doi: 10.1080/09518390010007647.
2   Alec Grant and Laetitia Zeeman, "Whose Story Is It? An Autoethnography Concerning Narrative Identity," *The Qualitative Report*, 17, no. 72 (2012): 1–12. Accessed January 1, 2016. www.nova.edu/ssss/ QR/QR17/grant.pdf. And Alec Grant, Nigel P. Short and Lydia Turner, Introduction to *Contemporary British Autoethnography*, eds. Alec Grant, Nigel P. Short and Lydia Turner (Rotterdam: Sense Publishers, 2013), 11.
3   The commoner's gown, when new, has the appearance of being worn to shreds: "What happened was that as the student went through his daily life, the gown became ripped and torn . . . Eventually . . . tailors started to make them in this abbreviated form. (Footnote: Modern parallels may be drawn with "distressed" denim jeans, sold with ready-made tears.)", Nicolas Groves, *Shaw's Academical Dress of Great Britain and Ireland* (The Burgon Society, 2011), 12.
4   Pauline R. Clance, and Suzanne A. Imes, "The Imposter Phenomenon in High Achieving Women: Dynamics and Therapeutic Intervention," *Psychotherapy: Theory, Research & Practice* 15, no. 3 (1978): 241–247. Accessed October 20, 2015. www.paulineroseclance.com/pdf/ip_high_achieving_women.pdf.
5   In the early stages of thinking up "Gown," I read Gill's article "Breaking the Silence: The Hidden Injuries of Neo-liberal Academia", 2009. Gill is Professor of Social and Cultural Analysis at Kings College, London.
6   Alec Grant, "Neoliberal Higher Education and Nursing Scholarship: Power, Subjectification, Threats and Resistance," *Nurse Education Today* 34, no. 10 (2014): 1280–1282. doi: http://dx.doi.org/10.1016/j.nedt.2014.06.004.
7   Research Excellence Framework, current name for the government quality-measuring exercise within UK higher education.
8   Miriam David, *Feminism, Gender and Universities* (Farnham: Ashgate, 2014), 40. David cites a 2011 ECU report which states that the ratio of male to female professors in UK higher education was 80.9 percent to 19.1 percent. The ECU—Equality Challenge Unit, an independent body concerned with higher education in the UK.
9   Steve Bearman, Neill Korobov, and Avril Thorne, "The Fabric of Internalized Sexism," *Journal of Integrated Social Sciences* 1, no. 1 (2009): 11.
10 Peggy Phelan in "Unmarked" argues that it is the invisible, rather than those made visible and thus vulnerable, who hold the power.
11 I am resistant to the pervasive reduction of menopausal symptoms to "hot flashes" without mention of other symptoms such as feelings of hopelessness, despair, and intrusive thoughts of suicide.
12 *Beyond Reason* (London: Hayward Gallery, 1996), 163.
13 Marguerite Duras, *Practicalities* (London: HarperCollins, 1990), 121–122.
14 Performed at the Institute of Contemporary Arts, London, 1995.
15 Viola Michely, "Agnes Richter," *Sammlung Prinzhorn*. Accessed November 11, 2015. http://prinzhorn.ukl-hd.de/index.php?id=63&L=3.
16 Duras, "Practicalities," 122.
17 Alec Grant, Nigel P. Short, and Lydia Turner, "Introduction," in *Contemporary British Autoethnography*, eds. Alec Grant, Nigel P. Short and Lydia Turner (Rotterdam: Sense Publishers, 2013), 4–5.

Bibliography

Bakhtin, M. M. (1981). *The Dialogic Imagination.* Austin: University of Texas Press.
Bearman, Steve, Neill Korobov, and Avril Thorne. (2009). "The Fabric of Internalized Sexism." *Journal of Integrated Social Sciences*, 1 (1): 10–47.
Beyond Reason. (1996). London: Hayward Gallery.
Brand-Claussen, Bettina, Viola Michely, and Brigitte Bernet. (2004). *Irre Ist Weiblich.* 1st ed. Heidelberg: Verlag Das Wunderhorn.
Clance, Pauline R., and Suzanne A. Imes. (1978). "The Imposter Phenomenon in High Achieving Women: Dynamics and Therapeutic Intervention." *Psychotherapy: Theory, Research & Practice*, 15 (3): 241–247. Accessed October 20, 2015. www.paulineroseclance.com/pdf/ip_high_achieving_women.pdf.
David, Miriam. (2014). *Feminism, Gender and Universities: Politics, Passion and Pedagogies.* Farnham: Ashgate.
Duras, Marguerite. (1990). *Practicalities.* London: HarperCollins.

Frank, Arthur W. (2005). "What Is Dialogical Research, and Why Should We Do It?" *Qualitative Health Research*, 15 (7): 964–974.

Gill, Rosalind. (2010). "Breaking the Silence: The Hidden Injuries of Neo-Liberal Academia." In *Secrecy and Silence in the Research Process: Feminist Reflections*, edited by Roísín Flood and Rosalind Gill, 228–244. London: Routledge.

Grant, Alec. (2014). "Neoliberal Higher Education and Nursing Scholarship: Power, Subjectification, Threats and Resistance." *Nurse Education Today*, 34 (10): 1280–1282. http://dx.doi.org/10.1016/j.nedt.2014.06.004.

Grant, Alec, Nigel P. Short, and Lydia Turner. (2013). "Introduction." In *Contemporary British Autoethnography*, edited by Alec Grant, Nigel P. Short and Lydia Turner, 1–16. Rotterdam: Sense Publishers.

Grant, Alec, and L. Zeeman. (2012). "Whose Story Is It? An Autoethnography Concerning Narrative Identity." *The Qualitative Report*, 17 (72): 1–12. Accessed January 1, 2016. www.nova.edu/ssss/QR/QR17/grant.pdf.

Groves, Nicolas. (2011). *Shaw's Academical Dress of Great Britain and Ireland*. The Burgon Society. Accessed December 5, 2015.

Miller, Nancy. (1991). *Getting Personal: Feminist Occasions and Other Autobiographical Acts*. New York: Routledge.

Parker, Rozsika. (2012). *The Subversive Stitch: Embroidery and the Making of the Feminine*. New York: I.B. Tauris and Co Ltd.

Phelan, Peggy. (1993). *Unmarked: The Politics of Performance*. Abingdon: Routledge.

Richardson, Laurel. (2001). "Getting Personal: Writing-Stories." *International Journal of Qualitative Studies in Education*, 14 (1): 33–38.

Schor, Naomi. (1987). *Aesthetics and the Feminine*. New York: Methuen.

Strong, Valerie. (2011). *The Secret Thoughts of Successful Women: Why Capable People Suffer from the Imposter Syndrome and How to Thrive in Spite of It*. New York: Crown Publishing.

10 Suck It Up, Buttercup! Or, Why Cu*ts Leave STEM

Kathryn Northcut

Between 1980 and 1996, female Ph.D.'s in geology increased from about 10% to about 22%; during the same period, the number of women receiving geology master's degrees rose by an impressive 50% (Cullicott and Tarrant 1997, 8). The numbers of successful female undergraduates soared, from around 25% of the total geology degrees to 36% (Cullicott and Tarrant 1997, 8), ostensibly reaching a threshold necessary for a gender-inclusive environment. Conferences celebrating women's achievements in geosciences were organized and memorialized. The end of the "good old boy" network seemed imminent.

As a female geology student in this era, I should have been buoyed by such changes in the field. Unbeknownst to us, although women were still a minority, we were studying geology in record numbers and percentages. Women were fighting bias, to be sure (Cullicott and Tarrant 1997, 8), but winning at least some of those fights, as evidenced in both the professoriate and industry. War stories of women barely scratching their way through academic programs and up the hierarchy were starting to look like historical relics by 1997. The National Academies addressed the issues of bias and barriers to women through a monumental effort led by Donna Shalala, culminating in a report in 2006 (see Shalala). Continual probing led Hill, Corbett, and St. Rose to document reasons, through a meta-analysis of the literature, for ongoing underrepresentation of women in STEM fields (2010). At this writing, the National Science Foundation continues to fund several multimillion dollar programs (NSF ADVANCE) designed to make campus environments more amenable to women and minorities in STEM. Despite having made progress, women have far to go in achieving equal representation in male-dominated fields. My story of leaving a STEM academic program because of harassment sheds insight into one of the important—and preventable—reasons that women veer away from STEM careers after committing themselves to that path.

My experience is admittedly anecdotal, but it is one data point in the constellation of narratives through which we can collectively understand the universe of the male-dominated STEM workforce. The rosy picture of 1997 failed to report attrition or to acknowledge the reality of the leaky pipeline (documented in Shalala 2006). Some of us quit because we had babies, some found interesting challenges elsewhere, and a few of us died. But too many of us quit because of the culture; we were excluded, disrespected, bullied, or harassed (Pollack 2013).[1] Where women in science survive, data demonstrate that they are paid less and take longer to achieve academic ranks (Shalala 2006; Shen 2013). Women simply have not reached parity with men in any professional area, in any demographic, by any age, race, or level of education (AAUP 2015; AAUW 2015). While vocal female scientists rightfully focus on successes, improved numbers, and both individual and group accomplishments, a lot of data to the contrary are missing from those reports (Pollack 2013; Shen 2013). Further, such reports tend to omit actions for departments or institutions toward retaining women students and faculty.

In short, my story is that I pursued a geology degree as an undergraduate at a small public college in the western U.S. Yet when I graduated in 1986, I had a BA in English and only a minor in geology. The reasons I switched had nothing to do with intelligence, aptitude, the ability to hike in the mountains, or the tedium of recording strike and dip. The culture of the department was one of exclusion, and I was excluded.

Some of the actions by the male students were silly and (almost) forgettable: turning my last name, "Northcut" into "Northcunt" on the field trip signup sheet. Snickering when I answered a question in class. Urinating directly in front of me. But other actions were predatory, designed to make it impossible for me to do work. During field camp, a weeks-long series of trips into the mountains where we did various mapping tasks, males I barely knew hassled me. The department loaned us Brunton compasses and altimeters for mapping. My equipment disappeared; some of it "turned up" later on. We were told to form teams; I was excluded from teams. During a memorable (for me) unsupervised night, a snake was put in my tent. I endured these insults, but before the course ended, I walked away from the campsite, and away from geology.

My departure from field camp was undramatic; I was a "good girl." I did not make a scene. No one from the geology program asked why I'd changed majors in my senior year. I was not invited to try field camp again the next year, when a different faculty member was teaching a different cohort. Instead, I became an English major. For the remainder of my undergraduate education and throughout two graduate degrees, I worked with professors, classmates, and administrators who acted with civility.

My story is emblematic in countless ways. I was isolated, as a woman in geology, and I represented difference. In linguistics, "marked" and "unmarked" forms are used to identify abnormal from normal. In geology at my college in the 1980s, we were all straight, White, American by birth, all male except for some rare young women. Looking back at photos from the era on Facebook confirmed those memories. No brown skin, no Asians, no Hispanics, no one with disabilities or non-typical gender identity. Because of their (male) homogeneity, my gender alone marked me as different. Marked forms are "the other." Otherness is an unwitting invitation to be noticed and potentially singled out by the majority.

Perpetuating the Ongoing Problem

Despite leaving college depressed and embittered in 1986, I returned to the academy twice for graduate degrees and secured an ideal academic job in a somewhat traditional English department. I achieved tenure in 2010 and promotion to full professor in 2016. English departments, as AAUP and AAUW reports confirm, treat women much better than STEM departments, where only 21% of full professors are women, and engineering, with only 5% of female full professors (Shen 2013).

Exceptions, however, exist. When the University of Colorado philosophy department was "found to be sexist," as reported by Jaschik (2014, n.p.), the story itself was moderately interesting, but the comments truly revealed the types of thinking that tolerate and promote sexism. The list of grievances against CU was long and detailed: sexual harassment, family-unfriendly policies, good-old-boy retreats at mountain cabins, resulting in observable, quantifiable inequities including attrition of faculty and uneven distribution of service obligations. To people like me, no doubt lingers that both the complaints and the findings of the investigating committee were legitimate.

Yet readers' comments focused on the veracity of the allegations, the *stasis* questions of whether harm was actually done and to whom, and constitutional issues of free speech. Predictable "political correctness" critiques were also invoked. An "attack the victim" mentality pervaded the skeptical side of the discussion, and the debate rapidly degenerated into *ad hominem* slurs in the form of snarky rhetorical questions. One skeptical commenter asked, if the facts reported were true, "Is this extraordinary? Is this . . . discrimination? There has to be more" (Jaschik 2014, n.p.). Such comments echo the negative voices inside the heads of victimized women, knowing that we cannot produce strong enough arguments and evidence to convince skeptics (much less perpetrators) that harm *is* being done, it *is* meaningful, it *is* preventable, and that our experience matters. The quote "there has to be more," takes on another meaning that the commenter didn't intend: that women want to work in a place where there *is* more: more equality, respect, and civility. That is why we leave. Then, as now.

When accusations of sexism are leveled, typical reactions are often negative rather than sympathetic and can be described in general terms including denial, victim-blaming, and gaslighting (Abramson 2014; Roberts 2016; Pickel and Gentry 2016). Denial, of course, is a negation of the facts of the case; it's her word against his. Victim-blaming, often associated with violent crime, turns the onus of responsibility on the victim (Roberts 2016). We are blaming the victim when we suggest that she deserved harassment or assault because of inappropriate attire, speech, or deed. Slut-shaming is a common form of victim-blaming, in which women are perceived to be "asking for it" (Pickel and Gentry 2016). The gaslight effect, a term originating with the eponymous movie *Gaslight*, is a form of psychological manipulation in which the perpetrator tries to convince the victim that she is incompetent (Abramson 2014). Gaslighting can appear civil to observers, but it is a technique of disinformation to cast doubt on the victim's outcry by challenging the victim's grasp of reality (Abramson 2014). Such reactions present obvious disincentives to women who have been harassed and explain why much sexism isn't reported.

Anecdotally, we know that sexism continues in academic fields. Data show us that women's careers are handicapped by virtue of gender. The NSF reports that women earn half the doctorates in science and engineering in the U.S. but are grievously underrepresented at the highest ranks (Shen 2013, n.p.).

Examining the chronicled experiences of two female geologists lends some insight into the current environment. One female geologist wrote about the prospect of sexism from her six years' experience at two universities (one being CalTech) as she was obtaining her Ph.D. at UT-Austin. When asked, "Have you encountered sexism as a geologist?" she answered, "Yes, but so what?" She concluded that the field's sexism was understandable by virtue of having been historically male dominated (Day 2014, n.p.). She believes that sexism is both rare and surmountable, advising women that "if you want to be a geologist, you will have to deal with it" (Day 2014, n.p.). Similarly, a geology post-doc (Ball 2013), recounting her fair treatment throughout her science education, writes that she had "unfortunately a rare experience" (n.p.) of *not* being discriminated against or unsupported in her pursuit of science. "I know women who have been ignored, propositioned, insulted, belittled, and ogled," writes Ball, "so I'm not unaware that the problem still exists, but I haven't been a target myself" (Ball, 2013, n.p.).

Looking back on my situation, I perceived what Day later suggested: I would, indeed, have to "deal with it," and that is the reason I left geology in 1985. The situation was too much for me to deal with; I could imagine my harassers being called out and responding by denying all my allegations, then teaming up to discredit me, then arguing that I had asked for it. I had little expectation that the male faculty would sympathize with me, because "boys will be boys," after all. Female faculty and students are not necessarily more supportive of female victims. When we look at the experiences recounted by Day and Ball, we see that Day's attitude is somewhat more cavalier than Ball's. Day experienced sexism and expects women in her situation to suck it up; Ball hopes that her experience of being treated fairly is not exceptional and offers to work to make that so.

Despite anecdotal evidence to the contrary as recounted by Day and Ball, sexism is not rare in academia (Baker 2014; Shen 2013) and women should not be taught to accept it: the AAUW, AAUP, and NSF, as well as countless institution-specific studies at universities and corporations, provide mountains of data about bias and discrimination. A 2010 survey of the American Association for the Advancement of Science (AAAS) found that "52% of women said that they had encountered gender bias during their careers, compared with just 2% of men" (Shen 2013, n.p.). In astronomy, one survey suggested that 57% of astronomists experienced gender-based verbal harassment and 9% physical harassment (Moskowitz 2016). The myth of fairness and impartiality is unfortunate when it's echoed by men and tragic when promulgated by women. The NSF ADVANCE[2] program description warrants that gender equity has not been achieved in terms of women in the professoriate and that institutions need to identify large-scale transformations as ways to change the culture of STEM fields to include more women (NSF 2016). Data on NSF's website reveal that although women obtain about half the STEM undergraduate degrees, they tend to leave STEM fields disproportionately, and women employed in STEM fields are more likely than males to have technician or other lower-level positions. Women are simply less likely to obtain advanced degrees in STEM fields (even after the exceptions like psychology are factored in). The reasons are not cognitive; they are cultural. Culture is created by people. We are all the perpetrators.

For that reason, it is important that campuses consider the forms in which harassment and discrimination are occurring. A climate study conducted on my campus (Careaga 2012) revealed some gender-based phenomena that help explain why female students may not feel comfortable locally, mirroring national trends and what they will experience in the workplace. My campus is overwhelmingly dominated culturally and demographically by males in STEM, mostly engineering (over 75% in gender and discipline). Results of our campus study showed that 18% of women reported harassment (compared with 11% of men) and 78% of those women attributed the harassment to gender, compared with 40% of men. About 14% of women experienced sexual harassment, which is considered typical. Numbers of female students who experience assault, unwanted advances, and rape on our campus were about the same as other universities in the U.S., according to the consulting firm of Rankin & Associates. Data repeatedly show that women experience sexism in predictable numbers regardless of where they are. Thus, the evidence both nationally (from the AAAS) and on my campus supports my claim that the problems that plagued me in the 1980s remain today. Campuses at which 14% of women perceive themselves subject to sexual harassment are typical, as are workplaces where half of the women have experienced bias. I should point out that my current institution is making extraordinary efforts to improve the status and representation of women at this moment; unfortunately, extraordinary efforts are what is required to change the culture of our campus. Whether current efforts will succeed remains to be seen.

Soon after I first posted to Facebook about writing this essay, a male STEM faculty member at my university cornered me in a coffee shop to make the point that *his* female graduate students don't want special treatment; they wanted to be treated just like everyone else. The problem is not about women demanding marked status; we are already marked. However, if males in geology treat each other respectfully, then being treated like one of the guys would be absolutely fine with us. The treatment I received that was "special" was directed only, and deliberately, at me. I was unable to negotiate a viable position in that group of males in 1985, and I have avoided telling this story publicly ever since because I knew the denial, victim-blaming, and slut-shaming that I invite by telling it.

Critical mass theory, supported by Virginia Valian and others, suggests that until a minority group reaches a threshold of 30%, they are unlikely to influence policy or culture. In the U.S., female full professors in science number only about 20% of the population, and in engineering, 5%, making it difficult for them to advocate successfully for themselves and their students (Shen 2013). In the UK, a social movement starting around 2010 agitated for 30% female representation on FTSE 100 corporation boards of directors in order to dismantle the good old boy network in British corporate culture (Gordon 2015). The 30% threshold and the concept of critical mass are more hypotheses to be tested than natural laws, and some feminists argue that 50%–100% of female representation is a better measure and guarantor of gender parity. On campuses where humanities departments have mostly female students and faculty, STEM units can have too few women yet not be forced to change because of the overall composition of the university. One net effect is lower pay for women across disciplines because humanities faculty earn less than science and engineering faculty. Another is continued disparity in culture from department to department, often visible through the difference between acceptance rates and graduation rates of women; recruitment, retention, promotion, and salaries of female versus male faculty can also be quantified and compared.

What Should Be Done?

Unfortunately, the burden of programmatic change cannot be entrusted to people who have no commitment to recruiting and retaining women in STEM fields. The burden of changing the culture will fall not solely on female faculty, but on those few faculty of either sex who will actively advocate for minority students (on the basis of gender or other demographics), despite potential risk to their own careers. Three recommendations follow: require that students are supervised by faculty advocates, take bullying seriously, and ask students why they changed majors. If people had acted on such guidelines in 1985 at my college, I might have enjoyed a career in geology. Knowing that women still leave STEM fields in too-large numbers, these suggestions merit consideration today.

Faculty Advocates Need to Supervise Students

Groups of students should not be unsupervised for overnight events, whether those events are raft trips, study abroad, field camps, or other university-sponsored activities. At best, off-site activities pose greater risks for vulnerable students; at worst, students are molested or coerced into doing things they would not otherwise do. As faculty, we simply cannot say, "Oh, they're good kids" and travel separately, as frequently happens. Knowing that fewer women survive the academic pipeline than men, we need to be aware that these activities and events have almost as much potential for detriment as for benefit to the students. Faculty need to be accountable for the well-being of the students in activities that they organize, especially because we are compensated for such service.

Universities need to incentivize invested faculty to lead and monitor those activities with the greatest potential for harm. Female faculty who can and do advocate for female students absolutely must be hired and retained. Unfortunately, too few strong female faculty advocates exist in many academic departments to ensure that field trips, for example, are supervised by faculty who will protect students, and not all women do work to prevent negative environments. As Enos (1995) recounts, she was in a female assistant professor's course (in graduate school in the humanities) where one of the most extreme situations occurred; the 80% male student body "was a sea of testosterone and male aggression" (25), yet a woman was nominally in charge in the course where "it was okay to offend the women in the classroom" (26).

Graduate students are even less likely to have the maturity to oversee groups in which sexual harassment is likely to occur. Staff are at-will employees and, therefore, cannot be given the responsibility of taking unpopular actions like sending a student home from a trip the student paid for and expects to receive course credit for. Similarly, non-tenured or pre-tenure faculty cannot be expected to confront students about bullying and discrimination when it has been tolerated, even systemically supported, for decades. Student expulsions are serious and run a real risk of repercussions to complainants; yet such extreme consequences need to be available even if only rarely used. When faculty seek action against students, administrators must be willing to follow policies that result in more than a proverbial wrist slap, while still preserving the university as a place where students can make mistakes and learn. It's no small charge, and that's in part why the problems remain.

Take Bullying Seriously

Instances of harassment need to be admitted and identified using clear language. When professors are identified as bullies through acts of discrimination or harassment, due process should result in appropriate responses. Otherwise, these faculty maintain contact with students, infect the departmental and institutional culture, and promote an environment where bias is the basis for decision making, while their seniority dictates that people who depend on them cannot resist without fear of retaliation. Subtle forms of intimidation and exclusion, especially discipline-based bias, are difficult to address, but can be challenged by tenured faculty in departments perceived to be weaker if they are protected by administrators committed to diversity.

When students are identified as harassing or bullying others, the incidents should be explained to the student body upon resolution. Although students who break laws tend to be more publicly visible (such as students who made threats via Yik Yak at the University of Missouri in 2015), most punitive actions taken against bullying and harassment are invisible in part because of FERPA, which ensures students' rights to privacy. The incidents can be reported to the community by identifying only the actions and the punishments without students' names. In the absence of such information, students tend to assume that no consequences were leveled against perpetrators.

When a student approaches a professor or administrator to ask for an intervention, it's likely that things have already gotten out of hand. In my case, the professor minimized the complaint I made, opening the door for escalation. If certain professors are oblivious or socially inept to the point that they can't supervise such situations and ensure the protection of students, they simply can't be allowed to lead activities that give students ample opportunity to isolate, harass, belittle, and hurt their peers.

New forums for harassment continually emerge in social networking systems, and this century has brought us the specter of cyberbullying. As much benefit as emerges from these networks, the harm that can potentially be done is important to acknowledge. On my campus, Yik Yak is often a site of hate speech, objectification, and harassment. Most offensive comments fail to break the law (and are protected under free speech) and are thus visible unless they are automatically filtered or until they are downvoted or reported by users on the site. As a staunch defender of free speech, I find myself somewhat conflicted when I read the postings on sites like Yik Yak; I do not want to see it shut down, but some of the commentary is admittedly brutal and much of it is judgmental and objectifying toward both sexes. In the case of Eastern Michigan University, a female professor felt so attacked that she argued that the teaching environment had become hostile and that she had been sexually harassed after she became aware of Yik Yak comments about her (Mahler 2015).

On a typical campus, Yik Yak postings might include "girls are crazy bitches" and suggestions that female students are pursuing "Mrs." degrees (looking for husbands, not seriously studying in their fields). In the case of anonymous cyberbullying that falls short of criminal activity, academic institutions can take only indirect action. Rather than eliminating the technology (which, to put it bluntly, won't work), alternative vehicles for networking need to be established and maintained, and women who experience depression or anxiety when subjected to cyberbullying need a strong counseling office and support network on which to depend. Educating students, staff, and faculty about what sorts of harassment occur on social media may work, but most trainings will result in preaching to the choir, with problematic personalities repeating predictable patterns of denial and victim-blaming. Addressing bullying and taking it seriously will mean universities attract the wrath of critics in the public, who claim for example that colleges are becoming sites of coddling and restriction of free speech. The differences between free speech and bullying can and should be made obvious. Bullying can be addressed appropriately without endangering constitutional rights or the privileges and benefits of civil disagreement.

Ask Students Why They Left

Students change majors constantly and relatively few are ever asked why or what might have prevented their departure.

As a faculty member, I know that advisees have changed majors only when they disappear from my advisee roster. However, this information is available through most university student records systems and can be accessed if requested. Department chairs or deans, depending on who's more astute with matters of discrimination and harassment, need to follow up when attrition happens, as faculty are likely to be a cause of the departure in some percentage of cases. Especially in STEM fields, attention to underrepresented minorities seems like a strong exigency for making this type of programmatic research part of an administrator's job: why did a female student change her major in her senior year, when her grades indicated that she was doing fine? What was the environment like for students in this major? What would be required in order for the student to have stayed? What does the student perceive about this profession? Conceivably, some students changing majors may be wooed back if intervention happens in a timely way.

An extension of such inquiries would be to work higher up the organizational chart and determine the causes of pipeline leaks. Are women still considered a bad investment, as Donna Shalala experienced in her early career (Shalala 2006)? Why do female graduate students leave? Female professors? In terms of the professoriate, NSF has attempted to encourage universities to adapt to increasing numbers of women in STEM fields. But female graduate student recruitment and retention may not be adequately addressed.

Academic leaders can do much to remove the barriers to women that exist within and outside STEM. We use our power unwisely at times or fail to use it at all. We may tend to hire people who look like us. We may choose to walk away when we see harassment and bullying. We may resist accountability. AAUW points to cultural factors (climate and bias) as the major reason STEM is so unbalanced (Hill, Corbett, and St. Rose 2010). As the most visible representatives of the culture to students, faculty do have responsibility for improving campus culture; unfortunately, the labor is often delegated to program staff lacking authority over (and sometimes access to) faculty.

Academic and industry leaders are clearly at fault for the imbalance in representation (in most fields of STEM) and in unequal pay (in all fields of academia). Academic leaders would do well to commit themselves to recognizing and eliminating the following behaviors:

- Denying that a problem exists,
- Blaming the victims,
- Perpetuating "good old boy" networks in all their guises,
- Making excuses for recruiting and successfully mentoring so few women into their fields,
- Ignoring people who leave.

The women I know who have successful careers in geology take their careers very seriously, and they echo the sentiment that geology is a better field for women today than it was in 1985. For example, women weren't then allowed on offshore drilling rigs in any capacity. In 2013, the first female casualty of the dangerous rigs involved a service worker who died in a helicopter crash. Today women working on the rigs are still a minority but not categorically excluded from such work. Inclusion came as a result of women asking for what then seemed like special treatment: to visit rigs, to work on them, to learn all the jobs associated with drilling and mining. The treatment was only special because they were women; they simply asked (and in some cases demanded) to be treated the same as male peers. These women relied on the support of supervisors and the tolerance of those to whom the presence of women was unusual and notable. Because of their success, many women today experience better treatment.

When I quit studying geology in the mid-1980s, I became one of thousands who left STEM careers and/or who have become disenchanted with academic environments because of experiences with sexual discrimination and harassment. In this chapter, I argue that decades-old cultural problems in STEM fields have been addressed but not solved. Three guidelines are proposed for leaders of academic programs, suggesting that faculty advocates should monitor student activities, that bullying should be taken seriously, and that attrition should be investigated thoroughly.

Notes

1   http://www.nytimes.com/2013/10/06/magazine/why-are-there-still-so-few-women-in-science.html.
2   Increasing the Participation and Advancement of Women in Academic Science and Engineering Careers.

References

Abramson, Kate. (2014). "Turning Up the Lights on Gaslighting." *Philosophical Perspectives*, 28 (1): 1–30. doi: 10.1111/phpe.12046.

American Association of University Professors. (March–April 2015). "Annual Report on the Economic Status of the Profession, 2014–15." *Academe*. www.aaup.org/list-tables-and-figures-annual-report-economic-status-profession-2014-15.

American Association of University Women. (2015). *The Simple Truth About the Gender Pay Gap.* Fall 2015 ed. www.aauw.org/files/2015/09/The-Simple-Truth-Fall-2015.pdfwww.aauw.org/files/2015/09/The-Simple-Truth-Fall-2015.pdf.

Baker, Kelly. (October 9, 2014). "Writing About Sexism in Academic Hurts." *Chronicle Vitae.* Web.

Ball, Jessica. (March 8, 2013). "My Experience as a Woman in the Geosciences." *AGU Blogosphere.* http://blogs.agu.org/magmacumlaude/2013/03/08/being-a-woman-in-the-geosciences/.

Careaga, Andrew. (November 2, 2012). *Missouri S&T News & Events.* http://news.mst.edu/2012/11/results_of_missouri_st_climate/http://news.mst.edu/2012/11/results_of_missouri_st_climate/.

Cullicott, Catherine E., and Christine M. Tarrant. (November–December 1997). *Putting Perspectives in Perspective: AWG Looks Ahead to the Next 20 Years.* p. 8. www.awg.org/images/news/1997/November-December1997.pdf.

Day, Mackenzie. (February 7, 2014). "Women in Science: Have You Encountered Sexism as a Geologist?" *Quora.com.* www.quora.com/Women-in-Science/Have-you-encountered-sexism-as-a-geologist.

Enos, Theresa. (1995). *Gender Roles and Faculty Lives in Rhetoric and Composition.* Carbondale, IL: Southern Illinois University Press.

Gordon, Sarah. (December 4, 2015). "The 30% Club: How Women Have Taken on the Old Boys' Network." *The Financial Times.* www.ft.com/intl/cms/s/2/43177e48-8eaf-11e5-8be4-3506bf20cc2b.html#slide0www.ft.com/intl/cms/s/2/43177e48-8eaf-11e5-8be4-3506bf20cc2b.html.

Hill, Catherine, Christianne Corbett, and Andresse St. Rose. (2010). "Why So Few? Women in Science, Technology, Engineering, and Mathematics." *AAUW.* www.aauw.org/files/2013/02/Why-So-Few-Women-in-Science-Technology-Engineering-and-Mathematics.pdfwww.aauw.org/files/2013/02/Why-So-Few-Women-in-Science-Technology-Engineering-and-Mathematics.pdf.

Jaschik, Scott. (February 3, 2014). "Philosophy of Sexism?" *InsideHigherEd.* www.insidehighered.com/news/2014/02/03/u-colorado-plans-change-culture-philosophy-department-found-be-sexistwww.insidehighered.com/news/2014/02/03/u-colorado-plans-change-culture-philosophy-department-found-be-sexist.

Maler, Jonathan. (March 8, 2015). "Who Spewed that Abuse? Anonymous Yik Yak App Isn't Telling." *New York Times.* www.nytimes.com/2015/03/09/technology/popular-yik-yak-app-confers-anonymity-and-delivers-abuse.html?_r=0www.nytimes.com/2015/03/09/technology/popular-yik-yak-app-confers-anonymity-and-delivers-abuse.html?_r=0.

Moskowitz, Clara. (January 6, 2016). "Astronomers Struggle to Translate Anger into Action on Sexual Harassment." *Scientific American.* www.scientificamerican.com/article/astronomers-struggle-to-translate-anger-into-action-on-sexual-harassment/.

National Science Foundation. (2016a). *ADVANCE: Increasing the Participation and Advancement of Women in Academic Science and Engineering Careers.* www.nsf.gov/funding/pgm_summ.jsp?pims_id=5383www.nsf.gov/funding/pgm_summ.jsp?pims_id=5383

———. (2016b). "Women, Minorities, and Persons with Disabilities in Science and Engineering." www.nsf.gov/statistics/2015/nsf15311/digest/theme2.cfm#overview.

Pickel, Kerri L., and Rachel H. Gentry. (2016). "Slut Shaming in a School Bullying Case: Evaluators Ignore Level of Harm When the Victim Self-Presents as Sexually Available." *Sex Roles,* 75: 7–8. doi: 10.1007/s11199-016-0662-6.

Roberts, Kayleigh. (October 5, 2016). "The Psychology of Victim-Blaming." *The Atlantic.* www.theatlantic.com/science/archive/2016/10/the-psychology-of-victim-blaming/502661/.

Shalala, Donna. (2006). "Preface." In *Beyond Bias and Barriers: Fulfilling the Potential of Women in Academic Science and Engineering,* xi–xiv. Washington, DC: National Academies Press.

Shen, Helen. (March 6, 2013). "Inequality Quantified: Mind the Gender Gap." *Nature,* 495: 22–24. doi: 10.1038/495022a.

11 Beyond the Old Boys Club? Gender Relations at UW–Madison Geography from the 1970s to the Present

Heather Rosenfeld

Disclaimers

And some notes for reading this zine ("legend," of sorts)

HI! I'M THE AUTHOR & SOMETIMES NARRATOR. THE CONTENTS OF THIS ZINE ARE BASED ON INTERVIEWS CONDUCTED IN 2013 & OBSERVATIONS (AS A GRAD STUDENT) SINCE 2011. TO PROTECT FOLKS' IDENTITIES * (& FOR FUN)...

TENURED (sometimes called "Old Guard") PROFESSORS ARE MONKEYS

ASSISTANT PROFESSORS & POSTDOCS ARE BIRDS

AND THESE BOT-CREATURES ARE GRAD STUDENTS. THEIR GEOMETRIES ARE INSPIRED BY SARAH BENNETT'S (2014) COMIC SELF-PORTRAIT.

MOST DIALOGUE IS CLOSELY PARAPHRASED, WITH THE EXCEPTION OF DIRECT QUOTES (IN QUOTES.

And CHARACTER NAMES ARE MADE UP, WITH SOME FOLKS' REAL EXPERIENCES SPLIT INTO TWO OR MORE CHARACTERS.

& 1992

★ Art Spiegelman's _Maus_ (1986), which uses different non-human animals to represent different peoples, is also inspirational here.

I STARTED THIS PROJECT **because of** **rumors** I'D HEARD ABOUT **women & feminists** IN GEOGRAPHY AT UW-MADISON HAVING AN ESPECIALLY HARD TIME, SOMETIMES LEAVING. THESE TURNED OUT TO BE **true,...**

ALTHOUGH...

even in these stories, there are...

ISSUES ABOUT WOMEN & FEMINISM

AND

ISSUES NOT NECESSARILY GENDERED

OR SPECIFIC TO UW

OR SPECIFIC TO GEOG

I think that this makes the project even more relevant: it speaks to issues of gender & geography, situated research, university politics, & workplace culture writ large.

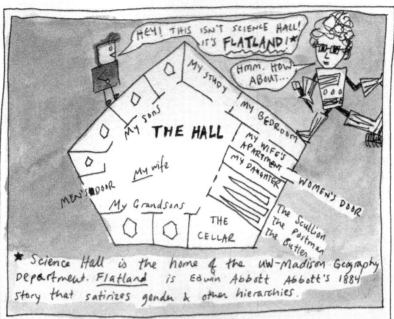

* Science Hall is the home of the UW-Madison Geography Department. _Flatland_ is Edwin Abbott Abbott's 1884 story that satirizes gender & other hierarchies.

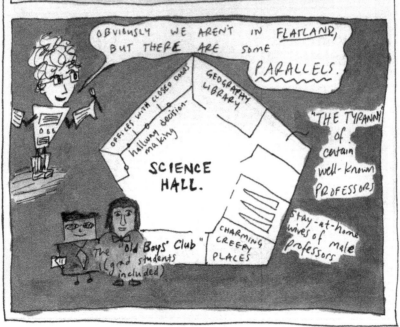

DURING MY FIELD WORK ABROAD, I WAS IN THE STREETS A LOT, WITH OTHER FEMALE ANTI-WAR PROTESTERS

I had to do **TWO PHD MINORS** because I wanted to minor in women's studies and geography profs said it wouldn't count.

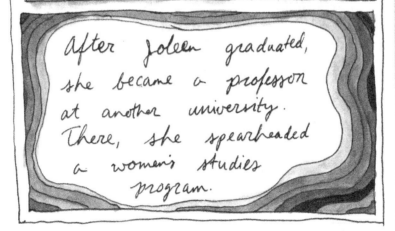

After Joleen graduated, she became a professor at another university. There, she spearheaded a women's studies program.

SEVERAL FEMALE FACULTY CAME AND QUICKLY LEFT IN THE 1970s AND 1980s

ONE OF THEM, THEY SHOULD HAVE LIKED HER — SHE WAS A NUMBER CRUNCHER ○○○○○○

MAYBE THEY DIDN'T LIKE HER BECAUSE SHE KNIT AT MEETINGS?

FOR EXAMPLE, PROFESSOR BERNICE...

WHERE I FINISHED MY PHD, THERE WERE A LOT OF STRONG WOMEN. WE WEREN'T DOING FEMINIST GEOGRAPHY, BUT IT WAS A VERY SUPPORTIVE COMMUNITY. IT WAS ALL ABOUT OUR WORK.

HALL OF SCI

GREAT TO HAVE YOU HERE!

INDEED!

PEOPLE WERE VERY WELCOMING AT FIRST — EVEN THE OLD GUARD BIGWIGS!

THERE WERE ISSUES OF FAMILY AND KIDS...

AND ONE PROF WAS KNOWN FOR WRITING LETTERS TO THE DEPARTMENT. SOMETIMES ABOUT ISSUES OF GENDER AND DIVERSITY.

Greetings!

1992 - 1994

"I see female administrators as power figures, savvy and brave enough to confront the harsh real world, and resourceful enough to create at the center of their campus a "playpen" for their male counterparts and for those women who can't quite hack it..." "Human geography has been subject to the full blast of deconstruction. Its House of Intellect is in ruins on covered graffiti..."

IN THE **LATE 1990s & EARLY 2000s,** A FEW THINGS CHANGED. SEVERAL NEW (GEOG) FACULTY LEFT FAIRLY QUICKLY. IN RESPONSE TO THIS, THE COLLEGE SET UP A MENTORING PROGRAM FOR NEW FACULTY. ~~AND~~ ALSO, MANY OF THE "OLD GUARD" WERE LEAVING OR RETIRING. AND NEW GENERATIONS OF FACULTY BEGAN CHALLENGING SOME OF THE TRADITIONS & CULTURAL NORMS THAT HAD ~~BEEN~~ PRESENT.

★ more transparency in decision-making,
★ fair divisions of labor

after ol got tenure... and then became chair, I DID THINGS LIKE CHANGE A FACULTY DINNER TO A POTLUCK, BECAUSE HOSTS, — OFTEN HOSTS' WIVES — TOOK DAYS PREPARING.

AT THIS POINT, IT SEEMS LIKE THE SITUATION AT UW-MADISON IN GEOGRAPHY WAS LESS EXCEPTIONAL — PROBLEMS & STRUGGLES & THE CLIMATE BECAME MORE AKIN TO ~~THOSE~~ THOSE OF OTHER GEOGRAPHY DEPARTMENTS.

2005

Greetings!
"What's new since the 1980s? Women's Studies is new, as is feminist theory." Neglecting women's studies "is increasingly seen as absurd if one is to know what makes society click...

Feminist theory is something else.[1]

It is not a theory -- not in any sense that a scientist understands --

and it is not a theory in the original Greek sense "spectator" -- someone who can see clearly because he stands above the fray.[2] Do ... fem... ist scholars really want to ... above the fray? D... be activi...

[1] ROSE (1993) DISTINGUISHES THESE TWO AS "SOCIAL-SCIENTIFIC MASCULINISM" AND "AESTHETIC MASCULINISM," RESPECTIVELY. THE FORMER ALLOWS THE INCLUSION OF WOMEN ~~THEM~~ AS A CATEGORY INTO RESEARCH ON A PRE-EXISTING, OBJECTIVE WORLD. THE LATTER ADMITS MORE VARIATION IN EXPERIENCES, ~~X~~ BUT OFTEN VALORIZES PARTICULAR (WHITE, CIS, MALE, BOURGEOIS) ONES.
[2] INDEED, MANY FEMINISTS (e.g. HARAWAY 1988) WOULD AGREE THAT FEMINIST (AND ALL) PERSPECTIVES CANNOT BE "ABOVE THE FRAY."

LAUREN AND KATE DISCUSSED THEIR EXPERIENCES AS GRAD STUDENTS IN THE LAST FEW YEARS...

Works Cited

Abbott, Edwin Abbott. 1884. *Flatland: A Romance of Many Dimensions*. London: Dover.

Bennett, Sarah. 2014. "Sway space and your inner Russian dinosaur." *Aether: The Journal of Media Geography*.

Haraway, Donna. 1988. "Situated knowledge: the science question in feminism and the privilege of partial perspective. *Feminist Studies* 14(3): 575-599.

Johnson, Louise. 1994. "What future for feminist geography?" *Gender, Place, & Culture*. 1(1): 103-112.

Katz, Cindi. 2001. "Vagabond capitalism and the necessity of social reproduction." *Antipode* 33(4): 709-728.

Pulido, Laura. 2002. "Reflections on a white discipline." *Professional Geographer* 54(1): 42-49.

Rose, Gillian. 1993. *Feminism and Geography: The Limits of Geographical Knowledge*. Cambridge: Polity Press.

Spiegelman, Art. 1986. *Maus I: My Father Bleeds History*. New York: Pantheon.

———. 1992. *Maus II: A Survivors Tale: And There My Troubles Began*. New York: Pantheon.

Tuan, Yi-Fu. "Dear Colleague letters archive." http://www.yifu tuan.org/archive.htm. Accessed May 30, 2016.
Specific letters referenced are from Feb. 1, 1992; May 1, 1994, & Mar. 15, 2005.

Finally, this project would not have been possible without the instruction & support of comics artist & professor **Lynda Barry**.

12 From Feminized to Feminist Labor

Strategies for Creating Feminist Working Conditions in Composition

Jennifer Heinert and Cassandra Phillips

> "[T]he major questions we must address, then, are why women in literacy do not say the truth; why do they do much of which is not in their best interest; why they have a stake in the system that is killing them; how, within the practices of literacy, women perpetuate the exploitation of the weakest members of society, among whom they number?"
>
> (Stuckey 1991, 106)

In 1991, J. Elspeth Stuckey posed these questions in "The Feminization of Literacy;" 25 years later, her questions are still relevant to and predictive of the feminized labor economy of higher education. Since its inception in Composition,[1] the feminization metaphor has provided a useful, if not complex and troubling, way to understand the problems with the way labor is valued in English and in higher education (see Holbrook 1991; Miller 1991; Stuckey 1991; Schell 1992; Flynn 1995). In "The Feminization of Composition," Schell (1992) identifies three characteristics of feminized labor: service courses intended to teach skills, low-paying and labor-intensive "drudge" work, and work performed primarily by women. That these characteristics still describe Composition underscores how academic values have not changed, especially when it comes to the teaching of writing (Schell 1992; Flynn 1995; Lauer 1995). While women now compose a larger portion of the academy, data from Modern Language Association (MLA) and American Association of University Professors (AAUP) reveal women's representation within the more prestigious ranks and positions remains significantly lower than their male counterparts'. In addition to the data about women's representation, analysis of employment trends shows that tenure track positions have become an increasingly smaller percentage of instructors at all types of higher education institutions, therefore increasing the reliance on contingent laborers, the majority of whom are women.[2] Because the teaching of writing is process driven and labor intensive in both instruction and assessment, those who do it are disproportionately affected by universal cost-saving measures and often have neither the time nor the political or academic capital to effect change.[3] As a result, teachers of writing have become even more vulnerable in political and budget climates that target feminized labor as expendable and non-essential (see Park 1996; Hogan 2005; Misra et al. 2011).

Both the discipline of Composition as well as the larger sphere of higher education acknowledge this problematic labor dynamic, but there has been little to no measurable progress with the issues identified by Stuckey and others in the 1990s. In fact, the case could be made that conditions have worsened, largely because solutions to inequity often focus on things that women should or should not do to become visible or valued in the current system rather than challenging the system itself.[4] What has largely been left out of the discussion is the outdated hierarchy of values and the assumption of meritocracy that have a stranglehold on higher education as well as on women's ability to progress within it (Boyer 1990; Park, 1996; Bird 2011). Creating feminist working conditions means engaging in the complex patriarchal system while simultaneously working to change the system itself.

In this chapter, we show how writing teachers can work to make disciplinary expertise both visible and valued, which we argue is a critical element to systemic change. We describe specific strategies designed to move feminized labor toward *feminist* labor—labor that relies on disciplinary expertise and supports changing working conditions. These strategies build on and develop from feminist theory and practice,[5] research on women in the professions, and disciplinary scholarship, specifically their discussions of collaboration, advocacy, and support. We outline deliberate actions that can challenge and destabilize traditional academic value systems and privilege the disciplinary expertise of Composition in its institutional contexts. In short, by resituating disciplinary work from feminized to feminist, it is possible to make progress toward substantive change that has eluded the discipline for so long.

From Collaboration to Coalition: Developing a Critical Mass for Lasting Change

As we will show, the foundation for feminist activism is collaboration. Compositionists have been saying for some time that writing teachers need to work together as part of a distinct discipline, with its own body of knowledge, values, and goals, regardless of the official status in an institution (see Lauer 1984; Hairston 1985; Harris 2000). Because of its feminized position in higher education, however, composition expertise can be excluded from informing curricular, labor, or governance decisions, even unintentionally by virtue of its relatively powerless position.[6] This absence reinforces a feminized Composition because its stakeholders are often precluded from advocating for resources and change, despite the large numbers of people performing that work. As such, writing teachers can use those numbers to develop their own support systems and employ strategic collaboration to identify, include, and support colleagues; develop common goals and strategies; challenge existing structures; and change working conditions.

However, over 30 years of static or worsening conditions have shown that collaboration alone is not an effective tool for systemic change because the system itself must also change. Finding writing colleagues who are willing and able to advocate for change can be difficult, as systemic exclusion complicates both collaboration and the ability to effect change. Much of the work that is valued and rewarded in higher education is individual (or presented as such), and people may be wary of relying on (and trusting) others with their work. For many women, the experience of collaboration is synonymous with doing the grunt work for a committee that does not recognize or give credit for their contributions (see Gee and Norton 2009). Pucino (2012) describes this phenomenon as characteristic of the "club culture" at academic institutions (90–92). Collaboration is also complicated by the material realities and power differentials at work in different contexts. For example, contingent writing instructors "have much in common with the proverbial housewife who contributes greatly to the running of the household (or the university) but gets no actual recognition for it (e.g. tenure, salary increases, office space, resources)" (Schell 1992, 58). It may also be difficult to collaborate with those who have already achieved success; having successfully navigated the channels of a meritocracy makes it much more unlikely they will find fault with the system: "Once a woman achieves success, particularly in a gender-biased context, her capacity to see gender discrimination is reduced" (Sandberg 2013, 163). These obstacles to collaboration are also indicative of the feminized labor dynamic that keeps the status quo in place. To change that dynamic, we need to reconceptualize that work in a feminist way: change requires not only collaboration but also collaboration in support of a strategic purpose: a coalition.

A coalition has common goals, works purposely toward them, and shares credit and responsibility for the work. Creating a coalition begins with identifying, including, and supporting colleagues who share values, concerns, and goals. On the surface, this may seem like an easy task, but it involves establishing regular communication and developing trust over time. Examining existing professional struggles may be a good place to begin identifying others who are experiencing issues with inequity. And that shouldn't be difficult to do—as Schell (1992) points out, "The large number of unpublished, hence untenured, part-time women composition teachers corresponds to deeply ingrained social and economic traditions that have designated teaching as women's work" (57). Creating a coalition of disciplinary peers who share the same values, concerns, and goals is the first step to destabilize the status quo of work environments that contribute to marginalization and devaluing of disciplinary work.

The key to an effective coalition is obtaining a critical mass. Essentially, a critical mass is defined by its effectiveness—once a given group is able to accomplish its goals, it has an established critical mass. By coordinating the efforts of even a small number of colleagues, a coalition has the potential to produce results (Sandberg 2013, 164). Having a majority group is ideal, but having even two people on a committee who can argue for the logic of a shared disciplinary position can make a significant difference. When individuals work alone, especially those who are already marginalized, they can quickly spend their political capital, making their efforts less effective. With a coalition, a critical mass of colleagues increases the political capital and disburses the workload. Finally, individuals who repeatedly call out inequity are often disregarded and ignored over time (Sandberg 2013; Williams and Dempsey 2014) but a coalition can help negate this phenomenon.

Mentoring is both an example of coalition building as well as a sustainable strategy for achieving one. There are many advantages to using mentoring as coalition building, namely that mentoring is an effective way to establish consistent communication about disciplinary issues and it is often work that women are already performing formally or informally (see Gee and Norton 2009). Research on women in the professions shows that women are already more likely to develop others and are more likely to develop women: "73% of women who were developing others were developing female talent compared to only 30% of men who were developing female talent" (Dinolfo, Silva, and Carter 2012). The key to strategic mentoring is creating bridges that navigate history, experiences, and values in a way that will identify and make plans for long-term change. To the extent that mentees often become future mentors, this strategy is both sustainable and a strategic way to build a coalition.

There are many ways to initiate and enhance mentoring and coalition building, both by working within and outside of established academic environments. Conferences, local or national, can be a purposeful way to identify and connect with colleagues at other institutions who can help support, or welcome support from, fellow writing teachers. In cases where institutional funding or support limits conference attendance, social media can provide ways for people to connect, particularly when the material conditions of women's lives precludes their involvement in traditional forms of networking. Facebook, Twitter, blogs, and other social media offer platforms to identify and connect with peers who share similar concerns and goals. National and regional organizations offer listservs that can facilitate connections and future actions as well as the access to resources like position statements, expertise, and possible funding opportunities. It is also important to not underestimate the affective value of these forms of support. Making these connections a regular part of a work day helps support the emotional labor component felt by so many writing instructors (see Micciche 2002).

Ultimately, it is important to remember that writing teachers are already providing an increasing amount of the labor in their departments, are already working with each other in a variety of ways, and already outnumber those who benefit from the feminized labor dynamic. Intentional collaboration—working like a coalition—can combat the isolation, disengagement, or even hopelessness that so often accompanies marginalized institutional positions. Even a small number of colleagues strategically working toward shared goals can improve working conditions for the majority and begin to change how disciplinary work is valued.

Advocacy: Working to Redefine What Is Valued

Changing the visibility and value of disciplinary work cannot be done without intentional and strategic forms of advocacy. Making discipline-related successes, accomplishments, and progress public is an inherent goal of advocacy. Sandberg (2013) discusses the central role of communication in changing cultures: "The simple act of talking openly about behavioral patterns makes the subconscious conscious" (148). Engaging in discussion is a form of advocacy and is the primary public responsibility of a coalition: this means intentionally discussing disciplinary approaches and values related to teaching, research, and service in multiple ways, and whenever possible, documenting them. For Composition, this means making the intellectual work of teaching, research, and service public in multiple contexts.

However, advocacy is not just about making successes public; it is about making the values that define those successes public, a problem that Composition has struggled with for a long time. In 1995, Flynn framed questions about Composition's disciplinarity: "Too often we have allowed other fields to dictate to us, not recognizing the importance of having research questions and methods grow out of our own problems and questions" (366). In many ways, the marginalization of the field is mirrored in how departments value the academic work of teaching Composition. It is important for a coalition to work intentionally and publicly against the forces that contribute to Composition's feminized status by advocating for standards or best practices as informed by the research in the discipline. By identifying, articulating, and using disciplinary values to define the quality of research, service, and teaching, a coalition can work to align department values with disciplinary ones.

The work of a coalition, then, is to prioritize disciplinary values in disciplinary work. For example, disciplinary research can inform and support the value of research-based teaching practices, helping us move away from traditional value structures that create inequity. In addition to reconceiving of disciplinary teaching as a form of advocacy, research can take up the disciplinary questions about student learning, governance and policy changes, approaches to pedagogy, the need for resources, and other avenues for change. An example of how effective such research can be is in the case of evaluating the teaching of writing. This process has often been disconnected from what we know about effective teaching in the discipline. Many teaching assessment processes do not allow for discipline-specific assessment or feedback about teaching effectiveness. Hindman (2000) notes how the assessment of teaching has privileged teacher-centered pedagogies instead of "student-centered, feminist, critical pedagogies" (13) that are associated with the best practices in our discipline. Indeed, many institutions use a tool that measures the instructor's "performance" in the classroom, and research on these tools has shown how ineffective those tools are for assessing teaching quality.[7] In response to this problem, Hindman (2000) piloted her own disciplinary teaching assessment tool focused on rewarding student-centered teaching with the goal of "re-shap[ing] students', teachers', and administrators' attitudes about the qualities that define effective teaching" (19). The tool she developed asks students about their experiences and the teaching of the course and gives them an opportunity to provide feedback on the assessment tool. Hindman's work in many ways exemplifies disciplinary approaches to teaching problems and can serve as an example of how research and teaching can be a form of disciplinary advocacy. By changing the values, she changes the conversation about teaching effectiveness in a critical, disciplinary way.

Disciplinary research can also inform the value of other parts of Composition's labor that contribute to its feminized status. Because Composition is seen a service discipline (see Adler-Kassner and Roen 2012), those who teach writing are often burdened with a heavy load of invisible service. Service work rarely is valued in a meaningful way despite its importance in quality program development (see Lauer's discussion of "women's work" in the field). However, much of the service associated with Composition is service that requires disciplinary expertise and knowledge, and as such can be an extension of research. The service work of Composition can be a form of advocacy—advocacy for quality curriculum and programming aligned with disciplinary standards, and advocacy for the value of this service in the form academic currency.[8] As Boyer (1990) articulates,

> To be considered scholarship, service activities must be tied directly to one's special field of knowledge and relate to, and flow directly out of, this professional activity. Such service is serious, demanding work, requiring the rigor-and the accountability-traditionally associated with research activities.
>
> (22)

Boyer's expansive and integrated definitions of faculty work illustrate the way that the intellectual work of service, research, and teaching intertwine in the discipline. Instead of "saying no" to service as is often advised, composition teachers should deliberately and strategically select service that is intellectual work and, in turn, advocate that it be recognized as such, using their critical mass to support that assessment. In this way, the act of engaging in service can gradually change how that labor is valued.

Integrating disciplinary values in this way has important implications for changing the public discourse surrounding effective teaching, research, and service. For example, a coalition can recognize and publicize accomplishments related to teaching and service as much as (or in equal proportion to) research and publishing successes. A coalition can also advocate for or facilitate teaching awards for instructors who can demonstrate evidence-based practices and disciplinary standards and should work to define the criteria for those awards. Public conversations are opportunities for a coalition to change the discourse about any area of an institution that is informed by disciplinary values. Some actions a coalition can take include supporting research that addresses local disciplinary inquiries, arguing for disciplinary standards to be used to judge teaching effectiveness, supporting instructors who spend time mentoring and assisting others with their development, acknowledging instructors who redesign a course to reflect shifting disciplinary standards, and supporting and valuing professional development related to instruction. Through advocacy—making the disciplinary values visible—a coalition can gradually work to decenter a system that marginalizes the work of writing teachers.

Sustainability and Support: Planning Ahead for Difficulties and Setbacks

Institutional and cultural change is incremental and requires a long-term commitment to the necessary labor required to sustain change. There will likely be many setbacks that accompany—or even outnumber—successes, and a great deal of emotional labor. Strategies to sustain activism include creating equitable and supportive communication backchannels, developing a plan that allows for sharing the labor and leadership, and being prepared to provide evidence in support of disciplinary practices.

An effective way to sustain a long-term commitment to activism is to create a supportive backchannel that operates as a safe space for colleagues to connect, work through questions and issues, and provide support in informal yet immediate ways. While the corporate culture version of networking often excludes women by design, social media and other forms of electronic communication close the access gap. It is possible to create support networks that are inclusive and effective and that can help people connect across institutions and states. This backchannel network provides a supportive venue for strategizing, feedback, and problem solving. Maddison and Shaw's (2012) research demonstrates the supportive and cooperative functions of such feminist backchannel communities. For example, one of their research subjects identified the value of a feminist community as "not feeling alone" and experiencing "alignment" and affirmation of her thinking that was difficult to find in any other forum (428). This experience is important because the work of advocacy and institutional change, especially in feminized labor conditions, is difficult, stressful, and relentless. Support in the form of cheerleading, commiseration, reassurance, brainstorming, or shared outrage can be invaluable and will often circumvent the negative consequences of missteps. A backchannel can also help with the creating and sharing of plans for and implementation to achieve disciplinary representation in leadership and other positions of power.

Backchanneling allows coalition members to coordinate the sharing of labor, both emotional and physical, of disciplinary advocacy, which is important for sustained activism. For example, it is important that many work-intensive committees include someone with expertise in Composition, especially those committees that serve evaluative or policy-forming functions. Because of the labor-intensive nature of such work, having a critical mass of colleagues with shared goals means that colleagues can cycle through that service and take turns. If those who are doing the work are not represented, the values will perpetuate the usual hierarchy. For example, as universities rely more and more on contingent labor, disciplines with high numbers of contingent instructors (like Composition) should be able to find ways to make sure they receive equal representation and input on important issues (McMahon and Green 2008; Mendenhall 2014). Yet contingent labor has little voice in the institution, even as they are doing more and more of the work. Ultimately, to change how feminized labor is valued, it is important that coalition members work toward serving in leadership positions in the institution. Chairs, deans, and roles in other governance bodies provide ways for the voice of feminized labor to be "at the table." Leadership provides the opportunity to advocate for disciplinary representation in hiring, work expectations and evaluations, retention, promotion, academic programs, policies, and merit. All of these aspects of an institution are influenced by this invisible work.

Finally, it is important to have a clear process not only for advancing change but also for responding to backlash and managing other challenging setbacks. As Williams and Dempsey (2014) discuss at length in *What Works for Women at Work: Four Patterns Working Women Need to Know*, women are often required to "prove" their work, often many times over (46). As a result, it is logical to expect skepticism and to be prepared to answer questions and provide evidence to support disciplinary work. Advocates should establish a culture of documentation and assessment when it comes to the work that they do as writing instructors. Accessible research and disciplinary standards can provide documentation and support that work is grounded in the discipline and not a personal agenda. National disciplinary organizations such as Council of Writing Program Administrators and National Council of Teachers of English have helped make standards visible and credible through position statements and electronic resources. These standards also allow for transparency; for example, when assessing the work of instructors, evidence can help demonstrate the relationship between effective teachers and disciplinary standards. What's more, such documentation need not be prepared in isolation. Coalitions can crowdsource support from disciplinary communities (listservs, system groups, and other disciplinary connections made through conference attendance or other meetings).

By creating communities of support, sharing the labor and leadership, and creating a culture of documentation and assessment, it is possible to sustain the work of culture change that it takes to address feminized labor.

Conclusion

The last 20 years of scholarship on Composition's labor read like prophecy in 2016. From the feminization of Composition to the feminization of service and labor, scholars have identified and analyzed labor conditions that contribute to gender and disciplinary inequities. Despite this work, Composition continues to grapple with the challenges of feminized labor, contingent staffing, and institutional marginalization. Yet changing the way that feminized labor has been valued for over 20 years means acknowledging how many scholars either directly or indirectly argue that engaging in feminized labor is something to avoid—even Stuckey stated that women "do much of which is not in their best interest." Instead, compositionists should work to demonstrate how this work is valuable and is in everyone's interests.

Moving from feminized to feminist labor requires a sustainable commitment to activism, despite the emotional and physical tolls of challenging existing power structures. This approach relies on feminist labor practices of

- Coalition building based on disciplinary values;
- Advocacy that centers on the value of disciplinary teaching, research, and service;
- Pursuing appropriate disciplinary representation in service, governance, and leadership.

While these goals may seem grand in scale, the focused strategies to achieve them are practical and possible. Doing so is the only way to challenge an academic system that relies on, indeed profits from, the marginalization of feminized labor at the expense of those who perform it.

Notes

1   Like Janice Lauer, we see Composition in the context of this article as writing instruction, not scholarship within the field of Rhetoric and Composition.
2   The number of part-time instructors has increased substantially every two years, and we have reached the point where part-time instructors make up almost 50% of our labor workforce (AAUP), while other studies indicate this may be as high as 70% (Kezar and Maxey 2013). Professional organizations including MLA, National Council of Teachers of English (NCTE), AAUP, and Association of American Colleges & Universities (AACU) have published many reports, studies, statements, and recommendations about labor in English and higher education, but none of these have amounted to any measurable change: the reliance on contingent labor to teach courses has only increased.
3   For example, most institutions do not follow the NCTE recommendations for course maxima of 15–20 students per writing class, recommendations based on estimated instructor time required for successful student learning. And institutions that have been able to maintain appropriate class sizes often accomplish this by exploiting the feminized labor dynamic: for example, graduate assistants teaching classes for tuition remission or minute stipends are the means to finance small class sizes rather than faculty with terminal degrees who are experts in their fields.
4   See Wilson (2012), Houston (2013, 2014), and Seltzer (2015) for examples of the advice to help women succeed in academia focusing on saying "no" instead of changing the system.
5   While the purpose of this chapter is not to discuss in detail feminist theory and practices as agents of change, we do want to acknowledge that the strategies we outline in this chapter are grounded in a feminist approach to activism. We are taking some of those concepts and using them to talk about ways to pursue change in how feminized labor, specifically the effective teaching of writing, is valued. For example, see Hassel and Launius (2015), specifically their discussion on feminist action (pp. 157–162).
6   Disciplinary organizations such as NCTE call attention to the feminized status of writing instructors even when writing position statements related to the problems of feminized labor in the discipline: See "CCCC Statement on Working Conditions for Non-Tenure-Track Writing Faculty" for an example.
7   See Boring, Ottoboni, and Stark's (2016) "Student Evaluations of Teaching (Mostly) Do Not Measure Teaching Effectiveness," which demonstrates problems with SET gender biases—findings that have significant implications for the evaluation of Composition courses, which are primarily taught by women.
8   The CWPA describes writing program work within the context of five categories of intellectual work: program creation, curricular design, faculty development, program assessment and evaluation, and program-related textual production (CWPA).

Bibliography

Adler-Kassner, Linda, and Duane Roen. (2012). "An Ethic of Service in Composition and Rhetoric: Serving the Profession Through Principle Doesn't Mean Teaching 'Service Courses.'" *American Association of University Professors*. Accessed December 20, 2014. www.aaup.org/article/ethic-service-composition-and-rhetoric#.WMGhNhiZPq0

Baker, Kelly. (2014). "Writing About Sexism in Academic Hurts." *Chronicle Vitae*.

Ballif, Michelle, D. Diane Davis, and Roxanne Mountford. (2008). *Women's Ways of Making It in Rhetoric and Composition*. New York: Routledge.

Bird, Sharon R. (2011). "Unsettling Universities' Incongruous, Gendered Bureaucratic Structures': A Case-Study Approach." *Gender, Work and Organization*, 18 (2): 202–230.

Boring Anne, Kellie Ottoboni, and Phillip Stark. (2016). "Student Evaluations of Teaching (Mostly) Do Not Measure Teaching Effectiveness." *Science Open*.

Boyer, Ernest L. (1990). *Scholarship Reconsidered: Priorities for the Professoriate*. Princeton: Carnegie Foundation for the Advancement of Teaching.

Conference on College Composition and Communication. (2016). "Statement on Working Conditions for Non Tenure Track Faculty."

Dinolfo, Sarah, Christine Silva, and Nancy M. Carter. (2012). "High Potentials in the Leadership Pipeline: Leaders Pay It Forward." *Catalyst*, 7: 1–20.

Flynn, Elizabeth A. (1995). "Feminism and Scientism." *College Composition and Communication*, 46 (3): 353–368.

Gee, Michele V., and Sue Margaret Norton. (2009). "Improving the Status of Women in the Academy." *The NEA Higher Education Journal*, Fall: 163–170.

Hairston, Maxine. (1985). "Breaking Our Bonds and Reaffirming Our Connections." *College Composition and Communication*, 36: 272–282.

Harris, Joseph. (2000). "Meet the New Boss, Same as the Old Boss: Class Consciousness in Composition." *College Composition and Communication*, 52: 43–68.

Hart, Jeni. (2008). "Mobilization Among Women Academics: The Interplay Between Feminism and Professionalization." *Feminist Formations*, 20 (1): 187–208.

Hassel, Holly, and Christy Launius. (2015). *Threshold Concepts in Women's and Gender Studies: Ways of Seeing, Thinking, and Knowing*. New York: Routledge.

Hindman, Jane. (2000). "Fostering Liberatory Teaching: A Proposal for Revising Instructional Assessment Practices." *WPA: Writing Program Administration*, 23 (23): 11–32.

Hogan, Katie. (2005). "Superserviceable Feminism." *The Minnesota Review*. Winter 2005 (63–64): 95–111.

Holbrook, Sue Ellen. (1991). "Women's Work: The Feminizing of Composition." *Rhetoric Review*, 9: 201–229.

Houston, Natalie. (2013). "Should You Say Yes Or No?" *The Chronicle of Higher Education*.

———. (2014). "Five Ways to Say No." *The Chronicle of Higher Education*.

Kezar, Adrianna, and Daniel Maxey (2013). "The Changing Academic Workforce." *Trusteeship Magazine*. Association of Governing Boards of Universities and Colleges. May/June. www.agb.org/trusteeship/2013/5/changing-academic-workforce.

Lauer, J. M. (1984). "Composition Studies: Dappled Discipline." *Rhetoric Review*, 3 (1): 20–29.

———. (1995). "The Feminization of Rhetoric and Composition Studies?" *Rhetoric Review*, 31 (2): 276–286.

McMahon, Deirdre, and Ann Green. (2008). "Gender, Contingent Labor, and Writing Studies." *Academe*, 94 (6): 16–19. *Professional Development Collection*. January 13, 16.

Maddison, Sarah, and Frances Shaw. (2012). "Feminist Perspectives on Social Movement Research." In *Handbook of Feminist Research: Theory and Praxis*, edited by Sharlene Nagy Hesse-Biber, 413–433. Los Angeles, CA: Sage Publications, Inc.

Mendenhall, Annie S. (2014). "The Composition Specialist as Flexible Expert: Identity and Labor in the History of Composition." *College English*, 77 (1): 11–31.

Micciche, Laura R. (2002). "More Than a Feeling: Disappointment and WPA Work." *College English*, 64 (4): 432–458.

Miller, Susan. (1991). *Textual Carnivals: The Politics of Composition*. Carbondale, IL: Southern Illinois University Press.

Misra, Joya, Jennifer Hickes Lundquist, Elissa Holmes, and Stephanie Agiomavritis. (2011). "The Ivory Ceiling of Service Work." American Association of University Professors. Jan/Feb. www.aaup.org/article/ivory-ceiling-service-work#.WNCnw1XyvIU.

Park, Shelley. (1996). "Research, Teaching, and Service: Why Shouldn't Women's Work Count?" *Journal of Higher Education*, 67 (1): 46–84.

Pucino, Janet. (2012). *Not in the Club: An Executive Woman's Journey Through the Biased World of Business.* Beverly Hill, CA: Deep Canyon Media.

Sandberg, Sheryl. (2013). *Lean In: Women, Work, and the Will to Lead.* New York: Alfred A. Knopf.

Schell, Eileen. (1992). "The Feminization of Composition: Questioning the Metaphors that Bind Women Teachers." *Composition Studies/Freshman English News,* 20 (1): 55–61.

———. (1998). *Gypsy Academics and Mother-Teachers: Gender, Contingent Labor, and Writing Instruction.* Portsmouth, NH: Boynton/Cook.

Seltzer, Rena. (2015). "To Find Happiness in Academe, Women Should Just Say No." *The Chronicle of Higher Education.* Web.

Stuckey, J. Elspeth. (1991). "The Feminization of Literacy." In *Composition and Resistance,* edited by C. Mark Hurlbert and Michael Blitz, 105–113. Portsmouth, NH: Boynton/Cook.

Williams, Joan, and Rachel Dempsey. (2014). *What Works for Women at Work: Four Patterns Working Women Need to Know.* New York: New York University Press.

Wilson, Robin. (August 5, 2012). "How Saying No Helps Professors Find Their Focus." *The Chronicle of Higher Education.* Web.

13 Surviving Sexism to Inspire Change

Stories and Reflections from Mothers on the Tenure Track

Krystia Nora, Rochelle Gregory, Ann-Marie Lopez, and Nicole A. Williams

In 1993, Deborah J. Swiss and Judith P. Walker introduced "The Maternal Wall"—referring to how having children stalls a career—and offered few viable solutions for climbing it. Now, over 20 years later, too many mothers continue to struggle with the demands of motherhood and their careers. Research shows statistically mothers are not as well paid or advanced as fathers (Mason 2013). Maureen Baker (2012) dubs this the "motherhood penalty," and Mary Ann Mason (2013) calls it the "baby penalty." Heightened awareness of this dilemma has fueled deeper inquires and produced varying results. For example, in the last five years, several Rhetoric and Composition (hereafter Rhet/Comp) scholars have published on how family-rearing is an enriching and rewarding part of their academic success (Cucciarre et al. 2011, 61; Pantelides 2013). Yet research by Amy Kittelstrom (2010), Mary Ann Mason (2013), and Kelly Ward and Lisa Wolf-Wendel (2012) shows that while academic women in all fields can find happy balances between motherhood and their careers, there are still long-term career penalties for choosing motherhood.

In order to lift the veil on what academic mothers in Rhet/Comp experience, as well as to propose potential avenues for future advocacy to diminish sexism, this chapter provides excerpts from anonymized surveys of more than 200 Rhet/Comp tenure track mothers. These show some of the complexities and joys of motherhood—a distinctly feminist issue—in our field. The positive situations described inspire us to imagine and work for better working conditions. The struggles shared here reveal how far many, if not all, institutions still have to go.

Surviving Stress

Over 80% of our Rhet/Comp survey respondents admitted having work difficulty because of being mothers. One of the largest issues shared is the feeling that there is never enough time. Motherhood demands the same invaluable commodities as academia—time and attention—and both are scarce resources. What makes composition studies stand out among other academic fields is its unique teaching demands: the writing development courses we teach are especially demanding time-wise due to reading, commenting on, and grading multiple drafts of papers. Add in time for work on scholarship and service, and the workload can get overwhelming. Our field exemplifies how "[a]cademic work is distinct in that it can be, quite literally, never ending" (Ward and Wolf-Wendel 2012, 54), much like parenting.

Balancing motherhood with Rhet/Comp is most intense in early years of parenting that coincide with the tenure track. As Mary Ann Mason and Eve Mason Ekman (2007) write in *Mothers on the Fast Track*, women in higher education are closer to 38 years old when they have their first child, a time that "coincides with their tenure year [and. . .] the end of their fertility curve" (42).

Over 70% of our respondents admitted that pregnancy and early childcare while on the tenure track affected their work performance. As Amy Kittelstrom (2010) explains, "Academic mothers *are* different than academic fathers. The differences are both sex-specific and time-limited, significant only during the intense years of childbearing and early caregiving—the years that matter most for academic careers" (para. 5).Women bear the brunt of childbearing (which can bring with it nausea and other temporary disabilities) and feeding of a child in the early years, especially when pregnant and nursing. Our participants offer several examples, like this one:

> Each time I was pregnant, [. . .] I'd be fairly debilitated for stretches. I started working in spurts—getting as much done as I could in the brief times I felt OK, and somehow I survived and seemed to even do well, but it was so stressful.

Although having no regrets, this participant admitted nursing was also difficult: "I never [had] more than two or three hours' sleep at a stretch." This underscores how motherhood brings with it certain uniquely female temporary handicaps.

One mother in our study, who was later in her career, reflects on how hard the early years were. While raising children, she struggled with

> less time, [was] more tired, [and] of course [had] less research and writing time. As my children grew up, I realize that was not just in my imagination. Not having them to care for, not having to be home to make supper or pick them up, meant I could work long and late at my own pace. When the children were young, I used to think maybe I used them as an excuse not to work. But once they were gone, I could see that was far from true.

Many academic mothers and those they work with hold on to the ideal worker model, dubbed by Arlie Hochschild (1995)—an ideal that can be impossible for mothers. Joan Williams (2000) in *Unbending Gender* describes how the ideal worker model typically privileges men since this model is "framed around the traditional life patterns of men" (24) who are expected to work full time—and even overtime—without significant responsibilities for child-rearing or housework.

When women do not live up to the ideal worker model, they can be targeted. One woman reports,

> There were times I couldn't stay late when meetings ran over because I had to go pick up my children from school or had to make a doctor's appointment or something. One time this happened, faculty from another department actually made fun of me. It was really hard.

Another states,

> There were many times I was told I was on the "mommy track" and that having children meant I was less productive than what I could have done without them—no matter how many more top-tier publications I had than that particular speaker/voice.

Nearly 35% of our respondents say they had struggles with colleagues over their choice to be mothers, but those who do not experience such discrimination provide models on how departmental colleagues can mitigate maternal stress. Compare the previous experiences with the mother who reports, "I am lucky to work in a child-friendly department. We all have kids of various ages, and they all kind of grow up together as extended members of the department. It is awesome for them, and us."

Many mothers do not experience stressors individually. The effects of multiple stressors are illustrated by a tenure track mother:

> I was in college for most of my kids' lives. I remember my first breakdown, at the ironing board, no less, very well. [. . .] I stopped, halfway done with a [child's] pant leg, and began to cry. I cried because I was exhausted and overwhelmed. I was teaching a full load. I was attending classes myself. I was taking care of kids and a home. [. . .] I'll often wonder what the cost is to my family and career and how I can best negotiate that price for both.

Academic mothers can be overwhelmed by the second shift—the work of the home and caregiving (Crittenden 2010; Hochschild 2012)—and can be idealists striving for excellence in every sphere.

More than a third of our survey respondents reported dealing with the "Superwoman" stereotype, a term that suggests that the woman can do it all superbly and easily. One survey respondent explains the toll this can take:

> I taught on a Tuesday, gave birth on a Wednesday, friends of mine did library exercises and showed movies for two weeks, and then I went back to work with the baby in a sling. I'd nurse her in the office one hour before class, put her in a sling, and she'd fall asleep as I walked to class. Luckily, she stayed asleep every time as I taught. But it was totally exhausting.

This experience illustrates how mothers feel pushed to be superwomen, to the point of not taking appropriate maternity leave, in order to be successful. One respondent found the term flattering

> in the sense that I appear to have everything together. But I really don't. I just laugh because in my mind, I am barely holding everything in my life together. I only appear polished to those who don't see me very often.

Even when pleasing, such labels do not leave any room for imperfections. A woman related, "I think I worked twice as hard to fight the perception that I wasn't pulling my weight." Indeed, Joan C. Williams and Rachel Dempsey (2014) found that "women, unlike men, are judged based on their achievement rather than their potential" (25).

On the other hand, other women report that they benefit from being mothers, becoming more productive, self-disciplined, and accomplished. A couple mothers, such as this one, say,

> I think it makes scheduling issues complicated. But, I also think I'm a better teacher, administrator, and scholar now that I have children. I am also more productive (overall) than many of my colleagues who don't have children. So, ultimately, I think it positively affects my ability to perform my work.

Similarly:

> I feel productive; I am getting good annual reviews. I don't know if I work harder than others or not to make that happen. [. . .] my husband is great, and we share work pretty equally. I guess I'm saying that I'm working hard on the tenure track and choosing to run around for the kiddos' activities, even lead the Girl Scout troop. And, overall, I like my groove right now.

Some mothers, like the one in the previous example, have spousal, departmental, and/or institutional support—allowing them to enjoy their roles as mothers and academics. Others do not.

In fact, over 95% of those answering "How far do we still need to go [. . .]?" say we must support mothers far more. Participants call for more backing from administration and/or family, as well as for better access to high-quality childcare and aftercare. This echoes Bonawitz and Andel's (2009) findings: "Women faculty report the greatest stress on women faculty comes from lack of support from administration, current economic conditions, biases of tenured colleagues, and family responsibilities" (1). In our study, one scholar exemplifies common family stresses: "I am often sacrificing time during normal hours to do family stuff and making up for it all night. My husband does far less of that, even though my job provides a majority of our income." Because most housework can fall on the woman, securing childcare and taking time off if childcare becomes unavailable/unaffordable often rests on mothers. About 30% of our respondents wrestled with these issues when discussing what kept them from excelling.

While several mothers emphasized, "childcare is so expensive," our participants cite childcare issues as stressful on multiple levels. For example:

> Even though my schedule is flexible, all of our meetings are held when children are out of school (after school hours). Also, our school will not look into childcare facilities, and I had numerous childcare issues (from filing complaints against a childcare center for neglect and abuse) to handling a high-needs (medical problems) child in daycare.

Another mother notes,

> We had trouble finding decent childcare, and now I drive [one] hour and 45 minutes home so that I can pick him up at my in-laws at the end of the work day. I became involved in advocating for childcare on our campus—it will likely happen soon but not in time to be useful for me.

This mother sacrifices over three hours a day commuting for childcare because no other viable solution exists for her.

Participants report struggling to fulfill their professional responsibilities while handling their children's needs. A professor explains,

> My biological son is just 3 months old, and I have an hour-long commute to work each way. We're still figuring out what we'll do with schedule, daycare, etc. I have a 10-year-old stepson, though, and it's been very difficult for us to figure out school drop-off, pickup, etc.

While an academic's flexibility may appear ideal, it is not always the case. When staying home with her feverish infant and toddler several times one semester and supplementing her courses with online instruction, one participant reported being called in to talk with the department chair, and "though my chair said he was very much on my side, he did complain about those absences." As this mother continued:

> I was in a situation with no options. My single male department chair told me that plenty of people in academia do this all the time, and I needed to figure out how to do my job and be a mom. He provided no suggestions how, didn't mention any options for what to do with sick kids who cannot go to daycare, was not finding my having class online sufficient enough, and pointed out no resources in the department or university (because there are none) that could help me.

Supportive partners, family, and close friends, as well as time management skills and the ability to "manage the details of everyday work and family life with great efficiency," often mean the difference between success and "opting out" in higher education (Mason and Ekman 2007, 53). However, as much as a mother learns to navigate and manage these details, not all have the support network that make the successful path possible. Workplace policies and backing are crucial factors in a successful career.

Building Better Attitudes, Policies, and Practices

Most of our participants emphasize the need for a universal shift in attitudes, practices, and policies for academic mothers. For many academic mothers, unfortunately, as Mason and Ekman (2007) argue, success is right now as much about luck and being able to work with "understanding colleagues and institutions" (53) as it is about hard work and talent. One professor exemplifies this, noting that with clear tenure policies, campus models, and a strong women's studies programs as well as supportive administrators, she still struggled to locate stable childcare:

> I went through three daycare facilities, each which I could afford less than the one prior. [. . .] The first two clearly had issues, and both have closed since. One of these [was] a campus daycare. The third was perhaps just going through growing pains, but the outside observer report I received showed I was not being informed about important issues.

This story's author says that much of her success relied as much on luck as it did work, but strong university policies, programs, and attitudes that supported parents were key. Even when the campus childcare failed, other policies and programs provided necessary support. Another scholar similarly praises her ability to succeed thanks to well-formulated policies as good luck:

> I had the good fortune of being on leave during the quarter after my children were born. I also have the good fortune of stopping the tenure clock for two years, one year per child for up to two children. I did not expect to perform my regular duties while caring for an infant, and my colleagues did not expect me to do so either. So even though I did not get any work done in the early months of caring for my children, I was able to bounce back once my children were old enough to go to daycare.

As a third mother explains, clear tenure policies can allow one to invest what is needed in her workplace, and then complete her academic work with even more fervor in later years after the demanding family years pass by:

> I often feel that I am being judged on probably the most unproductive academic years of my life. I am doing the minimum for tenure (and I do think I'll get it), because my kids mean more. As long as I get it, I can do amazing, superstar things later. Right now I only have them full time for a blip in my life, a short 18 or so years.

Colleges and universities should, as the universities in the three previous examples do, retain the cultural capital that academic mothers offer to departments through well-designed, explained, and documented tenure, promotion, and leave policies.

Too many of our survey respondents had the opposite experience of the ones reported earlier, describing a lack of support on multiple levels, unclear expectations from their university, and/or denial of tenure when they had thought they were doing enough. One woman reported, "I was told years later that my absences from evening social events with my department colleagues were noted." Such prejudiced responses to an inability to be available to the academic sphere perpetually, as may be true for the "ideal worker," can have dire consequences. For example, one mother was denied tenure despite a policy-allowed clock stoppage:

> I was taken to task for doing a lot of scholarship at the end of my probationary period (rather than produce it consistently). Consistency of scholarly activity is not a criterion for T&P, and when I was most inactive was in the middle of the probationary period when my first child was born and was in NICU for two months followed by intense at-home care for several months.

This story is reminiscent of the cases described in Joan C. Williams and Jessica Lee's (2015) article, "It's Illegal, But It Happens All the Time." Federal law prohibits against such discrimination and, in fact, requires accommodations be made for temporary disabilities associated with motherhood, but discrimination happens.

In another case, the participant was not worried about job security but regretted the levels of stress being unable to take a leave caused because her institution lacked an official leave policy:

> Due to the arrangement I had with my department, I was back at work two weeks after a C-section (though it was a two- course load). [. . .] It took me much longer to recover from my C-section because of the speed of which I returned to work. The first year, I have never been so exhausted in my life.

Though this academic mother notes that she "would not change anything," despite being able to have a third child after tenure, she observes that, like many working mothers, "I was completely stressed during the first four years of my second child's life; I would give anything to get that time back." Williams (2000) writes that for universities "the time has come to challenge the employer's right to define the ideal worker as someone who is supported by a flow of family work most men enjoy but most women do not" (24). The "Ideal Academic" model—one who can attain professional success because he or she is free from all domestic responsibilities—impedes academic mothers' economic equality and professional success and reinforces sexist barriers in higher education. A survey respondent counters this ideal, arguing that motherhood cultivates what bell hooks calls "engaged pedagogy":

> I feel less of a temptation to act like I am a higher caste than my students; I am more grounded when I go home to food in my hair and cleaning my house and nurturing my young children (the vulnerable).
> (24)

Amy Kittelstrom (2010) argues that we should acknowledge the unique labor of mothering in our vitas and packets—showing how as these demands dissipate, what further potential we have for even more productivity in the long haul.

Academic mothers bring their own cultural capital; thus, college and universities should adopt "family-friendly policies" like "promoting a second job for dual-career couples, discounting resume gaps attributable to parenthood, ending faculty meetings by 5:00 p.m., and carefully mentoring new parents through the tenure process" (Mason and Ekman 2007, 108). Throughout our survey data, respondents similarly advocate for such policy changes in addition to a need for childcare options. One respondent suggests, "The institution needs to recognize that these are family issues and to bifurcate motherhood/parenthood from research and teaching is problematic." In fact, Mason and Ekman (2007) emphasize that family-friendly policies attract the best and brightest faculty and graduate students to institutions and help maintain a competitive edge (108).

Academia also needs stop stigmatizing part-time and non-tenure track positions, as the "second-tier" track is predominantly populated by women with children. Mason and Ekman (2007) explain that "there are increasing numbers of women Ph.D.'s, particularly mothers, who will take the jobs" (85) despite the fact that those "in the second tier almost never compete for a position in the tenure track; their years in the second tier automatically discount their eligibility as scholars qualified for the first tier" (80). One study participant—who taught at a local community college while a graduate student and single mother of two children—challenges this stigma:

> I was rebuked frequently by my academic advisors who warned me that I would never be able to graduate while working full time and, if I graduated, would never be able to secure a tenure track job if I stayed longer than a year or two. [. . .]
>
> I reject such a narrowed definition of the "Ideal Academic" and could not care less whether I am "damaged goods" having taught so long now in the "second tier." I am a valuable asset to my college, and I focus instead on fostering relationships with my colleagues and economically and socially marginalized students while enjoying my freedom to research, present, and publish where I deem most worthy of my time and efforts.

For many academics, part-time or full-time non-tenure track positions present a workable compromise. Such positions enable them to "remain involved in professional life while escaping the stress of balancing upward mobility against the demands of family life" (Mason and Ekman 2007, 70). Hiring, tenure, and promotion policies should account for resume gaps by creating second chances for mothers who took time off or accepted full-time non-tenure track positions. For those who prefer employment in non-tenure track positions, they should be offered "job security, benefits, and pay that better represents their training and contribution" (Mason and Ekman 2007, 114).

As We Go Forward

Far more research is needed. For example, further inquiry can examine what percentage of compositionist mothers are disabled, single or married, living with a mate, LGBTQ, and so forth—exploring how each of these factors uniquely impacts a mother's journey in academia. We could further scrutinize the correlation between career trajectories and primary care roles for parents, regardless of gender. We could also look at the effects of physical-ableness and/or personalities of parents and/or children.

The positive stories in our research praise academia for being flexible and understanding and an ideal job for mothers, showing that there are institutions that respect academic mothers. All the stories—especially the heartbreaking ones where women did not make it in their careers because of a lack of support—show that all universities and colleges should aspire to do the same.

Our study supports research that shows two sorts of university policies need to be enacted universally. First, there is a need to increase awareness and sensitivity to parental and caregiver issues—particularly those faced by academic women, which can be accomplished through required workshops, educational programs, forums, support groups, or online courses. Joan C. Williams and Jessica Lee (2015) are helping design such an online program. These options can provide certificates of completion for dossiers, lines for vitas, and inspire research on these issues. Second, policies need to provide multilayered structural support for mothers. This can include the following:

- Accommodations for necessary leaves of absence for births, bonding, and care for family emergencies encouraging both women and men to have healthy family lives;
- Methods of finding pay for parents who need to be on leave;

- Facilities for pumping and nursing throughout campus;
- Equal pay and promotion policies for women;
- Equivalent pay and benefits policies that would help "second-tier" employees;
- Clearly delineated rules for how and when online elements can be incorporated into face-to-face classes, with programs to help find face-to-face substitutes if necessary;
- Clearly delineated hiring, tenure, and promotion policies;
- High-quality childcare facilities and a network of qualified babysitters organized by the university;
- Childcare provided for major events and meetings (when needed by participants);
- Options for sick child care;
- Generally pro-employee, humane health policies that include considerations for family, disabilities, caregiving, and so forth.

Building respect and understanding of academic motherhood's unique challenges can be inexpensive and relatively simple to implement, and institutions applying such policies on both the awareness and structural support fronts already have productive and happy Rhet/Comp mothers. Our research indicates all institutions should follow their example.

References

Baker, Maureen. (2012). "Gendered Families, Academic Work, and the Motherhood Penalty." *Women's Studies Journal*, 26 (1): 11–24.

Bonawitz, Mary, and Nicole Andel. (2009). "The Glass Ceiling Is Made of Concrete: The Barriers to Promotion and Tenure of Women in American Academia." *Forum on Public Policy: A Journal of the Oxford Round Table*, 5 (2): 1–16.

Crittenden, Ann. (2010). *The Price of Motherhood: Why the Most Important Job in the World Is Still the Least Valued*. New York, NY: Picador.

Cucciarre, Christine Peters, Deborah E. Morris, Lee Nichoson, Kim Hensley Owens, and Mary P. Sheridan. (2011). "Mothers' Ways of Making It—or Making Do? Making Over Academic Lives in Rhetoric and Composition with Children." *Composition Studies*, 39 (1): 41–61.

Hochschild, Arlie R. (1995). "The Culture of Politics: Traditional, Postmodern, Coldmodern, and Warm-Modern Ideals of Care." *Social Politics*, 2 (3): 331–346.

———. (2012). *The Second Shift: Working Families and the Revolution at Home*. New York, NY: Penguin Books.

Kittelstrom, Amy. (February 12, 2010). "The Academic-Motherhood Handicap." *The Chronicle of Higher of Education*. Accessed January 14, 2014. http://chronicle.com/article/The-Academic-Motherhood/64073.

Mason, Mary Ann. (August 3, 2013). "The Baby Penalty." *The Chronicle of Higher Education*. Accessed January 14, 2014. http://chronicle.com/article/The-Baby-Penalty/140813.

Mason, Mary Ann, and Eve Mason Ekman. (2007). *Mothers on the Fast Track: How a New Generation Can Balance Family and Careers*. New York, NY: Oxford University Press.

Mason, Mary Ann, Nicholas H. Wolfinger, and Marc Goulden. (2013). *Do Babies Matter?: Gender and Family in the Ivory Tower*. New Brunswick, NJ: Rutgers University Press.

Pantelides, Kate. (2013). "On Being a New Mother—Dissertator—Writing Center Administrator." *College Composition and Communication*, 65 (1): 28–29.

Swiss, Deborah J., and Judith P. Walker. (1993). *Women and the Work/Family Dilemma: How Today's Professional Women Are Confronting the Maternal Wall*. Hoboken, NJ: Wiley.

Ward, Kelly, and Lisa Wolf-Wendel. (2012). *Academic Motherhood: How Faculty Manage Work and Family*. New Brunswick, NJ: Rutgers University Press.

Williams, Joan C. (2000). *Unbending Gender: Why Family and Work Conflict and What to Do About It*. New York, NY: Oxford University Press.

———. (2003). "Beyond the Glass Ceiling: The Maternal Wall as a Barrier to Gender Equality." *Thomas Jefferson Law Review*. n.p.

Williams, Joan C., and Rachel Dempsey. (2014). *What Works for Women at Work: Four Patterns Working Women Need to Know*. New York, NY: New York University Press.

Williams, Joan C., and Jessica Lee. (September 28, 2015). "It's Illegal, Yet It Happens All the Time: How Pregnant Women and Mothers Get Hounded Out of Higher Education." *Chronicle of Higher Education*. Accessed January 10, 2016. http://chronicle.com/article/Its-Illegal-Yet-It-Happens/233445.

Embodied Gender

14 On the Edge of Knowing

Microaggression and Epistemic Uncertainty as a Woman of Color

Saba Fatima

Did It Really Happen the Way I Saw It?

Something—which was, perhaps, nothing—happened a long time ago. I was a graduate teaching assistant and I had just come out of a meeting with the professor for the class. He went over the final exam with all 12 TAs. Downstairs, in the library, I saw a student from my section preparing for the finals with a friend of hers who was not in my section. The student and I smiled at each other as our eyes met, and I wished her good luck. She said something about freaking out about the exam, and I said to her in an encouraging tone, "I just saw the exam, it's not that bad." At this moment, we were still at a considerable distance from each other. Her friend's eyes lit up and she called over, "Hey! . . . Come here."

I realize that this may be considered a strange incident to recount. I know this, because I can read my words as written. Her friend's statement seems benign on the surface. But in that moment, I felt humiliated.

It was a terse command. I remember my body heating up, possibly with anger or perhaps with embarrassment, I am not certain which. I am medium built, brown, and have visible markers of being an immigrant woman. Perhaps she thought I was a janitor and had inadvertently seen the exam. I have no idea who she mistook me for. Perhaps, she didn't mistake me for anyone. My student hurriedly said, "That's my TA." The friend had a slight change of expression. My slightly embarrassed student then quickly said goodbye to me as I walked away. Since I began working on this project, countless people (all White) have told me that the friend must have mistaken me for another student. This may be possible since at the time I was only one year out of my undergraduate studies. But each time someone offers that explanation, I am reminded of the sense of inarticulation I felt then, of being unable to explain to others (again, mostly Whites) why I felt insulted—all the while, thinking that perhaps I had no reason to feel that way, that perhaps I was being paranoid.

Knowing/Not Knowing

The sorts of experiences I am interested in examining are *not* the ones that can be easily classified as racist—or even those that are clearly *not*. In many cases, I *know* that racism, sexism, or prejudice is at play, for example, when campus police arbitrarily stops and harasses Black faculty or students, or when the dean keeps speaking only to the White male members of your department while barely making eye contact with the sole woman of color.

I am more interested in several different sorts of encounters where women of color (WOC) cannot tell the motivation of the other or where we may experience attributional ambiguity. Attributional ambiguity is when members of groups that experience social stigma find it challenging to determine whether the feedback they receive is based upon their personal deservingness or if it is discrimination against them because of their social identity (Crocker and Major 2003).

I am also interested in experiences where we *know* that racism and sexism were in play, but we either become unsure of that and lose epistemic ground with each passing moment often because no one around us saw it the same way, or because we don't quite know how to quantify in words why it was, indeed, an instance of microaggression. Microaggression is characterized as "brief and commonplace daily verbal, behavioral, and environmental indignities, whether intentional or unintentional, that communicate hostile, derogatory, or negative racial, gender, and sexual orientation, and religious slights and insults to the target person or group" (Sue 2010, 5). I am interested in exploring the social conditions around the epistemic border of thinking of oneself as paranoid and of being secure in one's perception of reality. The sorts of experiences I have in mind are:

- Having criteria that are applied stringently to you ("we are simply following the rules"), while discretionary goodwill is bestowed on your White male counterparts ("this is within the spirit of the rule").
- Being told by your well-meaning, White freshman student how to conduct your classroom, in order to make it more organized, intellectual, or just better, or whatever it is he or she thinks it needs to be.
- Despite having more publications than your White counterpart at the time of being hired or evaluated, still not knowing if you are at the table because you are a "diversity hire."
- The anxiety and unsureness of being a WOC at an academic conference. Often at conferences, WOC experience a heightened sense of anxiety. Being at a conference is not simply about presenting and receiving feedback on one's paper, but also part of the experience is also about talking with people in between sessions, having lunch or dinner with them, and so forth. At such an event, for some of us, our privileges afford us and our scholarship some degree of positive visibility. I am not simply referring to skin color or socioeconomic privilege, though that matters quite a bit, but other things as well, such as our appointment status: being at an R1 institution versus at a small unknown college. And because privilege *does* play a role, it is sometimes very unclear exactly when it is doing its work (Does my work suck, or do other people just carry more privilege around?).

Advice on How to Deal with Paranoia

As a WOC, I am continually aware of the small percentage of non-Whites within my discipline, Philosophy in particular, and how this impacts WOC's ability to speak about their experiences with an expectation of being understood by our White and male counterparts. Sometimes, when undergoing an experience, it is difficult to recognize certain patterns of disrespect motivated by racism, sexism, and xenophobia. The recognition itself can help us in responding more appropriately (emotionally and otherwise). As these sorts of incidents began to pile up through graduate school and my career, I began to notice two competing narratives on how WOCs should process their experiences. Both narratives appealed in varying degrees to my intellect and emotions.

Be Rational

The first set of advice I received appeared quite sensible, mostly because it was an appeal to rationality. White colleagues were often quick to ask me to consider *all* the possibilities of what a particular incident might have meant, gather the evidence, and pick the interpretation that appears most "reasonable." I have been told many times that to assume prejudice in cases of microaggression is irrational. Many suggest that I need to be more open and objective in assessing my experiences.

Of course, one of the ways that one confirms one's own perception of reality and assesses one's own doubtful experiences is through validation by one's peers, and for WOC, those peers are generally very differently socially located, that is, they are mostly White males. For example, the number of women being awarded Ph.D. in the discipline of Philosophy in the United States has stayed at a steady 27% for the past 30 years. And as of 2011, fewer than 125 out of 11,000 members of the American Philosophical Association are Black, with fewer than 30 Black women (Gines 2011). Thus, the appeal to rationality is often an attempt to reframe the incident to fit the worldview of the majority, such that the person making the appeal can remain blind to uncomfortable truths.

Be Strong

If I hadn't met other philosophers of color, or other feminist philosophers, I would have probably left the discipline of Philosophy long time ago. This is because very few of the visible voices reaffirmed how I experienced my reality. It was not only very alienating, but also often it fueled imposter syndrome, that is, I had a difficult time internalizing my own achievements, and often thought of myself as incompetent to do philosophy even in the face of contrary evidence.

When I did happen to meet senior women and people of color in the field (very seldom from the latter category early in my career), and on the slim chance that we talked about anything deeper than the session we had just attended, I almost always received reaffirmation of how I had felt my reality. But more importantly, other WOC emphasized that when I do think that I am being subjected to microaggression, I should never doubt myself. *Being unintelligible to one own self is not epistemologically sustainable long term, and we as WOC need to be able to retain our knowledges in the face of gaslighting.*

Push to the Edge of Knowing

Early in my career, a student athlete in one of my introductory level classes kept loudly referring to me by my first name, despite having corrected him on a couple of occasions ("Hey Saba, wassup?"). He regularly walked in late and slouched in his chair at the back of the class, with his legs spread as wide as possible, and occasionally passed *almost* inaudible comments to those around him during lecture. When I would ask him to refrain from talking during lecture, he would simply smile nonchalantly and say something to the effect of "just chill" or "no need to get upset, I was just saying . . ." followed by a pseudo–class-related comment. He had also once taken the trouble to explain the sport of basketball to me. He did not just simply explain the rules with the "here, *in America*" clause, but he condescendingly elaborated on unnecessary details of the game. As I look back, I am convinced his disrespect toward me was fueled, in part, because he saw me as an immigrant woman slow to understand American culture and one not worthy of respect given to a professor. At the time, though, I could not see his behavior as such because of the dismissive response I received from others. When I told a few other professors, many said, "We all get disgruntled students."

But he wasn't the sort of disrespectful student that one *just* gets. He was disrespectful to who he saw at my core, a brown immigrant woman. It wasn't a misery contest, but it mattered to me that people could not differentiate between the "regular" disgruntled student and the benignly xenophobic and sexist one. And until I related the experience to a few women at work, I *doubted myself* in how I should see his behavior. Serena Easton (2012) writes about such challenges in "On Being Special," whereby authority of WOC is constantly challenged by students in ways that it is not for our White counterparts. Easton writes,

> Only I was forced to pull up statistics, photos, theories, graphs, and charts constantly as evidence that what I was saying was true . . . only I as the sole black member of the cohort had to overprepare every week for discussion sections that often made me feel as if I was being cross-examined on a the witness stand.

(153)

Not only do such experiences of challenges to intellectual authority occur more frequently for WOC (especially earlier in the semester), but they can push WOC to begin to doubt their expertise over their subject matter, instead of seeing the experiences as a function of other people's biases. There may be many reasons why WOC may doubt ourselves, and here I comment on three major ways in which one may be pushed to the edge of knowing.

Emotions and Rationality

Emotions of certain people are not only considered worthless but also, in fact, are *signifiers* of their worthlessness in academia. Alison Jaggar (1989) writes,

> When unconventional emotional responses are experienced by [subordinated] isolated individuals, those concerned may be confused, unable to name their experience; they may even doubt their own sanity. Women may come to believe that are "emotionally disturbed" and that the embarrassment or fear aroused in them by male sexual innuendo is prudery or paranoia.
>
> (160)

When my student pointed out my anger at his behavior, it was not to highlight the egregiousness of his own conduct, rather it was meant to show I was not in control of my emotions, that I was irrational or hyper-sensitive. Marilyn Frye (1983) writes in "A Note on Anger" that instead of focusing on the harm that has been committed, the perpetrator turns it into an assessment of character and sanity of the wronged woman in question, part of which is perhaps about what the perpetrator thinks the wronged is entitled to.

This question of assessment of sanity is not the case when a White, able-bodied, male in academia expresses his "justified" anger. In that situation, it is a testament to what a good person he is that he has the capacity to recognize the opportunity for moral outrage. His anger appears civil and righteous. One of my White male peers who observed another class of mine later expressed incense at an overtly racist student, and it was his outrage that served as proof, as verification, to some of my earlier testimony about that student. Furthermore, my colleague's outrage attested not to his irrationality, but rather to the fact that he was a good ally.

Frye (1983) states, "Anger implies a claim to domain" (87) and "By determining, where, with whom, about what and in what circumstances one can get angry and get uptake, one can map others' concepts of who and what one is" (94). WOC do not have the luxury to express their anger at injustices dealt out to them or to other minorities. We are subject to both micro- and macroaggressions, while simultaneously existing in an atmosphere that demands "civility" in the face of unrelenting racism/ sexism/xenophobia and so forth. This demand for civility is often "used to silence those with less social power on the grounds of both how they present what they say, and the topics which they raise" (Reiheld 2013, 74). WOC have to guard our emotions, such that we do not lose credibility in the eyes of those who hold power over our careers. This regulation of emotions is not merely externally enforced, but minorities often self-regulate as well. Kristie Dotson writes about *testimonial smothering*, a coerced truncation of one's testimony. Testimonial smothering occurs when a speaker recognizes her audience as unwilling or unable to give the appropriate uptake to her testimony and, in response, limits and shapes her testimony in order to "insure that the testimony contains only content for which one's audience demonstrates testimonial competence" (Dotson 2011, 244).

One aspect of testimonial smothering is being aware that many of our White colleagues are too keen to police the tone of our speech and to reinforce their bias of our irrational nature, while being blind to the harm that elicits those emotions in the first place in WOC. This is especially true when the harm is difficult to quantify, as in the case of microaggression. Jeanine

Schroer (2015) writes about the shift toward quantifying, what she calls, "the 'feely' aspects of living in raced (and other stigmatized) bodies" (91). This particular move highlights how raced bodies are heard and believed. She compares the reception of stereotype research and micro-aggression research. Because stereotype research can be quantified by "objective" scientific studies, it has now been deemed credible. On the other hand, uptake of research on microaggression relies on how credible target audience finds the testimony of people of color. That is to say, for WOC, our emotions are not credible indicators of actual harm without independent verification. Here, I claim that if the only way that a woman of color's testimony is given any uptake is if dominant members of academia verify it, then we have *already discounted the epistemic credibility* of the speaker, regardless of how much of an ally one thinks of themselves to be.

One of the concerns that Schroer highlights is how "objective" verification of harm discounts the humanity of minorities. She writes,

> The focus on quantifying the harm, ignores the significance of expressing the hurt. . . . It testifies to the central import of interpreting and experiencing one's life, including the pain, through sharing it with others, not to *prove* your injury, but instead to demonstrate your humanity.
>
> (104–105, emphasis mine)

Schroer's point about expressing pain as a testament of our humanity really struck me at the core of partly why we relate our experience of microaggression to other WOC. When we hear about the experiences of other WOC, we empathize because we can relate to each other's challenges. But there are many dominant members who have not had similar encounters. And so any emotions that our specific WOC bodies exhibit is seen not as a testament of our humanity but as primal and animalistic, devoid of reason that is specific to humans.

Heterogeneity of the Nature of Discrimination

I have often wondered where I belong in the academic circles. Who are my own people? Who can I vent to with an expectation that not only will they validate my experience but also feel my pain as their own, because they see me as their own? And a more painful thought is: what are some of the barriers that *do not allow me* to see the humanity in others?

When I related the incident to other WOC about my student's friend who had called me over in the library, I had an almost instant recognition of a pattern of disrespect on their part that is unique to WOC. In the case of the student athlete, Americans (WOC or not) had a harder time seeing my reality than international faculty. "Here, in America" is almost always a code for asserting immigrants' status as perpetual outsiders who can never understand American culture. As WOC, our experiences are far from homogenous. African Americans, Latinas, Native Americans, Asian Americans, international faculty from Africa, South America, and Asia—we all have experiences unique to our social location, and certain sorts of experiences are more easily recognizable to those closer to our social locations.

Research shows that the nature of discrimination and macroaggression varies across different racial and ethnic groups experiences (cf. Solorzano and Yosso 2000; Szalacha et al. 2003; Araújo and Borrell 2006). According to one study, "Latino/ Hispanics and Black groups reported high levels of *Assumptions of Inferiority* microaggressions. . . . The opposite, however, [was] true for Asians." On the other hand, "Asian and Latino/Hispanic participants endorsed higher rates of experiences of *Exoticization and Assumptions of Similarity* than Blacks" (Forrest-Bank and Jenson 2015, 156–157). The authors note, "Important differences in microaggression experiences among racial and ethnic groups found in the current study suggest that interventions need to be adapted to meet the needs of young people from different backgrounds" (158).

While my immigrant body may be disrespected, it happens in ways that is very different from the discrimination attached to Black bodies. It is dangerous for me to assume that simply because I am a WOC and that I am at some axis of discrimination myself, that I can now cast judgment on WOC's experiences situated *differently* from myself. Certainly, differently situated WOC are more likely to understand each other's experiences, but if we are not careful, we can dismiss WOC testimony with far more authority and in much more damaging ways than our White counterparts. Audre Lorde (1984) writes,

> Anger is loaded with information and energy. . . . The woman of Color who is not Black and who charges me with rendering her invisible by assuming that her struggles with racism are identical with my own has something to tell me that I had better learn from, lest we both waste ourselves fighting the truths between us. . . . And yes, it is very difficult to stand still and to listen to another woman's voice delineate an agony I do not share, or one to which I myself have contributed.
>
> (127–128)

High Frequency of Microaggression

While it was the only time that a student had explained basketball to me, it was definitely not the first time a student or colleague had explained rudimentary things about American culture without being asked to do so. In fact, it has happened so many times, that I have now stopped expressing my negative views about American football, gun culture, or the "infallible" founding fathers, lest someone engages in ways to remind me of my outsider status. In fact, it is precisely because it has happened so many times that I can recognize it from a mile away. Each incident on its own, though, is difficult to explain to others differently situated.

Because of their "micro" nature, some have characterized microaggression as a case of minorities yet again being too sensitive to even the slightest of slights. This characterization furthers the feeling of paranoia, since we begin to question ourselves about becoming overly sensitive, especially if no one else recognizes the slights as insults.

Regina Rini (2015) wrote an insightful response to a widely circulated article on microaggression by Campbell and Manning (2014), in which Rini highlights how the recognition of microaggression is symbolic of the times we live in, where minority voices can be heard. So it is not that minorities have become too sensitive or steeped in victimhood as Campell and Manning claim—but rather we are able to connect and hear other similar minority narratives. We feel *safer* to crowdsource our experiences and express solidarity with each other.

But as Rini and others note, in acts of microaggression, the damage of the singular act is very hard to explain. On its own, it often may not appear harmful. However, it fits into and perpetuates a larger framework of systemic racism. So, it is not any single act, but rather a lifelong accumulation of indignant experiences that begin to shape the marginalized experience.

One of the common responses to hearing someone tell of an incidence of microaggression is an attempt to offer either alternate explanations of what the listener thinks *actually* happened or an alternate account of the *well-meaning motivations* of the perpetrators. They may offer explanation such as 'I don't think he meant it like that,' or 'It is very possible that she was actually trying to help you.' They may also suggest other benign possibilities such as 'well, I know it is not common that they do this, but they are simply following the letter of the law,' etc.

If the person from the marginalized social location is unsure about how to process the said microaggression, the listener's explanation compounds his or her doubt. For most part, these alternate explanations are rooted in the listener's own biases. Even when the listener knows and understands how implicit bias works and knows about the prevalence of bias, *he or she has a difficult time "seeing" the patterns of systemic institutional racism in individual cases of discrimination.* In each individual case, the listener attempts to conjure up convoluted "explanations" of individual life choices of the perpetrator and the minority person concerned. The listener is able to rationalize generally because of the following:

1. It makes the listener feel that the system is essentially fair on this particular matter, because if it isn't, it may imply that the listener had an unfair and unearned advantage. That is to say, the listener may be a beneficiary of the very system that is keeping the other person down; thus, it is in the listener's interest to remain in willful ignorance and epistemically blind to the other person's oppression (Pohlhaus 2012; Medina 2013).
2. The listener may honestly believe that the person relaying his or her experience of microaggression has epistemically flawed beliefs. Privileged individuals have the affirmation of everyone around them. They are certain that they see the truth and that the other person has, indeed, become too sensitive and sees racism at play where it does not exist.

Some Final Thoughts

It is not only difficult to explore and explain any one particular incident of microaggression but also almost near impossible. Reconsider the following examples:

•   The student who most probably didn't mean anything but whose behavior fell in line with the countless other students who dismiss intellectual authority of WOC academics.
•   The tenure committee members who believe themselves to be fairly applying the rules to *everyone* but their discretionary goodwill surfaces only for other White "hardworking folks."
•   The people who advocate diversity in *solely* in abstract terms but let their bias arbitrarily find flaws in individual cases of qualified candidates all in the name of meritocracy or where they compare solely the weakest element of a WOC application to the strongest elements in a White candidate.
•   The average disrespectful student who feels slightly more permissive and emboldened when the course is taught by a WOC.

Each of these incidents when examined on its own is hard to explain to those who occupy privileged social locations. The precise nature of microaggression purposely obscures the exploration of the intentionality of perpetuator and the quantification of the harm committed. The act fits neatly into a system that privileges some and validates their reality to themselves and to the rest of us. Thus, reasonable and well-meaning people often cannot see any individual case as symptomatic of the larger pattern of discrimination unless the discrimination is overt and blatant. They evaluate each particular incident of microaggression on its own "merit," disconnected from how implicit bias functions *within their self* and disassociated from the larger patterns of discrimination.

   While incidents of microaggression are hard to articulate to others, we cannot exempt ourselves from the possibility of fallibility when individual cases arise. In light of what has been discussed here, it would be helpful to keep the following in mind:

1. **Understand Experiences as Complex:** It is conscientious on our part to recognize that although we may think that we know what prejudice looks like, the way implicit bias works and how discrimination functions, we may still not be able to understand the experiences of those situated differently from across various axis of oppression.
2. **Don't Offer Alternate Explanations:** When a minority confides in you about a microaggression, especially when it involves a power hierarchy between the minority and the perpetrator, resist your first instinct to cast doubt on their testimony and to deny their sense

of perception. Don't offer an explanation of what you think happened. In that moment, recognize that there might be bias at work within you, and try to stay uncomfortable in that thought.

3. **Think Big:** It is always better to look at the larger structures of racism, sexism, homophobia, ableism, xenophobia, and so forth than to figure out the intent of the perpetrator. Try and understand microaggression within a sociohistorical context that connects to cumulative chains of interactions and to larger patterns of discrimination.

References

Araújo, Beverley Y., and Luisa N. Borrell. (2006). "Understanding the Link Between Discrimination, Mental Health Outcomes, and Life Chances Among Latinos." *Hispanic Journal of Behavioral Sciences*, 28 (2): 245–266.

Campbell, Bradley, and Jason Manning. (2014). "Microaggression and Moral Culture." *Comparative Sociology*, 13 (6): 692–726.

Crocker, Jennifer, and Brenda Major. (2003). "The Self-Protective Properties of Stigma: Evolution of a Modern Classic." *Psychological Inquiry*, 14 (3&4): 232–237.

Dotson, Kristie. (2011). "Tracking Epistemic Violence, Tracking Practices of Silencing." *Hypatia*, 26 (2): 236–257.

Easton, Serena. (2012). "On Being Special." In *Presumed Incompetent: The Intersections of Race and Class for Women in Academia*, edited by Gabrielle Gutiérrez y Muhs, Yolanda Flores Niemann, Carmen G. González, and Angela P. Harris, 152–163. Logan: Utah State University Press.

Forrest-Bank, S., and J. M. Jenson. (2015). "Differences in Experiences of Racial and Ethnic Microaggression Among Asian, Latino/Hispanic, Black, and White Young Adults." *Journal of Sociology & Social Welfare*, 42 (1): 141–161.

Frye, Marilyn. (1983). "A Note on Anger." In *The Politics of Reality: Essays in Feminist Theory*, 84–94. New York: Crossing Press.

Gines, Kathryn T. (2011). "Being a Black Woman Philosopher: Reflections on Founding the Collegium of Black Women Philosophers." *Hypatia*, 26 (2): 429–443.

Jaggar, Alison M. (1989). "Love and Knowledge: Emotion in Feminist Epistemology." *Inquiry*, 32 (2): 151–176.

Lorde, Audre. (1984). "The Uses of Anger: Women Responding to Racism." In *Sister Outsider*. Reprint 2007, 124–133. New York: Crossing Press.

Medina, José. (2013). *The Epistemology of Resistance: Gender and Racial Oppression, Epistemic Injustice, and Resistant Imaginations*. New York: Oxford University Press.

Pohlhaus, Gaile. (2012). "Relational Knowing and Epistemic Injustice: Toward a Theory of Willful Hermeneutical Ignorance." *Hypatia*, 27 (4):715–735.

Reiheld, Alison. (2013). "Asking Too Much? Civility vs. Pluralism." *Philosophical Topics*, 41 (2): 59–78.

Rini, Regina. (September 28, 2015). "Microaggression and the Culture of Solidarity." *The Splintered Mind: Reflections in Philosophy of Psychology, Broadly Construed*. http://schwitzsplinters.blogspot.com/2015/09/microaggression-and-culture-of.html.

Schroer, Jeanine W. (2015). "Giving Them Something They Can Feel: On the Strategy of Scientizing the Phenomenology of Race and Racism." *Knowledge Cultures*, 3 (1): 91–110.

Solorzano, D., M. Ceja, and T. Yosso. (2000). "Critical Race Theory, Racial Microaggressions, and Campus Racial Climate: The Experiences of African-American College Students." *Journal of Negro Education*, 69 (1/2): 60–74.

Sue, D. W. (2010). *Microaggressions in Everyday Life: Race, Gender, and Sexual Orientation*. Hoboken, NJ: Wiley.

Szalacha, L. A., S. Erkut, C. C. Garcia, O. Alarcon, J. P. Fields, and I. Ceder. (2003). "Discrimination and Puerto Rican Children's and Adolescents' Mental Health." *Cultural Diversity and Ethnic Minority Psychology*, 9, 141–155.

15 "I Have Always Felt Like a Trespasser"

Life Histories from Latina Staff Members in Higher Education

Mary Louise Gomez

Holland et al. (1998) argue that selves always are forming and re-forming. They are negotiated achievements between past and present moments. Identities, then, are personal accomplishments formed within what they term "historically contingent, socially enacted, culturally constructed worlds" (7). Holland et al. contend that identities are fashioned via interactions among persons. Allied with the sociohistorical school of psychology (as developed by Bakhtin, Leontiev, Voloshinov, Vygotsky), Holland et al. (1998) explain that a self acts in " socially and culturally constructed realm[s] of interpretation in which particular characters and actors are recognized, significance is assigned to certain acts, and particular outcomes are valued over others" (54). Identity generally means the traits of a person or how that person defines, recognizes, and distinguishes herself from others. Holland et al. argue that identities are "imaginings of self in worlds of action." They are lived "in and through activity and so must be conceptualized as they develop in social practice" (5). These imaginary worlds mediate persons' behavior, form and re-form over time, and inform how we and others view the contexts in which we live and what we know and believe we can do. As Holland and colleagues explain:

> The dialect we speak, the degree of formality we adopt in our speech, the places we go, the emotions we express, and the clothes we wear are treated as claims to and identification with social categories and positions of privilege relative to those with whom we are interacting.
>
> (127)

In other words, persons position themselves according to hierarchies we perceive others have created. Bakhtin (1981) explains that the spatial and temporal contexts in which we are situated are keys to what persons know, do, and understand. We often invoke authoritative discourses with which we have been imbued over time and across occasions from institutions and groups with which we have been affiliated. Authoritative discourses represent external authorities such as religious institutions, politics, schools attended, and the values of the communities in which persons were raised. Another kind of discourse is that which is internally persuasive, what we might think about as words and ideas that are persuasive to us as individuals and appropriated as we change over our lifetimes.

This chapter explores the academic life histories and identity development of two Latina higher education staff members, Sofia Arenas and Isabella Torres-Bello (all names of persons, institutions, and geographic places are pseudonyms). Both are administrators in different schools in a predominantly White Midwestern university campus. Sofia is a doctoral student and has worked in various units, but now is Assistant Director of First Scholars, a program enrolling students of color at State University and is an academic advisor for the students enrolled. Nearly 40 years old, Sofia has worked at State for 16 years. Isabella is an assistant dean in one school of the university and also is a lecturer in three departments on campus. She holds bachelor's, master's, and doctoral degrees. Now in her mid-50s, she has worked at State University for 20 years. Seeking to understand what their work experiences are, and how these affect their identity development, I ask the following research questions:

- How do two Latina staff members articulate their identities on a predominantly White Midwestern university campus?
- How do race, ethnicity, and social class figure in shaping who they are and what they and Whites with whom they work think they know and can do?

Literature Review

Higher education campuses across the United States and around the world are attempting to diversify their faculty and staff to better reflect the racial, ethnic, and language backgrounds of their students (Gay, Dingus, and Jackson 2003; Ladson-Billings 2005). Despite such efforts, people of color often remain underrated in terms of their contributions and underestimated with regard for their knowledge and skills.

Challenges that staff members of color face in higher education, particularly on predominantly White campuses, include five key components, two of which are feelings of being an "Other" or different from mainstream Whites while positioned as tokens of their race or ethnic background (e.g., Jackson and Flowers 2003; King and Watts 2004; Sue 2010; Wolfe 2010) and being viewed as so-called "experts" on all campus matters pertaining to diversity (Stanley 2006). Further, staff of color frequently report stress and frustration provoked by constantly negotiating a campus ethos contrastive with their familiar family values and traditions (Johnsrud and Sadao 1998; Sadao 2003; Segura 2013). Additionally, staff of color state they often feel exhausted from continually needing to prove their knowledge, skills, and abilities while scrutinized by their supervisors, colleagues, and students (Gutiérrez y Muhs et al. 2012). Finally, staff of color report feeling isolated from a lack of mentorship and limited rapport and connections with colleagues (e.g., Aleman 1995; Canul 2003; Viernes Turner, Gonzalez, and Wood 2008). These intersecting dimensions of their professional lives provide additional pressure and strain for staff of color from that of White peers.

This text adds to scholarship concerning staff of color in higher education via stories told by two Latinas. They both are longtime employees at State University who exemplify challenges faced by staff members interviewed for this research.

Context

Cole and Knowles (2001) underscore the important link between an individual's life and contexts in which it is lived. They argue that life history research "is about understanding the relationship, the complex interaction, between life and context, self, and place" (11). Given this connection between where we live and work and how we think about ourselves, it seems salient to describe State University, Lake City and Lake County, the community and county in which the institution is located.

Lake City, a community of 250,000 persons, reflects the nation with a growing population of people of color. In the city and county in which it is located, rates of poverty, unemployment, and admissions to the prison system are high for African Americans and contrast with lower rates for Whites (Dean *Lake City Times* 4/2/14). There also are low high school graduation rates for persons of color in comparison with Whites and school behavioral referrals and achievement rates reflecting the disparities between African American, Latino, and White students (Lake City Schools 2012; Dean 2014).

State University enrolls a predominantly White and economically well-off student body. The university enrolls 77% White undergraduates (State University Data Digest 2015) with out-of-state students' family incomes averaging $100,000 or more, and in-state students' family incomes averaging $80,000 (State University Data Digest 2012). Classified staff members (who hold non-teaching positions in the university) compose 5,270 persons; more than 85% are White (State University Data Digest 2015).

There have been several incidents on campus in the last few years generating concerns about racism. For example, a conservative group critical of what they called "racial preferences" for university hiring and admissions held a press conference in 2011, naming State as discriminatory in favoring persons of color. At a campus party, an effigy of a Black superhero was viewed hanging from an apartment balcony, suggesting executions of African Americans in the past. On another occasion, White students allegedly shouted racial slurs and threw drinking glasses at two African American females walking near their fraternity house. Such events as these have created tensions for staff members of color on campus. While the Black Out; Blind Side; Young, Gifted, and Black; and Black Lives Matter movements have worked to create a safe environment for all persons, the campus continues to experience racially motivated events. Given the county, city, and university contexts, it seemed important to investigate the work environment for staff of color at the university.

Methodology

Data Generation and Collection

Working with two graduate assistants, I drew on life history methodology to generate and collect data from interviews with staff of color (ten women and five men). Following permission from the State University Institutional Review Board to interview, "snowball" sampling primarily was used to locate staff of color for data collection (Flint and Atkinson 2004). Interviews were conducted between 2012–2014. Participants worked in a variety of units from student affairs to health services and career advising. Many had worked at State for between 10 and 25 years and expressed how challenging it was to labor in a predominantly White environment.

In this study, I focus on the academic dimensions of staff members' lives, examining how their prior life experiences, particularly schooling and employment experiences, affect their identity development and work at State University. Recognizing that it is not possible to recount all of a person's life, particularly in a few multihour interviews (Viernes Turner 2008), my goal is to describe salient events that led two participants to their past and current understandings of who they are and what they can do.

Data Analysis

I employed both inductive and deductive methods of analysis (Graue and Walsh 1998). I read the interviews multiple times, combing the data for patterns within and across interviews. Inductive themes that surfaced from the participant interviews include participants' dissatisfaction with their work lives, beliefs by staff of color that they are positioned as primarily responsible for enacting campus "diversity initiatives," and that supervisors in their units, as well as students with whom they work, often doubt their knowledge and skills.

Analyses also were deductive as I read the patterns of data in relation to a research literature describing and analyzing the experiences of staff of color in predominantly White institutions of higher education (e.g., Gutiérrez y Muhs et al. 2012; Jackson and Flowers 2003; Stanley 2006). Next, I read the data with regard for my personal experiences as a woman of color in the United States. I was socialized into a working-class family in the Northeastern United States with a

Latino father whose first language was Spanish, and a White, English-speaking, monolingual mother. While both of my parents graduated from high school, my father hid his talents under a "class clown" demeanor and graduated from high school after five years (in a four-year program) of study. Following my paternal grandfather's early death, my father and his siblings worked in low-paying factory or service sector jobs to support their mother, who spoke little English. I know from my father's stories how challenging it is to grow up in poverty and speak a language other than English. His stories sensitized me to ones I heard from staff members of color at State, particularly those featuring ethnicity and social class as impediments to their feeling secure and respected in their professional lives.

Participants

Sofia Arenas

Sofia Arenas self-identifies as Mexican American, and is the sixth generation of her family to live and work in the United States. She and her family experienced discrimination in the small west Texas community where they lived. Despite this, Sofia was placed in a class for gifted and talented children in third grade, the only child of Mexican heritage in the class for several years. She said, "All the way through high school I was the only one (Mexican) in all of those honors classes." She explains, "There was always racial tension in town—always, you know; I understood that."

Sofia earned two bachelor's degrees at a Texas university where she often was the only person of color in classes of 50 or 60 persons. She said,

> There were a lot of rancher families, all of them were White. . . . I didn't have any culture shock. It was no big deal. It was the same thing I had been dealing with since I was 6. I never had any trouble with anyone. I knew what to expect [from Whites].

Sofia shared a story from undergraduate school that illustrates challenges facing persons of color in the contexts in which she grew up. She recounted that a visiting faculty member from Barbados had earned her doctorate from State University and had been teaching at Sofia's university for a year. Sofia said this may have been the first Black teacher whom many of her White peers ever had encountered. Becoming angry when receiving lower grades than they expected, students complained and won overturns of their original grades by an assistant dean. Sofia was infuriated when she understood what had occurred.

Making an appointment with the dean, she was greeted rudely. Slouching in his chair, he said, "So, what did *you* (her emphasis) need to talk about?" He proceeded to berate the visiting faculty member as a professor. He told me, "So and so's dad is a district judge (one of the students who complained)" and he needed to keep him happy.

Sofia then phoned her mother to complain about this encounter. Her mother insisted that she meet with Sofia and the dean. She did not want Sofia to retreat but wanted her to learn how to respond to authorities when they have erred. Sofia recalled saying,

> What bothers me about this is how you are undermining a professor of color, someone you invited here. I received As in those classes. . . . I hope in the future, you don't handle things in this manner. It's really disrespectful to the professor.

She recalls her father's reminders that "once you have your degree, 'they' [implicating Whites] cannot take it away from you. You get your education, and then what are they going to say?" He saw it [education] as an effective tool to combat the racism we experienced.

At State, Sofia said,

> People know you are Mexican here—your skin color and hair. You need to know that people think they know who you are and how you can perform. What happened at my university in Texas is not unlike what happens here. People are just quieter about what they have done [here].

She said,

> One thing people should know is that this state is a really rural one. Students are very ignorant to issues related to the world in general, particularly people of color, and that is not necessarily from a lack of interest but derives from ignorance. . . . In general, the university does not have enough tools at its disposal to help [students] do this self-reflection that they have to do. . . . They [students] have a sense of entitlement, that sense of not really understanding cultures, and people not taking a step back and reflecting.

Sofia said that Whites cannot hear this need for reflection only from faculty, staff, and students of color; rather they require hearing it also from their White counterparts. Sofia sees White students as reflecting the authoritative discourses of their families, schools, and communities regarding people of color and receiving little support from White administrators or faculty on campus to alter their thinking and talk.

Sofia also notes that she has an obligation to help other persons of color on the State campus, "The people who have been my mentors have always said, you need to turn around and pick up the people behind you who look like you [racially or ethnically]." She said, "I kind of see helping others' as a sense of duty." Sofia believes that persons of color need to give up what she calls an "individualistic perspective," arguing that academic culture celebrates "publishing or perishing" and "climbing on top of everybody else because you want to do whatever." She keenly feels that she neither got to State on her own nor achieved any success in her work life by herself, but credits her family and mentors for support and inspiration.

Isabella Torres-Bello

Born in San Juan, Puerto Rico, Isabella moved to New York City as a toddler. With a Puerto Rican father and an Irish mother, Isabella was raised Roman Catholic. Early in her life, she recognized the inequities present in the church, where priests often lived very well contrastive with nuns who worked in relative obscurity and poverty. Thus began a life grounded in "questioning authority," especially questioning institutions, whether these represent the church or the university.

Isabelle's family moved to Long Island when she was a middle school student. There, she became aware of social class privileges braided to economic privileges she previously had not encountered. Isabella did well in her middle school courses but acquired an uneven high school record. She says she was tracked for the "secretarial pool" saying,

> I had flunked typing and shorthand, so getting a job was kind of hard for me. I got a job in a stock market office and there was a very educated man there who talked to me about important writers and encouraged me to go to school. So, I did, at night.

She completed her degree in the daytime program. Then, her parents sent her to Puerto Rico to a women's Catholic college, where she worked for political and social change, particularly for women. Later, she earned a master's degree from a Puerto Rican university and a doctorate from another Midwestern university.

Isabella says that despite her academic and professional success, she

> always feels like a trespasser. I always feel like I'm trespassing when I am around wealth and privilege. There's so much racism, that includes my own family from many different Latin American locations. Racism is not just specific to the United States.

She refers to the intersecting dimensions of race, ethnicity, and social class, arguing this is not solely an American phenomenon.

She also says,

> One thing I have recognized here at State U. is that if you question the status quo, you get branded as a troublemaker. When I came here, I wanted to open up the gates here in terms of multicultural affairs and I hit a brick wall. We have student groups fighting over crumbs for funding, and there were only a few rooms in an old building for a multicultural center.

Isabella Found that Her Stance on Questioning Authority Was Unappreciated on Campus

Naming a (now retired) powerful White administrator on campus, she said, "She basically hated me; she made that very clear. . . . She complained that I was belligerent because I questioned her." Isabella uses this administrator as an example of her treatment by Whites in authority at State University. When questioned, they found fault with you, rather than with the questions being asked, particularly if these were related to social justice and equity.

Isabella also recognizes that there is a "colonial" system in academia that is hard to penetrate as "academic materials become properties for building people' reputations . . . it is people building academic empires of their own." Because she fails to support such a system and questions its existence, she also is suspect. She said, "Early on in academia, you are taught not to rock the boat but to fit in." This she has failed to do and has paid a price for her questioning of the status quo. Like Sofia, she has fought perceived injustice and consistently has been rebuffed, especially by senior White university administrators. These experiences have left her frustrated and irritated but not defeated. She sees herself as always fighting battles, particularly with senior White administrators who see themselves as more knowledgeable than any staff member of color.

Discussion and Conclusion

Sofia and Isabella are enmeshed in webs of assumptions about who they are and what they know and can do. Their gender, social class, and ethnicity is assumed as fitting them for certain kinds of labor on behalf of particular people. Haslanger (2012) asks us to critique these discursive and conceptual frameworks, laying them open for examination and potential alteration.

If we do as Haslanger suggests in critiquing discursive and conceptual systems, I envision five approaches to enhancing the professional and personal lives of women of color at State University and other predominantly White campuses.

- First, increase connections to communities of color, particularly women, on and off campus, and strengthen ties within and across groups. Frequently, people of color work in "diversity silos" and have few people with whom they can problem solve.
- Building coalitions of institutional and national-level groups for female staff of color can reduce feelings of isolation, strengthen personal and professional support for one another, and increase individuals' political knowledge.

- Developing mentoring programs can better prepare female staff for their future employment, preparing them to deflect racism and build alliances with others (Viernes Turner, Gonzalez, and Wood 2008). Campuses also can increase attention to pay equity, rewarding staff for their knowledge, skills, and assets (Renzulli, Grant, and Kathuria 2006). Fostering intergroup dialogues across campus around race, ethnicity, social class, and sexism and developing programs focused on diversity can further assist staff of color (Pope and LePeau 2012). Then, they are not alone in speaking on issues of equity and social justice.

All of these are only partial remedies. Substantial changes will not come about as long as most persons on campus are White and have no incentives to alter their behavior. Until that time when there are more staff of color populating higher education, and a more diverse student population, dilemmas like the ones narrated by Sofia and Isabella will prevail.

References

Aleman, Ana M. Martinez. (1995). "Actuando." In *The Leaning Ivory Tower: Latino Professors in American Universities*, edited by Raymond Padilla and Rudolfo Chavez, 67–76. Albany: State University of New York.

Bakhtin, Mikhail M. (1981). *The Dialogic Imagination: Four Essays*. Translated by Caryl Emerson and Michael Holquist. Austin, TX: University of Texas Press.

Canul, Kathleen. (2003). "Latina/o Cultural Values and the Academy: Latinas Navigating Through the Administrative Role." In *The Minority in the Minority: Expanding the Representation of Latina/o Faculty, Administrators, and Students in Higher Education* edited by Jeanett Castellanos and Lee Jones, 167–175. Sterling, VA: Stylus.

Cole, Ardra, and J. Gary Knowles, ed. (2001). *Lives in Context: The Art of Life History Research*. Walnut Creek: AltaMira.

Dean, K. (April 2, 2014). *Q&A: Erica Nelson Is Personally Motivated to Shrink Racial Disparities in Dane County*. Lake City: Lake City Times.

Flint, John, and John Atkinson. (2004). "Snowball Sampling." In the *Sage Encyclopedia of Social Science Research Methods*, edited by Michael Lewis-Beck, Alan Bryman, and Tim Liao, 1044–10445. Thousand Oaks, CA: Sage Publications.

Gay, Geneva, Jeanine E. Dingus, and Carolyn W. Jackson. (2003). *The Presence and Performance of Teachers of Color in the Profession*. Landover, MD: Community Teachers Institute. Accessed August 18, 2011. www.communityleaders.org/reports.

Graue, Mary Elizabeth, and Daniel J. Walsh. (1998). *Studying Children in Context: Theories, Methods, and Ethics*. Thousand Oaks, CA: Sage Publications.

Gutiérrez y Muhs, Gabriella, Yolanda Flores Niemann, Carmen G. Gonzalez, and Angela P. Harris. (2012). *Presumed Incompetent: The Intersections of Race and Class for Women in Academia*. Logan, UT: Utah State University.

Haslanger, Sally. (2012). *Resisting Reality: Social Construction and Social Critique*. New York: Oxford University.

Holland, Dorothy, William Lachicotte, Jr., Debra Skinner, and Carole Cain. (1998). *Identity and Agency in Cultural Worlds*. Cambridge, MA: Harvard University Press.

Jackson, Jerlando, and Lamont A. Flowers. (2003). "Retaining African American Student Affairs Administrators: Voices from the Field." *College Student Affairs Journal*, 22 (2): 125–136.

Johnsrud, Linda K., and Kathleen C. Sadao. (1998). "The Common Experience of 'Otherness': Ethnic and Racial Minority Faculty." *Review of Higher Education*, 21: 315–342.

King, Kimberley, and Ivan E. Watts. (2004). "Assertiveness or the Drive to Succeed?: Surviving at a Predominantly White University." In *A Long Way to Go: Conversations About Race by African American Faculty and Graduate Students*, edited by Darrell Cleveland, 110–119. New York: Peter Lang.

Ladson-Billings, Gloria. (2005). "Is the Team All Right? Diversity and Teacher Education." *Journal of Teacher Education*, 56 (2): 229–234.

Lake City Schools. (2011–2012). *Lake City Schools Data*. Lake City: Data Bank.

Pope, Raechele L., and Lucy L. Le Peau. (2012). "The Influence of Institutional Context and Culture." In *Why Aren't We There Yet? Taking Personal Responsibility for Creating an Inclusive Campus*, edited by Jan Arminio, Vasti Torres, and Raechele L. Pope, 103–130. Sterling, VA: Stylus.

Renzulli, Linda A., Linda Grant, and Sheejita Kathuria. (2006). "Race, Gender, & the Wage Gap: Comparing Faculty Salaries in Predominantly White and Historically Black Colleges and Universities." *Gender and Society*, 20: 491–510.

Sadao, K. C. (2003). "Living in Two Worlds: Success and Bicultural Faculty of Color." *Review of Higher Education*, 26 (4): 397–418.

Segura, Denise A. (2013). "Navigating Between Two Worlds: The Labyrinth of Chicana Intellectual Production in the Academy." *Journal of Black Studies*, 34: 28–51.

Stanley, Christine A. (2006). "Coloring the Academic Landscape: Faculty of Color Breaking the Silence in Predominantly White Colleges and Universities." *American Educational Research Journal*, 4 (4): 701–736.

State University Data Digest (2014–2015, 2011–2012). Lake City: State University.

Sue, Derrick Wing. (2010). *Microaggressions in Everyday Life*. Hoboken, NJ: John Wiley & Sons, Inc.

Viernes Turner, Caroline S. (2008). "Pathways to the Presidency: Biographical Sketches of Women of Color Firsts." *Harvard Educational Review*, 77 (1): 1–38.

Viernes Turner, Caroline S., Juan C. Gonzalez, and J. Luke Wood. (2008). "Faculty of Color in Academe: What 20 Years of Literature Tells Us." *Journal of Diversity in Higher Education*, 1 (3): 139–168.

Wolfe, Barbara L. (2010). *When Being Black Isn't Enough: Experiences and Persistence Strategies of Six African American Administrators at a PWI*. Austin, TX: University of Texas-Austin.

16 Mother-Scholars

Thinking and Being in Higher Education

Yvette Lapayese

The invisibility of mother-scholars and their ways of knowing reflects a much larger academic trend (Lapayese 2012). Literature reveals that even though more women pursue academic careers, becoming a mother in academia negatively impacts women's professional advancement. Mason and Goulden's (2002) study, examining the effect of early pregnancy on women's academic careers, shows that women with early babies are less likely to achieve tenure than women with late babies or no children Further, female academics have the highest rate of childlessness, at 43% (Hewlett 2006). The American Association of University Professors (2011) confirmed in their statement on Family Responsibility and Academic Work:

> Although increasing numbers of women have entered academia, their academic status has been slow to improve: women remain disproportionately represented within instructor, lecturer, unranked positions; more than 57 percent of those holding such positions are women while among full professors only 26 percent are women; likewise among full-time faculty women, only 48 percent are tenured whereas 68 percent of men are.

Equally alarming is the scarcity of research on academic mothers. Not only do mothers and academia have a negative relationship, but also there is a limited amount of information on what the relationship implies for those of us in it. How do we survive? How can maternal identity be a source of empowerment in intellectual spaces? This chapter hopes to ignite, expand, and deepen the conversation on the relationship between maternal identity and academic identity. Through mother-scholar narratives, I hope to theorize the synergy between the intellect and the maternal and evidence how maternal thinking and doing transforms higher education.

Maternal Thinking

Feminists assert that maternal knowledge can be applied outside the immediate context of family. This knowledge can inform and benefit other social arenas and concerns such as politics, community relationships, peace, and environmental justice. I begin with Adrienne Rich's monumental contention that, even when restrained by patriarchy, motherhood can be a source of empowerment and political activism. From there, I investigate the work of eminent scholars who explore the deep relationship between mothering and cognition. Adrienne Rich's *Of Woman Born: Motherhood as Experience and Institution* highlights the maternal subject as complex, thoughtful, and in dialogue with current ideologies concerning maternity, with what Rich terms the "institution" of motherhood. This institution is, in Rich's view, shaped by patriarchal conceptions of women. As such, her 1976 observation of motherhood as "experience" and "institution" was a breakthrough. For Rich, the term "motherhood" signifies the patriarchal institution of motherhood, while mothering refers to women's lived experiences of child-rearing.

While mothering is not described or theorized in *Of Woman Born*, the text made feminist work on mothering possible by distinguishing mothering from motherhood and identifying the potential empowerment of mothering—particularly with those works that analyzed mothering as a site of power and resistance for women. As such, in *Maternal Thinking: Toward a Politics of Peace*, Sara Ruddick (1995) addresses the political and epistemic implications of maternal work. Her work is groundbreaking, as she is the first to suggest that maternal activities give rise to unique ways of thinking. Ruddick defines maternal thinking as focused on the preservation of life and the growth of children. She argues that the work of mothering demands that mothers think; out of this need for thoughtfulness, a distinctive discipline emerges. Patricia Hill Collins extends Ruddick's work through the lived experiences of African American mothers. Collins produces a description of maternal practice that is tangibly distinct from Ruddick's nearly universal version. Collins's construction of mother-work, based on the lives of mothers of color, produces a more specific list of mothering activities than Ruddick's does. Collins argues that survival, identity, and empowerment "form the bedrock of women of color's mothering" (Collins 1994, 7).

Despite groundbreaking works by Rich, Ruddick, and Collins, one of the most pertinent barriers the mothers' movement faces is the systematic silencing of their voices as mothers in higher education. This silencing is a significant emerging theme in various writings on motherhood. Some of the major collections that describe the unique experiences of mothers, of struggling, succeeding, and silencing in the academe are *Mama, PhD: Women Write about Motherhood and Academic Life*, *Motherhood, the Elephant in the Laboratory: Women Scientists Speak Out*, and *Parenting and Professing: Balancing Family Work with an Academic Career*, all of which include first-person narratives that depict, among other things, obstacles to obtaining tenure, accounts of isolation in university departments, gossip among faculty and department members, women getting pregnant just before their review for tenure, and so forth. Although they face the same type of oppression that women do among other professions, mothers in academia face a unique set of challenges and impasses.

Recent feminist scholarship on mothering shifts from the challenges of mothers in academia to the empowering dimensions of maternal identity in academia. In *Mother Outlaws: Theories and Practices of Empowered Mothering*, O'Reilly (2004) assesses the ways in which mothering can be empowering. In viewing feminist, lesbian, and African American mothering as sites of resistance, O'Reilly renews our interest in how to shift our mother-work, rather than simply document the constraints of the patriarchal conditions under which we mother. In O'Reilly's 2006 book, *Rocking the Cradle: Thoughts on Feminism, Motherhood, and the Possibility of Empowered Mothering*, and her 2008 book, *Feminist Mothering*, she argues that feminist mothers can transcend beyond the socially constructed confines of patriarchal motherhood (Green 2004). Further, Fiona Green focuses in her 2009 text, *Feminist Mothering in Theory and Practice, 1985–1995: A Study in Transformative Politics*, on feminist mothers who parent in a self-empowering and transformative way within a patriarchal context.

Mother-Scholar Standpoint(s)

It is important to highlight the methodology that grounds this work. As a feminist researcher, I turn to standpoint theory and qualitative methods to privilege the voices and lived experiences of mother-scholars (Harding 2004; Intemann 2010). Standpoint theory itself is a direct challenge to Eurocentric, male concepts of objectivity. Developing a standpoint from the perspective of the marginalized, in this case mother-scholars, gives researchers an epistemological, political, and scientific advantage over researchers who fail to account for alternative knowledge claims (Harding 2004, 2009).

Also a noteworthy feature is that standpoint theory does not deny a political agenda. In fact, standpoint theorists understand that a political agenda leverages marginalized knowledge claims, gives them power, and prompts subsequent research. Harding (2004) writes, "Political engagement rather than dispassionate neutrality, was necessary to gain access to the means to do research" (6). Harding continues, "Political struggle develops insights" that render a more complete understanding of oppression (7). Granting epistemic privilege to mother-scholar modes of knowledge provides a more exhaustive account of androcentric oppression in academia and insights into new possibilities.

Who We Are

I selected 22 mother-scholars through purposive sampling at universities across the United States. This work stems from a previous study I conducted on mother-scholars in the field of education. Through these in-depth interviews, I was introduced to other mother-scholars in different disciplines. Mother-scholars in education often formed deep alliances with mothers in other disciplines across their universities. In addition, I distributed the request for participants through Women's Studies listservs at these and other universities across the United States, as well as motherhood conference presentations at select Sociology and Anthropology conferences in the United States.

The mother-scholars in this study are full-time university faculty members. The group is diverse in age, race, sexual orientation, class and ability and included mothers who are single and coupled, women with one and several children, and women who plan and did not plan their pregnancies. I included narratives from mother-scholars in the beginning stages of tenure line, mother-scholars who are non-tenure track, and mother-scholars (both tenure line and non-tenure line) in the middle of their career.

The mother-scholars represent diverse disciplines. The breakdown of mother-scholars according to discipline is women's studies (5), sociology (4), political science (2), philosophy (1), education (5), mathematics (2), theology (1) and Chicana/o studies (2).

In-depth interviews with each participant consisted of three general areas: (1) information on the participant and her experiences in academia as a mother, (2) knowledge and beliefs about motherhood and their respective discipline, and (3) course plotting between the maternal and the intellect. The interviews lasted between one and two hours. The questions were guided by academic motherhood research, maternal thinking research, and feminist analyses of higher education.

The mother-scholars were asked to participate in journaling exercises. I asked them to describe significant experiences as a mother-scholar in higher education. The journal writing exercises spanned six months, providing a reflective space to record a variety of experiences.

The data collection and analysis conformed to the highest standards of qualitative research, using the common qualitative tools and technologies of triangulation, member checks, thick descriptions, and audit trails. I used two types of triangulation: investigator and theory triangulation. Theory triangulation relies on the use of multiple perspectives to interpret data. In this study, I relied on research emerging from the fields of psychology, sociology, education, and women's studies to triangulate the data. As I collected the data, I conferred continuously with emerging themes. I also used my own position and intuition as a mother-scholar to provide insight in collecting and analyzing the data (Denzin and Lincoln 2000).

To further maintain the integrity of the data, I conducted regular member checks by selecting participants to review, analyze, and confirm that the working themes resonated with their individual experiences. I incorporated their feedback into the final narrative. Moreover, by directly quoting the participants' accounts of their lives, I used thick description to keep the analysis consistent with the data. To ensure accuracy, I maintained an audit trail by keeping detailed records of all data collection and analysis stages (Marshall and Rossman 2011).

Maternal Thinking and Doing in Academia

Within and without their respective universities, mother-scholars in higher education fuse maternal and academic identities. Through their scholarship and within situated moments of agency, mother-scholars uniquely and differently engage academia.

According to mother-scholars, maternal thinking erupts and interjects itself in their academic scholarship. What fuels this is an explicit acknowledgment that the binary of public/private is false. According to most mother-scholars, the personal is political in that their work impacts not only their respective disciplines but also the field in ways that are connected to their children, and all children for that matter. Professional and private interests reach a converging point.

One sociology professor has researched and written about women of color and pornography for more than ten years. She only recently began to focus more acutely on young girls. She states,

> There is no doubt in my mind that being a mother of a young girl has influenced my research trajectory. I write now with a deeper sense of purpose, because even though these are not my biological girls, I feel a maternal sense about it. A maternal sense of protecting them, of advocating for them.

Another mother-scholar in Mathematics writes,

> I became interested in women and STEM from an early point in my career on tenure. Years later, and now as a mother of three young girls, my involvement in the STEM pipeline for young girls is personal. I have two large NSF grants under my name, and I'm not quite sure I would have pushed myself that hard if I didn't have that personal commitment as a mother of girls.

All mother-scholars evidenced scholarship informed by maternal thinking. They shared articles, book chapters, conference presentations, grants, and other forms of research fueled and grounded by their maternal-academic identity. In fact, all of the mother-scholars interviewed detailed ways their maternal identity informed and strengthened their academic thinking and writing. They shared research topics such as girls and body image; theology and virginity; boys of color and literacy; urban youth and eco-racism; language rights for children; STEM and Black boys; queer youth. A mother-scholar in Political Science expounds,

> I write about rape, migrant women, and human rights. Most of these women are mothers, but it wasn't until I became a mother that I got it. When I became a mother, wow did my interviews go deeper. I could relate to them in ways that I could not before. I was missing a part of the story and obviously a critical part of the analysis.

Further, mother-scholars search for alternative ways to disseminate knowledge. They question traditional formats for sharing one's work such as academic presses. As one mother-scholar posits, "Who really reads this stuff? Not the counselors at my site." Mother-scholars are not necessarily interested in being recognized as the hotshot academics in a male-driven academic world. Instead, there is a sense of urgency in disseminating their research to women and men outside the academy. Mother-scholars talked about publishing in newsletters, magazines, and online blogs. Although these mother-scholars evidence a strong track record for publishing in traditional ways, such as top-tier research journals, their opting-out is purposeful. A tenured mother-scholar in Political Science writes,

> I am finally writing the way I want to write. Blogging. It allows me to organize and share my ideas and research in a relevant way. I connect with other thinkers, not necessarily in academia, to brainstorm

and to deepen our thinking, to think of solutions, and to put me in contact with activists I otherwise would not have had access to. . . . But don't get me wrong. I'm surrounded by old male conservatives and traditionalists in my department. I do not share my work with anyone. I am not interested in their input. But I sure do love that my kids read the blog!

The mother-scholars also clarified that maternalizing the public sphere is not without struggle. They recounted experiences of discrimination, belittling, and sabotage specifically related to their positionalities as mothers in academia. For instance, mother-scholars *sans* tenure expressed deep concerns about publishing research grounded in maternal thinking. Three scholars articulated "back-burner" projects they were working on but that would have to wait, since this type of scholarship was not accepted by rank and tenure guidelines. One top-tier researcher states,

> To incorporate motherhood and research has always been a struggle for me. I trained at a top research university and was hired as an assistant professor at an R1 right after graduate school. It was nonstop publishing for three years, and then I got pregnant. I was back in the classroom after nine weeks. I was overwhelmed. I was the first young mother in my department at a research university that never had to "deal" with this. They didn't know what to do with me, so I just kept up the pace. I still do. There isn't a space for motherhood and research. It is always in the back of my mind that the work I do benefits my daughter and all children, but it is far, far back in my mind. I would say it was when she started kindergarten at a charter school that my work began to take a different direction. I was less preoccupied with the volume and pace of publications and more focused on the immediate impact of my research. I spent more time in the field, less time at the university. I wrote grants to buy out my teaching so I could conduct fieldwork at her school site and other nearby charters. I'm still questioned, though. I hear comments that I spend too much time at my daughter's school. In those cases, my researcher identity is somehow incompatible with my maternal one. It's either one or the other.

Situated Agency

How mother-scholars fuse maternal and academic identity emerged as an equally important theme to the work we do. In the face of patriarchal systems and processes in academia, how do mother-scholars sustain and deepen their work? In the following paragraphs, I provide concrete ways mother-scholars navigate higher education and its completing goals without invalidating their maternal identities. The situatedness of mother-scholars within historically specific material contexts lies at the heart of their individual agency in the pursuit or maternal scholarly work. They contextualize their strategies, which permits a more fluid, shifting, and often contradictory form of agency.

Commitment to contextualized moments offer mother-scholars some breathing room. Mother-scholars articulate that resisting patriarchal oppression in universities cannot become a way of life. To effectively combat oppression, the mother-scholar must shift from a position of constant conflict to a position that allows her to inhabit all of her contradictory identities and choose where to engage. One mother-scholar stipulates,

> It is critical to find ways to survive a male-dominated world that forces us to choose between mommy and scholar. This is totally false . . . and it is set up that way to make us feel inadequate in both worlds and to make us have to fight all the time . . . so you are left tired and exhausted. I cannot live my life in a way where I am always fighting back all the time. I want to be me in whichever way I see fit at that time, and I want that middle world to bring some peace to my life.

Another scholar adds,

> If I subject myself to black-and-white thinking, right and wrong, I will not survive academia. I embrace these different identities I embody, and I accept that there will be times when they clash. Academia lives and breathes these binaries. You are a professor here, a mother at home. I view my willingness to engage and disengage as pushing back on the pressure to have to act accordingly.

These mother-scholars are aware that, within the patriarchal context of higher education, contextualized moments allow them to flow in and out of their identities as mothers and scholars. They emphasize contextualized moments in order to contend with the fierce dialectic of maternity and intellect. Thus, the mother-scholar standpoint is marked by a unique tolerance for ambiguity. This tolerance provides relief from turmoil while facilitating their ability to live in the middle land between two worlds, *los intersticios*, or the space in between identities (Anzaldúa 1987, 20). One mother-scholar in English noted,

> Look, being in academics sucks for a mother. It just does. Once I was able to distance myself from most of it, the meetings, the egos, the politics, I felt better, more alive as a writer. When I really think about when that distancing happened, it was when I became a mother. With motherhood came a much wiser perspective that floating on the periphery was a safer and more productive space to occupy.

The discussion around the *Lean In* discourse bubbled up in several of my interviews. The women understand the importance of assuming leadership positions, but as mother-scholars, they define leadership uniquely, and contest oversimplified tactical positions, such as "leaning in." Instead, their academic leadership positions were often framed as "on the side" and/or "under the radar." There was an understanding that more public or "prestigious leadership positions" would negatively impact them in the private sphere. A mother-scholar and full professor in Women's Studies adds,

> I've tried the traditional leadership roles of department chair and associate dean. I found myself psychologically battered and drained for a variety of reasons. I would come home to small children and find it difficult to prevent the toxicity of the university spilling into my home. I had to question my intentions for assuming those positions and gain clarity on what exactly I wanted to accomplish as a leader in academia. It became clear to that those positions no longer resonated with me a mother-scholar. Instead, I focused my attention on mentoring and smaller-scale leadership roles, which ironically, resulted in impacting academic policies and processes.

Patricia Hill Collins's construct of outsider-within resonates with mother-scholars. Collins uses the trope to describe "the location of people who no longer belong to any one group," as well as "social locations or border spaces occupied by groups of unequal power" (5). Thus, in her formulation, outsider-within refers not to mere duality/plurality but to the power relations which are implicated therein. Outsiders-within are able to gain access to the knowledge of the group/community which they inhabit (or visit) but are unable to either authoritatively claim that knowledge or possess the full power given to members of that group.

Collins sees Black women as ideal outsiders-within, in that they were both dually marginalized (as women and as Blacks), yet able to move among a variety of communities. She perceives the result of this boundary crossing to be a particular collective viewpoint known as the Black feminist standpoint. This kind of multiplicity is a fruitful theoretical location for Collins, because unlike elite or oppositional knowledge, derived from resisting only one kind of oppression, outsider-within positions "can produce distinctive oppositional knowledges that embrace multiplicity yet remain cognizant of power" (8). Mother-scholars inhabit the halls of academia and gain knowledge of the academic community but are ultimately unable and, more importantly, unwilling to access the full power of academe. Intellectually, they flourish in the outsider-within space. What is significant in some of their journeys as mother-scholars is the unwillingness to become an insider. It would require a giving up of their emotional and spiritual trajectories that at this moment in their lives would be intellectual suicide. A mother-scholar in theology adds,

> My department is majority male and not necessarily open to feminist ideas or theories. This has already been a struggle for me. So I've taken another route which is the university platform. I have been involved in and spearheaded a number of significant committees that are trying to advocate for women and mothers in academia. This allows me to come back to my department meetings and advocate for the same things, all under the pretense that the university is moving in this direction.

In addition, mother-scholars found ways to incorporate maternal identity into public spaces, like lectures and conference presentations, by physically bringing their children with them. I shared the following:

> Frequently I have been the only mother who explicitly talks about my children in conference presentations. Or who physically brings them in, where they sit quietly playing their DS while I do my thing. I can feel they don't know what to make of it. There's always this hesitation or awkwardness, and that's just it, it doesn't fit.

Another mother-scholar discussed bringing her children to class to teach her students how to conduct qualitative interviews with children. By lecturing with a piece of her personal life, she was able to effectively present her maternal identity to her students:

> I assign a qualitative project in my class and one of the skills I need my students to demonstrate for me is how to conduct interviews with children. My children kept asking me to invite them to class, they wanted to see what I do, so I figured maybe I could create an activity where my students interviewed my children. I underestimated the power of that lesson. Not only did my students walk away with a hands-on demonstration of the complexity of interviewing children, but they walked away with a shift in perception of me as a researcher. You just do not see researchers as mothers.

For these mother-scholars, scholarship and agency are deeply anchored in their maternal identity. With full recognition of the phenomenology of mother-scholars, we reorient debates in a variety of disciplines in a relevant way. Placing a mother-scholar's standpoint at the center of a story changes it profoundly. Mother-scholar rethinking challenges academia, its core concepts, central assumptions, and institutional policies and processes. Adding mother-scholars and acknowledging mother-scholar epistemology *as relevant* forces us to deepen our interrogation and to rethink higher education's bias toward male bodies, experiences, and knowledge claims. As such, we begin to witness the transforming of higher education toward greater justice.

References

Anzaldúa, G. (1987). *Borderlands/La frontera: The New Mestiza*. San Francisco: Aunt Lute.

Collins, P. H. (1990). *Black Feminist Thought: Knowledge, Consciousness, and the Politics of Empowerment*. Boston: Unwin Hyman.

———. (1994). Shifting the center: Race, class, and feminist theorizing about motherhood. In Evelyn Nakano Glenn, Grace Chang, and Linda Rennie Forcey, *Mothering: Ideology, Experience, and Agency*, 45–66. New York: Routledge.

———. (2000). "Gender, Black Feminism, and Black Political Economy." *Annals of the American Academy of Political and Social Science*, 568: 41–53.

Denzin, N. K., and Y. S. Lincoln eds. (2000). *The Handbook of Qualitative Research*. Thousand Oaks, CA: Sage Publications.

Green, F. J. (2004). "Feminist Mothers: Successfully Negotiating the Tension Between Motherhood as 'Institution' and 'Experience.'" In *Mother Outlaws: Theories and Practices of Empowered Mothering*, edited by A. O'Reilly, 31–42. Toronto: Women's Press. AND In *Motherhood to Mothering: The Legacy of Adrienne Rich's 'of Woman Born'*, edited by A. O'Reilly, 125–136. Albany, NY: SUNY Press.

Harding, S., ed. (2004). *Feminist Standpoint Theory Reader: Intellectual and Political Controversies*. New York: Routledge.

———. (2009). "Standpoint Theories: Productively Controversial." *Hypatia*, 24 (4): 192–200.

Hewett, H. (2006). "Talkin' Bout a Revolution: Building a Mothers' Movement in the Third Wave." *Journal of the Association for Research on Mothering*, 8 (1–2): 34–54.

Intemann, K. (2010). "Standpoint Empiricism: Rethinking the Terrain in Feminist Philosophy of Science." In *New Waves in Philosophy of Science*, edited by P. D. Magnus and Jacob Busch, 198–225. Basingstoke, UK: Palgrave Macmillan.

Lapayese, Y. (2012). *Mother-Scholars: (Re)imagining K-12 Education*. Boston, MA: Sense Publishers.

Marshall, C., and G. B. Rossman. (2011). *Designing Qualitative Research*. Thousand Oaks, CA: Sage Publications.

Mason, M. A., and M. Goulden. (2002). "Do Babies Matter? The Effect of Family Formation of the Lifelong Careers of Academic Men and Women." *Academe*, 88(6): 21–27.

O'Reilly, A. (2004). *Mother Outlaws: Theories and Practices of Empowered Mothering*. University of Virginia: Women's Press.

———. (2006). *Rocking the Cradle: Thoughts on Feminism, Motherhood, and the Possibility of Empowered Motherhood*. Toronto: Demeter.

———, ed. (2008). *Feminist Mothering*. Albany, NY: SUNY Press.

Rich, A. (1976). *Of Woman Born: Motherhood as Experience and Institution*. New York: Norton.

Ruddick, S. (1995). *Maternal Thinking: Toward a Politics of Peace*. Boston: Beacon Press.

17 Catcalled in the Cafeteria

Managing and Teaching through Sexism from Students

Carol L. Glasser

Sexism is institutionalized in the U.S. workplace, including in academia. Women faculty face sex discrimination on campus that can range from lower rates of promotion[1] and pay,[2] to bullying,[3] to unbalanced job expectations, such as higher service and advising loads compared with their male colleagues.[4] Notably, these problems are even worse for women of color. Women faculty face sexism not just from colleagues and administration but also from students. A study of over 500 faculty at 100 U.S. universities found that 91% of faculty experience some type of incivility, bullying, or sexual harassment from students, with women, younger, and minority faculty most likely to have these experiences.[5] A survey at a Midwestern university reported that one-third of students admitted to engaging in the sexual harassment of faculty and over half of the faculty indicated being sexually harassed at least once.[6] Men and women faculty experience similar rates of sexual harassment and unwanted sexual attention from students,[7,8] but women experience more negative psychological outcomes from these experiences.[9,10] Sexism has negative consequences on women's emotional and mental health. Even less overt acts of everyday sexism are correlated with PTSD (Post-Traumatic Stress Disorder) among women (Berg 2006).[11] Sexual harassment from students has specifically been found to have an impact on faculty, with women and non-tenured faculty experiencing more anxiety and depression as a consequence than their male and tenured counterparts.[12]

Though sexual harassment from students is a pattern across academia, it remains insidious because when it happens it feels very specific to that individual situation, interaction, and student. Though sexism often seems specific, there are some consistent traits: the seemingly individualized nature of each attack, the ways that multiple sites of identity (e.g. age, race, gender, and class) intertwine, an emphasis on physical appearance and the sexualization of women, and the undue burden women face in being either blamed for or expected to stop the sexist behavior they experience.

In this chapter I discuss interpersonal instances of sexism that women professors face from students as well as potential responses to these situations. I will center this discussion around several of my own experiences in my first year as an assistant professor. I am a White female assistant professor in my early thirties at a medium-sized state school in the Midwest. We have a traditional student population, and over 85% are US-born, White students. I will also reflect on my own reactions within in a framework of feminist pedagogy. Feminist teaching strategies offer a potential way forward in these situations that can empower the target of this sexism while also providing a potential learning moment for the student.

Feminist Teaching

Feminist pedagogy, as conceptualized by Shrewsbury, has three key components: empowerment, community, and leadership.[13] Within the framework of feminist teaching, instructors teach and students learn in a more collaborative, empowering environment than the traditional classroom, with the hopes helping students develop the leadership skills needed to apply their learning to the real world in a positive and active manner. To allow this to happen, traditional classroom models "where knowledge flows form the top down and is unquestioned"[14] must change. Everyone in the classroom should actively engage in a take ownership of the learning process, making learning a less individualistic experience and developing a sense of community and "mutuality with others"[15]. Shrewsbury identifies leadership as the successful culmination of feminist pedagogy in action[16]: "Leadership in its liberatory aspect as an active element of praxis is the third crucial concept in feminist pedagogy. Leadership is the embodiment of our ability and our willingness to act on our beliefs." Ultimately, a feminist teacher should be a role model of leadership and the classroom experience should create empowered students who seek to act as leaders within and for their communities.

Achieving this goal can be challenging in the face of sexism, but these moments can also provide fertile ground for feminist teachers to model appropriate responses to sexism, teach students about community by creating appropriate learning environments, and helping students apply classwork to real-world needs, in a way that empowers students to actively engage in the production as well as the consumption of knowledge. If done well, not only can teachers confront sexism in the university setting but they can also help students learn to recognize when their own behaviors are problematic.

Experiencing Sexism in the Classroom

Gendered Expectations

> A White male student had missed about one-third of classes and was also getting low scores on his reading homework assignments. One day he asked to talk to me about his grade on an assignment. When we were alone in the classroom he pounded his fists on the desk and raised his voice at me in a threatening manner. Though he admitted he had not completed any of the necessary reading for the assignment, he remained angry and confrontational about his grade. He glared at me, stormed in and out of the classroom, and remained hostile for the remainder of the semester. I was nervous and sometimes scared when he walked past or approached me. Halfway through the semester he sought out my male colleague, who was in no supervisory role, hoping he would convince me to change my class policies.

Gendered expectations were reflected by this student's assumptions of my lack of authority as well as through the gendered norm of using aggressive behavior to compel a reaction. Inherent in sexism is the notion that men and women are fundamentally different and should or do have different roles and abilities. These gender role norms bleed into the labor force so that men and women are often held to different standards both at work and in the home, often in a contradictory manner. For example, women are seen as the primary caregivers of children so that while they may be viewed negatively socially if they don't have children,[17] they may also be discriminated against at work for having them.[18]

Gendered role expectations impact the work lives of women professors who, compared to their male counterparts, have higher service and mentoring obligations,[19] are expected to be more nurturing,[20,21] are rated lower on student evaluations,[22] and may be assumed to have less authority, as the previous vignette highlights. Women faculty may also informally be put into nurturing roles they do not choose for themselves. In a *New York Times* opinion piece, philosophy professor Carol Hay describes the all-too-familiar experience of students crying in women professors' offices.[23] I was initially confused as to why so many students cried in my office. A simple, "Hi. How is the semester going?" has led to crying over everything from mental health struggles to wedding planning challenges. Most often topics that I did not bring up, and often that students likely would not have brought up or cried over in a male professor's office. Hay explains the phenomenon as resulting from a lack of available cultural scripts to understand women in positions of authority: "I'm not their mother. And I'm not their girlfriend either. I'm their university professor. At times I encounter students, both male and female, who don't quite grasp this, and I consequently find myself in a whole host of awkward situations, trying to subtly remind them that I'm neither going to make their bed nor go to bed with them."[24] These gendered expectations mean that for the same behavior students may evaluate men and women professors differently (e.g., "bitchy" versus strict) and assume that men have more status and power than women. They may also have different expectations of what is appropriate behavior to engage in.

One way in which I tried to manage these issues was by clearly creating boundaries between myself and students, such insisting students call me "Dr. Glasser" rather than "Carol." Though this strategy might have had the impact of creating a boundary that would prevent some expressions of sexism, the strategy is potentially problematic in light of implementing feminist teaching strategies. Feminist pedagogy seeks to reorient the student-teacher hierarchy in a way that allows teachers to remain experts at the same time that students also come "to view themselves as viable and legitimate sources of knowledge"[25]; however, the demarcation of status by title reasserts a hierarchy in the learning environment.

In light of these concerns, women professors teaching within a feminist framework have the dual challenge of establishing and asserting appropriate boundaries that can help to curtail the influence of sexism in the classroom at the same that they create collaborative learning environments. In this particular class I utilized project-based group learning in order to foster collaboration and independence in the learning process, a model that has been found to be in line with feminist pedagogy.[26]

A more responsive approach could have entailed strengthening these aspects of the class by developing activities that addressed these issues within the context of this class, for example, a workshop surrounding effective group work to address how communication is influenced by cultural norms surrounding gender, race, class, ability, and more. This type of approach would have allowed all students in the class, not just the student who I was having trouble with, to understand their own sense of belonging and agency while also making them more aware of the positionality of others, thereby creating a more tightknit community as well as ownership over one's own behavior.

Intersectionality

> As I exited the cafeteria in the student center I heard a man catcall me: "Hey, yo! What's up? You! Come over here." I turned around to see two male students sitting at a table. The companion of the catcaller sunk in his seat, embarrassed. I heard him mumble something like, "Dude, it's a professor, what were you thinking?" The catcaller laughed with embarrassment, assuring me he didn't realize I was a professor. I approached them, both Black men. I told him how he made me feel and asked why he engaged in this behavior. We talked for about five minutes and I felt it was a good conversation, when he said that "in some cultures" being called out to is appreciated by women. I cut him off. I told him that at the university the culture is foremost a culture of learning and that women should be valued primarily for their intellect and should not be put in situations on campus where they might potentially feel uncomfortable.

There are multiple sites of inequalities at play simultaneously when sexist behavior is occurring. The concept of "intersectionality" was introduced by Kimberlé Crenshaw[27] in 1991 to describe how Black women's experiences of sexism and racism could not be compared directly to the experience of White women or Black men, respectively, because gendered and racial biases impact Black women in unique ways based on their simultaneous gender and race statuses. Sexism never exists in a vacuum and the intersectional nature of our identities is always important. It means that there are imbalances of power, social histories, and contextual differences that lead to different interpretations and experiences of sexism. In this situation, my singular focus on gender alone led to my mishandlings of a potential teaching moment in reaction to being catcalled. Rather than addressing the issue the catcaller was highlighting when he discussed "cultural differences" (i.e. possible racial, ethnic, and cultural differences in gendered interactions), I silenced him.

Feminist teaching encourages empowering students and a key way to do this is through a reorientation of the student-teacher relationship.[28] However, in silencing the student's concerns and demanding that my interpretation of the situation was the only accurate interpretation, without giving voice to his concerns, I reasserted a hierarchical, disempowering, top-down model of teaching.

Further, I did not acknowledge that he was potentially articulating that, as a racial minority on an overwhelmingly White campus, his experiences might differ from my own. A more successful teaching strategy would have been to foster a sense of community through dialogue with both the catcaller and his friend. This would involve not just talking to the students, but listening to them as well. In doing this I could have acknowledged not just my experience of sexism, but also their potential experiences of racism or other issues they want to share. This could have opened a deeper conversation about race, gender, and privilege—creating in the process deeper and more critical thinking, as well as a sense of commonality and community between us.

Sexualization/Objectification

After the first week of class I received the following email from a White male student:

I feel terrible for dropping your class, but coming into today, i was unsure of how exactly my schedule would work out. . . . I'm sure you're confused as to why I am saying sorry. The last thing I want is for you to feel neglected as a professor, or if a student doesn't like you or your teaching ways. . . . Another reason i dropped the class, which I understand is extremely unprofessional, is because I have never had an attractive teacher/professor in my entire life, which throws my attention out the window. This wasn't needed in the email, but I'm a pretty direct person myself.

You're a very brilliant teacher that really strives to help students learn, so this has nothing to do with you.

About a week after receiving this email I saw the student on campus and asked if he would speak with me. We talked for about 15 minutes in the hallway. I explained how he made me feel, why his email was not flattering, and that his behavior could have serious real-world consequences. I provided some examples of sexism in the workplace context and we discussed his feelings and reactions to these scenarios.

Women are often reduced to their physical appearance and sex appeal so, while the workplace and classroom should extend beyond the corporeal aspects of a person, women professors are still often sexualized within this space. This email highlights both the sexualization that is often a characteristic of sexism as well as the belief that women are responsible for the objectification that is imposed on them. This student clearly acknowledged that it is not appropriate to recontextualize our student-teacher relationship in the context of sex (i.e., "I understand [this] is completely inappropriate . . ."; "This wasn't needed in the email . . ."). Nonetheless, he did so anyway while I assumed the blame for his inability to focus. The student believed he had no responsibility to create any separation between his sexual desires and his educational pursuits.

This notion of a mind-body separation is the Madonna-Whore Complex of the professional world; smart women should not be attractive if they are to be taken seriously, at this same time that there is an expectation that women who are successful and competent should be well put together. This leaves women professors at a loss for acceptable self-presentation. The expectation of a mind-body separation supports a system of victim-blaming (women should "control" their appearance) and perpetuates unachievable and contradictory expectations for women professors. At the same time, the myth of the mind-body divide provides men an excuse for "coercive and unrestrained"[29] sexual behavior. Potts describes men's privilege to use their physical desires as an excuse for inappropriate sexual behavior as stemming from our cultural belief that, for men, the "penis-brain" overtakes the rational brain.[30] In other words, when men are sexually interested we give them a pass not to be completely in control of their actions.

My response to this student's email took the focus off of myself and my appearance and put it back onto the student. In our confrontation following the email, I sought to regain my own sense of worth and power in the situation. Doing this in such a way that confronted the student prompted him to acknowledge his behavior and how he might act differently in the future. Students playing an active role in and taking ownership of one's own learning and role in the community are key features of feminist pedagogy.

Through direct confrontation and conversation, I helped to facilitate this process, though in many ways I was reactionary. This situation might have been improved by removing the coercive nature of the meeting (I caught him on the spot) and providing a context with more time and well-thought-out teaching and engagement strategies. Even so, it provided the potential for the student to take ownership of his mistake and learn from it.

Conclusion

As this volume exposes, sexism in academia is experienced by students, faculty, and staff. In this chapter, I use my own experiences in my first year as a tenure track professor as a lens through which to contextualize student-to-teacher sexual harassment. The goal of this chapter was not just to understand that this type of sexism happens, but how as women faculty, we can turn these moments on their head and use them as teaching moments.

Sexism is about power—it is the act of positioning women as powerless. Good teaching is about empowerment and that is why teaching through sexism is so challenging. To teach through these moments requires regaining a sense of power in the face of sexism while also empowering the person who engaged in the sexist behavior. If done correctly in these situations, for the target of sexism, this can potentially become an empowering moment while at the same time becoming a transformative learning moment for the student. As Shrewsbury notes, a feminist classroom will empower students, develop a sense of community among students, and encourage students to be leaders. Some key strategies for teaching within this framework in the face of sexism include confronting instances of sexism head on, creating open dialogue during these confrontations, and acknowledging the complex and individual nature of each instance of sexism while not ignoring the underlying systemic causes of the problem.

That sexism is systematic is something women faculty know intellectually but often don't feel in moments of sexism, as each instance feels very specific and personal in nature. At the same time, there are always aspects of sexist interactions that are unique to that situation. It is important to understand the intersectional nature of all oppressions to fully acknowledge the depth and interplay of power relationships between student and teacher that will be specific to each instance of sexism. Within this context, confronting sexism head on is important to be able to create powerful learning moments. These confrontations may be in the context of a conversation or within a classroom setting, but the issue of sexism must be directly addressed so that students assume ownership of their own behavior. Importantly, these confrontations must also be a back-and-forth. Teachers must share their power in this learning process. A key way to do this is through open dialogue. To avoid a top-down model of learning teachers must not only talk to students but also listen to them and be willing to learn from them.

Notes

1   Joya Misra, Jennifer Hicks Lundquist, Elissa Holmes, and Stephanie Agiomavritis, "The Ivory Ceiling of Service Work," *Academe* 97, no. 1 (2011): 22–26.
2   Jonah Newman, "There Is a Gender Pay Gap in Academe, But It May Not Be the Gap That Matters," *The Chronicle of Higher Education Blogs: Data Points*, April 11, 2014, http://chronicle.com/blogs/data/2014/04/11/there-is-a-gender-pay-gap-in-academe-but-it-may-not-be-the-gap-that-matters/.
3   Loraleigh Keashly and Joel H. Neuman, "Faculty Experiences with Bullying in Higher Education: Causes, Consequences, and Management," *Administrative Theory & Praxis* 32, no. 1 (2010): 48–70.
4   Joya Misra et al., "The Ivory Ceiling of Service Work."
5   Claudia Lampman, "Women Faculty at Risk: U.S. Professors Report on Their Experiences with Student Incivility, Bullying, Aggression, and Sexual Attention," *NASPA Journal About Women in Higher Education* 5, no. 2 (2012): 184–208.
6   Eros DeSouza and A. Gigi Fansler, "Contrapower Sexual Harassment: A Survey of Students and Faculty Members," *Sex Roles* 48, no. 11–12 (2003): 529–542.
7   Eros DeSouza, and Fansler, A. Gigi, "Contrapower Sexual Harassment."
8   Except see Claudia Lampman, "Women Faculty at Risk," who found that men experience sexual harassment more often
9   Jim Matchen and Eros DeSouza, "Brief Report: The Sexual Harassment of Faculty Members by Students," *Sex Roles* 42, no. 3–4 (February 2000): 295–306.
10   Claudia Lampman, "Women Faculty at Risk."
11   Susan H. Berg, "Everyday Sexism and Posttraumatic Stress Disorder in Women: A Correlational Study." *Violence Against Women* 12, no. 10 (October 1, 2006): 970–988. doi:10.1177/1077801206293082.
12   Eros DeSouza, and Fansler, A. Gigi, "Contrapower Sexual Harassment."
13   Carolyn M. Shrewsbury, "What Is Feminist Pedagogy?" *Women Studies Quarterly* 25, no. 1/2 (1997): 166–173.
14   Rachel Robinson-Keilig, Cynthia Hamill, Annalisa Gwin-Vinsant, and Matthew Dashner, "Feminist Pedagogy in Action: Photovoice as an Experiential Class Project," *Psychology of Women Quarterly* 38, no. 2 (2014): 292–297.
15   Carolyn M. Shrewsbury, "What Is Feminist Pedagogy?"
16   Ibid., 171.
17   Kristin Park, "Stigma Management Among the Voluntarily Childless," *Sociological Perspectives* 45, no. 1 (March 1, 2002): 1–20.
18   Mary Ann Mason, "The Baby Penalty." *The Chronicle of Higher Education*, August 5, 2013. http://chronicle.com/article/The-Baby-Penalty/140813/; Shelley J. Correll, Stephen Benard, and In Paik, "Getting a Job: Is There a Motherhood Penalty?," *American Journal of Sociology* 112, no. 5 (2007): 1297–1338.
19   Joya Misra, "The Ivory Ceiling of Service Work."
20   Myra Green, "Thanks for Listening." *The Chronicle of Higher Education*, October 19, 2015. http://chronicle.com/article/Thanks-for-Listening/233825.
21   Carol Hay, "Girlfriend, Mother, Professor?" *NYTimes.com*, January 26, 2016. https://mobile.nytimes.com/blogs/opinionator/2016/01/25/girlfriend-mother-professor/.
22   Anne Boring, Kellie Ottoboni, and Philip Stark, "Student Evaluations of Teaching (Mostly) Do Not Measure Teaching Effectiveness." *Science Open Research* (January 7, 2016). doi:10.14293/S2199–1006.1.SOR-EDU.AETBZC.v1.
23   Carol Hay, "Girlfriend, Mother, Professor?" See also: Myra Green, "Thanks for Listening";
24   Carol Hay, "Girlfriend, Mother, Professor?"
25   Rachel Robinson-Keilig et al., "Feminist Pedagogy in Action: Photovoice as an Experiential Class Project," 293.
26   Ibid.
27   Kimberlé Crenshaw, "Mapping the Margins: Intersectionality, Identity Politics, and Violence against Women of Color." *Stanford Law Review* 43, no. 6 (1991): 1241–1299. doi:10.2307/1229039.
28   Rachel Robinson-Keilig et al., "Feminist Pedagogy in Action: Photovoice as an Experiential Class Project."
29   Annie Potts, "The Man with Two Brains: Hegemonic Masculine Subjectivity and the Discursive Construction of the Unreasonable Penis-Self." *Journal of Gender Studies* 10, no. 2 (2001): 145–156.
30   Annie Potts, "The Man with Two Brains: Hegemonic Masculine Subjectivity and the Discursive Construction of the Unreasonable Penis-Self."

Bibliography

Berg, Susan H. (October 1, 2006). "Everyday Sexism and Posttraumatic Stress Disorder in Women: A Correlational Study." *Violence Against Women*, 12 (10): 970–988.

Boring, Anne, Kellie Ottoboni, and Philip Stark. (January 7, 2016). "Student Evaluations of Teaching (Mostly) Do Not Measure Teaching Effectiveness." *Science Open Research*, 1–11.

Correll, Shelley J., Stephen Benard, and In Paik. (2007). "Getting a Job: Is There a Motherhood Penalty?" *American Journal of Sociology*, 112 (5): 1297–1338. doi: 10.1086/511799.

Crenshaw, Kimberlé. (1991). "Mapping the Margins: Intersectionality, Identity Politics, and Violence Against Women of Color." *Stanford Law Review*, 43 (6): 1241–1299. doi: 10.2307/1229039.

DeSouza, Eros, and A. Gigi Fansler. (2003). "Contrapower Sexual Harassment: A Survey of Students and Faculty Members." *Sex Roles*, 48 (11–12): 529–542.

Green, Myra. (October 19, 2015). "Thanks for Listening." *The Chronicle of Higher Education*. http://chronicle.com/article/Thanks-for-Listening/233825.

Hay, Carol. (2016). "Girlfriend, Mother, Professor?" NYTimes.com. Accessed January 26, 2016. http://opinionator.blogs.nytimes.com/2016/01/25/girlfriend-mother-professor/.

Keashly, L., and J. H. Neuman. (2010). "Faculty Experiences with Bullying in Higher Education: Causes, Consequences, and Management." *Administrative Theory & Praxis*, 32 (1): 48–70.

Lampman, Claudia. (2012). "Women Faculty at Risk: U.S. Professors Report on Their Experiences with Student Incivility, Bullying, Aggression, and Sexual Attention." *NASPA Journal About Women in Higher Education*, 5 (2): 184–208.

Mason, Mary Ann. (August 5, 2013). "The Baby Penalty." *The Chronicle of Higher Education*. http://chronicle.com/article/The-Baby-Penalty/140813/.

Matchen, Jim, and Eros DeSouza. (February 2000). "Brief Report: The Sexual Harassment of Faculty Members by Students." *Sex Roles*, 42 (3–4): 295–306. doi: 10.1023/A:1007099408885.

Misra, Joya, Jennifer Hicks Lundquist, Elissa Holmes, and Stephanie Agiomavritis. (2011). "The Ivory Ceiling of Service Work." *Academe*, 97 (1): 22–26.

Newman, Jonah. (April 11, 2014). "There Is a Gender Pay Gap in Academe, But It May Not Be the Gap That Matters." *The Chronicle of Higher Education Blogs: Data Points*. http://chronicle.com/blogs/data/2014/04/11/there-is-a-gender-pay-gap-in-academe-but-it-may-not-be-the-gap-that-matters/.

Park, Kristin. (March 1, 2002). "Stigma Management Among the Voluntarily Childless." *Sociological Perspectives*, 45 (1): 21–45. doi: 10.1525/sop.2002.45.1.21.

Potts, Annie. (2001). "The Man with Two Brains: Hegemonic Masculine Subjectivity and the Discursive Construction of the Unreasonable Penis-Self." *Journal of Gender Studies*, 10 (2): 145–156. doi: 10.1080/09589230120053274.

Robinson-Keilig, Racheal A., Cynthia Hamill, Annalisa Gwin-Vinsant, and Matthew Dashner. (May 2014). "Feminist Pedagogy in Action: Photovoice as an Experiential Class Project." *Psychology of Women Quarterly*, 38 (2): 292–297.

Shrewsbury, Carolyn M. (Spring–Summer 1997). "What Is Feminist Pedagogy?" Women Studies Quarterly, 25 (1/2): 166–173.

18 Dress for Success

Dismantling Politics of Dress in Academia

Katie Manthey

> Dress codes make room to turn a lot of 'isms' into policies—especially since typical standards of professional dress are, at the core, racist, sexist, classist, and xenophobic.
>
> —Carmen Rios, "You Call It Professionalism; I Call It Oppression in a Three-Piece Suit"

This chapter uses narrative story as a methodological approach to theorizing a lived experience of sexism in the academy. This chapter investigates notions of "professional dress" through implicit academic dress codes, ultimately arguing that all dress codes are sexist. This chapter offers the idea of "ethical reading" as a methodology to engage with other people—people who write their stories on their bodies and discusses the idea of "feminist microaggressions" as potentially productive spaces.

Scene 1: Job Group, First Meeting

I'm sitting in a small conference room in the rhetoric and writing department. I am nervous but excited. It's the first meeting of our annual "job group"—a mentorship group led by tenured faculty in rhetoric and writing to help those of us with three-plus dissertation chapters and dreams of careers in higher education find jobs in an increasingly complex market. This year, there are only three of us—two of us are straight cis women and one self-identifies as a queer sex positive femme.[1] It's the first time on the job market for all of us. The group is led by a middle-aged, White, cis, male and a middle-aged cis woman of color. It's April, and the MLA job list comes out in five months. This first meeting is to provide an overview of what will happen within the next year and give us "homework" to complete before we start meeting regularly in August.

One of the first things we are told is that the job market is a weird, shitty thing that won't always make sense. We are told that the job market, in many ways, represents the worst of academia as an institution: decisions are made on the basis of things other than merit, many of the people on committees are (subconsciously) biased toward certain types of applicants, it's very expensive, and so forth. Basically, it's still an old White boys' club. We are told that while, yes, this is terrible, especially for women and people of color, part of the purpose of this group is to offer mentorship to help us navigate the heterosexist patriarchy of the academy in strategic ways so that we can not just get jobs, but get *good* jobs—jobs where, hopefully, we can work to make things a little less terrible for other people.

Got it. I appreciate the transparency. I'm listening.

Over the course of the hour we talk about timelines, about having an emotional support system, about the financial cost of the next year. In addition to being assigned to finish at least three chapters of our dissertations and start looking at samples of job letters and other materials, we are told to think about doing some shopping.

In the way of most mentoring, the advice about what to wear for the job market is mostly presented in anecdotal, ad hoc sorts of ways: here's what so and so did. Here's what I did. Here's a story about something that was terrible—learn from it. Pack an extra pair of panty hose. Always have a pair of flats in case you need them.

And then the conversation changes a little. Two of us (myself included) are going to be read in very traditional, "straight ways." One of us, the queer femme, can probably "get away" with looking less "traditional" because her scholarship is part of who she is as a person. Her appearance, identity, and scholarly work all connect in ways that may allow her more "room" to have options with her dress practices: she shouldn't have to change who she is and how that manifests through her dress practices for the job market.

This is one of the last things we talk about that day. It's supposed to be one of the more light-hearted parts of the job market experience—after all, who doesn't love shopping?

At the very end of the meeting, when we were packing up to leave the room, one of the mentors—the woman of color, who is also on my dissertation committee—comments offhandedly to me: "So, Katie, this means you will need to buy some pants."

Scene 2: In Front of My Closet

It's the morning of the first job group meeting, and I'm standing in my bedroom in my pjs and looking into my closet. "I have nothing to wear," I think to myself. Really, the truth is that I have too many options. I see a sweater dress from Old Navy in two different prints, a casual pencil skirt in three styles, and an array of t-shirts, button downs, and blazers. I love clothes. I enjoy manipulating my body through physical garments in order to portray a certain version of myself to the world. I take pleasure and power from purposefully not hiding parts of my body, especially my legs and my arms. I know I can't make myself (much) taller, but I can certainly command attention by dressing a certain way and showing off strategic parts of my body.

I haven't always been this way, though.

In a previous part of my life, my partner encouraged me to hide my arms and legs. He told me that they were embarrassing. I didn't wear skirts, dresses, or shorts. I wore t-shirts or tank tops only if I had a cardigan over them. My sartorial vocabulary was limited. This desire to control my body went beyond my clothing and encompassed all aspects of renowned dress scholar Joanne Eicher's multifaceted definition of "dress." Eicher (2008) explains that dress is a uniquely human practice that includes "actions undertaken to modify and supplement the body in order to address physical needs in order to meet social and cultural expectations about how individuals should look" (4). This definition includes not only clothes and makeup but also things like body hair, odor, and body fat.

In this previous life, I was told (and believed) that my self-worth and love-ability was directly related to the size of my waistline and the number on the scale. At one point, my partner told me that if I ever weighed more than 200 pounds he wouldn't love me anymore. I remember thinking to myself that he must be kidding—who could ever be that shallow? But Maya Angelou was right—"when someone shows you who they are, believe them." After years of trying to keep my body "under control" and hiding it when I couldn't through slimming clothes that cut off circulation and prevented me from movement, the relationship ended . . . and suddenly a relationship with my body began. My body could be anything I wanted it to be. In this moment, standing in front of my closet in my pjs the morning of my first job group meeting, I am 5'4" and 235 pounds and I am actively working on loving myself.

My personal recovery from those experiences has been bolstered by my complete rejection of waistbands that are not elastic. For me, non-elastic waistbands are a physical representation/

reminder of the rigidness of a hetero-patriarchal idea of what it means to have an "acceptable" body. The waistband doesn't allow for the body inside to get bigger or smaller and still be able to wear the pants. My body (like all bodies) is in a constant state of flux: calories in, calories out. In the last few years my weight has fluctuated over 80 pounds. The recovery from this previous life deeply influenced my scholarly work—I am writing about body positivity and dress as multi-modal rhetorical action. My dissertation investigates how self-identified fat fashion bloggers make meaning through their dress practices in ways that are rhetorical, material, and embodied. I write for body positive activist websites like The Body Is Not an Apology. I practice radical self-love by embracing the silhouette that leggings give me and by refusing to feel guilty when clothes don't fit anymore. Clothes are replaceable—I am not. At the time of the first job market meeting, my closet options are dresses, skirts, and black, thin (but not sheer), elastic waistband, cotton-spandex blend leggings from Kohl's. There are no "pants."

I do not wear "pants."
Ever.

Standing in front of my closet, I ultimately choose a button down shirt, a bright blazer, and one of my many pairs of leggings. I put on flats and put my curly brown hair into a bun on top of my head. I put on natural-looking makeup and go to campus, excited for the first job group. Today is the beginning of the next chapter of my academic career. Today I start the transition from graduate student to faculty member. Today is important.

And that day was important: it was the day that I realized that I would never be safe from microaggressions about my appearance.

Interlude: Ethical Reading

I'm telling you these stories as a way to take ownership of the experiences I have had—the experiences of trying to help other people read my body in a certain way. Story can be a powerful methodology; Thomas King (2003) posits that "the truth about stories is that that's all we are" (2). In addition, story can also be a vehicle for engaging in what I call "ethical reading." Briefly put, ethical reading is an approach for "reading" bodies in a way that keeps in mind that the only thing we can know about another person on the basis of their appearance (that is, without the addition of story) are our own biases. For example, young men of color are often written off as "thugs," fat people are seen as "lazy," and a woman who researches fashion and rhetoric who wears spandex to an interview could be seen as "unsavvy," as my mentor commented in a more public forum[2] (see Figure 18.1):

Ethical reading means that the only way to know anything about why the person in front of you looks the way he or she does is to ask. In the rest of this chapter, I will discuss how my experiences after the first day of job market group show the sexism around dress that permeates the academy.

> I hate to tell you all this but leggings are NOT interview appropriate by themselves 😊 Leggings under a skirt with boots? sure. Dresses/skirts w/tights? sure. Remember, the goal of "interview" clothes is to help you make your possibly-future colleagues comfortable. If someone who writes about fashion & whose diss is on the rhetoric of clothing is wearing spandex leggings in the interview instead of all of the equally comfortable options open to her, I'm gonna wonder how rhetorically savvy she actually is... Just sayin'
> Yesterday at 3:00pm · Unlike · 👍 4

Figure 18.1 I Hate to Tell You This but

Scene 3: Campus Visit #1

I'm at a sprawling state school for an interview. A tall, thin, White, middle-aged man is giving me a campus tour. It's starting to rain. I pull out my umbrella and try to balance holding it with the bag I'm carrying. It wasn't heavy this morning when I left my hotel, but it's starting to feel like it weighs 40 pounds now.

> The tall, thin, White, middle-aged, unencumbered man has a long gait.
> "Let's just cut across this grass here so we can get to the building faster," he suggests.

I am wearing kitten heels and the heels of my lovely, comfortable, fashionable shoes sink into the mud with every step. I try to move quickly as the wind picks up and plays with my knee length skirt. With one hand I grasp my umbrella and carry my bag. With the other I clutch my unruly skirt.

> He doesn't even notice how far behind I am.
> I **almost** wish I were wearing pants.
> Please don't ever tell my mentor.

Scene 4: Campus Visit #2

I'm sitting in an office chair across a wide desk from an old White dude. He's an administrator at this small, private university and has sway with the search committee. He is wearing pants. His legs are crossed as he sits back in his chair. We both don't know it yet, but this search will be one of many that fails this year. We sit in silence for a moment. He makes eye contact with me for the second time since I sat down almost 20 minutes ago.
"I don't think embodiment is a real *thing* as you've been describing it," he says to me. He pauses.

> I'm not wearing pants.

I'm wearing a dress from Torrid. It takes everything I have not to pull up the top of my dress in this moment. It's too low cut. I know that. I knew that earlier when I tried it on—that it had the potential to sit pretty low on my already protruding chest. Given half a chance, this dress will betray me. Sure enough, in this moment it makes it impossible to not notice that I have a shape—a shape very different from the human across the desk from me. I hear my mentor's voice in the back of my head—"remember, the goal of 'interview' clothes is to help you make your possibly-future colleagues comfortable."

> Goddammit.
> I'm annoyed.

I'm annoyed with this dress and the stretchy fabric that keeps stretching the wrong way. I'm annoyed with my mentor for being right. I'm annoyed by this guy sitting across from me who oscillates between not giving me the time of day and being borderline aggressively rude. I toy with the ring on my finger instead of yanking up the slipping neckline.
I take a breath. A deep one. I purposefully bend down to adjust the buckle on my shoe unnecessarily. I don't care if it makes him uncomfortable anymore.
"Well, I can see that we have two very different ideas about what embodiment can mean. I think my understanding of the concept comes from a different disciplinary place than yours.

I appreciate what you are saying, though. I think we will have to agree to disagree here," I say in an easy, even tone. I refuse to break eye contact.

He does this thing that's part laugh, part eye roll, part disgruntled huff. He uncrosses his legs and sits forward in his chair. He asks me if I have any final questions for him. I think he thinks this meeting is very much over.

I'm here for a writing center/writing across the curriculum job. I've done my damn homework. I refuse to leave this meeting on this note.

I ask: "How would you describe the climate on this campus for faculty collaboration, especially in regards to campus-wide writing initiatives?"

Without missing a beat, he simply replies:
"Hostile."
This meeting is definitely very much over.

Scene 5: Campus Visit #3

I'm sitting at dinner with the search committee. I arrived into town an hour ago and they wanted to do a casual dinner this first evening before the long day of meetings and interviews tomorrow. I haven't had a chance to change, so I'm wearing my "airport" clothes: dark jeggings, pointy flats, a flowing black-and-white polka dot tank top, and a pink v-cut cardigan.

We are sitting outside on the patio at a circular table with drinks. It's May and warm this evening. Next to me is a very thin, older White woman with a shock of brilliant color-crayon orange hair. Next to her is a young woman of color who has a similar body shape to me. She's wearing a maxi dress from Target that I'm pretty sure I have in my closet at home in a different color. The administrator is the odd one out in a sharp, well-tailored pantsuit. I don't feel out of place. The conversation is easy and the meal is enjoyable. We don't talk about the job until I bring up the fact that we haven't talked about the job.

"We do things differently at a women's college, Katie," the administrator says to me.

Later in the evening, before we leave the restaurant, the woman with the bright orange hair leans over and says to me conspiratorially: "You know, we planned tonight on purpose to sort of ambush you. We wanted to see what you would be wearing normally—not all that, you know, fancy interview stuff. We wanted to see the *real* you first."

I am in love.

Scene 6: Writing Center Orientation

I've been an assistant professor and writing center director for about two weeks. I was fortunate to be offered a tenure track job at the women's college that I visited in May. Today is writing center orientation. In front of me are 11 self-identified women. They are all so young. Most of them are first-year students and this is their first "professional" job. They live in an array of bodies—tall, short, thin, fat, Black, White, Brown. They are wearing pjs, tank tops, super low-cut shirts. I see bra straps, boobs, and lots of curves. I see unruly femininity. My internal sexist voice tells me that they need to dress more professionally when they work here.

They listen when I tell them things. I think they believe me when I talk. It's a total power trip. This is a huge responsibility.

On the agenda for today is the *Bedford Guide*, using the payroll and scheduling system, and talking very explicitly about what it means to dress professionally in our writing center. This is, after all, my area of expertise.

We start by talking about mental health. Being a writing consultant can be very draining, especially for people with social anxiety. I encourage them to be aware of their fatigue during the semester and to let me know when they need to be given some space. One girl lets out a deep breath and the whole room pauses. We all sort of turn to look at her. "It's just so great to hear someone actually talking about mental health," she says with what look like tears in her eyes. She reminds me of myself—short, curvy, and showing a lot of cleavage. My internal sexist voice tells me that she needs to cover up. Then I look at my own outfit and realize that my top is basically transparent. My internal sexist voice tells myself that I need to cover up.

Together, after some discussion, we decide that for our writing center on this campus, dressing professionally means, "dressing in a way that honors your mental health, body, and the space around you." I silently vow to not judge my staff on the basis of their appearance—and to have productive conversations with anyone who comes with a complaint and to handle all microaggressions swiftly. This work space will not reproduce systems of power that hurt people. We plan to post our dress code along with other "writing center commandments" in a public place in the center. Right now, this is my approach to handling the implicitly problematic nature of dress codes at my place of work.

I'm not entirely sure how well this approach will work. I feel like I need to reinforce the idea that in different contexts, their appearances (especially as young women, many of whom are women of color) will be read in many different ways. I teach them about the rhetorical situation of writing: considering audience, context, purpose, genre, and style for each individual piece of text. I teach them about the rhetorical appeals: ethos, pathos, and logos. I teach them these things not only so that they can help others with their writing projects, but also so that we have a shared critical vocabulary for talking about dress. I try to teach them about how rhetoric can be a tool for both recognizing and resisting systems of power.

Rhetoric is always embodied.[3]

Conclusion

All of these scenes have sexism woven in them. In the case of the first job market group meeting, the advice about how to best be read was laden with implicit cis sexism, racism, sizeism, and classism. It's important to note that this advice, although delivered by someone who didn't necessarily hold to those views, was indicative of the implicit biases of our ultra-conservative (read: racist, cis sexist, sizeist, ageist, classist) peers. The idea that some bodies are more restricted than others reinforces the implicit problematic dress codes of the academy.

In the example of the first campus visit, the well-intentioned man giving me the tour didn't think about my footwear situation. He wasn't malicious—but unconsciously assumed I could keep up with him. He was wearing jeans and sneakers. He was unencumbered. It was mostly innocuous—but it was still sexism through dress.

In the second campus visit, I will never know how much my clothing impacted the administrator's opinion of me. I know, though, that I was uncomfortable because of the neckline and because of this internalized sexism about my own body and the perceived comfort of old White males.

When your work is embodied (and, yes, this is a real thing) you can't separate it from your everyday life. That was part of the reason that the third campus visit was so refreshing—the search committee seemed to understand that my appearance was always already part of my performance of self. They didn't claim that how I looked didn't matter—but by modeling a transparency of expectation, they allowed me to fully show myself and be more comfortable.

In the final example of my new position as a mentor with a group of young women in the writing center at a women's college, I realize that I am in a position to discipline the bodies of the people around me. It seems to me that there is no way not to do this—I owe it to my staff to give them the tools they need to not just survive in a patriarchal society but also to be able to make change. Is it enough to simply talk with them about theoretical circumstances of dress? Or do I owe it to them to have them practice dressing for a (racist, cis sexist, sizeist, classist, ageist) audience?

Suddenly, the context around my mentor's comment makes sense as an example of a *feminist* microaggression. I posit that while all microaggressions are rooted in moments of unbalanced power, a feminist microaggression might be a moment when we purposefully enact hetero-patriarchal practices in order to call attention to these very same practices. It is important to remember that everyone has a different experience of a moment, and each individual response/recollection is valid; what seems like a microaggression (feminist or otherwise) to one person might not seem like one to another. Similar to the idea of ethical reading, we have very little power over how others interpret what we say to them; it's best to be as transparent as possible when delivering feminist microaggressions.

Because not/wearing pants can be a way to work within a dress code and to be subversive at the same time, I created a digital space for people to share their stories about how dressing professionally is a type of personal performance. Dress Profesh (www.dressprofesh.com) is an activist gallery that features user-submitted images and text of how people perform what I call "profesh" (as opposed to "professional"). Since its creation in 2015, the site has garnered over 13,000 followers across social media platforms (Tumblr, Twitter, Facebook, Instagram). Dress Profesh is a place where people can tell their own story about their appearance and find a supportive community of other folks who think critically about how systems of power influence what we wear. My hope with this space is that it continues to function as a place where dress codes can be interrogated and challenged. Maybe things can be a little less terrible for future groups of people who go on the job market.

What I have learned from the experiences described in this chapter, then, is that we can't effect change *solely* by not wearing pants. People simply aren't going to understand the larger context of our sartorial choices—ethical reading tells us this. This doesn't mean that we shouldn't push at the boundaries of systems of power through our embodied dress practices; I still dream of the day that I attend an academic conference in my pjs. But it's critical to note that it takes a very particular kairotic moment for someone to safely be unsafe. In my case, I am able to be subversive in my dress practices because I carry an enormous amount of privilege—I am White, young, middle class, able bodied, and cisgender. Not everyone is able to inhabit the same moments in the same way—this is my concern for my staff. Decolonial feminist rhetorical scholars tell me that the best way to effect change is by working on the boundary of the patriarchal structures I already inhabit (Anzaldua 1997; Collins 2000; Mignolo 2011; Tuhiwai Smith 1999). This means that sometimes choosing to wear pants is not a resignation—it's the most practical and subversive way to effect feminist egalitarian change. This I learned, at last, from my mentor.

Notes

1   While writing this chapter, I asked her for her self identification.
2   I am using this Facebook comment with my mentor's permission. The process of writing this chapter has given me a chance to talk with her about everything that happened that year. She has read this manuscript, and we are both happy with it.
3   For more, see "Embodiment: Embodying Feminist Rhetorics" (Johnson et al. 2015).

References

Anzaldua, Gloria. (1997). "La conciencia de la mestiza: Towards a New Consciousness." In *Writing on the Body: Female Embodiment and Feminist Theory*, edited by Katie Conboy, Nadia Medina, and Sarah Stanbury, 233–247. New York: Columbia University Press.

Collins, Patricia Hill. (2000). *Black Feminist Thought: Knowledge, Consciousness, and the Politics of Empowerment*. New York: Routledge.

Eicher, Joanne B., Sandra Lee Evenson, and Hazel A. Lutz. (2008). *The Visible Self: Global Perspectives of Dress, Culture, and Society*. 3rd ed. London, UK: Fairchild Publications.

Johnson, Maureen, Daisy Levy, Katie Manthey, and Maria Novotny. (2015). "Embodiment: Embodying Feminist Rhetorics." *Peitho*, 18 (1): 39–44.

King, Thomas. (2003). *The Truth About Stories: A Native Narrative*. Minneapolis, MN: University of Minnesota Press.

Mignolo, Walter D. (2011). *The Darker Side of Western Modernity: Global Futures, Decolonial Options*. Durham, NC: Duke University Press.

Rios, Carmen. (2015). "You Call It Professionalism; I Call It Oppression in a Three-Piece Suit." *Everyday Feminism*. February 15, 2015. http://everydayfeminism.com/2015/02/professionalism-and-oppression/.

Tuhiwai Smith, Linda. (1999). *Decolonizing Methodologies: Research and Indigenous Peoples*. New York: St. Martin's Press.

Section 2

Feminist Strategies for Action

Changing Material Conditions

19 The Aftermath of Activism

Combating and Surviving Sexism at One Southern University

Laura Jennings and Lizabeth Zack

Introduction and Background

The spring of 2014 opened a period of deep unrest at our small southern public university. Following uproar in the state legislature over a freshman book with LGBT content, and facing pressure from conservative politicians regarding our annual Bodies of Knowledge Symposium, the university administration decided to cancel the satirical lesbian coming-out performance piece which was to kick off the symposium. Then, after commencement, with most students and faculty gone for the summer, administrators sent an innocuously titled email containing a hidden bombshell: the sudden unilateral administrative decision to close the campus Center for Women's and Gender Studies (CWGS). Students and faculty protested the decision in a variety of ways, public and private. The administration's ineffective and disingenuous response caused further outrage and accusations of violations of shared governance policy. The CWGS announcement was followed by the equally sudden and unilateral decision to close the Burroughs Child Development Center (BCDC), and metaphorical hell broke loose on campus.

CWGS had long attracted controversy on campus, with many believing its woman-centered mission had been usurped by "fringe" LGBTQ programs and concerns. This belief was widespread despite well-publicized programming and collaborations addressing women's history, women in science, girls' studies, and intersections of gender and race. BCDC, however, was an uncontroversial point of pride on campus. It was one of only two nationally accredited child development centers in the area, was a great recruitment tool for prospective employees and students with children, and was vital for training purposes for several academic programs including psychology and education. It was also staffed entirely by women, most of whom earned fairly low wages. The decisions to close these centers, then, disproportionately affected women and other marginalized groups. The closure announcements occurred not in a vacuum but against a backdrop of everyday sexism (top administrators who were mostly White males, mentorship and promotion of junior White men over others, and administrative scolding and condescension in interactions with women faculty) and occasional vicious incidents including pornographic graffiti following significant corrective raises given to three women faculty.

Out of the uproar, a core group of women faculty—including these authors—formed with a specific intention to fight the center closures and a general desire to improve the status of women on campus. Our battle could be viewed as at least partially successful; while BCDC was rapidly closed, its staff laid off and facilities dismantled, CWGS remains open and in full operation, its leader in place and its programming active. The efforts of this core group to spread information, to generate public discussion and support, and to publicize the negative effects of unilateral administrative decisions were instrumental in bringing about a faculty vote of no confidence against the chancellor in spring 2015. In early fall 2015, the chancellor announced his intention to step down; by early 2016, the search for a new chancellor was underway.

These victories did not come without cost to members of the core group. The struggle at times consumed our lives and affected our relationships. In many ways we are still dealing with the aftermath of our activism. What impact does collective public activism have on the lives of women who choose to fight sexism in the academy?

Literature on Activism

Research on the broad question of how individual activists are impacted by their activism is rather limited. For a long time, scholars of social movements and political protest were focused on explaining the rare occasions when activist campaigns emerged and on identifying the conditions leading to their success or failure in changing the policies and institutions activists targeted, not what happened to the participants themselves as a result of being involved in those campaigns (Guigni 2008; Meyer 2003). Even once scholars began to reexamine the myriad outcomes and effects of social movement participation, research on the "biographical" consequences of political activism has been limited to analyzing the long-term life-course effects and varying levels of future engagement among activists from a limited set of social movements (Corrigall-Brown 2012; Guigni, McAdam, and Tilly 1999; McAdam 1989; Van Dyke, McAdam, and Wilhelm 2000).

Literature addressing feminist activism often focuses on the complex nature of problems (Baumgardner and Richards 2005; Mitchem 2005). Sara Ahmed (2010) uses a metaphor of a family table at which many topics of conversation are off-limits. Feminist activists disturb the peace, raising issues others would rather not discuss, threatening the comfort and hierarchical seating of all present (Ahmed 2010; Bailey 2006; Hart 2008). Those threatened by feminist consciousness-raising react by relegating problems activists expose to the background while renaming feminists themselves as the problem (i.e., as angry, pushy, unreasonable) (Ahmed 2010; Burrow 2005), a common political strategy for diverting attention from activists' messages to their tone or style of presentation (Bailey 2006; Burrow 2005; Mitchem 2005). This resistance causes weariness, self-doubt, and the need for a "safe haven . . . where rest is possible" (Mitchem 2005, 128; also see Ahmed 2010; Burrow 2005).

Methodology

To answer the question "What impact does collective public activism have on the lives of academic women?" we approached the core group of women faculty involved in activism on our campus in 2014 and 2015. Most (six including the authors) agreed to participate; four had tenure at the time of activism. We collected information from the activists through open-ended questionnaires, interviews, and follow-up group email conversations, asking participants how they had first become involved in the recent activism, how their involvement had proceeded, how (if at all) the activism had affected their relationships, and how (if at all) their career plans or goals were affected by their activism. Follow-up questions addressed the effects of the time commitment and stress during the period of intense activism, whether participants considered the activist period to be over, and whether they experience any lingering effects. Participants' identities were kept confidential; each was sent a draft of the paper before it was submitted so that she could elect to exclude her information if she saw fit. None did.

Findings

This section describes how the group of women faculty became involved in campus activism, what happened to them during the campaign, and what followed from this experience.

Getting Hooked

Activists differed in their initial reaction to the news of closing CWGS. All were surprised, but they expressed different feelings about it. Four of the six felt strong shock and anger. Three of the four who were affiliate faculty of CWGS and taught gender- or sexuality-themed courses were worried, especially about the loss of a safe space for LGBTQ students. Two indicated more ambivalence; one said, "I remember feeling some concern and surprise but not necessarily a strong, visceral reaction. I didn't have strong connections to CWGS." The other initially blamed the Center's director for the closure for too much emphasis on LGBTQ issues and worried about implications for the nascent African American studies program.

Participants also framed their reaction slightly differently. Almost all pointed to controversies during the preceding academic year as important conditions leading to the announcement. Some highlighted the administration's poor handling of the public controversy over the gay-themed freshman book in the fall and their decision to cancel the lesbian performance piece in the spring. One activist focused on the administration's mismanagement of a budget crisis during the year, saying "the closure . . . looked like yet another confusing and bumbling move . . . to get things in order."

Activists differed as well in the way they became more actively involved and committed to the campaign. Half felt strongly committed to challenging the CWGS decision as soon as it was made. After attributing her anger and activism to multiple moments during the preceding academic year, one noted that

> what pushed me over the edge was [the decision] to close CWGS . . . I called the director . . . her despair coupled with my anger spurred me into action. From that moment, I actively pursued ways and other faculty supporters to stop what I believed was a dismantling of the university I knew and loved.

Three protested directly to senior administrators, by letter, phone, or in person. Most felt, as one activist put it, "energized on some level and ready for a fight." Two of the activists agreed more reluctantly to take action to save CWGS. One noted, "I ended up supporting . . . the center" only after realizing that "things were not as I thought." The other did so once she saw the closure "in a new light," as more than simply another misguided administrative decision, after hearing others talk about it. All joined a meeting in late May to discuss a formal response to the closure.

If half were firmly committed to challenging the decision at this point, three continued to feel ambivalent through the initial protests. One participant, concerned about her untenured status, said, "the shift happened when I moderated the forum [the meeting about CWGS with the chancellor in late June]," which showed her that she "couldn't be behind-the-scenes anymore." For two others, it was the administration's closing of BCDC that really pushed them into the fight. One had served on the so-called BCDC Task Force that was "making headway" when they were abruptly "shut down." One, who had a young daughter in BCDC at the time, says, "I can still feel the anger, the sadness and the bewildering sense of disorientation that filled me up . . . we now had two centers to defend, and I was ready." Thus, for some, getting hooked was an abrupt and immediate experience while for others it was reluctant and gradual.

During the Campaign

Although participants described very different points of entry into this activism, the effects were similar. All six noted the vast amounts of time and energy spent on research, networking, meeting, and composing documents, as well as in thought and worry over campus events. All remarked on the intense effort involved: "It was exhausting work, psychologically and physically—we all lost sleep," and "Much of my time was spent researching, finding the concrete data that was used to back up arguments," and "I look back at a lot of those conversations and a lot of that mobilizing, and ALL the FUCKing work that we did."

Most said the campaign took a toll on personal relationships. Participants wrote, "My domestic partner commented at times that I seemed to have forgotten how to talk about anything else," and "[My partner] asked jokingly one night if I was married to [another group member]" and "As I got more involved . . . I grew more preoccupied and stressed, and less emotionally available . . . At some point, he told me . . . [he] was worried about our relationship." This activist made adjustments to devote more time and energy to her relatively new relationship; another wrote, "I began to make efforts to keep work talk to a minimum at home. I also had to stop reading emails close to bedtime because I had such terrible 'stress dreams' regarding our efforts."

Participants also reported engaging in balancing acts in their professional roles, to win colleagues over to the cause without pressuring them or to remain involved in the struggle without compromising job responsibilities. A participant who had moderated one of the public forums described neutrality as the main requirement of the adjudicator role but said that "it felt . . . almost disingenuous" because while as moderator she had to allow the chancellor equal time to speak, she found herself hoping to "leave enough rope for him to hang himself. So it was sort of this double-edged sword. . . . I wanted to work in an ethical way." Another participant wrote that she "was extremely careful not to do or say anything that would give the appearance of me having any undue influence on any of the faculty in my division."

One of the most disillusioning aspects of the work involved co-workers. In some cases, colleagues expressed sympathy or agreement but offered no help; in other cases, colleagues initially perceived as allies refused to become involved or worked against the group's efforts. The core group had been conscious from the beginning of the vulnerability of untenured faculty and had tried to shield them from taking a large or visible role in the activism, but lack of support from tenured colleagues was more difficult to understand. One participant described a conversation with a close friend and colleague who, upon learning of the plan to close CWGS, said, "Oh, wow, that sucks. Oh well." and then seemed ready to move on. Another participant characterized the situation as "an emotional firestorm," saying, "People I had admired for their integrity . . . not only refused to fight for the Centers but also refused to stand on principle for the policies that had been violated." She concluded, "I don't know that I was justified in feeling betrayed, but I did." Another participant, too, mentioned feelings of betrayal when "colleagues who I thought would have been clear allies" of CWGS instead defended the closing. This participant continued, "I thought a lot of people were using the chaos—the power vacuum—as an opportunity to promote their own careers, and that . . . made me sick." Some participants mentioned the gendered nature of involvement; while some male colleagues stepped up and offered vocal support for the centers, signed letters of protest, and participated in meetings and other activist efforts, the core group of activists consisted entirely of women. A member of the group wrote of her discouragement "when one male colleague said he supported our side but wasn't going to sign the letter because of fears about tenure and then wished me 'good luck in your fight'." She reflected, "That pretty much summed up the reality of sexism on our campus. Child-rearing and gender inequality are still women's fight."

Several described periods of self-questioning or discomfort with some aspect of their activist role. Two mentioned that the constant collaborative nature of the core group was difficult for them and at times caused them to feel ambivalent about their involvement. An untenured member who had been singled out for a one-on-one meeting with a top administrator described the experience as awkward "though it did make me feel like I had some sort of agency." She said she felt as if she "was cavorting with the enemy, in a way that made the other members of the group view me as . . . [a] narc or spy . . . Why would he single me out?"

Almost all participants needed to temporarily withdraw or rest at times during the activist period, especially from the constant email communications of the group. One chose not to read activism-related email while on vacation, saying, "I felt like I owed it to my family to give them my undivided attention and not be a ball of stress all week." Another said that she and another core group member had made a pact to take a temporary break from the email conversations. All conveyed the sense that this activism was like having an additional part-time job.

Four participants lamented the public portrayal of the activist group and its members as problems. Administration and colleagues opposed to the activism downplayed the issues and the extent of campus discontent, framing problems as small, temporary, and enflamed by a few women faculty with their "hair on fire," to quote the senior vice chancellor. A participant wrote,

> I know that a . . . colleague reported me to my chair for including her in . . . efforts to organize CWGS support. She said she felt pressured to participate by me, and a different colleague later told me that she had reported me to [the university president] for "bullying."

Another was conscious of the fact that

> some people . . . likely responded to me as a loud-mouthed Black woman, maybe aggressive . . . I think [the chancellor] tried to position himself sometimes to let the mean Black lady beat up on him to gain sympathy so I began to rein in my emotions.

A third wrote of her frustration and sense of isolation when every action the group took seemed to bring complaints: "When we decided to wear red shirts to a public meeting . . . people complained that . . . was somehow placing unfair pressure on them." Even mentioning to people "that we were writing and collecting signatures on letters of protest . . . was sometimes seen as intimidation," and "when we sent information . . . people complained that we were flooding their inboxes." A fourth group member was verbally attacked and silenced in a faculty senate meeting, and members of the academic program most opposed to the activism then applauded her silencing. She described feeling angry and terribly hurt but realizing now, "in retrospect, it's a consequence, of . . . working against the status quo, and being a woman, at a university in the South. . . . It's a consequence of being outspoken."

Despite these difficulties, five of the six participants reported a sense of empowerment from speaking out, even if the feeling was at times offset by discouragement. One described the chancellor bringing his "entire cabinet with him, perhaps to intimidate" to a moderated forum; she was shocked when he "appeared weak. . . . By the end, it was clear we had outdone him. We could, indeed, do battle with these high-level administrators . . . on the field of logic and facts. And this was empowering." Of a special senate meeting she wrote,

> [This] was taking our activism to a new level as we were going before the faculty, our peers, in a public forum and asking them for support. That was a big deal. We did a good job of making our case

and "won the vote overwhelmingly," bringing more feelings of victory and empowerment. Another described a conversation with the chancellor:

> I told him that if he closed [CWGS] I was going to chain myself to the door and call the media. I think he had to know at that point . . . that this was not going to be easy for him.

Four participants had a sense that participation in the activism had altered their campus identity, both positively and negatively. One stated that the very victories that had helped empower us "also made us the public face of resistance to the administration, which won us both allies and detractors." Another wrote,

> My profile was elevated and as people came to know me better they respected me and my opinion. I think that the perception of me that resulted enabled me to bring some folks along to vote [No Confidence] because they trusted me.

A third mentioned feeling more visible on campus but added,

> I pressed the chancellor hard in some of the public meetings, and I think that some people . . . didn't think that was okay. It was not long after some of those meetings that the university unveiled a civility policy. . . . We wondered if it was an attempt to control us.

All participants noted the importance and role of "the group"—in providing information, support, relief from isolation, and a safe place to strategize. Participants stated that group members who had been near-strangers before had helped them through rough spots in the activist period, sustained their involvement in the activism, and often were the only people they could trust on campus. "The group . . . kept me sane through what was really a very traumatic two years," said one. Another, who had been treated disrespectfully at a faculty senate meeting, said, "[T]hat hurt a lot, but I had you guys as a community. . . . You know, it really felt GOOD that someone leapt to my defense." She relayed talking another core group member out of calling for a public apology at the next senate meeting and how touched she was at the other woman "wanting to do that . . . to be that sort of protector." Others described the deep respect, affection, and trust that grew among group members in a remarkably short time. No one was under the illusion that the group or membership in it was perfect; participants mentioned having tensions and disagreements to work through, difficult conversations, and one wrote, "I almost left the . . . group a few times because it was sometimes . . . too collaborative and consensus building for me," and because she "wanted to maintain my independence and to own my own voice." Despite difficulties, the core group remained intact. One participant reflected,

> While we may disagree, I have great respect for the courage and tenacity shown by these women. We worked through various disagreements as a group, and the whole experience seemed . . . supportive and healing even when it was stressful.

After the Campaign

Some of the effects of this activism have outlasted the activist period itself. Participants spoke of the importance and closeness of the group in present tense, referring to other members as friends and trusted colleagues with whom they had shared a unique and difficult experience. Some mentioned lingering pain or trauma, requiring healing. Participants also spoke of empowerment in the present tense, alluding to a hypothetical future when they might feel compelled—and would be ready—to stand up and fight again.

Some participants found their views of career or employer altered. As one stated, "[T]his made me . . . less apathetic about faculty governance. . . . I'm also open to leadership opportunities if they present themselves." Another wrote that she now avoids work social events and tries "to get in and out of work as quickly as possible," keeping her "office door shut or cracked to avoid most of my colleagues." Long-term, she says,

> I've realized that I don't see myself in academia for the rest of my life, I don't care that much about academic advancement, and I've found that not caring liberates me to be a useful tool in any future rebellion.

Acknowledging the toll taken by our sustained activist efforts, she concludes, "I think that my recent detachment from my career is probably a very healthy reaction to promote self-healing after a very, very traumatic two years." One participant accepted an academic position in another university in a more liberal part of the United States. She described her new department and university as more open to women and LGBTQ people in visible leadership roles and to discussion of varying viewpoints, "unlike the conversations that you'd hear in upper administration [at our university], where the other side would be dismissed." Of the likelihood of such openness at our university she said, "I . . . don't know if that world's possible . . . or if I would even be allowed into that world. It's so depressing." A fourth participant mentioned new interest in shared governance but added that it is fortunate that she has never had administrative ambitions because she thinks her activism scuttled her chances. A fifth participant said that before the activism-precipitating events she had "been largely happy with the . . . administration and with my work environment." Now, however, she views her "administrative work through a different lens . . . not wanting to make the same mistakes our administrators did." The sixth participant wrote that her "pride in working here and [feeling] appreciated for who I was and the work I did" had gradually eroded. "As various individuals showed themselves to be corrupt and/or incompetent," she explained, "I lost faith and confidence in the ability of the administration to run the university effectively. . . . The prospect of a new chancellor doesn't relieve me of my disillusionment."

Discussion

Two major points emerged in our analysis: the complexity of the battle and the ongoing nature of its effects on the activists.

What Were We Fighting?

Was it sexism? In many ways, closing CWGS had the hallmark features of sexism. Yet, as participants described their reactions to the closure, they did not frame the problem simply as "sexism." Perhaps it was there in the subtext of their testimony, obvious to them without needing to be labeled as such. Perhaps the first closure was not universally understood, or at least articulated, by the activists as "sexist," nor was their desire to resist it interpreted by them as "fighting sexism" separately from other issues.

In a way, the fight to keep the centers *became* more clearly a fight against sexism as the process unfolded and pushback began. As the activists pursued their campaign to keep CWGS open, they were dismissed and belittled by administrators and other faculty for "nagging" about the issue. Complaints were filed against activists for "bullying," being "intimidating" and "putting pressure" on colleagues, terms unlikely to be applied to men engaged in the same activities. Once the administration targeted BCDC, their behavior acquired an increasingly "sexist" cast. To the activists, the two closures were linked together as the vulnerable being preyed upon by a gender-biased administration (We quickly incorporated saving BCDC into our campaign, while joking that the university slogan had become "Women and Children First (In Budget Cuts)!").

Ultimately, "saving the centers" was a deeply intersectional problem. The BCDC closure introduced a class dimension to the problem considering the low salaries of eliminated staff and the fact that students who relied on the childcare services were often low-income single parents. White, well-paid, heterosexual men and their allies had targeted two centers that were primarily serving and staffed by women, some of whom were poor, poorly paid, of color, or queer. Our campaign to "Save the Centers" operated on multiple fronts—against gender, racial, and class bias, against homophobia, and against conservative politics, the politics of austerity, and administrative incompetence. Perhaps the main reason why we did not frame our campaign squarely as a "fight against sexism" was that the fight itself was never disaggregated from these other issues.

In the Aftermath

What happened to the activists while the campaign proceeded can only be described as mixed, as uplifting and demoralizing, and full of trade-offs. This is in line with research on political activism in general and feminist activism more particularly. The exhaustion that comes from carrying out all of the necessary behind-the-scenes work, as well as the emotionally charged atmosphere that develops around interpersonal relationships and the contentious process of constructing a group identity, are common experiences for activist groups (Goodwin, Jasper, and Polletta 2001; Polletta 2002). Despite the individual and collective empowerment experienced by the activists and the victories they achieved, they were under no illusion that the deeper problems were resolved or that the work was nearing completion (Ahmed 2010; Bailey 2006; Baumgardner and Richards 2005; Burrow 2005; Hart 2008; Mitchem 2005).

The more interesting finding emerges from the activists speaking in the present tense, in the near-term aftermath of the campaign. Some describe feeling battered, almost traumatized by the experience; others refer to distrust and disillusionment, and even leaving academia. There is a dark undertone and sense of loss in some of the testimony. These are not the sentiments one expects to accompany victory. And, by many accounts, the long campaign these activists fought, which started with saving the centers and ended with ousting the chancellor, was largely successful. Why so little joy?

Perhaps the lack of celebration is a sign of the heavy emotional and psychological toll of the relentless, painstaking politicking they engaged in for a year, and this period is the respite that necessarily follows from it, a time to recuperate. With more time and recovery, perhaps the darker feelings will dissipate, making room for some of the activists' prior feelings toward the university—trust, loyalty, security, and so forth—to return. But it may be that the losses—the closure of Burroughs, the public shaming, the loss of friends—exacted too much of a cost, one that cannot be recovered.

It is also possible that what the activists feel now, in the aftermath, is what happens to those who fight sexism in the academy. Initially unconcerned by their relegation to the foot of the table, we feminist killjoys spoke up upon seeing some members of the family excluded. Not only did we kill the joy of others by raising uncomfortable topics, we also killed our own joy by exposing unpalatable conversations at the privileged end of the table. Repulsed by what we found, we lost our sense of our institutional home as a decent place to work and build a career. Perhaps this is the bigger trade-off in the aftermath of activism.

Conclusion

Though limited, this study of women faculty fighting campus sexism suggests important lessons for others in similar circumstances. Our focus on a small group of activists who fought a particular battle on a particular campus very recently means that we cannot yet see the long-term effects of the activism on them or their institution. It is also difficult to know whether these findings are generalizable beyond this single case, to what degree the experiences of these activists are typical of others, and to what extent the findings shed light on other cases of fighting sexism in the academy. This case does, however, highlight the need to build the right affinity group for activists fighting sexism in the academy, one that can sustain the backlash, emotional toll, and demands for energy and time that accompany those campaigns. The case also points to the need for strategies of rejuvenation in the aftermath of those campaigns, even campaigns marked by measurable successes.

References

Ahmed, Sara. (Summer 2010). "Feminist Killjoys and Other Willful Subjects." *The Scholar and Feminist Online*, 8 (3): 1–8.

Bailey, Courtney. (2006). "'Taking Back the Campus': Right-Wing Feminism as the 'Middle Ground.'" *Feminist Teacher*, 16 (3): 173–188.

Baumgardner, Jennifer, and Amy Richards. (2005). *Grassroots: A Field Guide for Feminist Activism*. New York: Farrar, Straus, and Giroux.

Burrow, Sylvia. (2005). "The Political Structure of Emotion: From Dismissal to Dialogue." *Hypatia*, 20 (4): 27–43.

Corrigall-Brown, Catherine. (2012). "From the Balconies to the Barricades, and Back? Trajectories of Participation in Contentious Politics." *Journal of Civil Society*, 8 (1): 17–38.

Giugni, Marco. (2008). "Political, Biographical, and Cultural Consequences of Social Movements." *Sociology Compass*, 2 (5): 1582–1600.

Giugni, Marco, Doug McAdam, and Charles Tilly. (1999). *How Social Movements Matter*. Minneapolis, MN: University of Minnesota Press.

Goodwin, Jeff, James M. Jasper, and Francesca Polletta. (2001). *Passionate Politics: Emotions and Social Movements*. Chicago: University of Chicago Press.

Hart, Jeni. (Spring 2008). "Mobilization Among Women Academics: The Interplay Between Feminism and Professionalization." *NWSA Journal*, 20: 184–208.

McAdam, Doug. (October 1989). "The Biographical Consequences of Activism." *American Sociological Review*, 54: 744–760.

Meyer, David. (2003). "How Social Movements Matter." *Contexts*, 2(4): 30–35.

Mitchem, Stephanie Y. (Fall 2, 2005). "Coloring Outside the Lines." *Journal of Feminist Studies in Religion* 21: 128–130.

Polletta, Francesca. (2002). *Freedom Is an Endless Meeting*. Chicago: University of Chicago Press.

Van Dyke, Nella, Doug McAdam, and Brenda Wilhelm. (2000). "Gendered Outcomes: Gender Differences in the Biographical Consequences of Activism." *Mobilization*, 5: 161–177.

20 Professors and (M)Others

Smashing the "Maternal Wall"

Michelle Rodino-Colocino, Molly Niesen, Safiya Umoja Noble, and Christine Quail

Flexible work schedules and job security make faculty jobs seem ideal for mothers' career advancement. Stalling equity for women in the academy is the "maternal wall," discriminatory workplace practices and beliefs that halt career progress (Williams and Dempsey 2014; Williams and Segal 2003). Because 82% of U.S. women are mothers, including 76% of women with advanced degrees, the maternal wall may constitute a more formidable barrier to career advancement and pay equity than the "glass ceiling" (barring women from top positions; Williams and Dempsey 2014). The maternal wall may contribute to men's constituting most tenured faculty at U.S. colleges and universities and women's holding most precarious, low-pay contingent and adjunct positions (men hold 59% of tenured positions; women hold 51%–61% of contingent ones; Lubrano 2012; MacFarlane 2012; Steiger 2013). It may also account for apparent inequity in work–life balance, as women faculty have fewer children than do male peers (Mason 2013) and are more likely to divorce or never marry (70% of tenured male faculty are married compared with 44% of women faculty). Additionally, women who have "early career babies" (within five years of earning Ph.D.'s) are less likely to survive in the academy, whereas men enjoy a "fatherhood bonus" of increased pay and promotion (Mason 2013; Miller 2014).

The maternal wall is constructed by external discrimination as well as internalized cultural beliefs that demands women's all-consuming labor (Cowan Schwartz 1983). Feminist media scholars Susan Douglas and Meredith Michaels (2004) call cultural demands that women put motherhood ahead of all else "the new momism." "Supermom" expectations that mothers exceed professionally and personally may also result in burnout (Hunt 2015). Furthermore, colleagues may internalize such beliefs about all-consuming mothering. When academic mothers but not fathers are late to a meeting, colleagues assume she has childcare issues (Williams and Segal 2003). Mothers also experience discrimination when workplaces fail to accommodate physical requirements of motherhood that include time to recover from childbirth and breastfeeding.

Intersecting systems of race and gender thicken maternal walls, driving down wages and status for women of color and erecting institutional barriers (Collins 2012). Mothers of color report hitting the maternal wall more often than do White women, 63% to 56% (Williams and Dempsey 2014). Women faculty of color often negotiate being a department's only underrepresented person which results in assuming additional "diversity" committee work. Notions of the "maternal sex" also compel childfree women to prove they are not primarily "people who have domestic ties" (Cockburn 1991, 76).

Drawing on our experiences as tenure track faculty in the U.S. who became early career mothers and analyzing policies at our home universities, we argue that the maternal wall constitutes a significant career barrier. Specifically, we discuss our experiences becoming mothers as graduate students, during transitions from graduate school, and as new faculty. We situate these experiences in relevant research and policies. This chapter also shares what has enabled us to survive this form of sexism in the academy. Our conclusion calls for collective action to smash the maternal wall. We begin by discussing how policies and their application have built the maternal wall in the U.S. and for this essay's authors.

Policies that Build the Maternal Wall

Parental leave promotes parents' and children's emotional and physical health and is good for business. Longitudinal data show that longer paid leaves lower infant and child mortality, problems breastfeeding, and incidence of postpartum depression (McGovern 2011; Ogbuanu 2010). Parental leaves also decrease employee turnover (Kantor and Streitfeld 2015).[1]

Despite such positive outcomes, few universities offer paid parental leave. One survey of 168 U.S. four-year colleges and universities found that 18% of public and 34% of private schools offer paid parental leave (Yoest 2004). Public universities that offer leaves tend to emphasize research as faculty's primary duty. Thus, leave-takers risk being viewed as opportunists seeking to boost research productivity. Although U.S. women are allowed 12 weeks of unpaid time off under the Family and Medical Leave Act (FMLA), the authors have been discouraged from taking time off, encouraged to make maternity leave coincide with university breaks, and persuaded not to "stop the tenure clock" (adding time to the probationary period in a tenure track job). For example, one study found that stopping the clock raises the likelihood of achieving tenure but may decrease subsequent pay (even more drastically for men who stop the clock) (Jaschik 2012).

Our experiences suggest that academic women of color may not enjoy protection by campus policies because they are not made aware of them. Safiya, an African American woman and one of authors of this chapter, gave birth in the final year of her graduate program and learned about graduate student union provisions for leaves after graduation. Thus, she taught as a new mother while transitioning from graduate student to tenure track assistant professor. Although breastfeeding, she was not covered by FMLA or her new university's leave policy because she had not been employed the requisite twelve months.

Even before the maternal wall appears, women of color may be "presumed incompetent" (Gutiérrez y Muhs, et al. 2012). In Safiya's case, not pursuing leave options also reflected the wisdom of other African American academic mothers who counseled her that doing so may heighten perceptions about her competence. None of her African American faculty mentors took extended or unpaid leave around the birth of their children for intense fear of retribution. One faculty member reported feeling forced by her department chair to continue teaching through her delivery date against doctor's recommendations of bed rest. Safiya's African American mentors shared stories of grading papers in the hospital within hours of giving birth fearing negative student evaluations and colleagues' reprisals. Such stories underscored African American academic mothers' difficulty in taking advantage of university policies and general precarity, consistent reports from graduate students of color (Swarts 2016).

Applications of leave and tenure clock-stopping policies also strengthen maternal walls by individualizing ways of coping with motherhood. Experiences of women faculty at Penn State University (PSU), where author and White associate professor Michelle Rodino-Colocino teaches, illustrate this individualizing dynamic. Parents interviewed by PSU's Commission for Women found that despite having paid parental leave policy since 1994, decisions regarding leave tend to be local. Department heads and college deans influence leave-taking decisions above university-wide policy. Thus, some parents described a "supportive" environment that boosted their feelings of "loyalty" toward the institution, while others described the opposite (Dolberstein et al. 2010, 8). One dual-appointed mother felt "alienated" in one department whose head and faculty were older and childfree but supported by the other where faculty were parents of small children (7). This mother described how such discrepancies affect faculty leave taking at Penn State, "I'm sure there are some university-wide policies, but boy, the implementation of those has really looked different depending on who your head was and how kind of assertive they were on your behalf" (6).

The policy's wording contributes to its uneven application. Penn State's "Guideline 18 Paid Parental Leave" was designed, paradoxically, to encourage *and* limit universal application of the policy across programs: "[i]t is the intent of this guideline to provide consistency throughout the University community in granting paid parental leaves (and workload accommodations) without limiting any flexibility held by faculty and administrative heads" (see https://guru.psu.edu/policies/OHR/hrg18.html). Additionally, the policy implicitly blames those on leave for any "hard feelings" or loss of "departmental harmony" during the leave-taker's absence when it advises dividing the leave-taker's work fairly among employees to avoid such discord. Thus, the policy may also boost faculty's fear of post-leave backlash and may more strongly impact faculty of color who fear perceptions of incompetence. As the PSU report put it, "a woman who is the first in her department to request a leave may face pressures not to do so" because she fears less favorable evaluations, perceptions that she is less committed, and that she may be "cheating" by working on publications while on leave (Dolberstein et al. 2010, 8). Untenured and contingent academic mothers may be further disadvantaged by flexible, individualizing policies because professional women have also been socialized to believe that "balancing" mothering and careers is determined by individual choice. Thus, leave policies themselves may contribute to the "motherhood penalty" (Correll, Benard, and Paik 2007) and perceptions that women are on the "mommy" rather than "tenure" track.

Like leaves, "stopping the tenure clock" policies are unevenly applied. At PSU, de jure authority is central and de facto authority is local: administrators advise faculty on tenure clock-stopping decisions by interpreting university policy. The Commission on Women's report described this contradiction, "in some cases, department heads discouraged expectant faculty from stopping the tenure clock. In other departments, the department head was knowledgeable about policies for stopping the clock and submitted the required paperwork promptly" (Dolberstein 2010, 6).

Two male supervisory administrators discouraged Michelle from stopping the clock during her first year despite joining Penn State with her 6-month-old baby, lacking daycare, and breastfeeding. During her campus interview, administrators assured her that she could to stop the clock for this particular baby if she so desired. When she requested leave during her first year, however, her department-level supervisor walked her over for an impromptu meeting between the two of them and a college administrator who advised that articles accepted and published off the clock would not "count" (including one essay that had come out that year) in the tenure dossier. University policy on clock stoppage made no such stipulation. Although Michelle countered that she was not contributing to her publication pipeline that year and, thus, forecast an upcoming publication gap, the two men judged Michelle's track record up to that point as productive enough to impress tenure committees who would ask, "How does she do it"? It felt as if Michelle were being compared to a "supermom," and given Michelle's specific situation, the supervisors implied that she might appear to be asking for special treatment by stopping the clock. In contrast to such advice, male faculty in the program who became fathers or encountered health problems were offered time off the clock prior to and during Michelle's probationary period. Not realizing this and persuaded by the men's arguments, Michelle chose not to stop the clock during her first year, bore the risks of continuing, and felt the "decision" was hers to make.

Penn State's policy on clock stoppage also encouraged faculty to approach such decisions as individual choices. According to PSUs "HR 23 Promotion and Tenure Procedures and Regulations" policy, the executive vice president and provost may grant clock stoppage if they judge that a faculty member's work would be "adversely affected" by: "the responsibility as primary caregiver after the birth or adoption of a child, a serious personal illness, the provision of care for a seriously ill family member, or any similar situation." Thus, College and department administrators vet decisions before sending them to top university administrators for approval. Herein lies the wiggle room that allows for some faculty women to gain support in meeting demands of work and motherhood.

Michelle appreciates the work of colleague and faculty mother Esther Prins, who chaired a PSU faculty senate committee to improve clock stoppage policy. New language allows up to two years instead of one year, makes foster parents explicitly eligible, and requires that evaluation committees and external reviewers be explicitly directed to judge candidates for their record during the number of years on the clock without holding them to higher standards. If applied evenly, this new policy change may, indeed, decrease the maternal wall for faculty mothers by reducing risks of clock stoppage.

The experiences of two chapter authors suggest that taking time out to have a baby and tend to a sick child may prove especially alienating at teaching-intensive comprehensive regional universities, where, unlike research-heavy ones, a culture of presence prevails. When Molly, author and White assistant professor, took advantage of FMLA leave policy during her first year at a tenure track job, she felt punished. As soon as she announced her pregnancy, she dealt with bureaucratic confusion that continued before, during, and after her leave. She took 12 weeks of unpaid FMLA leave. Supervisors told her that she was among the first faculty to take a leave for childbirth. At first, she was asked to find her teaching replacement for the 12 weeks. This work proved difficult because the leave of absence was 12 weeks, but the semester was 15. After learning that she was expected to resume teaching for the semester's final three weeks, Molly was able to negotiate extra service assignments in lieu of an awkward return to the classroom.

Making matters worse, she faced the "catch-22" of working on leave but being informed that university policy stipulated that work on unpaid leave could not be included in her first tenure portfolio, which was due only weeks after her return. While on leave, Molly clearly worked: she advised students, attended faculty meetings, and presented research to the department and at conferences, where she won a top paper award. After being denied a request to postpone the review, she submitted her portfolio (with only three weeks of paid work time to report), making sure to detail, as requested by the university, "what she accomplished" over her "break." Unsure of how (and if) her achievements would be evaluated, Molly was given mediocre evaluations for teaching and service (the third lowest ranking out of four or one above possible termination). When she asked why she received this evaluation, supervisors explained that she had not performed teaching duties and only had a few weeks of service assignments. There was no palatable decision to make here: the leave meant less of her work "counted" but not taking it would have made balancing working and mothering impossible. This faculty member hit the maternal wall and was left alone to figure her way up and over it.

Worried about the confusion over her first year, Molly decided it was in her best interest to submit paperwork to stop her tenure clock. This action created even more confusion, because her department's annual review committee asked her to remove accomplishments from her first year because some had interpreted "stopping" the clock as "discounting" accomplishments (Michelle was told something similar). The matter was finally resolved after a formal grievance was filed with her faculty union. The grievance was decided in her favor, and she was, indeed, told that all of her accomplishments "counted" whether or not she stopped the clock. This story is one of many wherein unions are critically important in providing legal protections for faculty.

Additional challenges face faculty mothers where faculty are required to be present four full days per week. This aspect of the culture of presence proves difficult for pregnancy and parental leave. Christine, author and White associate professor, was required to submit her campus attendance record to the university (a regional teaching-intensive university, with a 4–4 teaching load). Sick leave policies allowed for excused faculty absences (1.25 allotted sick days per month could accumulate and be traded for paid sick leave). Accumulating "sick days," however, proves difficult because working from home, on weekends, and around-the-clock before children rise does not count as presence. Christine worked for one year before a pregnancy, but between needing to use sick days for tending an ill toddler and for prenatal exams (in a hospital located in a neighboring town), she accrued only ten days of "paid parental leave." While on her paltry leave, one university official phoned her at the hospital two hours after she gave birth (on a Saturday) to ask how her class would be covered the following Monday. For the two weeks of her "paid leave" (expanded by deferring sick days), Christine worked. Although she found colleagues to cover some classes, she arranged to have student presentations videotaped to avoid burdening overworked colleagues. Her typical day involved sitting in bed, recovering from a difficult pregnancy and birth, nursing her newborn, tending to a 3 year old, grading students' presentations and final exams, and figuring final grades. Christine seemed a supermom, indeed.

Such stories may partially account for gender pay inequity in the U.S. where women faculty earn on average 77% of male faculty's pay. This pay gap is further complicated when rank and institution are included: fewer women are promoted to full professor rank, awarded endowed chairs, and named to upper administration positions. Additionally, men are overrepresented at higher-prestige and higher-paying universities, whereas women are disproportionately visible at two-year colleges and other lower-paying institutions (Newman 2014). Moreover, women are often punished with lower pay and promotion following the request for a leave of absence. One study demonstrated that academic mothers accumulate 29% less than do men in their retirement fund due to parenting leaves and responsibilities—with each child further reducing her lifetime pay (Mason 2013).

The maternal wall may also present in subtle ways. For example, at regional universities student evaluations are influential in renewal, tenure, and promotion decisions. When Christine was pregnant with one of her children, she received anonymous course evaluations commenting on her pregnancy. Several students wrote, "good luck with the baby," which, on the surface, symbolizes kindness and support. She interpreted the comments as such but also noted that they documented her pregnancy in her teaching portfolio. More troubling was one student's insidious claims that Dr. Quail had "gotten fat" and was using the pregnancy to hide weight gain. It is difficult, still, to unpack these problematic statements. Of immediate concern was how her pregnant body became a source of student evaluation and whether that evaluation would negatively impact renewal decisions. Thankfully administrators strongly supported her, and she assumed that they would not interpret this student's remark as a credible evaluation. Nevertheless, having her pregnancy become part of the teaching dossier speaks to the ways in which pregnant bodies' public visibility and source of public comment can constitute a hidden element of the maternal wall.

The maternal wall also blocks women on the job market. Each time Christine searched for faculty jobs she had an infant. When a breastfeeding mother of a small infant has two-day long interviews, capped on either end by travel, the physical demands are significant. Like Safiya's mentors, Christine's mentors advised her not to ask for additional breaks, because the stakes are too high to risk seeming "needy." Thus, Christine (and Safiya) experienced significant physical discomfort, rushing through interview dinners to express breast milk discreetly in the bathroom or hotel. Michelle had a positive experience interviewing while 8½ months pregnant for a job she accepted at Penn State. Although no one asked her about her pregnancy during her campus visit, she told the search chair ahead of time. He showed support by scheduling the interview far enough before her due date for travel. Michelle took bathroom breaks without reprisal.

Breaking Through the Maternal Wall

The authors have found resources to scale the maternal wall. We feel indebted to our unions, administrators, mentors, and informants. The maternal wall is a labor issue. Thus, Molly's union played a pivotal role in her scaling it when her union's grievance officer helped determine materials to include in her tenure portfolio post-leave.

Administrators are also critical for creating and fostering family-friendly work environments in which all faculty and students benefit. At Penn State, Michelle enjoyed support from her department head to reduce new course preparations after her third semester, locking her into a 2-2 (two sections of the same course per semester) schedule that opened up time for her to publish. Michelle also received useful advice about how to interpret student evaluation comments that she breastfed in her office (advice she received from colleagues was to proceed with work as usual and brush off the comments). Informal conversations with faculty and administrators proved valuable to Michelle's ability to form strategies and sustain the energy needed to push through the wall. After receiving a formal evaluation that noted her paltry publication pipeline, one senior colleague at Penn State advised, "just keep doing what you are doing" and gaps in her publication record would be outweighed by publications submitted during year two. Michelle's experience underscores the importance of hiring leadership supportive of family-friendly practices.

Mentors are also key. Molly appreciated support from fellow faculty mothers, one of whom is an amazing professor and single mother of four who spoke up when she thought Molly experienced discrimination because of her maternal status. Michelle also credits surviving the probationary years to early support for her pregnancy among colleagues at the University of Cincinnati, where Michelle worked for three years as tenure track faculty. In her last year there, she became pregnant and had her baby. Upon learning of her pregnancy, she received a large office to accommodate a mobile playpen for her newborn child. Women faculty across ranks poured out of the woodwork to assure Michelle that she would be able to stop the tenure clock to accommodate time lost while recovering from labor and mothering. One colleague promised to help her pump (calling herself "the pumping queen"). Still ringing in Michelle's ears is the advice of one senior faculty mother about negotiating unexpected work/motherhood conflict: "Sometimes you punt." These microencouragements and structural supports proved invaluable in enabling Michelle and Molly to surmount the wall.

Some faculty are lucky enough to enjoy supportive on-campus daycare with hours that enable long workdays. In Michelle's case, the Bennett Family Center (BFC) at Penn State, with hours from 7:30 a.m. to 6:00 p.m., proved invaluable for supporting the long workdays necessary for achieving tenure. Although the care center is also the most expensive in town, Michelle and her family viewed the cost as worth the experience and were fortunate to afford it. In addition to its convenient campus location, BFC administrators conducted research recognized for instilling best practices in early childhood development. Although Michelle's child was waitlisted until she was 2 years old, another center cared for her when she turned 1 during Michelle's second semester at Penn State. Similarly, Christine enjoyed university-affiliated daycare. When two of her four courses were scheduled in the evening, Christine was fortunate to find a caregiver employed by the same university-affiliated center so that her family enjoyed consistency of care. Molly used state subsidies to pay for childcare that enabled her to finish her Ph.D. Unfortunately, these benefits are on the chopping block in many states, but our experiences suggest they should be expanded.

The demands of tenure production also require faculty to work beyond daycare hours; thus, supportive family and friends can ease childcare burdens to help tenure seekers work around the clock. Molly and Safiya thank family who minded their children while they finished their Ph.D.'s. Christine's supportive neighbors tended to her children when classes started prior to the children's schooldays, and she traded in-home childcare with another faculty mom. Michelle and Safiya credit their partners, parents, and friends for enabling long work hours by minding children and partners who assumed most household duties. Earning a high enough household income allowed for Michelle's family to purchase a house with a home office, where she could immerse herself in writing before the rest of the family awoke. Michelle's first semester at Penn State with an infant without daycare was especially challenging but survivable because she found a babysitter who met her with the baby at her classroom's door. We are grateful for support networks, which may be non-existent for tenure track faculty who move away from such networks because of job scarcity.

Mothers, Not Others

Entirely eradicating the maternal wall requires support from campus administrators, collective faculty action, and cultural shifts. We arrive at this conclusion because we realize our daily work in scaling the maternal wall has been draining, risky, and never ending. We credit our significant labor and luck for surviving in the academy thus far (the labor and luck of finding supportive faculty, administrators, babysitters, daycare, spouses, and friends who support our tenure aspirations). Rather than deem the burden of scaling the maternal wall as an individual faculty member's to bear, however, we view the maternal wall first as a leadership issue. It is one in which university presidents, provosts, deans, and department chairs should commit to smashing through supportive policies and their even application.

We also call for academic labor movements to mobilize against the maternal wall. Academic labor unions and associations like the American Association of University Professors (AAUP) support model leave and clock-stopping policies.[2] Academic labor movements should also form coalitions to secure broader policy change that specifies mothers as a protected group needing equal opportunity protection. Because women of color face an even higher maternal wall than do White women, intersectional coalitions among anti-racist, LGBTQ (lesbian, gay, bisexual, transgender, and queer), differently abled, and workers' rights groups is key.

Ensuring that faculty mothers are not oppressed "others" may also require that administrators and activists use Title IX to pursue equal access to employment. Given recent campus policy changes following federally mandated anti-sexual assault policies at U.S. college campuses, the authors view Title IX as a useful tool toppling the maternal wall (Bishop 2015).

To make broader social change, it is important to connect with non-academic parents and in solidarity with caregivers (e.g., with individuals giving eldercare). If parenting and care were treated as human rights (i.e., the right to parent, the right to give care), as they are in other countries, then institutions and unions would enjoy support of broader social policies such as extended federally mandated leaves, monthly child benefits, and affordable, accessible daycare. In Canada, for example, federal mandates guarantee longer leaves, split parental leaves, a universal paid child benefit to the parent of each child under 7 years old, and income-dependent monthly benefits paid at a sliding scale. McMaster University in Canada, where Christine now works, awarded a flat raise to every woman faculty member after a campus-wide study found pay inequity. While this is certainly a step in the right direction, much more needs to be done to eradicate the maternal wall in Canada (and to McMaster's credit, continuing studies are underway).

Finally, razing the maternal wall requires that academics reconsider the quantity of work demanded of tenure track faculty who, like mothers, are expected to "do it all" on a shift that seems endless. Faculty at state-funded universities may feel additional pressure to produce as state budget cuts have meant hiring freezes, job creep, growing class sizes, teaching loads, and taking on additional administrative duties (Gardner et al. 2014). In this climate, faculty and administrators should rethink tenure demands that overwork faculty. Knocking down the maternal wall should make room for life outside of work, instead of only opening more time for ever-growing work demands.

In ways big and small, administrators, activists, and policy makers must unite to smash the maternal wall.

Notes

1   https://www.nytimes.com/2015/09/02/upshot/big-leaps-for-parental-leave-if-workers-actually-follow-through.html?_r=0.
2   See www.aaup.org/issues/women-academic-profession; www.aaup.org/issues/balancing-family-academic-work.

References

"Balancing Family & Academic Work." (n.d.). AAUP.org. www.aaup.org/issues/balancing-family-aca demic-work.

Bishop, Tyer. (September 11, 2015). "The Laws Targeting Campus Rape Culture." *The Atlantic*. www.theat lantic.com/education/archive/2015/09/the-laws-targeting-campus-rape-culture/404824/.

Cockburn, Cynthia. (1991). *In the Way of Women: Men's Resistance to Sex Equality in Organizations*. Ithaca, NY: Cornell University Press.

Collins, Patricia Hill. (2012). *Black Feminist Thought: Knowledge, Consciousness, and the Politics of Empowerment*, 2nd ed. New York: Routledge.

Correll, Shelley J., Stephen Benard, and In Paik. (2007). "Getting a Job: Is There a Motherhood Penalty?" *American Journal of Sociology*, 112 (5): 1297–1339.

Cowan, Ruth Schwartz. (1983). *More Work for Mother: The Ironies of Household Technology from the Open Hearth to the Microwave*. New York: Basic Books.

Dolberstein, Melissa, Kelly D. Davis, Barbara Schaefer, and Auden Thomas. (2010). *Work Family Balance at Penn State*. http://equity.psu.edu/cfw/docs/work_family_balance_psu_09.pdf.

Douglas, Susan J., and Meredith W. Michaels. (2004). *The Mommy Myth: The Idealization of Motherhood and How It has Undermined Women*. New York: Free Press.

Gardner, Susan K., Amy Blackstone, Shannon K. McCoy, and Daniela Véliz. (2014). "The Effect of State Budget Cuts on Department Climate." *AAUP.org*. www.aaup.org/article/effect-state-budget-cuts-department-climate#.V0iKLJMrL-Y.

Gutiérrez y Muhs, Gabriella, Yolanda Flores Niemann, Carmen G. Gonzalez, and Angela P. Harris. (2012). *Presumed Incompetent: The Intersections of Race and Class for Women in Academia*. Boulder: University of Colorado.

Hunt, A. N. (2015). "The Role of Theory in Understanding the Lived Experiences of Mothering in the Academy." In *Teacher, Scholar, Mother: Re-Envisioning Motherhood in the Academy*, edited by Anna M. Young, 3–12. Lanham: Lexington Books.

Jaschik, S. (June 14, 2012). "A Stop the Clock Penalty." *Inside Higher Ed*. www.insidehighered.com/news/2012/06/14/study-finds-those-who-stop-tenure-clock-earn-less-those-who-don't.

Lubrano, Sarah C. Stein. (October 31, 2012). "Tenure and Gender." *The Harvard Crimson*. www.thecrimson.com/column/exodoxa/article/2012/10/31/gender-tenure-women-professors/.

MacFarlane, Alexandria. (April 19, 2012). "Gender Gap Persists Among Tenured Faculty." *The Brown Daily Herald*. www.browndailyherald.com/2012/04/19/gender-gap-persists-among-tenured-faculty/.

McGovern, Patricia, Rada K. Dagher, Heidi Roeber Rice, Dwenda Gjerdingen, Bryan Dowd, Laurie K. Ukestad, and Ulf Lundberg. (2011). "A Longitudinal Analysis of Total Workload and Women's Health after Childbirth." *Journal of Occupational and Environmental Medicine*, 53 (5): 497–505.

Mason, Mary Ann. (June 17, 2013). "In the Ivory Tower, Men Only." *Slate*. www.slate.com/articles/dou ble_x/doublex/2013/06/female_academics_pay_a_heavy_baby_penalty.html.

Miller, Claire Cain. (September 6, 2014). "The Motherhood Penalty vs. the Fatherhood Bonus." *New York Times*. www.nytimes.com/2014/09/07/upshot/a-child-helps-your-career-if-youre-a-man.html?_r=0.

Newman, Jonah. (April 11, 2014). "There Is a Gender Pay Gap in Academe But It May Not Be the Gap That Matters." *Chronicle of Higher Education*. http://chronicle.com/blogs/data/2014/04/11/there-is-a-gender-pay-gap-in-academe-but-it-may-not-be-the-gap-that-matters/.

Ogbuanu, C., S. Glover, J. Probst, J. Liu, and J. Hussey. (2011). "The Effect of Maternity Leave Length and Time of Return to Work on Breastfeeding." *Pediatrics*, 127 (6), 114–127.

Steiger, Kay. (July 11, 2013). "The Pink Collar Workforce of Academia." *The Nation*. www.thenation.com/article/academias-pink-collar-workforce/.

Swarts, Susan E. (2016). "Socialization Experiences of Doctoral Student Mothers: 'Outsiders in the Sacred Grove' Redux." Dissertation submitted to the University of California, Los Angeles.

Williams, Joan C., and Rachel Dempsey. (2014). *What Works for Women at Work: Four Patterns Working Women Need to Know*. New York: New York University Press.

Williams, Joan C. and Nancy Segal. (2003). "Beyond the Maternal Wall: Relief for Family Caregivers Who Are Discriminated Against on the Job." *Harvard Women's Law Journal*, 26: 77.

"Women in the Academic Profession." (n.d.). AAUP.org. www.aaup.org/issues/women-academic-profession.

Yoest, Charmaine, and Steven E. Rhoads. (2004). "Parental Leave in Academia." Report to the Alfred P. Sloan Foundation and the Bankard Fund at the University of Virginia. www.faculty.virginia.edu/family andtenure/institutional%20report.pdf.

21 Motherhood and Leadership in Academia

Getting Beyond Personal Survival Mode

Diane M. Hodge

The "personal is political" is not just the rallying cry of the second wave feminist movement; it's been my mantra every day since graduate school. I keep telling myself this simple truth because I still believe it holds the key to change in the academy. Very little has changed in the 25 years since I started my journey in higher education, a journey that has been lonely, yet universal. My story of surviving in the academy is not unique, but in providing this autoethnography, I demonstrate how my personal became political and continues to inform the changes I am making in the academy for mothers. Motherhood, in my experience, intensified both the individual and institutional sexism that I've experienced, given the complex interplay between social expectations of motherhood with outdated work expectations. Mothers remain less likely to stay in full-time employment, are paid even less than single women, and are overall undervalued in the workplace (Crittenden 2001; Dominici, Fried, and Zeger 2009; Mason 2013). It's time to bring some grassroots change to allow mothers to not just survive but also thrive in the academy. If more women are to become academic leaders, we not only have to get them into the academy but also keep them there, particularly through one of the toughest periods of time for women, the pre-tenure/ motherhood years.

My Experience in the Academy

It is sadly ironic that I decided to get my doctorate in social work and have a career in higher education because of how difficult it was working full time as a social worker in the direct practice field. I was on call, had to be flexible in dealing with crisis situations, worked long hours, and received low pay. How could I possibly have children with hours like this? Academia seemed like the perfect career choice. Not only did I love being a student but also teaching had comparable work hours and breaks with children's schools and professors seemed to have flexible day hours, good pay, and stimulating work. As a child of the 1970s feminist movement, I never considered not working when I had children, and work was a necessity. Growing up on a farm with a mother who was not "allowed" to work, I knew I would need a career to have my own money and maintain my independence and equality. My journey through doctoral studies also began my own feminist journey. Both were eye opening.

Clearly, I was naïve and not prepared for the struggle to begin before I was even accepted into a doctoral program. My interview at one doctoral program was apparently to ascertain my commitment to doctoral work because, I was told, some faculty members were concerned that I would just get married, have kids, and not stay in the program, let alone stay in the academy. Why provide the support for study to someone who was not going to make it anyway? When I was finally accepted into a doctoral program, it was because another woman had dropped out just before starting and I was able to enroll on short notice. I was told point blank that the program was willing to "take a chance" on me. Once admitted, I continued to find everyday sexism, both overt and covert. Comments were made about my appearance, I was denied opportunities for financial support because I "probably had support from my parents or boyfriend," and I endured criticisms that my dissertation topic was "not scholarly" (qualitative research on depressed young women). Through feminist mentors who provided role modeling and readings (Hochschild 1989; Mason 1992; Petchers 1996; Crittenden 2001), I started to connect the realities of sexism to my own life. One mentor reminded me that the bigger the perceived threat to the status quo, the more sexism I would face. She would know. I lost female mentors every year while working on my doctorate as those women did not make tenure themselves, losing valuable support and time in completing my own dissertation.

I managed to forge ahead and complete my doctorate, only to find that the academic job market also questioned my commitment to the academy. I stopped wearing my wedding rings to interviews and ignored questions about future children, when I managed to get an interview. One interview, by a senior woman faculty member no less, ended the minute I walked in the door. All she could say was "Honey, you're so young, these boys will eat you alive and you'll never get tenure." That was it. After two years on the job market, I finally obtained a tenure track position at a comprehensive university for relatively low pay.

By the end of my first year teaching, I was 33 years old and ready to start a family. Seeking advice, I was surprised that my female director suggested I "plan" for having children during the summer, as it would be less disruptive to my work and the department. She also noted that the university did not provide formal maternity leave so I should not expect anything beyond documented sick leave. Unfortunately for me, it was not an uneventful pregnancy, and I struggled with complications and exhaustion while trying to keep up at work. My son was born in mid-June and despite additional birth complications, I was told to report by mid-August with no considerations for my health or the need to breastfeed. I went straight back to teaching mostly night classes, pumping breast milk in my office on breaks, and being pushed to provide more committee service as I struggled to make tenure. Perhaps due to my exhaustion, I did what I had to do without asking permission or apologizing: I often brought my child to work (setting up a playpen in my office), ate snacks at meetings, and asked to be phoned into meetings so I could breastfeed. Either no one had the audacity to question me or they were afraid to appear unsympathetic. There was, after all, no real precedence or support at my university. It would be years later that Mason, Wolfinger, and Goulden (2013) would document the research of this same experience of making decisions about family formation on the basis of the needs of an academic career. Mason (2013) also notes that family formation negatively affects women's but not men's academic careers, as more women elect to work in "second-tier" academia (part-time, adjunct, non-tenure). Either way, having children has the biggest effect on whether women stay in the academy.

The struggle didn't stop with my work schedule. Half of my take-home pay went to daycare. I tried to rely on my spouse more, but he was also dealing with the entrenched roles/sexism at his work while also working toward tenure and promotion. Two years later, I was pregnant again, but this time, I had a crushing miscarriage during university final's week. There was no acknowledgment of my loss at work, but the loss heightened my resolve to get pregnant with a second child on my own schedule. This time, I was fortunate to have a new department head who supported me as much as she could, but because of the timing, I had to again report after only eight weeks while still recovering from a second cesarean. I had no idea how I was going to manage this time, so I looked to anything I could cling to: working mother–type magazines and books (Blades and Rowe-Finkbeiner 2006; Evans 2006; Mason and Mason 2007), academic research on the topic (Young and Wright 2001; William 2004), and wiser colleagues. No matter what I did, every day left me with a sense of *Sophie's Choice*: do I stay with a sick child or go into work; attend a child's soccer practice or work on a manuscript; leave the family to attend a conference or risk the lack of networking? When I was finally ready to apply for tenure and promotion, I was struck that a few senior male colleagues were hesitant to support my application, with one noting that I should "take motherhood more seriously."

I thought I had made it once I was tenured and promoted, yet I still struggled for work–life balance. I did my work after my children were in bed, stayed very organized, made schedules, and tried to negotiate work and family time with a spouse also on the tenure track. However, I ended up disregarding my own desires, health, and emotional well-being. The constant work at the university and at home played into my decision to not have a third child, sadly referred to as the "career killer" (Chávez-García 2009). Mason, Wolfinger, and Goulden's (2013) research was my reality: my career was making the decisions for my life. I was surviving, not thriving. Most of the academic men had stay-at-home wives such that few understood that any unexpected illness or schedule change was a crisis at my home: sudden snow days declared with no alternative childcare, getting a sick child to the pediatrician when both of us had classes to teach, or exhausting weekends with children's soccer practice. Seeking some consideration and assistance, I was told to get stress management, find more back-up help, stop taking time to cook dinners or clean, leave kids in daycare ten hours a day—anything to not disrupt work. This was the height of the "mommy wars" and "supermom" labeling, so working meant that I had to figure out how to "have it all."

At that time, Bennets (2007) wrote eloquently on women giving up too much for work, and I refused to give up everything in the name of work. Then and now, it is not actually a choice for many mothers who can't afford housekeeping, meal service, the best childcare. Yet the notion of choice continues to be used to justify impossible hours, low pay, lack of advancement, forced choices about limiting the number of children, and leadership opportunities. Not working means long-term consequences of less retirement money and difficulty in returning to the job market when children were older. As Slaughter (2012) notes, there are many "half-truths" that surround "having it all. In my case, it was not that I was not committed or didn't have the right spouse or didn't sequence my life; it was because working academic mothers are stuck in a system that has not evolved.

Perhaps it should not have been a surprise to be diagnosed with cancer at age 45. I took one semester off for treatment and reflection. I had been pushed to the point of wanting to leave the academy altogether despite making it to full tenured professor status and even completing a year as the interim director for the department. I had already declined staying on in the position of leadership solely because I was "burned out" and the expectations for the position versus the realities of being a mother in the academy were unchanged in the last 15 years. I realized that I needed to return to my social work roots and "be the change I wanted to see in the world." Five years later, I had another chance to be the department head and I took it, not because of changes in the institution, but because I wanted to make institutional changes and the position would allow me to do that. With now 20 years of experience in the academy, I still do not have all the answers on how to get beyond a daily struggle of surviving as a mother in the academy, but I want to share what I have been able to do.

Leading for Change

Having survived in the academy, I am slowly moving toward thriving in it. As a woman, mother, social worker, and professor, I bring my experiences and understandings to the academy. My personal is political. While I continue to contend with sexist assumptions and expectations of mothers, I feel empowered. With at least 25 years of research and discussion about mothers in the academy, it is clear that we need to just do the hard work of change, using the proposed solutions that have been suggested by many (Slaughter 2015). After the long struggle to leadership, I can no longer wait on sweeping legislative change, policy enforcement, fair pay, or social/conscious/structural change from peers and the academy. I am making my own grassroots changes, modeling those changes for other department heads, and documenting the results of what it means to provide feminist leadership and a supportive academic environment to mothers. I did not plan for a leadership position in the academy, but I want to be in the system making incremental changes rather than dropping out or sitting back hoping the work environment will change someday.

My leadership has been questioned to the extent of being offered leadership conferences to attend so I can "learn" to be a leader, as if there is only one way to lead. I start there, by challenging one model of leadership, one path through the academy. I also continue to work on the mythical work–life balance, while realizing that everyone working for me will have different ideas and solutions for their work–life balance. But I've consciously stopped reinforcing individual blame/solutions, as if there is the holy grail of a skill set that will magically make work and life more balanced for everyone. For me, I still keep up that family calendar, but I accept my limitations; I have my personal stress relievers, but I also advocate for the "political" and making of institutional changes for university childcare, summer funding, stopping the tenure clock, increasing salaries every chance possible, supporting flexibility and diversity, and addressing discrimination when I see it. There are many ways to provide leadership to implement strategies for change.

Transitions and Options

To make any change in the academy that promotes mothers staying in the academy and promotes female leadership requires that we first need to keep women from leaving the academy. Without their voices on the issues that affect them the most, talking about their experiences and perspectives, mentoring and supporting others in the academy, there is little incentive to consider the needs of mothers. The overall academic environment has been slow to change in encouraging women and mothers to stay in the academy, such that we have been hemorrhaging women at all levels of the academy for many years (Slaughter 2015). Dominici, Fried, and Zeger (2009), among others, have already noted sufficient evidence of low salaries, low rank, slow promotion, low retention, and less recognition for mothers in the academy. For being the supposed supporters of liberal thinking, those in the academia have been some of the least progressive, least supportive employers for working women (Mason 2013).

Mason (1992) found, almost 25 years ago, that Title VII failed moms in the workplace because, while women did not want special treatment, there was no alternative to the male work model of short and narrow career paths in the academy, not even in female-dominated professions. Consequently, Wolfinger, Mason, and Goulden (2009) suggested "sequencing of transitions," such that there could be multiple trajectories or career paths toward tenure and promotion. Traditional paths in academe provide no alternatives or flexibility in transitions or the timing of those transitions, yet the academy has evolved into using more adjuncts, part-time faculty, and limited contracts for faculty with most of these positions now filled by women. Why can't these positions also count toward tenure and promotion? I have several women on my faculty who started in non-tenured positions that were converted later to tenure track positions. They were allowed to count their time working in non-tenured positions toward tenure. Other faculty changed positions after they were supported in getting their doctorates while working for the department, what we refer to as "growing your own." Likewise, colleagues working in temporary or part-time positions often moved toward permanent and full-time positions once they could ramp up their work hours. Having the department be flexible about hours and positions made those faculty more likely to stay, to be part of the team, and to be self-motivated on the job. Investing in workers through their transitions provided needed stability in my department and it certainly can work in the academy as a whole.

Mentoring and Supporting Leadership

Few women are specifically recruited for administrative ranks, and women presidents especially are less likely to be married or have children (Mason 2009). Klein (2010) found that the lack of female leadership results in a lack of female voices on research agendas and a shortage of role models. While there has been more leadership training aimed at women in the academy, what is actually being taught about leadership? Are women leaders being trained to accept the status quo or mute their own voices (Anyikwa et al. 2015)? Like tenure lines, leadership in the academy does not need to be so narrowly defined and of a single model. Accepting of multiple forms of leadership would encourage more women to take these positions. Placing value on caring and emotional intelligence, along with the ability to delegate, coordinate, prioritize, and be efficient are qualities that are enhanced with motherhood (Ellison 2006). Models, such as Jean Baker Miller's Cultural-Relational model, recognize the need for relational understandings in the workplace (Anyikwa et al. 2015). Training on feminist leadership would encourage more women to value the wisdom that comes from motherhood and encourage them to take leadership positions using their own voice. Likewise, making those leadership positions more attractive by allowing for greater flexibility of hours and tangible support could encourage more mothers to "lean in" (Sandberg 2013). While women in the academy may experience less respect as leaders or be left out of informal networking, I've sought out other women leaders on campus and at other universities to informally network on my own. I make it a priority to sit on committees that work to improve the climate for women on campus. That camaraderie and sharing of experiences remain one of the most rejuvenating ways to motivate me for leadership and change. Now when I am asked about my leadership style, I use a play on *All I Really Need to Know I Learned in Kindergarten* (Fulghum 2004): all I really need to know about leadership I learned from motherhood. Delegating, prioritizing, multitasking, role modeling, and mediating have been developed skills. Ellison (2006) notes the positives of having a "mommy brain"—an increase in caring, perception, efficiency, motivation, resiliency, and emotional intelligence—all necessary leadership skills. Likewise, Slaughter (2015) makes the analogy that workplaces celebrate marathon runners for their abilities but fail to recognize mothers for similar abilities to organize, prioritize, and work beyond exhaustion.

Maternal Wall

To keep women in the pipeline for the profession and moving toward leadership, how do we deal specifically with the "maternal wall"? Williams (2004) uses the term "maternal wall" to point out the specific bias that mothers encounter. Some of that bias includes negative competency assumptions that are thought to be due to pregnancy (being irrational, overly emotional), problems around maternity leave (or lack of it), and returning to work with additional needs, such as breastfeeding and childcare. Other *attributional biases* are made about mothers that range from assumptions that any time at home is spent caring for children to being poor mothers if one works long hours (Williams 2004). Women end up caught between the ideal worker who works 60 hours per week and the ideal mother who is always available for her children. In addition, there is a benevolent assumption that a mother does not want to serve on too many committees, travel, or do summer teaching/research. It is one thing to be thoughtful, but it is another to limit opportunities. The simple solution, of course, is to just ask! In my experience, many of those mothers had already made childcare plans to accommodate extra work or were traveling to conferences where extended family lived. Assumptions do not just affect work options but Mason (2009) also notes that motherhood is the "single most important factor in explaining the wage differential between men and women" (para. 14).

Family Care

How do we get past perceptions and assumptions about parenting? It is particularly difficult when childless faculty, who may be asked to cover workloads for new mothers, are set up to resent anything that appears to advantage mothers: family paid leave, flexible career tracks, and childcare assistance. Crittenden (2001) writes that "the gift of care can be both selfless and exploited" (8). And with women providing the majority of family care, all women could benefit from greater flexibility in the academy for providing care. Types of caretaking, whether providing for childcare, care of elderly parents, or even care of pets, need to be an accepted reason to be away from work. To have a sense of work–life balance for everyone, the academy needs to provide time for care to anyone and not marginalize it as a motherhood issue.

When everyone feels that their priority to care is respected, colleagues are less likely to grumble about helping to cover classes or committee work. It is, therefore, crucial to include men/fathers who also want work–life balance to care for family members. As Leonard (2013) points out, the suggestion that men are not doing their share of parenting or caring just takes the focus off the academy and how institutions fail all families. Slaughter (2015) suggests a need to build an "infrastructure of care" such that daycare, eldercare, paid family and medical leave, and part-time/flex work is available to all workers. As a director, I think it is critical to provide as much support for colleagues providing care as possible and to develop a team sense of caring so that everyone feels that they can provide care when they need to with no penalty.

Travel

Traveling to conferences is an expectation in the academy. But traveling when you have children creates many issues not addressed by the academy. Recently, Jaschik (2015) shared issues with bringing children to conferences, and Harris (2015) noted the lack or expense of childcare at conferences. Social work, a field significantly more female dominated, has failed to address these issues at major conferences. I have personally voiced my concern that conferences have been scheduled during holidays and at non-family friendly venues. On the other hand, computer science, a male-dominated field, has provided childcare/kid camp, child events, and family tours at major professional conferences in an effort to attract more women to the conferences.[1] Clearly, if it is a priority, changes can be made.

Similarly, problems with not bringing children to long conferences are not addressed, such as issues of pumping breast milk (refrigeration, equipment, TSA rules) or the amount of prepping of meals, taking care of appointments, and childcare prior to going to a conference, particularly if one is a single parent. Given these considerations and the increasing cost of travel, my department has reconsidered travel requirements, allowing faculty to attend interdisciplinary conferences rather than social work–only conferences. We also share information on conferences that are family friendly. I also encourage mothers to get on conference boards to add their voice. We could also reconsider how critical is travel in the academy. With Skype, conference calling, Google docs, and other technology, the need to travel extensively seems unnecessary. In my department, we value local presentations, community presentations, and local conferences for tenure and promotion. As a comprehensive university, we are expected to have a community focus so our work in the community should be valued as much as national presentations.

Work Schedules

Working long and varied hours in the academy has been a long-standing issue for mothers. Flaherty (2014) recently found that professors are working 61-hour weeks, 10-hour days, with additional research on weekends. Students and university administration expect emails to be answered within 24 hours, such that those in the academy are now on call all day, every day. Teaching has become 24/7 as online courses blur boundaries even more. While Slaughter (2015) notes that work doesn't happen from just 8 to 5, it is constant for academics. I do agree with her that this makes it impossible to work in the 21st century and that this "culture of overwork" is not just a woman's or mother's problem.

The Society for Human Resource Management (2008) found almost 10 years ago that slowness to change may be due to perceived cost or difficulty. There has been a fear that people will take advantage of flex time or compete for days off. This has not been my experience; flexible schedules have provided better coverage time in our department as classes run all day, six days a week, on two campuses. Faculty request the schedule and classes that work best for them, and when accommodated, they have greater productivity and increased moral and retention. This is particularly helpful for mothers who want to schedule classes when their children are in school or daycare. In my experience, working mothers are more likely to work in the mornings when children are in school and work over winter breaks when children are back in school while universities are still closed. Many other faculty in my department prefer teaching in the evenings or on weekends. Both are greatly needed and equally appreciated. Assumptions about mothers being the only ones needing flexible hours mask the wider issue of gender discrimination, whereby all women are disadvantaged by a workplace that recognizes only an ideal worker. Similarly, Gunn (2013) suggests that flexible time options may keep women from moving up because of the stigma of a "mommy track." I think we have had this fear of segregated work, but given the never-ending requirements of work, flexibility is something that is not gender based. Promoting true flexibility in hours, committee assignments, meetings, and teaching schedules has to become the norm for everyone (Wolfinger, Mason, and Goulden 2009).

Conclusion

We need to change the conversation when it comes to motherhood and leadership in the academy. Beyond what mothers need to thrive in academia, we need to talk about what they bring to the institution. As a mother of two, and as a school director, I know that my colleagues who are mothers don't sleep in, ever. They are up every day, every weekend caring for their families and, yes, working. They work irregular hours around everyone else's needs. They work through academic breaks, they are usually the first ones at work in the morning, and they are ones who are focused and socialize less because they know they have to be productive while they are at work. They bring their mothering skills of efficiency, negotiating, finding solutions, and recognizing individual strengths. Mothers bring an awareness and commitment to their work that needs to be more valued in academia and not looked at as a deficit. Small changes in how we work and our expectations will encourage more mothers to remain in the academy and take positions of leadership, changing the work environment for everyone to have a better work–life balance.

Note

1   Other examples include the American Historical Association, Conference on College Composition and Communication, and Modern Language Association's provision of childcare grants, and the American Sociological Association and American Political Science Association's provision of childcare on-site.

References

Anyikwa, Victoria A., Christina Chiarelli-Helminiak, Diane M. Hodge, Rhonda Wells-Wilbon. (2015). "Women Empowering Women." *Journal of Social Work Education*, 15 (4): 723–737.

Bennets, Leslie. (2007). *The Feminine Mistake: Are We Giving Up Too Much?* Voice.

Blades, Joan and Kristin Rowe-Finkbeiner. (2006). *The Motherhood Manifesto*. New York: Nation Books.

Chávez-García, Miroslava. (September 28, 2009). "Superprofessor Meets Supermom." *The Chronicle of Higher Education*. http://chronicle.com/article/Superprofessor-Meets-Supermom/48613/.

Crittenden, Anne. (2001). *The Price of Motherhood: Why the Most Important Job in the World Is Still the Least Valued*. New York: Metropolitan Books.

Dominici, Francesca, Fried, Linda P., and Scott L. Zeger. (July-August, 2009). "So Few Women Leaders." *AAUP*. www.aaup.org/article/so-few-women-leaders#.VoSMkfkrKbg.

Ellison, Katherine. (2006). *The Mommy Brain: How Motherhood Makes You Smarter*. New York: Basic Books.

Evans, Carol. (2006). *This Is How We Do it: The Working Mother's Manifesto*. New York: Hudson Street Press.

Flaherty, Colleen. (April 9, 2014). "Research Shows Professors Work Long Hours and Spend Much of the Day in Meetings." *Inside Higher Ed*. www.insidehighered.com/news/2014/04/09/research-shows-professors-work-long-hours-and-spend-much-day-meetings.

Fulghum, Robert. (2004). *Everything I Really Need to Know I Learned in Kindergarten*. New York: Ballantine Books.

Gunn, Dwyer. (March 28, 2013). "The Flex Time Ruse: Does Working Flexibly Harm Women?" *Slate*. www.slate.com/articles/double_x/doublex/2013/03/flex_time_is_not_the_answer.2.html.

Harris, Rachel S. (September 16, 2015). "Child Care Shouldn't Be an Issue." *Inside Higher Ed*. www.insidehighered.com/views/2015/09/16/essay-says-child-care-shouldnt-still-be-issue-scholarly-meetings.

Hochschild, Arlie R. (1989). *The Second Shift*. New York: Avon Books.

Jaschik, Scott. (September 8, 2015). "Poli-Sci's Baby Ban." *Inside Higher Ed*. www.insidehighered.com/news/2015/09/08/political-science-association-criticized-agreeing-keep-babies-out-exhibit-hall.

Klein, Tovah. (July 22, 2010). "Why Women Leaders Are MIA from Academic Life." *Washington Post*. http://views.washingtonpost.com/leadership/guestinsights/2010/07/why-women-leaders-are-mia-from-academic-life.html.

Leonard, David J. (July 26, 2013). "Blame the Institution, Not Just the Fathers." *Chronicle of Higher Education*. http://chronicle.com/article/Blame-the-Institution-Not/140405/.

Mason, Mary Ann. (July 1992). "Standing Still in the Workplace: Women in Social Work and Other Female-Dominated Occupations." *Affilia*, 62 (3): 447.

———. (September 16, 2009). "How the 'Snow-Woman Effect' Slows Women's Progress." *The Chronicle of Higher Education*. http://chronicle.com/article/How-the-Snow-Woman-Effect/48377/.

———. (June 17, 2013). "In the Ivory Tower, Men Only." *Slate*. www.slate.com/articles/double_x/doublex/2013/06/female_academics_pay_a_heavy_baby_penalty.single.html.

Mason, Mary Ann, and Eve Mason Ekman. (2007). *Mothers on the Fast Track*. New York: Oxford.

Mason, Mary Ann, Nicholas H. Wolfinger, and Marc Goulden. (2013). *Do Babies Matter? Gender and Family in the Ivory Tower*. Rutgers, NJ: Rutgers University Press.

Petchers, Marcia K. (1996). "Debunking the Myth of Progress for Women Social Work Educators." *Affilia*, 11 (1): 11–38.

Sandberg, Sheryl. (2013). *Lean In*. New York: Alfred A. Knopf.

Slaughter, Anne-Marie. (July–August 2012). "Why Women Still Can't Have It All." *The Atlantic*. www.theatlantic.com/magazine/archive/2012/07/why-women-still-cant-have-it-all/309020/.

———. (September 8, 2015). "A Toxic World." *The New York Times*. www.nytimes.com/2015/09/20/opinion/sunday/a-toxic-work-world.html?_r=0.

Williams, Joan C. (November-December 2004). "Hitting the Maternal Wall." *Academe*. www.provost.umich.edu/faculty/family/resources/pdf/Hitting-the-Maternal-Wall-Williams.pdf.

Wolfinger, Nicholas H., Mary Ann Mason, and M. Goulden. (2009). "Stay in the Game: Gender, Family Formation and Alternative Trajectories in the Academic Life Course." *Social Forces*, 87 (30): 1591–1621.

"Workplace Flexibility in the 21st Century." (2008). *Society for Human Resource Management*. www.shrm.org/research/surveyfindings/articles/documents/09-0464_workplace_flexibility_survey_report_inside_finalonline.pdf.

Young, Diane S., and Ednita M. Wright. (2001). "Mothers Making Tenure." *Journal of Social Work Education*, 27 (3): 555–568.

22 Organic Mentorship

A Feminist Model to Support Scholars and Leaders

Jen Almjeld, Meg McGuire, and Kristine L. Blair

While women make up the majority of students in both undergraduate and graduate programs in the United States, they make up less than half of full-time faculty in the academic workforce (Curtin 2011). Further, women account for only 29% of full professors, and just one in four college presidencies are held by women (Ward and Eddy 2013). One area where women do lead, however, is in "service" work that is often overlooked and unaccounted for by the academy, especially work done outside the university walls (Masse and Hogan 2012). Methods for countering this gender inequity in public universities, including strategies that focus on faculty and student recruitment, equitable assessment, and preparedness are now mandated by most institutions of higher education. One popular tactic for encouraging racial and gender diversity is mentorship programs.

A 2006 study by Omofolasade Kosoko-Lasaki, Roberta Sonnino, and Mary Lou Voytko found that mentoring is "an important element in promoting academic excellence for both faculty and students" (1449), most importantly for underrepresented populations. Universities often create formal mentorship programs characterized by hierarchies: faculty mentor undergraduate and graduate students, and senior faculty members are assigned to mentor "junior" faculty. While such programs are well meaning, they are sanctioned by institutions and, thus, embedded in the existing power structures of the academy. These are the very structures that frequently impede the academic and professional advancement of women and deny them access to leadership positions on campuses across the United States.

As women working within the systems that perpetuate these power structures, we understand mentorship as beneficial for our own careers and posit it as a tactic for subverting sexist limitations frequently faced by professional women. But for us, the mentoring systems now prevalent in many schools are less effective than mentoring that springs from organic relationships grown in informal ways and rooted in a feminist "ethic of care," as advocated by Carol Gilligan (1982) and others. Such mentoring relationships are not mandated but instead evolve from relationships established in personal connection, reciprocity, and a valuing of one another as more than academics.

In this chapter, we share our own stories as a three-generation mentoring lineage spanning more than a decade and representing various career stages. Through these experiences, we present strategies for women particularly to mentor one another so that we may thrive and lead as underrepresented faculty. Specifically, we identify strategies for better acknowledging this sort of work, thus allowing women mentors to advance their own and others' careers. We also offer advice for making mentorship sustainable and living, including recognizing it as scholarly and vital service work, fostering reciprocal relationships, naming shared goals for mentoring, and adopting feminist but not gendered models for mentoring. Our own mentoring experiences working with graduate and undergraduate mentees may then be a fruitful space for reframing the often invisible and undervalued mentorship so often taken up by women and minority faculty and might allow increased recognition for this important work in our current academic economy of rewards.

Mentoring "Others"

Mentorship comes in many forms and is prevalent in corporate and academic settings with many theories of mentorship developed in the wake of the 1972 passing of the Equal Rights Amendment for Women. Often such programs are established to recruit and retain job candidates of color and women. One such academic initiative is the Committee on Institutional Cooperation's (CIC) Summer Research Opportunities Program (SROP). Danielle Joy Davis (2008) explains, "The national initiative, implemented on various campuses throughout the United States, seeks to establish a diverse faculty by encouraging the enrollment and completion rates of minority doctoral candidates" (278). Davis's study of the program finds,

> Faculty mentorship plays a key role in fostering the academic socialization processes of future minority scholars. This holds particularly as it pertains to mentorship's influence upon the individual, interpersonal, group, and extra-programmatic realms of participants' lives.
>
> (282)

Kosoko-Lasaki, Sonnino, and Voytko's (2006) study also focuses on the importance of mentoring programs for underrepresented faculty and student populations. Focusing on women and minorities in the health sciences, the study found that mentoring is "an important element in promoting academic excellence for both faculty and students" (1449). The authors define mentoring as "the process of providing younger and less-experienced individuals with support, counsel, friendship and constructive example in order for them to succeed in their careers and life" (1449) and find this mentoring is particularly necessary when it comes to the professionalization of women.

Scholarship on mentorship frequently points to key features and characteristics of mentoring programs. For example, "*Dyadic structure* refers to aspects of the relationship that increase the likelihood of meaningful and frequent interactions, a recognized feature of high-quality informal relationships," according to Tammy Allen, Lillian Eby, and Elizabeth Lentz (2006, 569). Their study focuses on the dyadic structure of formal mentorship programs, including physical proximity, the need to pair mentors and mentees from different areas within an organization, and also the importance of pairing people of differing ranks. They inevitably conclude that "formal mentoring is better than no mentoring but not as effective as informal mentoring" (567).

This preference for less-structured models of mentorship may be related to the inherent power dynamics embedded in any official relationship. As Gail M. McGuire and Jo Reger (2003) state, "a traditional mentoring relationship is a hierarchical one in which one person serves as teacher, sage, and sponsor to another one in order to facilitate the other's professional and career goals" (56). The mentee is thus an apprentice and may inadvertently be molded into a copy of the mentor rather than more productively supported in ways to achieve personal goals in a given academic community. Such relationships may make it difficult for mentees to establish their own intellectual and research agendas or to establish academic reputations separate from their senior mentors. These traditional mentorship programs are often mandatory, with senior faculty assigned a junior faculty member, resulting in relationships limited to professional aspects only. Mentors may unintentionally focus only on what a mentee needs to do professionally without accounting for personal interests, needs, family responsibilities, or goals beyond the classroom or publication venue.

Additionally, as mentorship is often viewed as gendered work, these traditional, structured mentorship programs are often carried out by female faculty members, strictly because they are female. This can become discriminatory in that mentoring becomes service that often goes unrecognized and uncompensated. Assigning such undervalued work to women and minority faculty may unintentionally result in even greater inequity, as these mentors may become overwhelmed by the weight of unrecognized "service" work and be unable to advance professionally. In a 2004 report from Stanford on the Status of Women Faculty, Judith Glazer-Raymo (2007) notes that "among their findings were heightened concerns among women faculty regarding greater work-load pressure related to advising and mentoring, particularly among women of colour" (172). While the report offered six strategies to counter this and many other concerns (173), there is no mention of making such work visible or honoring it in our academic economy of rewards.

In a related study, Maike Ingrid Philipsen (2012) reflects on the recent proliferation in articles about "work–life balancing in academe" (203) and looks specifically at the ways these balancing acts seem to differ on the basis of gender. Many female faculty, particularly those early in their careers, noted that "ill-defined expectations" for tenure and other academic rewards was particularly frustrating and one noted that what most often got cut from an overfull schedule was "anything that had to do with taking care of herself" (207). One way women in the study dealt with this issue was to cultivate "networks, friendships, support groups and . . . collaborations" (212). Such strategies are a step toward more mutually beneficial feminist mentorship models that may actually support and lessen—through sharing—one's workload rather than adding to it.

Enacting an Ethic of Care

On the basis of these academic reward structures, we advocate a less formal but, for us, more meaningful mentoring approach based on Carol Gilligan's ethic of care. Mentoring may be considered a feminist ethic of care as introduced in Gilligan's 1982 work *In a Different Voice: Psychological Theory and Women's Development*. Gilligan considers differences she noted in female experiences related to moral development and, according to Mary Jeanne Larrabee (1993), Gilligan's "work thus trumpets aspects of women's experience found defective, deficient, or undervalued by the broader culture" (5). Her work, and its discussion of the role of caring in the moral development of women, is key to our project as we consider ways caring, connection, and relationship may matter differently to women than men in the academy. This sort of authentic connection may be more difficult to foster in mandated mentorship programs defined by required meetings, hours spent, and the foregrounding of departmental or organizational goals over personal ones. Mentorship by choice rather than university mandate is bedrock to our own feminist mentorship experiences.

Like Gilligan, we feel relationships entrenched in mutual commitment and desire offer not only richer and perhaps more sustainable results but also might offer differently inspiring and motivational mentorship situations for female faculty members particularly. As Gilligan's (1982) work sought to counter ideas that women's thoughts and development were somehow lesser to males by instead "offer[ing] a representation of their thought that enables them to see better its integrity and validity" (3), our work seeks to legitimize the advising and networking approaches many female faculty seem intuitively drawn to but are not always recognized for. The three of us have participated in a variety of mentoring relationships—some formal and institutionally sanctioned, some with male colleagues whose advice is limited to professional roles, some with peers who enhance our personal lives but offer little professionally, and a select few that sustain us personally and professionally. While mentoring relationships founded on an "ethic of care" are impossible to mandate and difficult to plan, we can foster them by making space in mentorship scholarship to share stories from those who have benefited from such relationships.

Stories Matter

Stories matter a great deal in feminist mentoring relationships and in feminist research generally. Knowledge drawn from personal experiences, particularly the often less visible experiences of women, can change individual lives and larger academic culture. Sandra Harding (1987) argues that feminist research situated in women's experiences, political struggles and their attempts to change cultural conditions can impact the way the world is shaped (8). For this reason, it is important for us to articulate the ways feminist mentoring has impacted our own careers and helped us navigate the often sexist power structures prevalent in the academy. We offer our three stories as sites of meaning making—intertwined and individual, spanning multiple generations, institutions, and career levels. Including these personal narratives speaks not only to feminist principles but also, according to Allen, Eby, and Lentz (2006), to a need for story in mentorship theory as well. The authors point to a "gap in the literature" of mentorship scholarship in "the omission of the mentor's perspective" (568). We hope to speak to this disparity by providing our own viewpoints and experiences as both mentors and mentees. We also hope to reveal the deeply personal, situated, and sustainable nature of mentorship that is rooted in choice and caring rather than institutional directive.

Kris's Story

I have always self-identified as a materialist feminist, as this particular framework focuses on the lived experiences of individuals and groups and the material conditions that impact and mediate access and empowerment in a range of cultural contexts. This includes the shifting working conditions of the academy in general, and rhetoric and composition in particular, and the impact of those conditions upon our roles as mentors. Our mentoring roles in preparing future female faculty must address how labor issues, as Rosemary Hennessy and Chrys Ingraham (1997) identify, are tied to race, gender, sexuality, and nationality. What are the labor conditions in which rhetoric and composition specialists find themselves in a field that has historically been seen as feminized? And how do these conditions impact women? Certainly, decreases in the state share of support continues to plague institutions around the United States, with universities being asked to do more with less, including hiring fewer full-time faculty and more adjunct faculty, with fewer faculty replacements for retirements in an aging professoriate and the need for remaining faculty to take on more labor and responsibility.

Given this larger economic context surrounding the academy, I have been concerned about my own role as a mentor. How do I foster feminist critique and activism about these issues for graduate students? How do I introduce graduate students to the material realities of the profession they are entering? Because I have worked with many graduate students, my primary role has been to provide opportunities for professional development and research collaboration. For example, it has been important for me to involve graduate students in outreach to the community, including a five-year technology camp I co-directed with graduate student women, The Digital Mirror Computer Camp For Girls. For me, this effort represented what Theresa Enos (1997) has referred to, in a feminist sense, as "(wo)mentoring," or a process that moves away from "hierarchical concepts of master, tutor, or model to that of advisor, supporter, and sponsor, with these latter terms suggesting a reciprocity among individuals and groups" (138), something I certainly experienced with the camp. The experience with Digital Mirror, in turn, has allowed many of the students I have mentored to assume such roles themselves or engage in similar feminist initiatives, as my co-author Jen Almjeld has with the camp she developed with her own graduate students at New Mexico State University, Girlhood Remixed. Although our close working relationships with students foster these important forms of activism, we might, as Enos suggests, find ourselves overworked as a result, given the larger numbers of female graduate students seeking careers in rhetoric and writing and the more limited numbers of tenured or senior female faculty expected and obligated to serve them. Many people equate mentoring with mothering, a 24/7 type of availability and often invisible labor that is deemed "women's work," and is thus deskilled and devalued in comparison to other academic measures of performance.

I have found myself becoming just as concerned about mentoring students into the realities of life as an assistant professor or as non-tenure track faculty. Will my students be in tenure track positions, and if so, will they be awarded tenure through their labor on a computer camp for girls, or for the demands of mentoring that our increasingly diverse student populations require? Will the jobs they take allow them to be recognized for such labor? Is such labor gendered? In many ways, it is certainly classed because of the limited power untenured or non-tenure track faculty have to resist hierarchical structures that create differential workloads, including service on more committees, assumption of administrative roles pre-tenure, and admittedly, expectations of increased availability among students and faculty colleagues, particularly women faculty of color, to assume mentoring roles. Thus, Sheree Wilson (2012) advocates conducting "cultural audits to 'assess' the temperature of the climates in academic units" and within institutional structures and to provide "an educational environment that welcomes and supports all of its participants, regardless of race, ethnicity, or gender" (77).

But how do we mentor all future faculty, not just women, to assume those roles and responsibilities and to benefit equally from those efforts? Feminist graduate educators must determine how we better mentor our graduate students for a broader range of academic realities that impact their success as both faculty and as feminists: increasing numbers of NTT positions, limited incentive and reward for mentoring opportunities, particularly for female faculty of color, and static criteria for tenure and promotion. How do we articulate feminist mentoring as active, political, and rhetorical listening to the material and cultural conditions I have outlined, and to the types of working environments that are becoming more the rule than the exception for our students? In short, as feminist mentors, we need to do more than mentor to help our graduate student women not only get the job, but also how to survive and thrive in the job, fostering a culture where multiple forms of labor, including mentoring, are valued and recognized rather than exploited for both current and future generations of women faculty.

Jen's Story

While studying my job materials for my first tenure track job nine years ago, my advisor, mentor, and friend Kris Blair told me that the toughest challenge I would likely face would be saying no. As a doctoral student at Bowling Green State University, the newness of the field to me and my own enthusiasm led me to take on many tasks—some recognized on my vitae and some not—and prompted Kris to advise me to think strategically about the work I could do and the work I want to do. Conversations like this one with Kris were never limited to the classroom or office but often happened over coffee dates at conferences, friendly phone calls and hasty pleas for help in Facebook messages. Through this informal mentoring relationship and in my own eventual work with graduate and undergraduate students, I began to recognize this mentoring as both vital to my career and also wholly unrecognized on Kris's annual performance reports or vitae. Tammy Allen, Lillian Eby, and Jean Rhodes (2007), in their introduction chapter for *The Blackwell Handbook of Mentoring: A Multiple Perspectives Approach*, explain that "faculty mentors are a primary mechanism for indoctrinating students into a professional field and the relationship can have profound effects on students' professional identity and career plans" (13). This certainly has been true of my own career trajectory, as Kris's mentoring encouraged my focus in digital media and girlhood studies, resulted in several joint conference presentations, a co-authored chapter, and a textbook. It also modeled for me ways to invest my professional and personal energies in students in ways that are mutually beneficial and sustainable.

I believe the mentoring I received from Kris not only shaped my career but also impacted the field, as it is reflected in my own work as a mentor and in my mentees' future work with others. My co-author Meg McGuire and I first worked together in a graduate course at New Mexico State University. Perhaps because Meg and I were friendly prior to the course, we met often and unofficially (much like Kris and I had) and found ourselves discussing syllabi, assignments, her personal and scholarly goals, and ways those could be blended with the goals of the course she was enrolled in as a doctoral student. I shared with Meg—and graduate teaching assistants I now mentor at James Madison University—what works for me in the classroom, what flopped, and ways I embed my own scholarship in my class as well as how my teaching feeds my publications. This sharing of ideas goes both ways, as students share cool assignment ideas and help me brainstorm approaches for my own teaching and research projects. With Meg, these exchanges often took place when she passed by my open office door, when I dropped into her hours at the campus Design Center, and through text messages. Even while sharing a pint at our local brewpub, our conversations always came back to pedagogy and current writing projects. In an early article on mentorship, Robert Blackburn, David Chapman, and Susan Cameron (1981) explain,

> Within the academic profession, mentorship most often occurs in the informal, but special, sponsorship that a graduate student receives from a senior professor during graduate school. The mentor provides a role model, academic advice, and eventually, assistance in gaining access to the profession.
>
> (315)

Since working with Meg, I have mentored several undergraduate and graduate students. These mentoring relationships resulted in co-authored book chapters, conference presentations, and shared leadership in engagement projects including a girls' technology camp and after-school digital storytelling programs. While the artifacts that sometimes result from these relationships are often valued in the academy, the time and emotional investment spent in such mentoring relationships go unseen and perhaps are even discouraged as less important than focusing on my own scholarship. For example, at my Young Women's Leadership Camp, mentoring happens at multiple levels including a graduate student serving as the assistant camp director and an undergraduate camp counselor. I have held one-on-one meetings, exchanged multiple emails, and helped conceptualize ways this work might speak to both of these women's future career goals. While this informal mentoring might be recognized when included in a narrative like this one, it is otherwise invisible because there is no space on my annual performance report to list such work that is subsumed by the camp itself and, thus, shuffled into service. By not making this work more explicit, I not only add to my own uncompensated workload but also fail to model for other scholars ways this sort of work should be displayed and rewarded.

While the personal, specialized, and very human feminist model of mentorship we present here recognizes the uniqueness, complexity, and depth of relationships rooted in personal connection and genuine reciprocity, the lack of formal structure does, however, have a downside. It seems this sort of work is silently added to an ever-growing list of tasks faculty continue to take on for free. The meetings I hold with graduate students to discuss their teaching or research projects are completely delightful but also consume hours in my day that I can't spend grading, meeting with other students, or writing. I have chosen, as Kris advised me so many years ago, what to say no to—and mentorship, though often unrecognized, offers too many benefits to me personally and professionally to be on that list. In my mind, the benefits of these mentoring relationships far outweigh the costs, but making this sort of behind-the-scenes community building work more explicit might validate the work so many female academics are already doing. It's hard to honor and reward a practice until we name it.

Meg's Story

Unlike many of my peers who entered the Ph.D. program straight from their Master's degree or from adjunct teaching, I started my Ph.D. program after many years of working as a technical writer. There were a lot of challenges in this transition: from a new home, and a new job, to acclimating to a new professional discourse and culture. I often felt as though I was, as David Bartholomae (1986) argues, "Inventing the University" along with my freshman students. What helped in these transitions were the relationships I was able to cultivate with my former professor and current co-author, Jen Almjeld, and other faculty in my graduate program. Jen's openness and encouragement to talk about ideas helped to, as Priya Dua (2007) states of feminist mentorship, "empower others by helping them realize that they are their own sources of truth, knowledge, judgment . . . that they have the capacity within themselves to maximize their own potential" (600). I began to gain confidence in myself and in my new identity and see that I did have a place in the academy. Because our relationship was unlike a more structured mentorship with mentors and mentees strategically paired or sought out in order to excel in a hierarchical system, I feel this feminist model of mentorship prepared me for my career in ways traditional mentorship might not have.

Jen and I worked together on many different projects including presentations at conferences, where I have often been on panels with Jen and Kris, who have introduced me to others in the field. Additionally, because of our similar research interests, I was given the opportunity to teach a class Jen had originally developed. She shared her curriculum, but I was encouraged to make it my own. We often met and shared what was working in this class or not working. In this way, we resembled McGuire and Reger's (2003) definition of co-mentoring. "Each person in a co-mentoring relationship has the opportunity to occupy the role of teacher and learner, with the assumption being that both individuals have something to offer and gain in the relationship" (55). Although Jen and I were professor and student, there was still a reciprocal relationship where we could exchange ideas and learn from each other. It was important that our relationship did not feel hierarchical or one-sided because I knew Jen was not necessarily being compensated for this time with me. Therefore, I often viewed us as colleagues working together to forward a shared project rather than as teacher-student.

This relationship has had long-lasting impact on me. The guidance I received from Jen in graduate school sustained me through my own professional transition to non-tenure track faculty, helped me situate myself within our field with this position, and to decide what that means for the trajectory of my career. It has helped me navigate through the more formal, structured mentorship I currently participate in. It has also guided my role as Internship Coordinator for my department where the largest, but most overlooked, component of my work is the mentorship I provide to undergraduate students in their career paths that sometimes continues after graduation. This includes everything from mock interviews to pep talks before the first day of their jobs—all things that are not necessarily acknowledged but elements that I enjoy nonetheless. Because of this, I have successfully argued for a course reassignment in order to have an open door and more time to provide the mentorship that I benefitted so strongly from. Although this does not count as scholarship, it is still honored in my workload and is an example of how this work may be situated in the economy of rewards in academia.

Strategies for Feminist Mentoring

Reflecting on our experiences as mentors and mentees working within feminist models of mentorship allows us to recognize commonalities in approaches—and concerns—related to mentoring and to offer specific strategies and cautions that might impact universities striving to more fully engage women in the professoriate and other academic leadership roles. Feminist mentorship, with a focus on organic relationships growing in informal but important ways, may offer alternatives to more prevalent systemic mentoring. And this mentoring model may beget mentorship in multiple sites and for multiple populations including graduate and undergraduate students, instructional and adjunct faculty, professional staff, and other women in need of support in our universities.

Because of the invisible and often individual female labor mentoring often represents, several options exist to better share responsibility and meet diverse student and faculty needs:

- **Graduate students, particularly women of color, and those with disabilities, may not benefit from a one-size-fits-all mentoring model.** Thus, programs should develop needs assessment surveys to determine specific types of issues students may face on the basis of cultural background, family needs, and professional goals. On the basis of those needs, a broader range of departmental faculty and advanced students can be tapped to support newer students. Similarly, at the end of a student's program, exit interviews can provide the type of cultural audit Wilson (2012) calls for and foster necessary updates to existing initiatives.

- **Undergraduates and adjuncts deserve mentors too.** While much of the scholarship on mentorship at the university level seems focused on graduate students and faculty early in their careers, younger students and adjunct faculty can benefit from reciprocity and making mentorship a visible arm of scholarship and service as well. Faculty might choose to collaborate on scholarly articles with undergraduate students, for example, in relationships that honor the mentorship experience as much or more than the final scholarly product. Similarly, working with adjunct faculty to co-create curriculum may forward the teaching goals of both parties.

- **Having and discussing shared values and goals for the relationship is vital.** Relationships that are mutually beneficial and enjoyable, like those discussed by McGuire and Reger, tend to grow naturally and to move beyond the walls of the institution. Whether it is similar research interests, teaching styles or approaches to a work–life balance, these are what help people feel comfortable with each other. Additionally, articulating what each person wants to accomplish in the relationship is helpful. Ideally, these goals could include working on an article, developing curriculum, creating new departmental or university resources, or presenting at conferences—tangible outcomes that highlight work the mentor and mentee have done that is productive to all parties involved. These goals also help the sustainability of the relationship as participants move to different institutions.

- **Reciprocity should be a driving force in mentoring relationships.** Making these sorts of long-term, personal mentoring models sustainable for faculty means recognizing the true give-and-take that should be bedrock to such relationships. Mentors provide guidance, ideas, new perspectives, and important feedback, but mentees also have valuable personal and professional experiences and insights that might enrich their mentor's life and because work needs to be done to make mentorship visible and beneficial, it is important that such relationships reward mentors and mentees in intrinsic and extrinsic ways. Mentoring should not be a one-way street and should not be understood as a mentor "gifting" a mentee. A foundation of mutual contributions not only eases the burden on the mentor but also allows the mentee more agency to begin to see herself as a co-equal rather than a permanent novice.

- **Both student and faculty mentees must better understand the demands of mentoring to acknowledge mentors in more tangible, public ways.** Such acknowledgments can include letters of support for tenure, promotion, and merit, nominations for internal and external awards, and invitations to mentors to speak at their new institutions, preferably in a compensated model to avoid reinscribing the limited value placed on a female faculty's mentoring work.

- **Build mentorship relationships to last.** Sustainability is important in a feminist mentorship model. Because these relationships arise from personal connections, it is important to think beyond the assigned amount of time spent together in one location and to consider the relationship after graduation or into a new position. Feminist mentorship should have the capacity to evolve and to extend to new connections that last multiple generations and institutions.

While formal mentorship programs are recognized as service for mentors with clear objectives from a department or university, feminist mentorship is often unrecognized, uncompensated, and rarely rewarded beyond personal satisfaction. Clearly, the academy must better acknowledge the work done to help women advance their careers, even when that work may occur outside the university walls. Our goal in this chapter is to make visible the informal feminist mentoring happening within our classrooms, offices, homes, and local coffee shops and to recognize that mentoring's impact on the material conditions of current and future women faculty as a valued labor force. In this way, we sustain the ethic of care that mentoring represents.

Bibliography

Allen, Tammy D., Lillian T. Eby, and Elizabeth Lentz. (2006)."Mentorship Behaviors and Mentorship Quality Associated with Formal Mentoring Programs: Closing the Gap Between Research and Practice." *Journal of Applied Psychology*, 91 (3): 567–578.

Allen, Tammy D., Lillian T. Eby, and Jean E. Rhodes. (2007). "Definition and Evolution of Mentoring." In The Blackwell Handbook of Mentoring: A Multiple Perspectives Approach, edited by Tammy D. Allen and Lillian T. Eby, 7–20. Malden, MA; Oxford: Blackwell.

Bartholomae, David. (1986). "Inventing the University." *Journal of Basic Writing*, 5 (1): 4–23.

Blackburn, Robert T., David W. Chapman, and Susan M. Cameron. (1981). "Cloning in Academe: Mentorship in Academic Careers." *Research in Higher Education*, 15 (4): 315–327.

Curtin, John. (April 11, 2011). "Persistent Inequity: Gender and Academic Employment." paper presented at "New Voices in Pay Equity" Panel, Washington, DC.

Davis, Danielle Joy. (2008). "Mentorship and the Socialization of Underrepresented Minorities Into the Professoriate: Examining Varied Influences." *Mentoring & Tutoring: Partnership in Learning*, 16 (3): 278–293.

Dua, Priya. (2007). "Feminist Mentoring and Female Graduate Student Success: Challenging Gender Inequality in Higher Education." *Sociology Compass*, 1 (2): 594–612.

Enos, Theresa. (1997). "Mentoring—and (Wo)mentoring—in Composition Studies." In *Academic Advancement in Composition Studies: Scholarship, Publication, Promotion, Tenure*, edited by Richard C. Gebhardt and Barbara Genelle Smith Gebhardt, 137–145. Mahwah, NJ: Lawrence Erlbaum.

Gilligan, Carol. (1982). *In a Different Voice*. Cambridge, MA: Harvard University Press.

Glazer-Raymo, Judith. (2007). "Gender Equity in the American Research University: Renewing the Agenda for Women's Rights." In *Women, Universities, and Change: Gender Equality in the European Union and the United States*, edited by Mary Ann Danowitz Sagaria, 161–178. New York, NY: Palgrave Macmillan.

Harding, Sandra, ed. (1987). *Feminism and Methodology*. Bloomington: University of Indiana Press.

Hennessy, Rosemary, and Chrys Ingraham, eds. (1997). *Materialist Feminism: A Reader in Class, Difference, and Women's Lives*. New York: Routledge.

Kosoko-Lasaki, Omofolasade, Roberta Sonnino, and Mary Lou Voytko. (2006). "Mentoring for Women and Underrepresented Minority Faculty and Students: Experience at Two Institutions of Higher Education." *Journal of the National Medical Association*, 98 (9): 1449–1459.

Larrabee, Mary Jeanne. (1993). *An Ethic of Care: Feminist and Interdisciplinary Perspectives*. Psychology Press.

McGuire, Gail, and Jo Reger. (2003). "Feminist Co-Mentoring: A Model for Academic Professional Development." *NWSA Journal*, 1: 54–72.

Masse, Michelle A., and Katie J. Hogan. (2012). *Over Ten Million Served: Gendered Service in Language and Literature Workplaces*. Albany: SUNY Press.

Philipsen, Maike Ingrid. (2012). "Joining the Chorus: Work–Life Balancing in Academe for Women and Men." In *Women in Higher Education: The Fight for Equity*, edited by Marian Meyers and Diana Rios, 203–216. New York, NY: Hampton Press.

Ward, Kelly, and Pamela L. Eddy. (December 9, 2013). "Women and Academic Leadership: Leaning Out." *The Chronicle of Higher Education*. Accessed December 7, 2015. http://chronicle.com/article/WomenAcademic-Leadership-/143503/.

Wilson, Sheree. (2012). "They Forgot Mammy Had a Brain." In *Presumed Incompetent: The Intersections of Race and Class for Women in Academia*, edited by Gabriella Gutiérrez y Muhs, Yolanda Flores Niemann, Carmen Gonzales, and Angela Harris, 65–77. Boulder, CO: University Press of Colorado.

23 Career Navigation of Female Leaders in Higher Education

The Importance of the Mentor-Protégé Relationship

Missy Skurzewski-Servant and Marilyn J. Bugenhagen

Introduction

While an increasing number of women within the United States have achieved leadership positions in higher education over the last 45 years, gender equality is still not present. A 2013 report from the U.S. Department of Education indicates that more women than men achieve higher-level degrees (i.e., associate, bachelor, master, and doctoral), yet men outnumber women who achieve full-time tenured faculty status from degree-granting post-secondary institutions (i.e., 125,836 male professors versus 55,694 female professors and 87,720 male associate professors versus 67,675 female associate professors). A similar report indicated that females compose 54.9% of all management positions in these same higher education institutions (U.S. Department of Education 2014). However, Cook (2012) reveals that while the number of female college presidents has been increasing, they still compose only 26.4% of all U.S. college presidents. A gap also exists in pay for female versus male leaders in U.S. colleges and universities. Male full-time tenured faculty members are paid more (i.e., $123,899 for male professors and $84,507 for male associate professors) than their female counterparts (i.e., $108,031 for female professors and $78,723 for female associate professors) (AAUP 2014).

Barriers to equality still exist for women's inclusion and advancement in faculty and administrative roles in higher education. Hymowitz and Schellhardt (1986) and Hymowitz (2004) explored barriers for females along their career journey and were among the first researchers to explore the "invisible barrier [glass ceiling]" (4). This journey was later described by Eagly and Carli (2007) as navigating through "the concrete wall, the glass ceiling, and the labyrinth" (2). Hannum et al. (2015) explored the journey of 35 women to senior leadership positions in higher education, citing both formal mentoring programs and informal mentoring as support for leadership development to this level. From Hannum et al.'s 2014 *Stories from the Summit Trail: Leadership Journeys of Senior Women in Higher Education*: "Naturally, mentorship was a large component of this category and there were many stories of someone encouraging, nominating, or coaching these women through something that they might not have attempted on their own" (19).

Mentoring (i.e., formal and informal mentoring relationships) has been identified as a key strategy for assisting protégés in continuing to navigate past barriers to achieve their career goals. In this chapter, research is explored that exhibits the positive impact of mentors in helping protégés journey past barriers to leadership in academia.

Mentoring

Mentors and Protégés

Mentors and protégés are key members of a mentoring relationship who give and receive information along the path of development. The specific roles of a mentor and protégé have been outlined by many researchers including Phillips-Jones (1982), who defines mentors as, "influential people who significantly help you reach your major life goals" (21) and protégés as, "men and women who are helped to reach their career and life goals by mentors" (22). Kram (1985) also provides the following definition: "A mentor supports, guides, and counsels the young adult as he or she accomplishes this important task [to navigate in the adult world and the world of work]" (2). More recently, Rockquemore (2015) described mentors as "important because they provide you with information, resources, connections, and the wisdom of their experiences" (1). Mentors fill a critical role in providing advice to protégés as they work to navigate past barriers to their continued development and career advancement.

Mentoring Relationships

A commonly accepted conceptualization of the mentoring relationship is that which includes a mentor providing guidance to a protégé. Dunbar and Kinnersley (2011) state, "Traditional mentoring typically involves a hierarchical relationship: it is comprised of a senior person who advises and guides a junior or less-experienced colleague" (17). The structure of the relationship, dimensions of development focused upon, and how the relationship comes together has many variations. A key part of all types of mentoring relationships is the interaction between the mentor and protégé. According to Weil (2001), "All the activities of mentoring, but especially the nurturing activities, require interacting with those mentored, and so to be a mentor is to be involved in a relationship" (473). The interactions within a mentoring relationship can be created via formal or informal means and can involve cross-gender or same-gender pairings of mentor and protégé.

Mentoring relationships can be initiated as part of an organization's formal mentoring program that matches mentor with protégé. These relationships may also come together more informally when both individuals interact without set structure or parameters regarding the mentoring that is experienced in the relationship. Allen, Day, and Lentz (2005) differentiate formal and informal mentoring: "Informal mentorships develop spontaneously through the process of mutual attraction. One the other hand, formal mentoring relationships commonly begin based on an assignment or matching process initiated by a third party" (158). The structure of a mentoring relationship may evolve as circumstances surrounding the relationship also change. For example, formal mentoring relationships may become more informal if the mentor and/or protégé discontinue involvement in a mentoring program, yet choose to continue their interaction. Informal mentorships could also evolve into a more formal structure if both individuals become involved in a formal program and are linked together or even upon the request of a protégé specifically seeking sponsorship in place of mentoring:

> Sponsors are people who have power and influence and use it on your behalf to shape the story about who you are (and the importance of your work) behind closed doors when people are talking about you and you're not there.
>
> (Rockquemore 2015, 1)

While mentors and sponsors provide career navigation support, the delivery, audience, focus, and ultimate result in position attainment may vary.

Kram (1985) and Blake-Beard (2001) suggest that individuals should become involved in any types of mentorships that are available to them. Several other researchers (Allen, Day, and Lentz 2005; Burke 1984; Chao, Waltz, and Gardner 1992; Dunbar and Kinnersley 2011; Fagenson-Eland, Marks, and Amendola 1997; Ragins and Cotton 1999; Scandura and Williams 2001) suggest that informal mentoring can provide the most benefits to the protégé. There is a need for further understanding of the effectiveness of formal mentoring programs as organizations increase their support for and encouragement of staff into formal mentoring programs.

Other factors beyond means of initiation and structure of the relationship (i.e., formal or informal) may have an impact on the effectiveness of the mentoring relationship. Age, race, career experience, and the role in one's organization are some of these factors. Gender of the mentor and protégé is an additional characteristic that has been researched regarding the effectiveness of mentor and protégé interactions. Mentor-protégé dyads include same-gender mentoring relationships (i.e., male mentor—male protégé, female mentor—female protégé) and cross-gender mentoring relationships (i.e., male mentor—female protégé, female mentor—male protégé). Much research has concluded significant benefits extending from same-gender mentoring relationships (Burke, McKeen, and McKenna 1993; Ragins and Cotton 1991; Ragins and McFarline 1990; Scandura and Williams 2001). Similar to the need for further development of more formal mentoring programs and the benefits of such formal mentoring upon the development of protégés, further investigation needs to be conducted into the effectiveness of cross-gender mentoring dyads. Rhode and Kellerman (2007) express support for informal, same-gender mentoring, as well as the importance of gaining a further understanding of other forms of mentoring as well:

> The most effective mentoring relationships typically arise naturally among individuals who share important similarities, such as sex, race, ethnicity, background, and interests. This presents problems in organizations that have too few women in leadership positions to aid all those seeking assistance and too few powerful men who are comfortable filling the gaps. The problems are compounded when senior women are already overextended with work and family responsibilities if they direct all their mentoring to junior women.

> (cited in Kellerman and Rhode 2007, 22)

While informal and same-gender mentoring relationships have been found to be highly effective forms of mentoring, the opportunities available for individuals to become involved in mentoring relationships expands greatly by adding in the options of interacting in a cross-gender dyad and/or within a formal mentoring program. Continued investigation into strengthening formal mentoring programs is needed, as well as further understanding of how to foster productivity from cross-gender mentor-protégé pairings.

The Mentoring Impact in Academia

Mentoring has been determined to have a positive impact upon the career advancement of women in academic institutions, including those in faculty roles and those women working within administrative positions. Sherman, Muñoz, and Pankake (2008), for example, investigated female assistant superintendents and superintendents ($n = 10$) who expressed the importance of having mentors to help guide them on their career journey:

> If women who are in leadership positions recognize and identify practices that acted as roadblocks for them, they need to actively seek ways to help other women overcome them. Women, and men, should actively seek to identify potential leaders of all types and make it their duty to enhance and promote them.
> (254)

Women in academic institutions should seek out assistance for performance development and career advancement from mentors, and mentors in academia should also extend their willingness to guide and support protégés along their career journey.

The rationale behind active involvement in mentoring relationships was one focus of the work by Skurzewski (2013). In this study, female leaders ($n = 12$) in upper administrative positions in higher education (i.e., dean level or higher) all highlighted their experience as a protégé as influencing their desire to mentor others. Five of these female administrators emphasized a particular want to mentor other women. Other reasons they expressed for wanting to mentor others included an interest in people, collaboration, and community. They also identified their filling the role of mentor as a responsibility, obligation, and expectation, as well as the belief that development through mentoring was a focus of their institution and a part of the mission of higher education. Women in academic institutions should seek out assistance for performance development and career advancement from mentors, and mentors in academia should also extend their willingness to guide and support protégés along their career journey.

Female Faculty

Female faculty members expressed a positive influence of mentors on their career journey through the work of Gibson (2004) including: "(a) having someone who truly cares and acts in one's best interest, (b) a feeling of connection, (c) being affirmed of one's worth, (d) not being alone, and (e) politics are part of one's experience" (173). Mentors can provide guidance to and be an advocate for female faculty members as they navigate the tenure and promotion process. Mentoring of these faculty members can also have a ripple effect upon students, as faculty are often targeted as ideal individuals to provide support and guidance to students.

Female Administrators

Mentoring has been found to positively impact female administrators (Dunbar and Kinnersley 2011; Switzer 2006) wanting to be successful in their current roles and seeking to advance their positions in education. Dunbar and Kinnersley (2011) explored the mentoring experiences of female administrators in higher education ($n = 239$; 90% informal relationships) and found that the informal mentoring provided a positive impact on protégés and their professional development. Switzer (2006) also investigated female administrators in higher education, specifically focusing on college presidents ($n = 15$) and their mentoring experiences. These female college presidents attributed much of the guidance received along their career pathway to their mentors.

The female higher education administrators interviewed by Skurzewski (2013) expressed the barriers they encountered along their career path, their involvement in mentoring relationships, and the meaning of these relationships. Eight of the women in this study identified barriers they encountered throughout their career including their gender, credentials, attention to their family and children, a need to relocate for job advancement, and a lack of female role models. Mentoring was expressed by all the women in this study as a resource for assistance in navigating around these types of barriers for the achievement of leadership positions in higher education. All of the study participants had experience being protégés and mentors, and ten of them were continuing to be mentored at the time of the interview. Benefits specific to formal and informal mentoring were identified by the women in this study. Structure, consistency, and commitment were among the benefits of formal mentoring, as well as providing access to assistance. The emphasized benefits of informal mentoring relationships involved an open environment with trust and honesty, a lack of structure, and the development of friendships.

The Future of Mentoring Women in Academia

Mentoring relationships have been found to be effective in helping women navigate past barriers to achieve career opportunities in higher education. Continuing to seek understanding of how women become involved in mentoring relationships could help to increase those individuals who are mentoring and those who are receiving guidance. As expressed earlier, there is a continued need for helping organizations develop effective formal mentoring programs from which more mentoring relationships can begin and grow. Additional research could explore the experience of becoming a mentor involving a further understanding of one's readiness to mentor and the forming of a mentor identity. The understanding of the connections among mentoring, role modeling, coaching, and sponsorship could be expanded upon as well.

Formal Mentoring Programs

Much of the research surrounding the value of formal and informal mentoring includes greater subject pools of informal mentoring relationships investigated versus formal mentoring relationships (Allen, Day, and Lentz 2005; Chao, Walz, and Gardner 1992; Dunbar and Kinnersley 2011; Fagenson-Eland, Marks, and Amendola 1997; Ragins and Cotton 1999; Scandura and Williams 2001). There is a need for more research specifically into formal mentoring programs and best practices in helping these formal programs advance the development of individuals within various types of organizations including academia. Benefits of formal mentoring emphasized through the work of Skurzewski (2013) include structure, consistency, commitment, and access to assistance. Further research is needed to determine how formal mentoring programs could be organized to produce these benefits, maximize the opportunities for connecting mentors with protégés, and increase the effectiveness of their interactions regardless of gender, age, race, and other demographics that differentiate the dyads.

Readiness to Mentor and Mentor Identity Formation

Research is limited in the experience of recognizing one's readiness to mentor and accepting the role of mentor as a part of one's identity to determine if an individual is best suited for and prepared to provide effective mentoring. Research from Rosser (2005) involving an investigation of the mentoring experiences of for-profit organization CEOs ($n = 15$; all male) demonstrates a lack of acknowledgment for their role as mentor. According to Rosser (2005), "Although they [CEOs] discussed their mentors in detail, the CEOs did not feel comfortable identifying themselves as mentors" (533). Female mentors ($n = 13$) who were investigated by Mysyk (2008) also expressed a lack of clear understanding as to their readiness to mentor and acceptance of the role of mentor as a part of their identity. As stated by one of the participants in Mysyk's (2008) study, "I never set out to be a mentor. I think it became, it evolved" (214). The work of Rosser (2005) and Mysyk (2008) suggest that individuals don't actively seek to determine their readiness to mentor or recognize the formulation of their mentor identity before engaging in mentoring relationships as a mentor.

Understanding one's readiness to fill the role of mentor is becoming increasingly critical as more organizations are being encouraged to promote peer-to-peer mentoring among their employees. According to Ngunjiri, Longman, and Madsen (2015),

> Although mentoring traditionally has been viewed as involving a more senior person serving as a guide and support, the concept now includes peer mentoring among other types of "collateral" mentoring that encourage professional learning from a variety of sources and directions.
> (as cited in International Leadership Association, Routledge Freebook 2015, 155)

Guidance provided through traditional mentoring by a more senior-level individual as well as through one's peers increases the access females in academia have to the support they need.

Strategies to Accompany Mentoring

Other forms of guidance have been investigated in addition to mentoring including role modeling, coaching, and sponsorship. Role modeling involves one individual who models behavior and the other who works to replicate that behavior in his or her own actions. This type of guidance is most closely related to informal mentoring with a lack of structure to the relationship and varying degrees of interaction between the role model and the person shaping their behavior as a reflection of the role model's behavior. Role models are often designated by individuals on the basis of attraction to one's behavior and/or persona.

Coaching is more closely related to formal mentoring as it involves a coach linked with a coachee working to progress development. According to Frankovelgia and Riddle (2010),

> The goal of coaching is to improve the effectiveness of the leader, as well as his or her team and organization. Leadership coaching uses the relationship between the coach and coachee as a platform for questioning assumptions, stimulating reflection, creating or expanding options, and growing perspectives.
>
> (as cited in Van Velsor, McCauley, and Ruderman 2010, 126)

Extending beyond formal mentoring, coaching mainly targets accomplished leaders on their continued path of development and often designates individuals from outside an organization as coaches. Frankovelgia and Riddle (2010) state,

> Although it is sometimes aimed at remedying a gap or correcting a fault, coaching is increasingly used to help already successful leaders move to the next level—helping them prepare for increased responsibilities, accelerating their acclimation to a new challenge, and widening their ability to address complex challenges.
>
> (as cited in Van Velsor, McCauley, and Ruderman 2010, 126)

While this form of guidance has commonly included external coaches, more organizations are seeking options for internal coaches and formal mentors within their leadership development programs. Continued research is needed regarding the development of leadership development programs including formal mentoring and coaching. More organizations that invest in these forms of development for their employees may increase the guidance they are receiving along their career pathway and their productivity within the organization.

Sponsorship is another form of assistance for individuals looking to advance their career progress to accompany mentoring and coaching. Ibarra, Carter, and Silva (2010) found that not all mentoring is equal. Sponsoring engaged the mentor in "going beyond giving feedback and advice and uses his or her advice with senior executives to advocate for the mentee" (3). Ibarra et al. note that their research suggests that women are often overmentored and undersponsored in comparison with their male peers. This undersponsorship results in women as less likely to be appointed to top leadership roles. While mentors can be at many levels of the hierarchy, sponsors have influence at the senior level. Sponsors engage in getting their protégés opportunities for challenging assignments, while mentors are more likely to assist in how to navigate the politics (and have little influence to help their protégé gain opportunities).

Conclusion

Mentoring has been found to provide assistance to individuals along their career pathway. As stated by Ngunjiri, Longman, and Madsen (2015),

Mentoring, broadly speaking, can open doors for emerging leaders in ways that are critical to professional success. A mentor can tell you what you need to know about your competency and skill set, and what you need to do to cover any gaps.

(as cited in International Leadership Association, Routledge Freebook 2015, 154–155)

Females navigating past barriers to career advancement in academia have also been found to benefit from mentoring. Further research is needed to maximize the effectiveness of formal mentoring programs and cross-gender mentoring relationships in all organizations including those within academia, as well as helping individuals better determine their readiness to mentor others. Additional investigation into other sources of career assistance for females in academia include role modeling, coaching, and sponsorship.

References

Allen, Tammy D., Rachel Day, and Elizabeth Lentz. (2005). "The Role of Interpersonal Conflict in Mentoring Relationships." *Journal of Career Development*, 31 (3): 155–169.

American Association of University Professors. (2014). "Table 5: Average Salary for Men and Women Faculty, by Category, Affiliation, and Academic Rank, 2013–14." *2013–14 Annual Report on the Economic Status of the Profession*. www.aaup.org/sites/default/files/files/2014%20salary%20report/Table5.pdfwww.aaup.org/sites/default/files/files/2014%20salary%20report/Table5.pdf.

Blake-Beard, Stacy D. (2001). "Taking a Hard Look at Formal Mentoring Programs: A Consideration of Potential Challenges Facing Women." *The Journal of Management Development*, 20 (4): 331–346.

Burke, Ronald J. (1984). "Mentors in Organizations." *Group & Organization Studies*, 9 (3): 353–372.

Burke, Ronald J., Carol A. McKeen, and Catherine S. McKenna. (1993). "Correlates of Mentoring in Organizations: The Mentor's Perspective." *Psychological Reports*, 72: 883–896.

Chao, Georgia T., Patm Walz, and Philip Gardner. (1992). "Formal and Informal Mentorships." *Personnel Psychology*, 45: 619–636. doi: 10.1111/j.1744-6570.1992.tb00863.x.

Cook, Sarah G. (2012). "Women Presidents: Now 26.4% But Still Underrepresented." *Women in Higher Education*, 21 (5): 1–3. http://wihe.com/women-presidents-now-26-4-but-still-underrepresented/#.

Dunbar, Denise P. and Ruth T. Kinnersley. (Spring 2011). "Mentoring Female Administrators Toward Leadership Success." *Models of Leadership*, 77–73: 17–24. www.dkg.org/site/c.meJMIOOwErH/b.6511935/k.BE53/Home.htm.

Eagly, Alice H., and Linda L. Carli. (2007). *Through the Labyrinth: The Truth About How Women Become Leaders*. Boston, MA: Harvard Business School Press.

Fagenson-Eland, Ellen A., Michelle A. Marks, and Karen L. Amendola. (1997). "Perceptions of Mentoring Relationships." *Journal of Vocational Behavior*, 51: 29–42.

Frankovelgia, Candice C., and Douglas D. Riddle. (2010). "Leadership Coaching." In *The Center for Creative Leadership Handbook of Leadership Development*, edited by Ellen Van Velsor, Cynthia D. McCauley, and Marian N. Ruderman, 125–146. San Francisco, CA: Jossey-Bass.

Gibson, Sharon K. (2004). "Being Mentored: The Experience of Women Faculty." *Journal of Career Development*, 30 (3): 173–188.

Hannum, Kelly M., Shannon M. Muhly, Pamela S. Shockley-Zalabak, and Judith S. White. (2014). "Stories from the Summit Trail: Leadership Journeys of Senior Women in Higher Education." *Higher Education Resource Services (HERS)*. http://hersnet.org/wp-content/uploads/2014/07/StoriesfromtheSummitTrail.pdf.

———. (2015). "Women Leaders Within Higher Education in the United States: Supports, Barriers, and Experiences of Being a Senior Leader." *Advancing Women in Leadership*, 35: 65–75.

Hymowitz, Carol. (2004). "Through the Glass Ceiling." *The Wall Street Journal*, 7–10. http://online.wsj.com/home-page.

Hymowitz, Carol, and Timothy D. Schellhardt. (1986). "The Glass Ceiling: Why Women Can't Seem to Break the Invisible Barrier that Blocks Them from Top Jobs." *Wall Street Journal Special Report on Corporate Women*, 1–5. http://online.wsj.com/home-page.

Ibarra, Herminia, Nancy M. Carter, and Christine Silva. (2010). "Why Men Still Get More Promotions than Women." *Harvard Business Review*, 1–6.

International Leadership Association. (2015). *Becoming a Better Leader: Applying Key Strategies*. A Routledge Freebook. New York: Routledge.

Kellerman, Barbara, and Deborah L. Rhode, eds. (2007). *Women and Leadership: The State of Play and Strategies for Change*. San Francisco, CA: Jossey-Bass.

Kram, Kathy E. (1985). *Mentoring at Work: Developmental Relationships in Organizational Life*. Glenview, IL: Scott, Foresman and Company.

Mysyk, Noreen F. (2008). "Women Becoming Mentors: Reflection and Mentor Identity Formation as a Process of Lifelong Learning." *The International Journal of Diversity in Organizations, Communities, and Nations*, 8 (5): 207–217. http://ijd.cgpublisher.com/product/pub.29/prod.4.

Ngunjiri, Faith W., Karen A. Longman, and Susan R. Madsen. (2015). "Lessons to Enhance Women's Effectiveness in Leadership." In *Becoming a Better Leader: Applying Key Strategies*, International Leadership Association, A Routledge Freebook, 153–158. New York: Routledge.

Phillips-Jones, Linda. (1982). *Mentors & Protégés*. New York, NY: Arbor House.

Ragins, Belle Rose, and John L. Cotton. (1991). "Easier Said than Done: Gender Differences in Perceived Barriers to Gaining a Mentor." *Academy of Management Journal*, 34 (4): 939–951.

———. (1999). "Mentor Functions and Outcomes: A Comparison of Men and Women in Formal and Informal Mentoring Relationships." *Journal of Applied Psychology*, 84 (4): 529–550.

Ragins, Belle Rose, and Dean B. McFarlin. (1990). "Perceptions of Mentor Roles in Cross-Gender Mentoring Relationships." *Journal of Vocational Behavior*, 37: 321–339.

Rhode, Deborah L., and Barbara Kellerman. (2007). "Women and Leadership: The State of Play." In *Women & Leadership: The State of Play and Strategies for Change*, edited by Barbara Kellerman and Deborah L. Rhode, 1–62. San Francisco, CA: Jossey-Bass.

Rockquemore, Kerry A. (2015). "Essay on Difference Between Mentors and Sponsors in Academe." *Inside Higher Ed*, 1–4. www.insidehighered.com/advice/2015/06/03/essay-difference-between-mentors-and-sponsors-academe.

Rosser, Manda H. (2005). "Mentoring from the Top: CEO Perspectives." *Advances in Developing Human Resources*, 7 (4): 527–539.

Scandura, Terri A., and Ethlyn A. Williams. (2001). "An Investigation of the Moderating Effects of Gender on the Relationships Between Mentorship Initiation and Protégé Perceptions of Mentoring Functions." *Journal of Vocational Behavior*, 59: 342–363.

Sherman, Whitney H., Ava J. Muñoz, and Anita Pankake. (2008). "The Great Divide: Women's Experiences with Mentoring." *Journal of Women in Educational Leadership*, 6 (4): 239–259. http://cehs.unl.edu/edad/jwel/policy.html.

Skurzewski, Melissa L. (2013). "An Exploration of Women Leaders in Higher Education: Forming a Mentor Identity." Doctoral dissertation. Marian University.

Switzer, Jo Y. (2006). "Women College Presidents: Interviews About Journeys and Adaptations [Electronic version]." *Advancing Women in Leadership*. http://advancingwomen.com/awl/awl_wordpress.

U.S. Department of Education. National Center for Education Statistics. (2013). "Table 301.10. Enrollment, Staff, and Degrees/Certificates Conferred in Degree-granting and Non-Degree-Granting Postsecondary Institutions, by Control and Level of Institution, Sex of Student, Type of Staff, and Level of Degree: Fall 2010, Fall 2011, and 2011–2012." *Integrated Postsecondary Education Data System*. http://nces.ed.gov/programs/digest/d13/tables/dt13_301.10.asp?current=yes.

———. (2014a). "Table 314.30. Employees in Degree-granting Postsecondary Institutions, by Employment Status, Sex, Control and Level of Institution, and Primary Occupation: Fall 2013." *Integrated Postsecondary Education Data System*. http://nces.ed.gov/programs/digest/d14/tables/dt14_314.30.asp.

———. (2014b). "Table 315.20. Full-Time Faculty in Degree-Granting Postsecondary Institutions, by Race/Ethnicity, Sex, and Academic Rank: Fall 2009, Fall 2011, and Fall 2013." *Integrated Postsecondary Education Data System*. http://nces.ed.gov/programs/digest/d14/tables/dt14_315.20.asp?current=yes.

Van Velsor, Ellen, Cynthia D. McCauley, and Marian N. Ruderman, eds. (2010). *The Center for Creative Leadership Handbook of Leadership Development*. San Francisco, CA: Jossey-Bass.

Weil, Vivian. (2001). "Mentoring: Some Ethical Considerations." *Science and Engineering Ethics*, 7: 471–482.

24 Mentoring Women in Technical Communication

Building Safe Spaces through an Affective Mentoring Model

Kristen R. Moore, Lisa Meloncon, and Patricia Sullivan

For many women struggling to survive sexism in academia, the struggle is a lone one, as they (sometimes blindly) navigate the institutional particularities that dictate our success. Unsurprisingly, problems of sexism permeate the classroom, administrative work, and scholarly work alike. Consider for a moment the case of Elizabeth[1]:

> Elizabeth is in her fifth year as an assistant professor and recently was singled out for her admirable service work. Later, though, in a one-on-one conversation, her dean (the same one who openly praised her) admonishes her for taking on too many women's service roles. Elizabeth is understandably concerned. While she has participated in a network-mentoring program in the past, she feels alone because she does not know anyone in her network well enough to discuss this issue.

This example reminds us that sexism (or at least uneven treatment) is alive and well in the academy and that in order to survive, resist, and overcome sexism, scholars in academia need strategies and infrastructures. How can we help women overcome and thrive within existing institutional structures? Though many institutions boast mentoring programs (e.g., Darwin and Palmer 2009; Mullen 2009)—and some even with a focus on mentoring women—few mentoring programs overtly respond to sexism through infrastructural approaches as Women in Technical Communication (WomeninTC)[2] aims to do.

Women in Technical Communication is a nationally recognized organization that offers support for women in the field of technical communication, broadly construed. The organization seeks to (1) acknowledge that the challenges women face are often unique and (2) provide a safe space for women to discuss their concerns about their careers. In other words, the purpose of WomeninTC is to help women survive sexism, and it does so through a recursive, participatory approach to mentoring that values experiences over expertise, listening over directing, and relationships over rigid, institutionally sponsored structures.

Perhaps the most important finding from our research is that mentoring programs in and of themselves do not necessarily help combat, resist, and overturn sexism. Many scholars agree both that mentoring has the potential to support women (and other minorities) and that mentoring programs built through feminist frames most effectively does so. And yet even feminist approaches to mentoring do not adequately support women facing sexism in the academy.

This chapter offers a history of WomeninTC and overviews mentoring as it has traditionally been theorized and implemented. It then illustrates how WomeninTC's innovative model differs from existing models and, specifically, the ways that it addresses institutional structures that perpetuate sexism. Finally, the chapter describes two important aspects of the mentoring model we employ—how this model flattens power hierarchies through dialogue and how this model deploys affect through listening and recursive orientation. We present a model for mentoring that can usefully be replicated in other fields or disciplines, particularly as a feminist means of supporting those with limited power.

Women in Technical Communication's Recursive Participatory Mentoring Model

WomeninTC was founded in Spring 2013, when a group of women organized a luncheon at the Association of Teachers of Technical Writing annual conference. Given that many of us had experienced situations similar to Elizabeth's, the goal of the luncheon was to provide a safe space for women to come together and talk about issues and/or problems related to their careers. Over 50 women attended, and they overwhelmingly said, "We Need Mentoring!" From a simple lunch, a national organization was born. (For more specifics on the history of the organization, see the commentary: Simmons, Moore, and Sullivan 2015). Importantly, WomeninTC is affiliated with no single institution; it includes representatives from existing professional organizations in technical communication, and it has representation from all different levels of professorial ranks, all of which help to ensure WomeninTC addresses the needs of women at various points in their careers. Since the initial luncheon, WomeninTC has focused on building an approach to mentoring that might help women faculty in the field of technical communication be successful.

WomeninTC supports scholars like Elizabeth, whose story we sketch earlier and Kim, whose story provides another example of women's mentoring needs:

> Kim related that she has been assigned a mentor, a full professor and a leader in her department, who is meant to help with her professional development. Although Kim, the protégé in this case, is grateful for face time with a seasoned full professor, she reports feeling uncomfortable asking questions that might make her appear underprepared or unprofessional. Her mentor will be voting on her tenure, so it has been important to maintain a professional and competent image. This means: keeping her medical problems to herself—particularly those related to fertility, her feelings of loneliness and uncertainty, and her misgivings about departmental politics. Although Kim asked other faculty members for advice, these faculty members offered conflicting responses and, further, cautioned Kim to rely on her assigned mentor.

Both Kim and Elizabeth needed some support, and traditional approaches to mentoring often fall short of the needs of junior faculty—particularly women. Elizabeth and Kim demonstrate a need for support and guidance that may more safely originate outside of the political milieus of their own institutions. Our sense is that both Elizabeth and Kim (despite their differing situations) need a safe space to ask questions without fear of rebuke, retaliation, or humiliation. Do existing models enable or encourage these safe spaces?

In some ways, yes. Feminist approaches to mentoring are especially invested in the importance of trust and relational work. But as in Kim's case, even when mentors aim to help, the power relations protégés contend with limit the potential for safe spaces. Since it is beyond the scope of this brief chapter to exhaustively review mentoring scholarship (see O'Brien et al. 2008 and Sullivan et al. 2015 for in-depth examinations of existing models), we want to briefly discuss the ways traditional mentoring might fail to support Kim, Elizabeth, and other women struggling in the academy.

Existing mentoring models fall into one of three broad categories:

- Mentor-mentee: traditional one-on-one model often seen as the expert and protégé model and is usually tied to an institutionally created and run mentoring program,

- Co- or peer mentoring: broadens beyond one-on-one and takes into the experiences of multiple mentors,
- Networked: includes strong relational ties among its participants.

Kim's existing mentoring relationship is a traditional mentor-mentee, which fails to provide her spaces and support that can actually address her concern. Elizabeth could have reached out to her network, but she felt she needed to discuss her situation with someone with whom she had a more personal and connected relationship. Both Kim and Elizabeth's stories illustrate the need for a different kind of model than those dominating the landscape.

In response to stories like these, WomeninTC has been developing a mentoring model that draws on and extends existing models. What does our model look like? And how does it differ from existing models? In truth, the model is messier than it is straightforward because it emphasizes and is rooted in participatory, recursive practices. We purposely and actively engage with and listen to participants to enable the mentoring process (Sullivan et al. 2015, n.p.). That is, we have been building WomeninTC alongside members, listening to their needs and responding. This approach differs from existing approaches in the literature, which rely on programmatic structures. Specifically, our approach tends to four overlapping dimensions of mentoring: people, places, resources, and affect. As we demonstrate in Table 24.1, each dimension helps us consider the needs of our participants, the health of the field/academia, and what is needed moving forward.

The recursive, participatory model can be used to help achieve the ideal goals of mentoring and, to our minds, help to shift structures that perpetuate sexism. While our approach to mentoring draws on earlier models, it differently configures expertise and the ways we build and advocate for safe spaces. It does so through configuring power structures differently and incorporating the affective dimension, which we talk about in the next two sections.

Table 24.1 Four Overlapping Dimensions of Mentoring: People, Places, Resources, and Affect

Dimension	Importance of Dimension	Example from #WomeninTC Work
People	At the heart of WomeninTC is the desire to support people, to help them craft successful and balanced lives, and to generate a mentoring model that privileges people's individual needs, stories, and experiences.	Because we place listening at the center of our activities, our model builds from and with participants.
Places	WomeninTC recognizes that participants need opportunities to meet in a range of places, both face-to-face and online.	WomeninTC meets annually at various conferences, but we also maintain online spaces that are private (on Slack) and public (Twitter feed, Facebook page, www.womenintechcomm.org)
Resources	WomeninTC has been building resources in conjunction with its members. These resources cross the boundaries of scholarly/professional and personal resources.	WomeninTC maintains a shared mentoring bibliography, gathers teaching resources on particular topics, and also serves as a network of emotional and professional support for individuals.
Affect	WomeninTC recognizes that these other dimensions result in an affective dimension, which must be tended to through relational work, listening, and trust-building.	WomeninTC creates spaces of shared support and tend to the need for self-care and emotions.

Flattening Hierarchies Around Existing Power Structures

Key to our mentoring model is a flattened hierarchy, which shifts power relations to enable mentoring to extend into the affective realm. In other words, flattening out the hierarchy of mentoring enables mentoring program to respond flexibly, affectively, and consistently to the needs of its participants.

Indeed, some scholars report that women face particular barriers in attaining successful mentors because of their lower position of power in academia and organizations. O'Brien et al. (2008), for example, list individual, interpersonal, organizational, and societal barriers to successful mentoring. Drawing on Ragins and Sundstrom (1989), O'Brien et al. explain that because men typically hold positions of great power in organizations, women may have limited interactions with potential mentors and struggle with the "identification process that is critical to the development of mentoring relationships" (539). Although this research primarily references mentoring in the workplace rather than academia, the same struggles occur when women in academia seek mentors in their local institutions. Because men are disproportionately represented in full professorships and administrative roles (Dominici, Fried, and Zeger 2009), women may not have access to willing or appropriate mentors in positions of power. Moreover, we found that without specific attention to power structures and power dynamics in existing mentoring models, women would continue to be faced with issues normally linked with sexism.

Beyond these problems with mentoring access and experiences, a feminist critique of mentoring programs' central assumptions illuminates weaknesses with current mentoring programs. In particular, mentoring programs built within the academy are often structured upon the patriarchal values and power systems that make it difficult for women to succeed. Boddy, Agllias, and Gray (2012) suggest that building strong partnerships through mentoring is a key to success and that such partnerships are built through (1) trust, honesty, and commitment; (2) support, encouragement, and flexibility, and (3) perceived similarity, common ground, and reciprocity. Building from feminist strength perspectives, which focus on building from the strengths and knowledges of protégés, these scholars' approach can be contrasted against other foci on mentoring as knowledge transfer, which delivers information from expert to novice or mentor to protégé.

One goal of WomeninTC has been to promote mentoring structures that move outside of home institutions and also subvert dyadic relationships that dominate traditional notions of mentoring. How can mentoring be used to combat academic sexism so that it can be conquered, reduced, avoided, or at least tamped down? One way is through the recursive, participatory model that focuses on different dimensions and supports those like Kim in reaching out to different people to get the mentoring she needs. In this case, Kim needed a co-mentoring relationship, which flattens hierarchies, creates a supportive infrastructure, and provides support of people and resources that enable these types of relationships. Where much mentoring research and many programs work to pair individual protégés with senior mentors, our approach resembles a networked approach to mentoring and assumes some support can be offered by those who have lower or equal rank. Feminist scholars have promoted co-mentoring because it provides a non-hierarchical vision of mentoring (McGuire and Reger 2003). Bona, Rinehart, and Volbrecht (1995) write,

> Placing the prefix "co" before "mentoring" reconstructs the relationship as nonhierarchical; "co" makes mentoring reciprocal and mutual. This reciprocity means that over time the mentee and mentor roles may shift; no one is stuck in one or the other for the duration of the relationship. It does not, however, remove the elements of counseling, modeling, and teaching preserved in the term mentoring.
>
> (119)

Feminist models replace hierarchical and dyadic conceptions of mentoring with co-mentoring and often blend feminist cooperativeness with teacher research, action research, and/or collaboration, all of which are contributions to scholarship associated with women faculty. Models of feminist mentoring also feature McGuire and Reger's 2003 article because they tracked the origin of co-mentoring to ecological necessity—namely, there were not enough senior faculty mentors; future women faculty needed to band together and mentor each other if they hope to subvert the problematic power dynamics of the academy.

In adopting co-mentoring and flattened hierarchies, WomeninTC works toward subverting existing models that reinfuse the academy with patriarchal, hegemonic values. We started with rethinking academic notions of expertise. Since expertise is typically static and tied to rank, we instead tied mentoring to experiences, since women of all ranks had experiences that were valuable to be shared. In WomeninTC, flattened hierarchies have produced mentoring relationships where people of equal or even lesser ranks provide sound guidance. In Kim's case, the best advice for her situation might come from someone of equal (or nearly so) rank who has only recently navigated the same type of situation. Because Kim now has access to disciplinary mentors (in addition to institutional mentors), she receives feedback from individuals who have no immediate power over her or her career. This, we think, is one way WomeninTC redresses sexism: by moving outside of institutional homes, we revise power structures and offer safe spaces for solving problems.

Safe Spaces and an Affective Approach to Mentoring

In developing WomeninTC as a mentoring organization for those with less power (women), we looked to develop safe spaces and trustworthy relationships, and we knew that a structured mentoring program, with rigidity and rules and regular meeting times would not serve WomeninTC as effectively as a program that provides flexibility, that listens, that provides strategies for orienting oneself toward (or away from) an institution. We knew, in short, that we needed an affective approach to mentoring because mentoring is so often fraught with stress and emotion. And yet previous and existing models have failed to account for the intensities that between the bodies, between the people involved in higher education mentoring relationships. These emotional, affective visions of mentoring are deeply connected to the need for safe space and trust in mentoring.

These safe spaces exist both in face-to-face locations and virtually. Since we have had leadership roles with the field's other organizations, WomeninTC has been successful in bringing women together in face-to-face environments during dedicated times at existing conferences. In addition, we have created a number of communication channels in online environments that have varying levels of privacy to attend to the diverse needs and preferences of participants. In all cases, these spaces were recursively created on the basis of feedback we received. For example, we created a group in Slack because it affords more privacy than Twitter or Facebook because those wanting to participate have to be invited. These safe spaces provided an opportunity for dialogue, discussion, and support in order to mitigate feelings of having limited power and consistently being located in vulnerable positions. Graduate students and assistant professors—even associate professors—struggle to know who to trust, who to speak with openly, and whose support is reliable. WomeninTC provides a range of spaces suitable for women to ask questions openly (or privately) and discuss their concerns. These spaces have generally been women-only, or those who identify as women, and they have fostered conversations that merge the false dichotomy between professional and personal and that invite support that spans institutional bounds.

But creating safe spaces has required an attunement to affect. Beyond mere emotional intelligence (e.g., Chun et al. 2010), we turn to affect because it engages not just emotion but the body as well. In the recent "affective turn," scholars have emphasized neuroscience, the body, and emotions in the co-creation of meaning and in the experience of the world (Gregg and Seigworth 2010; Leys 2011; Massumi 2002). Affective resonances and power are not ideological but reactive. What does this mean for mentoring? And why does it help us to eschew the patriarchal and often sexist origins of the academy?

So much of mentoring for women faculty is dependent on the "intensities that pass body to body" and on the "variations between those intensities." Affect theory helps us understand these bodily resonances as part of women's experiences in academy, and it allows those experiences to be validated as cultural practices not only as psychological states keyed specifically to one's gender (e.g., Ahmed 2004; Micciche 2007; Micciche and Jacobs 2003).

Affective theory offers a shared commonplace, suggesting that all WomeninTC are in it together, that no one is alone; such a commonplace relies on a participatory framework, where participants actively contribute and inhabit roles they feel comfortable with. But our model moves beyond participation; instead we also pursue embodied, attuned approaches to mentoring. In other words, we tend not merely to resources or the people but to the affect of assembling these together: "Affect is found in those intensities that pass body to body . . . in those resonances that circulate about, between, and sometimes stick to bodies and world, and in the very passages and variations between those intensities and resonances themselves" (Seigworth and Gregg 2010, 1). For Kim, meeting with her mentor was preoccupied with the power differentials dictated by the institution. WomeninTC combats this preoccupation through a flattened hierarchy but also through an attention to listening and to orientation—both elements of affect theory.

We have yet to see overt discussions about affect and mentoring and, more specifically, we have not seen scholarly discussions wherein mentors attune themselves to the protégé and wherein listening and awareness dominate the mentoring relationship. Kim's case is particularly striking and demonstrates the importance of two affective aspects we want to bring to the forefront—rhetorical listening and orientation.

Rhetorical listening is a "stance of openness . . . that a person may choose to assume in relation to any person, text, or culture" (Ratcliffe 2005, 1); it allows room both for listening in the mentoring encounter and for a dialogic conversation to occur. This sort of listening is key to our example of Kim and also to our opening example provided by Elizabeth. In her case, Elizabeth is caught in an all-too-frequent situation where untenured women faculty members are approached by men with requests to serve (Neumann and Terosky 2007). As their service lists grow longer, those women may be criticized for not using their time well. This double standard and conflicting message requires attention to rhetorical listening from several angles: Elizabeth needs to discuss the event with a mentor who will listen beneath the surface for values in play that prompted the initial request to serve and a subsequent rebuke for agreeing to serve (namely, that service is "women's work" and is disproportionately done by women in the academy). Rhetorical listening affords the listener the ability to understand complex political, cultural, and ethical positions, which is important for mentors because of differences across institutions and circumstances. Beyond the aural acts of simply listening in a conversation, Ratcliffe's rhetorical listening invites (or demands) embodied listening, which builds a deeper trust, enables sharing and confidence, and empowers faculty to act.

Orientations (and reorientations) may not initially appear to represent an affective stance, but Ahmed (2006) and Massumi (2002) illuminate the ways orientation actually is affective. Ahmed sees orientation as a way bodies come to inhabit spaces, and this is vital in understanding how and why an iterative mentoring model has been successful. "Neither the object nor the body have integrity in the sense of being 'the same thing' with and without others" writes Ahmed. "Bodies as well as objects take shape through being orientated toward each other" (54). This conception extends the iterative participatory model into the affective real, as it illustrates that both the model and the participants take shape through activity [in this case, mentoring]. Orientation, then, is embodied, indeed, affective. If one is not properly oriented, they can experience a disorientation, often characterized by a visceral, embodied reaction of not belonging, not knowing which way to go, and not knowing what to do, which can manifest itself in any number of ways such as increased stress and anxiety, sleeplessness, anxiety, and lack of self-efficacy due to low (or lowered) morale.

In our work with WomeninTC, we have found that many women faculty struggle with orientation. Women in the academy often need help orienting themselves within their departments and institutions, as orientations are not automatic or simple. For example, women need strategies for controlling their professional persona and figuring out how that persona interacts with institutional policies and practices (e.g., reappointment and tenure documents or annual performance reports). We have to learn and adapt to new ecologies and, in doing so, learn the new visual and perceptual clues these new situations, places, and spaces present. As such, each manifestation of change within departments (e.g., change in department chair), colleges (e.g., new assessment coordinator) or institutions (e.g., new provost with a different vision) require women faculty to reorient themselves and their work to new people and/or new initiatives. This kind of reorientation involves a bodily perception, or a sixth sense, and our true orientation happens when women can combine what they see and what they feel into directed action that results in an increased comfort of expectations of the job (Massumi 2002, 178–183).

If Massumi (2002) gives us a way to think about how women in the academy come to locate themselves, then Ahmed takes it a step further because once the body is oriented, it needs to do things. For Ahmed, like Massumi, this perception "involves orientation; what is perceived depends on where we are located, which gives us a certain take on things" (Ahmed 2006, 27). Demands of the 21st century academy, however, require additional orientation outside of a sixth sense. Women need an awareness that their work culminates in high-stakes evaluation, namely: the levels and kinds of service they are expected to do, what it means when official documents say "good teaching," and how to decipher the often ambiguous language around research production. Both Kim and Elizabeth's stories have an orientation component. Both needed to be oriented to practices outside of their institutions, both needed orientations on how their actions may be perceived and valued and, finally, both needed orientations on what to do next.

Through mentoring relationships, Kim and Elizabeth were able to reorient themselves (and their bodies) and find ways to address their concerns. Massumi and Ahmed (though Ahmed is more overt) align orientation with politics, and for women in the academy, understanding political orientations is a necessary skill, as illustrated by Kim and Elizabeth's stories. In both cases, these women struggled to orient themselves, in part because the power dynamic was not in their favor. But, in both cases, they had someone to turn toward: the WomeninTC mentoring network. WomeninTC provides mentors who will listen and think through their situations collaboratively. Affect, orientation, and listening—on which we have only scratched the surface—provide glimpses of nuances associated with creating and sustaining successful mentoring networks. As we discuss the affective dimension of the iterative and participatory mentoring model we are developing, it is important to remember that what makes the model work is understanding that people—all people—experience affect because it "is the commonplace, labor-intensive process of sensing modes of living as they come into being" (Stewart 2010, 340).

Implications and Conclusion

WomeninTC and the mentoring approach we espouse works to protect women scholars in technical communication from sexism. We draw on the feminist co-mentoring model that flattens hierarchies and redistributes power more widely, and we adopt affective theories that sidestep the rationality that privileges traditional criteria (and that usually privileges men). Instead, we promote a more holistic and embodied approach to mentoring. This means listening carefully and thinking about mentoring as a daily, embodied practice.

We suspect persons of all gender identifications suffer ill effects that derive from the academy's masculine-favored procedures, habits, and criteria for career success and, thus, we do not contend that men drive actions that result in academic sexism. However, women more overtly and regularly deal with sexism and, therefore, need a particularly feminist approach to mentoring. The WomeninTC's recursive, participatory mentoring model provides new infrastructure that can help combat everyday sexism and provide women in the academy support networks they need to be successful.

Notes

1   All the examples are drawn from our multiyear research study and are based on actual experiences of participants at WomeninTC events. The names have been changed and institutional details are omitted to protect their identities. This research work is covered under Miami University IRB # 01731e (Michele Simmons, PI).
2   All three authors are members of the steering committee for WomeninTC.

References

Ahmed, Sara. (2004). *The Cultural Politics of Emotion*. Edinburgh, Scotland: Edinburgh University Press.
———. (2006). *Queer Phenomenology: Orientations, Objects, Others*. Durham, NC: Duke University Press.
Boddy, Jennifer, Kylie Agllias, and Mel Gray. (2012). "Mentoring in Social Work: Key Findings from a Women's Community-Based Mentoring Program." *Journal of Social Work Practice*, 26 (3): 385–405.
Bona, Mary Jo, Jane Rinehart, and Rose Mary Volbrecht. (1995). "Show Me How to Do Like You: Co-Mentoring as Feminist Pedagogy." *Feminist Teacher*, 9 (3): 116–124.
Chun, Jae Uk, Barrie E. Litzky, John J. Sosik, Diane C. Bechtold, and Veronica M. Godshalk. (2010). "Emotional Intelligence and Trust in Formal Mentoring Programs." *Group & Organization Management*, 35 (4): 421–455.
Darwin, Ann, and Edward Palmer. (2009). "Mentoring Circles in Higher Education." *Higher Education Research and Development*, 28 (2): 125–136.
Dominici, Francesca, Linda P. Fried, and Scott L. Zeger. (2009). "So Few Women Leaders." *Academe*. http://aaup.org/article/so-few-women-leaders#.VplanMArLbg.
Leys, Ruth. (2011). "The Turn to Affect: A Critique." *Critical Inquiry*, 37: 434–472.
McGuire, Gail M., and Jo Reger. (2003). "Feminist Co-Mentoring: A Model for Academic Professional Development." *NWSA Journal*, 15 (1): 54–72.
Massumi, Brian. (2002). *Parables of the Virtual: Movement, Affect, Sensation*. Durham, NC: Duke University Press.
Micicche, Laura. (2007). *Doing Emotion: Rhetoric, Writing, Teaching*. Portsmouth, NH: Heinemann.
Mullen, Carol A. (2009). "Re-Imagining the Human Dimension of Mentoring: A Framework for Research Administration and the Academy." *The Journal of Research Administration*, 40 (1): 10–21.
Neumann, Anna, and Aimee LaPointe Terosky. (2007). "To Give and to Receive: Recently Tenured Professors' Experiences of Service in Major Research Universities." *The Journal of Higher Education*, 78 (3): 282–310.
O'Brien, Kimberly E., Andrew Biga, Stacey R. Kessler, and Tammy D. Allen. (2008). "A Meta-Analytic Investigation of Gender Differences in Mentoring." *Journal of Management*, 36 (2): 537–554.
Ragins, Belle Rose, and Eric Sundstrom. (1989). "Gender and Power in Organizations: A Longitudinal Perspective." *Psychological Bulletin*, 105: 51–88.
Ratcliffe, Krista. (2005). *Rhetorical Listening: Identification, Gender, Whiteness*. Carbondale, IL: Southern Illinois University Press.
Seigworth, Gregory J., and Melissa Gregg. (2010). "An Inventory of Shimmers." In *The Affect Theory Reader*, edited by Melissa Gregg and Gregory J. Seigworth, 1–25. Durham, NC: Duke University Press.
Simmons, W. Michele, Kristen Moore, and Patricia Sullivan. (2015). "Commentary: Identifying the Mentoring Needs of Women Technical Communication Faculty." *Programmatic Perspectives*, 7 (2): 277–297.
Stewart, Kathleen. (2010). "Afterword: Worlding Refrains." In *The Affect Theory Reader*, edited by Melissa Gregg and Gregory J. Seigworth, 339–353. Durham, NC: Duke University Press.
Sullivan, Patricia, W. Michele Simmons, Kristen Moore, Lisa Meloncon, and Liza Potts. (July 2015). "Intentionally Recursive: A Participatory Model for Mentoring." Proceedings of the 33rd Annual International Conference on the Design of Communication, Limerick, Ireland.

Changing Ideologies

25 "You Are Too Blunt, Too Ambitious, Too Confident"

Cultural Messages that Undermine Women's Paths to Advancement and Leadership in Academia and Beyond

Anna Grigoryan

"Anna, can I talk to you for a minute?" asked Tony, as he led me to an empty cubicle at the edge of the large office space partitioned by dingy, gray-brown panels that seemed to have been there since long before I was born. It was the first week of my first job after college. Having suffered through a drawn-out job search and a year working my way up through temporary gigs, I had finally landed my first "real" job as a document reviewer at a university-affiliated, government-sponsored science and research institution. My excitement was tempered with relief and hope that my English literature degree had not been a waste of time and money, as I had feared. I was in my early twenties, and Tony, a short and stout journalism major a few years my senior, had been designated my trainer. As he addressed me, I sensed from his apparent gravitas and attempts to temper friendliness with authority that, in true Napoleonic fashion, he had decided that he was not just my trainer but my mentor as well.

The job was rather easy and consisted mainly of reading scientific articles, PowerPoint presentations, and abstracts submitted by over 3,000 engineers and scientists for clearance before external release to the public through journal and conference publications. After a week of training, I had enthusiastically thrown myself into the task of clearing as many documents as quickly as I could. "You may want to slow down a little," Tony whispered, as we stood in the middle of the empty cubicle. "Others may not like you taking all the jobs," he warned.

I was puzzled. Would not others be happy that the new hire was doing her part, pulling her weight? However, because I was new, and because he was my trainer, I agreed and slowed down, but not for long. Aiming for mediocrity just was not my style. Little did I know that this seemingly insignificant encounter reflected a general social and cultural attitude toward women who excel at what they do and do not apologize for it. I realize now that it was not others' feelings Tony was trying to protect, but his own. The little boy inside him was threatened by the new, young woman who had the potential to not only be more competent than him, but also who did not blindly accept him as an authority figure simply because of his gender and a couple of years' seniority.

It took me over a decade in the workforce to realize that the problems with Tony and others that I would encounter in the corporate sector as well as in international academic settings were not the result of intrinsic character flaws, but of the "prove it again" and "tightrope" gender bias patterns that most women in the workforce encounter. There is no simple way to overcome these forms of gender bias because every work environment has its own unique cultural and social context. In addition, implementing the advice on how to overcome these types of bias is no easy feat because the advice itself can be riddled with contradictions and also because the degree and manner in which the advice can be implemented varies on the basis of each organization's unique cultural context.

Thanks to my mother, in many ways, my personality exemplifies the feminist disregard for stereotypically "female" gender expectations and behaviors. Because my mother had suffered through gender expectations of traditional Armenian culture, which demand female silence, subservience, and chastity, and which she repeatedly insisted had "ruined" her life, upon immigration to the U.S., unlike many first-generation immigrant parents who worry about their child losing their native culture and impose even stricter versions of that culture on their offspring, my mother consciously encouraged me to shed the shackles of traditional Armenian femininity and embrace the values and opportunities of American feminism. Sometimes she jokes that she overdid it.

I expend little energy worrying if people like me. I work hard; aim to be as honest, ethical, and productive as possible; and expect my work to speak for itself. I have never suffered from the "impostor syndrome," a lack of confidence in their abilities and qualifications that makes women feel that they do not deserve prestigious jobs or opportunities (Sandberg 2013). On the contrary, I feel as if I could handle many more challenges and responsibilities than I am generally given the opportunity to tackle. Since overcoming the universal problem of low self-esteem that plagues most girls during adolescence, lack of confidence has not reared its ugly head. I have no problem being honest and "speaking my truth," as Sandberg advises, and sometimes I probably overdo it. I am polite and approachable, but I do not go out of my way to be "nice" in the stereotypically feminine way—to smile, be excessively friendly, or start every sentence with "I'm sorry, but I think . . ." I never suffered from what Jane Fonda in her memoir calls the "disease to please"; I feel comfortable saying "no" and setting boundaries, both at work or in my personal relationships. I generally feel strong and empowered. In meetings, I "lean in," as Sandberg encourages, and speak my mind. I also feel comfortable negotiating and asking for what I want, and I participate in job interviews with great ease and confidence. Upon completion of my graduate studies, I made the exciting transition from office drone to English composition instructor and, for the past ten years, I have worked in educational environments in the U.S., Kazakhstan, Turkey, Brazil, and the United Arab Emirates.

Despite my relative success and enthusiasm for making my dream of being a global educator a reality, throughout my international career, in spite of my best efforts to be collegial and collaborative, I have not been able to avoid the minefield that seems to underlay my interactions with colleagues or supervisors, which has often left me dazed and confused. I had to reevaluate my approach to workplace communication once again when, upon completion of my terminal degree and fruitless attempts to navigate the maze of the promotion application process in an international setting lacking clear-cut criteria for promotion, I realized that the same personality traits that had led to my professional success: ambition, confidence, assertiveness, had also led me to hit not so much a glass ceiling as a brick wall. I understood that my simple confidence and lack of conformity to traditionally "feminine" styles of interaction and communication may have reduced my likability and, hence, my chances of achieving a promotion.

The catalyst for my deeper understanding of the forces that made my road to promotion and advancement in academia an arduous and frustrating one was Sheryl Sandberg's (Sandberg 2010) widely circulated TED Talk about the social and cultural impediments that have led to the dearth of female leaders in business and government and her subsequent book publication on the subject entitled *Lean In: Women, Work, and The Will to Lead.* Just as I did not know that my low self-esteem as an adolescent was part of the universal female experience until my cultural studies courses, until faced with numerous studies on the all-encompassing shadow of gender bias that permeates our culture and work environment, I had not realized that my challenges in and outside of academia were not just the result of intrinsic personality flaws, but of the general cultural distaste for assertive women. This bias bore significant social and economic costs for women, and if pop culture icons and feminists like Amy Schumer, Jennifer Lawrence, and Lena Dunham were ready to tackle the issue, perhaps I too could no longer continue to ignore its role in my professional life.

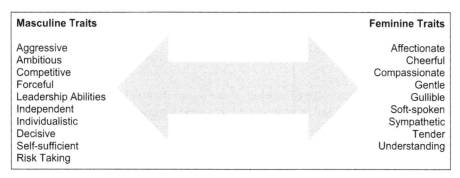

Masculine Traits		Feminine Traits
Aggressive		Affectionate
Ambitious		Cheerful
Competitive		Compassionate
Forceful		Gentle
Leadership Abilities		Gullible
Independent		Soft-spoken
Individualistic		Sympathetic
Decisive		Tender
Self-sufficient		Understanding
Risk Taking		

Figure 25.1 Stereotypically Male and Female Traits. Adapted from *What Works for Women at Work*.

In attempting to further understand the problem, I try to analyze my personality and locate my behavior within the spectrum of traditionally male and female traits outlined in the Bem Sex-Role Inventory (Holt and Ellis 1998), a widely accepted test used to assess perceptions of gender roles. In *What Works for Women at Work: Four Patterns Working Women Need to Know*, (Williams and Dempsey 2014) use the inventory to explain the "tightrope" bias women face in which they are criticized for their interpersonal skills when they act like men and are judged as less competent when they engage in traditionally feminine behavior. This bitch/bimbo tightrope was lampooned in an SNL sketch about the media portrayal of Sarah Palin as an attractive bimbo and Hillary Clinton as competent, but cold and masculine during the 2008 presidential campaign (Williams and Dempsey 2014).

Then I understand the futility of trying to evaluate my own behavior because the problem lies not in whether I consider myself aggressive, forceful, or competitive, but how *others* interpret my behavior and communication style. I can attest with confidence that few, if any, of my colleagues would ever describe me as "cheerful, soft-spoken, or gullible," but I think that I am understanding and sympathetic, when the situation requires. In considering the male characteristics, I recognize that there is nothing wrong with being independent, decisive, or self-sufficient in and of itself and that the appropriateness of acting "masculine" or "feminine" depends on the situation. Most importantly, I realize that what feels like "normal" behavior for me, which veers more toward the masculine than the traditionally "feminine" on the spectrum of gendered behavior, is likely seen as not feminine enough and, hence, problematic to others.

When asked to determine which of the characteristics would be most useful for success in a professional environment, especially in positions requiring leadership, most people would not hesitate to choose the masculine traits. Thus, if women want to achieve success in the modern workplace, they must act more "masculine," but if they do so, while they may increase their accomplishments, they may also garner dislike and be penalized for lack of femininity, which, in turn, can jeopardize the very success they were trying to reach through their accomplishments.

Numerous studies have found that women who display leadership qualities are not liked. One study found that when depicted as successful managers, women were characterized more negatively in interpersonal attributes than men (Heilman, Block, and Martell 1995). In another study, (Eagly and Karau 2002) found "incongruity" between traditional female gender expectations of women and leadership roles, which resulted in two forms of prejudice: favoring men over women for leadership roles and perceiving behavior appropriate for a leader less favorably when enacted by a woman. (Sandberg 2013) aptly summarizes the frustrating situation as follows:

> If a woman is competent, she does not seem nice enough. If a woman seems really nice, she is considered more nice than competent. Since people want to hire and promote those who are both competent

and nice, this creates a huge stumbling block for women. Acting in stereotypically feminine ways makes it difficult to reach the same opportunities as men, but defying expectations and reaching for those opportunities leads to being judged as undeserving and selfish.

(43)

Similarly, after interviewing over 67 women at the top of their field in government, academia, business, medicine, and the legal profession, (Williams and Dempsey 2014) conclude that "women need to act masculine enough so they are seen as competent at their jobs but feminine enough so they are seen as competent at being women" (295).

It seems that I had failed at "being a woman," which was rather unsurprising, considering I had put minimal time or effort into what I considered a tedious and unnecessary task. Did the behavior on which I prided myself—rarely wearing makeup or fixing my hair, avoiding heels or jewelry, prioritizing comfort over appearance, require reexamination? Was my embodiment of feminist values sabotaging my career? Studies show that people

believe not only that women are nurturing, but that they should be nurturing above all else. When a woman does anything that signals she might not be nice first and foremost, it creates a negative impression and makes us uncomfortable.

(Sandberg 2013, 43)

I was so "*un*-nurturing" that I had long ago made the decision to forego motherhood, which I had assumed had no relevance to my career, or could perhaps even bolster it, but now I wondered if the absence of a feminine nurturing impulse that all women were supposed to possess somehow oozed through my professional persona and, unbeknownst to me, contaminated my interactions. In fact, results of three experimental studies indicated that the negativity directed at successful female managers in terms of likability, interpersonal skills, and acceptance as a supervisor was reduced when "communal" aspects of being a woman, such as motherhood status, were emphasized (Heilman and Okimoto 2007).

Just as I expended minimal time and energy on my appearance, I made little effort thinking about how I expressed myself; I expressed myself as clearly, directly, and efficiently as possible. In other words, I veered more toward the "masculine" than "feminine" style of communication. Even though most of my colleagues were either from the West, or had been educated in Western universities, I recognized that I had been naïve in assuming that I could act "normal," act in what I considered a gender-neutral way without pandering to outdated gender expectations of female niceness (as in smiling a lot), friendliness (engaging in frequent small talk, showing interest with a nurturing attitude, giving compliments, smiling some more), accommodation (completing office housework, accepting classes and schedules rejected by male colleagues), helpfulness (not saying no, *ever*), and be accepted and treated fairly and equally to that of my male colleagues or females who did engage in stereotypically female behaviors. Hence, the same feminist values that empower us on a personal level can disempower us on a practical or materialistic level.

In view of the social and political penalty that women pay for counter stereotypical behavior, it is no surprise that studies show that success and likability are inversely correlated for women (Sandberg 2013). Unfortunately, promotion decisions depend as much on a person's likeability as competence. This helped explain why the promotion of a colleague who had taken twice as long as me to complete her degree and whose qualifications were comparable to mine, was supported by management, while I was advised to put my application for a promotion on hold for a "few years." Being the youngest person in the department did not help.

In addition to the backlash against counter stereotypical behavior, the lack of support for my promotion also exemplified the "prove it again" bias pattern in which women's performance is judged by higher standards than that of men and in which men are promoted on the basis of potential, while women are promoted on the basis of past accomplishments (Williams and Dempsey 2014). While I was completing my degree, I was periodically reminded that my continued employment was not guaranteed until I had done so, but once I did complete my degree and asked for a routine promotion, the message was "Hold on, hold on, not so fast!" Part of the "prove it again" bias is when objective requirements are applied strictly to women and leniently to men (Part I). In this instance, they were applied more leniently to a woman who *did* conform to stereotypically female behavior.

As both (Rezvani 2012) and Sandberg (2013) concede, we currently do not have a truly gender-inclusive workplace. Rezvani (2012) admits that women's concern about being penalized when negotiating for themselves is warranted: "When a woman assumes what psychologists call *agentic* behavior, such as being confident and ambitious, men and women *both* feel less comfortable with her than if a man were displaying the same attributes" (33). This statement helped explain the reasons behind that vague feeling of discomfort I sensed throughout some of my interactions with colleagues. However, she encourages women to "forge ahead" despite the danger of failure, which is precisely what I did in advocating for myself when asking for a promotion. However, it seemed that the more I explained why I was qualified, the less I was liked, and the less my supervisor, who was also female, was willing to support me. My experience with my nebulous application for a promotion reflects the "damned if you do, doomed if you don't" double bind described by Sandberg that affects women who own their success and attempt to negotiate on the basis of their accomplishments. When I did not have the degree, I was penalized for it. When I did get the degree and asked for a reward, I paid a social price and was probably even less liked as a result. However, if I had not asked for a promotion, I would have never have been considered for it and would be doomed to spending the rest of my career as a lower-ranked faculty. Being less liked would not have bothered me if I had at least obtained the promotion, but the latter seemed impossible without the former.

I now realize that I was mistaken in assuming that caring about being liked should be limited to adolescence angst and high school years and that unless I changed my behavior and communication style, my career was going to pay a hefty price. As Williams and Dempsey's (2014) research findings indicate, "women pay a price for counter stereotypical behavior" (71). As much as it felt like a betrayal of my feminist values and identity, I had to find ways to be more "feminine" to enhance my likability and find a passage through the brick wall standing in the way of my advancement. But how?

The advice on how women can navigate a biased workforce is riddled with contradictions. For instance, in the popular *Nice Girls Don't Get the Corner Office: Unconscious Mistakes Women Make that Sabotage Their Careers*, (Frankel 2014) lists both "needing to be liked" (83) and "not needing to be liked" (86) as mistakes women make. She encourages women to avoid "holding their tongue" (61) for fear of offending someone, yet warns that the "playing field" (23) in terms of assertiveness and direct communication is much narrower for women than men. No wonder I had given up trying to figure out what offends whom a long time ago and had decided to simply be myself!

In *What Works for Women at Work*, (Williams and Dempsey 2014) acknowledge that most of the advice that women are given about professional success is "wrong" because it is based on the assumption that women are too feminine and should "man up" without considering the social cost of doing so (9). However, they themselves cannot avoid the trap of contradiction when they advise that women work more to prove themselves again and again, yet caution that overt displays of ambition can backfire and lead to "backlash" because "ambition is stereotyped [as] masculine and successful women violate expectations of how women should act, which leads to a greater risk of prescriptive bias" (74). Sandberg (2013) also acknowledges the unavoidable paradox inherent in any piece of advice on female success in an environment steeped in gender bias when she advises that women negotiate in a way that does not violate stereotypical expectations of feminine behavior while recognizing that the very act of negotiation is inherently "masculine" and, hence, bears a high risk of social penalty. To ensure that the act of negotiation does not back-fire, she suggests that women focus on the communal rather than personal good of the outcome and that they ceaselessly smile throughout the ordeal.

A logical approach to overcoming the "prove it again" bias would be to simply list one's accomplishments; yet studies show that while men pay no social penalty for listing their achievements, women who do so in an interview may actually lower their chances of being hired because of the perception that they are engaging in traditionally masculine and boastful behavior: "When they advocate for themselves or point to their own value, both women and men react unfavorably" (Sandberg 2013, 45). Furthermore, people may not want to work with a woman who negotiated her salary because she is perceived as demanding and in violation of gender norms—she is supposed to be unselfish and concerned for others (Sandberg 2013). I suspect the same perceptions undermined my attempts to negotiate for a promotion.

The barriers women face when negotiating for themselves recently gained mainstream media attention when Jennifer Lawrence wrote an essay entitled "Why do I make less than my male costars?" for Lena Dunham's e-newsletter dubbed "Lenny Letter." Referring to her discovery, after the Sony hack, that she was earning less than her male costars in *American Hustle*, even though she was a bigger star at the time, Lawrence explains that she refrained from extensive negotiation because she did not want to be perceived as "spoiled" or overly demanding. She also recounts her frustration with having to constantly monitor her communication style to avoid causing offense: "I'm over trying to find the 'adorable' way to state my opinion and still be likable! Fuck that." Her words aptly sum up the attitude I had taken as an "empowered feminist" since my twenties, but the repercussions on my career had been disheartening.

At times, I find the daily struggle between speaking up and staying silent, between acceptance of gender bias and the impulse to rebel against it, between tolerance and resentment, between friendliness and authenticity, between ambition and the realization of its futility, exhausting. I wonder if feelings of burnout and disappointment with academia, at the ripe old age of 36, are normal. I contemplate the irony of expecting women to smile more in the workplace when a more appropriate response to the daily acts of social injustice they must tolerate would be anger and indignation.

A summary of the advice literature on how women should act in order to achieve success and likability can be summarized as follows:

1. Speak your truth, softly, gently, tenderly, and cheerfully;
2. Prove it again, without complaining or bragging about it;
3. Own your success, without showing off;
4. Be assertive;
5. Be confident;
6. Do your job well, but don't list your accomplishments or ask a for a reward;
7. Don't be afraid to say "no," but make it sound like a "yes";
8. Track your accomplishments, but don't talk about them;
9. Own your success, but be surprised by it (it may have been just luck);
10. Be competent, but not too confident.

To sum up, as my mother once counseled, "Don't be a bulldozer!"

With my deeper understanding of the intricate workings and contradictions of gender bias that permeate academic life, I observe my colleagues who seem to have succeeded in striking a delicate balance between competence and femininity. This observation has even allowed me to cultivate a deeper empathy for my female supervisor who I initially perceived as unsupportive. Upon deeper consideration, I have come to appreciate that she faces her own challenges at an institution where she is one of very few female leaders and that she too must daily navigate the treacherous tightrope of participating in decision-making processes without overstepping the narrow bounds of acceptable female behavior in the Middle East. I observe other successful and respected female colleagues, many of whom are both Muslim and American or European, who have a deeper and clearer understanding of local cultural norms, but who also have the credentials and values of Western academic culture. I see that they pick their battles, that they do not openly oppose or criticize situations, decisions, people, or management. They smile often and accept office housework or administrative duties without complaints. Some are mothers and easily transfer the nurturing parts of their personality to students or colleagues. They are able to laugh off sexist advice like "be more Asian" and do not overtly question the "prove it again" biases that result in bonus reductions. They collaborate and use benevolent sexism to their advantage. In other words, they make the best of the situation without burning out.

What will I do with my newfound understanding of gender bias in academia and beyond? How can I succeed without feeling that I am betraying my feminist ideals, values, and integrity? Armed with the understanding that the rules of the game are simply different for men, I can avoid or minimize the social and logistical penalties of engaging in unfeminine or gender-neutral behavior. Since my institution lacks clear criteria for a promotion, I have decided to "prove it again" by following Sandberg's (2013) advice and speaking to the head of my department in order to establish clear criteria and objectives that would make my future promotion feasible. I do not know if I can be "relentlessly pleasant" (48), as Sandberg suggests, but I will try to be "nicely persistent." In an effort to avoid making the mistake of focusing on results without worrying about pleasing others, I will focus on completing my publication and service goals. Most importantly, I will continue to incorporate themes related to gender bias in my teaching of composition to freshmen female engineering students who attend a university segregated by gender, but who will be entering an integrated workforce in a traditionally male-dominated field within a highly patriarchal culture.

References

Eagly, A. H., and S. J. Karau. (2002). "Role Congruity Theory of Prejudice Toward Female Leaders." *Psychological Review*, 109(3): 573–598. http://doi.org/10.1037/0033-295X.109.3.573.

Frankel, L. P. (2014). *Nice Girls Don't Get the Corner Office: Unconscious Mistakes Women Make that Sabotage Their Careers*, Revised ed. New York: Business Plus.

Heilman, M. E., C. J. Block, and R. F. Martell. (1995). "Sex Stereotypes: Do They Influence Perceptions of Managers?" *Journal of Social Behavior & Personality*, 10 (6): 237–252.

Heilman, M. E., and T. G. Okimoto. (2007). "Why Are Women Penalized for Success at Male Tasks? The Implied Communality Deficit." *The Journal of Applied Psychology*, 92 (1), 81–92. http://doi.org/10.1037/0021-9010.92.1.81.

Holt, C. L., and J. B. Ellis. (1998). "Assessing the Current Validity of the Bem Sex-Role Inventory." *Sex Roles*, 39 (11–12): 929–941. http://doi.org/10.1023/A:1018836923919.

Rezvani, S. (2012). *Pushback: How Smart Women Ask—and Stand Up—for What They Want*, 1st ed. San Francisco, CA: Jossey-Bass.

Sandberg, S. (2010). *Why We Have Too Few Women Leaders*. www.ted.com/talks/sheryl_sandberg_why_we_have_too_few_women_leaders?language=en.

Sandberg, S. (2013). *Lean In: Women, Work, and the Will to Lead*, 1st ed. New York, NY: Knopf.

Williams, J. C., and R. Dempsey. (2014). *What Works for Women at Work: Four Patterns Working Women Need to Know*. New York, NY: New York University Press.

26 Writing to Resist

Storying the Self and Audit Culture in Higher Education

Jessica Moriarty

In 2015, I was asked to peer review an article for an academic journal where the author identified the "busyness" of their individual office as a symptom of the neoliberal management culture that has begun to dominate higher education (HE). The author of the article argued that subconsciously, he wanted to be perceived as busy and hardworking and that even though he was under pressure and working hard, the mess and disruption of his work space articulated to his colleagues and managers that this was, indeed, true. The impact of neoliberal agenda had meant that the author felt this needed to be performed in order to be evidenced, in order for it to become tangible to those who might not otherwise see or believe it. His story was personal, it was honest, it was worrying. In this chapter, I explore my own processes of using my autobiographical and researched experiences with academia as data that can inform a dramatic text. I suggest that in this way, performance can offer a strategy that resists rather than complies with male, neoliberal discourses that continue to dominate HE and that this offers a potential tool for surviving sexism in academia, on an individual basis but also as a collective movement.

In earlier research,[1] I identified principles of neoliberal governance, such as the introduction of fees and the Research Excellence Framework (REF; which is the system for judging the quality of academic research in the UK as outlined by Sikes 2006[2]), as being potentially harmful because they give an illusion of self-management and freedom, maintaining an aspirational desire for academic autonomy while allying with business models and management structures that undermine this very notion.[3] Sparkes argues that the normalizing and naturalizing features of neoliberal discourses and practices need interrupting in order to "initiate the process of decomposing the neoliberal subjects we have become."[4] Sparkes goes on to suggest that we must challenge those in positions of power and influence instead of complying with neoliberal culture and accepting the damage to our professionalism and integrity.[5] By articulating their real experiences of the neoliberal culture and how it had driven them to perform their "busyness" via a messy and chaotic office environment, the author of the article under review had moved me to consider my own experiences, my own "busyness." As well as eliciting a personal and empathetic response, I was also inspired to explore and document my own lived and imagined experiences with the political shift in HE, a shift that I had found to be harmful.

Tedlock (2000) argues that "women's ethnographic and autobiographical intentions are often powered by the motive to convince readers of the author's self-worth, to clarify and authenticate their self-images"[6] and identifies this as a feminist issue. I suggest that storying oneself can offer the necessary detachment that is needed when seeking a viewpoint from which to examine one's lived experiences. This distance can provide a space for reflection that can trigger meaning making and offer powerful insight into one's own identity. My experience is that this process can offer women a method for authenticating self-image and recovering feelings of self-worth, allowing for a more expansive and liberated self that is able to critique and also resist oppressive cultures. I explore the process of developing a screenplay where I drew on my own emotional material and filtered it through a character with no connection to my autobiographical experiences and argue that this process provided me with the radical subjectivity and objectivity required to perform cultural and social critique. I agree with Hunt (2000) that for some women, "where the imagination sets to work on the raw material of the unconscious and turns it into art . . . engaging with their inner world has a strong self-developmental or therapeutic dimension"[7] and suggest that the process has been transformational, positive, liberating. I will argue that this process has been enabling, helping me to recover from experiences of sexism in academia and move past feelings of victimization in order to evolve as a survivor.

Background—The Emergence of a Neoliberal Agenda in Higher Education

Davies and Bansel (2010) maintain that the most prominent feature of neoliberal government is that "it systematically dismantles the will to critique, thus potentially shifting the very nature of what a university is."[8] They further argue that the impact of neoliberalism on HE is not just evident here in the UK but also internationally. While in this chapter I detail my own experiences of capturing and storying autobiographical experiences with academic life that have been effected by neoliberalism and the audit culture it has fostered (the emergence of fees, the REF, and the emphasis on universities as businesses first and places of research and learning second), this work is situated in a broader global context of neoliberal forms of governmentality which have been emerging in France and Germany since the mid-1970s, the U.S. from the late 1970s, and in Australia and New Zealand at the beginning of the 1980s.[9]

I am a positivist, humanist, feminist qualitative researcher in the humanities, seeking to engage readers in dialogues exploring the effects of the audit culture on academic(s) life and to use those discussions to imagine and facilitate ways of evolving beyond it. I identify autoethnography, and specifically autoethnodrama, as a methodology that can trigger such conversations and contribute to a strategy that critiques and also resists the neoliberal agenda. My approach is to use my research to inform my creative texts and to use a study of my writing process and the texts themselves to help audiences and readers consider how life potentially is and how it might also be. The effect of the audit culture had a damaging effect on my professional and personal life, and this has motivated me to explore and discuss the impact of neoliberalism via the production of evocative texts.

Sikes (2006) suggests that while there are shared experiences of the audit culture, its impact is also unique to every university and to every member of staff and these generalizations are problematic. She identifies the systematic restructuring, introduction of fees (here in the UK), and the increased pressure to function as a business as disturbing for the majority of academic staff, making them feel anxious and unclear about their professional identities and "leaving them feeling generally inadequate."[10] Sikes's research also indicates that while there are shared themes and issues with the neoliberal structure that permeate HE in this country and also elsewhere, these tensions are also unique and personal, generated by constructs of gender, conditions specific to each institution/school/staff member and a shift in emphasis on administration/teaching/research.

In the 1963 Robbins Report, academic freedom in the UK is described as the freedom to publish, to teach according to a teacher's own concept of fact and truth, and to "pursue what personal studies and researches are congenial."[11] In the 1988 Education Reform Act, the term was redefined to suggest that academic freedom enabled us to "question and test received wisdom, and to put forward new ideas and controversial or unpopular opinions, without placing themselves in jeopardy of losing their jobs."[12] Seismic economic cuts that have resulted in an almost business-like efficiency emerged as the driving force behind the management agenda in HE. This agenda has resulted in the creation of the REF which measures the impact of an individual academic's work and allocates funding to the university to which they are affiliated on the basis of this assessment leading to an increased pressure and busyness on some academic's lives. While my previous research and this chapter and focused on my own experiences, it is hoped that the ideas put forward here will have relevance elsewhere in the UK but also further afield where the impact of fiscal austerity and market forces on HE culture has also been noted (Davies and Bansell 2010).[13]

Cuts to funding across HE, but most specifically in the arts and humanities, means that academic research in these disciplines is increasingly restricted and yet we are still under immense pressure to seem relevant in terms of the REF and produce research that is deemed as having impact by a government hell-bent on cuts and developing a Higher Education Academy (HEA) that is motivated by wealth-creation rather than academic integrity. The Higher Education Funding Council (HEFCE) has been managed by the state since it replaced the UK University Grants Committee in 1992, and the effects of this change have gradually spread through HE. In keeping with Foucault's analysis of neoliberal governance,[14] many academics have consciously or unconsciously had to silently comply with pressure to do more for less and in the meantime, funding has all but evaporated, meaning that often "we no longer teach as we wish, but according to the logic of cuts and its attendant economics."[15] Docherty issues a call to arms: "Academic freedom is at the core of democratic intellect and a free culture. It must be fought for."[16]

In 2013, I was asked to write a chapter for an edited book entitled *Contemporary British Autoethnography*, where I talked about the process of completing an autoethnographic doctorate and simultaneously becoming a mother. I detail experiences of being undermined that were traumatic and led to feelings of anxiety and of not being good enough. Autoethnography "requires that we observe ourselves observing, that we interrogate what we think and believe" (Ellis 2013, 10)[17] in order to help us make sense of experience and offer insights into a particular culture or way of being.[18] This process seeks to democratize academic writing and resist dominant White, male, oppressive narratives that are synonymous with academic writing and academic life.[19] I argue that autoethnography can, therefore, engage academics in a process of self-study and storying the self that can help them to resist oppressive male discourses and that this can lead to a more enhanced sense of self. In the conclusion of that chapter, I wrote,

> Like Laurel Richardson in *Fields of Play* (1997), I hope "that by hearing about my intellectual and emotional struggles with 'authority' and with 'my place' in my texts, academic department, discipline—my life—will be of value to others who are struggling with their 'place.'[20] I hope it furthers the resistance. I hope it changes where HE is at and where I fear we might be heading."[21]

Now in 2016, I am still anxious about the direction HE is moving in, but I have been able to use my writing as a way of reflecting on why those fears are legitimate and to trigger discussion with colleagues who are experiencing similar anxieties that are reductive and oppressive. The result is that I feel less isolated. Many of us are responding to Docherty's call.

Autoethnodrama

Ellis and Bochner (2000) identify autoethnography as a methodological turn capable of producing

> meaningful, accessible, and evocative research grounded in personal experience, research that would sensitize readers to issues of identity politics, to experiences shrouded in silence, and to forms of representation that deepen our capacity to empathize with people who are different from us.[22]

In earlier research,[23] I identified autoethnographic work and specifically autoethnodramas that encouraged an enlightened reading as being potentially more democratic and inclusive, promoting civil and spiritual freedom and a resistance to dominant and anti-feminist structures, sometimes seen as synonymous with traditional academic work (Canagarajah 2002).[24] I devised an autoethnodrama entitled "Impact" that centered on a fictional university on the south coast and explored the effects of the audit culture on individual academics but particularly on one woman academic who was pregnant and completing a thesis, who experiences feelings of inadequacy and anxiety, engendered by the traditional male, oppressive environment that HE can generate. I identified autoethnodrama as a methodology which allows the voices of the researcher and the researched to come alive. It is a methodology that brings data to life but also offers a critical knowing.[25] Saldana adopts the term "ethnotheatre"[26] as a methodology that draws on interview data and journal entries in order to imbue performance texts with a personal story that is also social and cultural. For the purposes of my doctoral work, I adopted the term "analytical autoethnodrama" as the process by which the script was created, using a structure proposed by Anderson[27] for analytical autoethnography for which he advocates the following criteria:

1. (The writer must be) A full member in the research group or setting,
2. Visible as such a member in published texts,
3. Committed to developing theoretical understandings of broader social phenomena. (Anderson 2006, 373)

Autoethnodrama can encourage an empathetic reading of the research story that would be lost in traditional research analysis. As with other forms of experimental ethnography, the aim is to trigger meaning making on the part of the reader[28] by juxtaposing social theory and dramatized accounts to recreate and create events that say something about the social world under study. In this way, autoethnodrama and performance texts become "a way of knowing, a method of revealing and generating meaning"[29] (see Figure 26.1).

In writing the autoethnodrama "Impact," my intention was to offer an insight into my autobiographical experiences as a pregnant woman while carrying out the research. I also interviewed colleagues from across the University of Brighton at varying stages of their careers (early career researcher to professor) and used my analysis of the data to further inform the writing process. The autoethnodrama explores the contention between the historic and romantic view of academia and the realities of the existing culture and suggests that our personal and professional lives overspill and overlap and that this process is messy and has potentially negative, but also positive, effects. The processes of interviewing colleagues and using my own autobiographical experiences was ultimately transformative, and when I completed the doctorate I felt as if I had a better sense of myself and of academic life. Producing "Impact" was not a minor or secondary aspect of the research process; instead, it provided a method of understanding the social world under study that is supported by Richardson, who reasons that "Writing is also a way of knowing—a method of discovery and analysis. By writing in different ways, we discover new aspects of our topic and our relationship to it. Form and content are inseparable."[30] When I began the research and writing

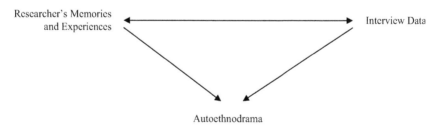

Figure 26.1 Triangulation of Research

processes for "Impact," I felt isolated, outside the HEA, and as if I would have to change in order to fit in. By the end of the doctorate and after my viva, I felt as if I were contributing to a body of academic work and a strategy that encourages conversations about the audit culture. This is indicative of how the process of production was transformative and ultimately empowering. I felt able to contribute to and also take on the academy as a lecturer and also as a mother, a role that had been used to undermine and reduce my professional identity during my pregnancy. I was aware that while autoethnography seeks to trigger research that resists male-oppressive discourses, there remains a limited amount of autoethnographic work that is explicitly feminist, and I sought to remedy this by outlining a process that had enabled me to not only recover from experiences of sexism in academia but also resist them in the future.

The Practice of Storying the Self

In 2014, I was approached by a film production company and asked if I would read a novel with a view to adapting it into a screenplay. The previous writer had dropped out and while the production company was still keen to adapt the novel, they recognized that the story needed serious reworking. I enthusiastically agreed having not read the book. When I finally did read it (as I am still under contract and the film has not been completed, I am unable to reveal the name of the book/film here), I was genuinely surprised that, knowing me as they did, the film company had still thought I might be able to undertake the project with any success. Firmly based in the chick-lit genre and with a gratingly heteronormative, non-feminist, conventional narrative, I was utterly despondent and daunted: what could I possibly bring to the story that would make it engaging to audiences anywhere? My first strategy was to completely overhaul the central character so that she went from being a chocaholic who was preoccupied with fashion and celebrity culture and desperate to get a husband to a cocaine-snorting, iron-willed fashion journalist, seeking to conquer the world on her own terms. Not surprisingly, perhaps, the film company sent it back saying they were not sure it would meet the criteria for a Parental Guidance certificate that they were keen to establish.

The problem was that I did not know the woman in the book. I know women trying to juggle a professional and personal life, and I respect and admire them. This was not how I felt about the protagonist, and I did not feel comfortable depicting a woman I could not respect and further perpetuating a view of women as dizzy, unprofessional, and able to achieve happiness only once they are married. What I did know something about was pressure at work (as detailed in my thesis), successfully and unsuccessfully balancing work and personal life (as I explored in "Impact"), and a desire to be viewed as something I actually was not (a conventional academic practicing traditional academic research), before accepting that who I really am was going to have to be good enough (at least some of the time). I also understood what it was like to be too busy to stop, stand back, and reflect on what the pressures of work were doing to me and if it was holistic and beneficial to my well-being. While the character and I were in many ways opposite, I began to see how our experiences might be aligned, and this helped me to come to know her and see why her story might matter:

> One of the most important elements of good mimetic fiction writing is that it enables the reader not only to get into the minds of the characters portrayed, but also to experience the emotions of the characters, as if they were real people, this implies that the author, when creating the work, was able to do so as well.[31]

By developing the character in the screenplay to foster elements of my own experience while maintaining characteristics and storylines that were distinct to her, I was able to connect with her, like her, respect her. Unlike the process of creating the autoethnodrama "Impact," however, I did not feel a responsibility to my interviewees or motivated to create a text that I recognized as authentic to my own life. Instead, Darcy (name of the central character) is struggling to succeed in male-dominated, audit culture, where she feels under pressure to project an image of an emotionless professional. The resolution of the story is that she realizes she is able to succeed on her own terms and stops pretending to be something she feels she has to be and instead is content to be who she is. There are elements of Darcy's journey that strongly mirror my own experience of academic life as detailed in my earlier research.[32] As I was writing the script I began willing her on, championing her to believe in herself, being kind to her when she had moments of doubt or fell back into earlier patterns of dealing with stress using alcohol or shutting out her friends and those who loved her.

Hunt argues that by fictionalizing our own autobiography, the writer is able "to move beyond entrapment in a single image of herself and to expand the possibilities for self."[33] In my earlier work, while the research process was transformational, the character I created to represent myself in "Impact" ultimately conformed to the pressures of the audit culture and their desire to be seen as "professional." By trapping myself in a narrative where I became a victim of neoliberalism and sexism, I was unable to explore a more expansive version of myself, and this restricted my desire to move past my self-imposed status as victim. Alexandra Symonds suggests,

> Helping a woman resolve her . . . fear of self-assertion, helping her to emerge with a more authentic identity to handle her hostility and the hostility of others, involves an additional layer of anxiety since she will differ from the expectations of the culture.[34]

Hunt argues that by storying the self, women are able to express themselves in a way that gives them permission to be different.[35] Creating Darcy helped to resolve my fear of asserting myself as an empowered academic with something critical and personal to say about the audit culture. I identify this process as offering the potential for a more democratic and inclusive way of working in qualitative research, where a woman may explore a more expansive and less anxious self in a way that promotes civil and spiritual freedom and resists dominant oppressive structures that are sometimes seen as synonymous with traditional academic work.

Autoethnography offers a platform by which to share stories of trauma with lived experiences and for these to provide a form of cultural critique that can offer the writer a pathway to recovery.[36] As a methodology, autoethnography enabled me to explore my own messy, lived experiences of academic life and culture that was ultimately transformative but which trapped me as a victim in my own narrative, where I had experienced sexism as a pregnant woman completing her doctorate. The process of fictionalizing my experiences via a character in a screenplay has meant that while my own emotional trauma has fueled the writing and specifically the development of the central character, it has also given me the necessary detachment required to view my inner turmoil and move past it. This process allows for the internal to become external and, for some, myself included, this can be therapeutic[37] and form part of a strategy for surviving sexism in academia. In this way, storying the self can offer a variety of autoethnography that resists criticism of being naval gazing and narcissistic and, instead, allows the writer to develop a self-knowledge and social critique that can be liberating and empowering. I suggest that fictionalizing the self can provide a viable contribution to work seeking to explore and also resist the effects of neoliberalism and male-hierarchical environments that are synonymous with HE, on individual lives and on academic culture. The process has been enabling and healing, and this has offered a direct contrast with earlier narratives where the central character was painted as a victim with suggestions of an inevitable dystopic future for HE. Instead, I now have a rejuvenated and more confident sense of self who is less fearful of what is to come. This optimism is perhaps necessary in order to contribute to the resistance to the non-inclusive, male-dominated culture that continues to prevail in HE in a spirit of social justice and fairness that is motivated and robust.

Conclusion

The relationship between creative and personal writing and academic work is evolving and strengthening within qualitative research, and this practice can be used to critique and explore the emerging audit culture in HE. Creative writing, and specifically analytical autoethnodrama, can potentially detail human experiences and locate them within a definite time and place while simultaneously providing the analysis and rigor to make this meaningful in academic work. The process of storying the self offers autoethnographers the potential distance and objectivity that is needed in order to critique the culture in which they are working. While I identify autoethnographies and specifically autoethnodramas as offering a potential lens by which to view and critique individual lives and lived experiences with the audit culture, I also argue that these stories can potentially trap women in repressed narratives. Using autobiographical experiences to imbue creative texts can provide a more expansive way of working that is more synonymous with more inclusive and democratic ways of being in academic work and academic life. The busy and anxious academic I detailed in the autoethnodrama "Impact" still exists, but by identifying existing and emerging work that seeks to provoke and engage with discussions seeking to resist the audit culture and offer other ways of being in academic work and academic life, she has started to feel less isolated, more empowered, less afraid. The realization of this transforming self has been discovered and documented through the creation of a film script where the central character resists the pressure to conform to the male-dominated hierarchical culture in which she operates and instead emerges with a surer sense of her expansive self. This story acts as a distorted mirror that is ultimately persuasive when held against my own life and experiences of working in HE. A year later and the landscape of HE is perhaps no less uncertain; the introduction of fees and shift to neoliberal governance in HE has done little to stem the culture of compliance. We need to be mindful of the voices in HE, the staff and their experiences that can help to inform and enrich the next chapter in HE history. I suggest that individual academics, institutions, and the HE academy as a whole must challenge traditional forms of academic writing and publishing in order to empower peripheral individuals and communities and democratize power and knowledge so that it is no longer controlled only by dominant forms of discourse and that this process may have particular relevance for women working in HE and who struggle with traditional, male hierarchical dominance that is synonymous with many prevailing academic discourses.

With higher student numbers than ever before, increased teaching, and the pressure to produce four-star-rated research, alongside deadlines for a film script and trying to maintain a positive family life, the busyness of my own academic life continues to intensify, and this is evident elsewhere in HE, both nationally and also internationally. Giving ourselves permission to step back and consider the real and possible effects of this emerging culture on our individual lives becomes even more important. Storying the self offers one possible way of distance and reflection, and it is my hope that reading about the process might facilitate similar spaces for the readers of this research and contribute to a more holistic and expansive academic culture that is democratic, inclusive, motivated, pleasurable. A culture that will promote and support women and allow them to prevail in academia on their own terms.

Notes

1 (Moriarty 2014)
2 (Sikes 2006, 555–568)
3 (Gillies 2011)

 4 (Sparkes 2013, 13)
 5 (Loughlin 2004)
 6 (Tedlock 2000, 455–486, 468)
 7 (Hunt 2000, 40)
 8 (Davies and Bansel 2010, 5)
 9 (Davies and Bansel 2010, 7)
10 (Sikes 2000, 563)
11 (Robbins 1963)
12 (Docherty 2012, 47)
13 (Davies and Bansel 2010)
14 (Foucault 1991a)
15 (Docherty 2012, 52)
16 Ibid., 54.
17 (Ellis 2013, 9–12)
18 (Ellis, Adams, and Bochner 2010)
19 Ibid.
20 (Richardson 1997, 2)
21 (Moriarty 2014)
22 (Ellis, Adams, and Bochner 2010)
23 Ibid.
24 (Canagarajah 2002)
25 (Bagley 2008)
26 (Saldana 2011)
27 (Anderson 2006, 373–395)
28 (Grant 2010, 577–582)
29 (Bagley 2008, 53–72)
30 (Richardson 2000, 923)
31 (Hunt 2000,16–17).
32 (Moriarty 2014)
33 (Hunt 2000, 75)
34 (Symonds 1991, 305)
35 (Hunt 2000)
36 (Grant 2013, 33–48)
37 (Hunt 2000)

Bibliography

Anderson, L. (2006). "Analytic Autoethnography." *Journal of Contemporary Ethnography*, 35: 373–395.
Bagley, C. (2008). "Educational Ethnography as Performance Art: Towards a Sensuous Feeling and Knowing." *Qualitative Research*, 8 (1): 53–72.
Banks, M. (2007). *The Politics of Cultural Work*. Basingstoke/ New York: Palgrave Macmillan.
Canagarajah, A. S. (2002). *Geopolitics of Academic Writing*. Pittsburgh, PA: University of Pittsburgh Press.
Daves, B., and Bansel, P. (2007). "Neoliberalism and Education." *International Journal of Qualitative Studies in Education*, 20 (3).
Ellis, C. (2013). Carrying the Torch for Autocthnography. In *Handbook of Autoethnography*, edited by Jones S. Holman, T. E. Adams and C. Ellis, 9–12. Walnut Creek, CA: Left Coast Press.
Ellis, C., T. E. Adams, and A. P. Bochner (2010). "Autoethnography: An Overview [40 paragraphs]." *Forum Qualitative Sozialforschung / Forum: Qualitative Social Research*, 12 (1), Art. 10, http://nbn-resolving.de/urn:nbn:de:0114-fqs1101108.
Foucault, M. (1991a). "Governmentality." In *The Foucault Effect: Studies in Governmentality*, edited by G. Burchell, C. Gordon, and P. Miller, 87–104. Chicago: University of Chicago Press.
Gillies, D. (2011). "Agile Bodies: A New Perspective on Neoliberal Governance." *Journal of Education Policy*, 26 (2): 207–223.
Grant, A. (2010). "Writing the Reflexive Self: An Autoethnography of Alcoholism and the 'Impact' of Psychotherapy Culture." *Journal of Psychiatric and Mental Health Nursing*, 17 (7): 577–582.
———. (2013). "Writing Teaching and Survival in Mental Health: A Discordant Quintet for One." In *Contemporary British Autoethnography*, edited by N. Short, L. Turner, and A. Grant, 33–48. Rotterdam: Sense Publishers.

Hunt, C. (2000). *Therapeutic Dimensions of Autobiography in Creative Writing*. London, Philadelphia: Jessica Kingsley Publishers.

Loughlin, M. (2004). "Quality, Control and Complicity: The Effortless Conquest of the Academy by Bureaucrats." *International Journal of Humanities*, 2 (1): 717–724.

Moriarty, J. (2014). *Analytical Autoethnodrama: Autobiographed and Researched Experiences with Academic Writing*. Rotterdam, Boston, Taipei: Sense.

Richardson, L. (1997). *Fields of Play*. New Brunswick, NJ: Rutgers University Press.

———. (2000). "Writing: A Method of Inquiry." In *The Handbook of Qualitative Research*, 2nd ed., edited by N. Denzin and Y. Lincoln, 923–948. Thousand Oaks, CA: Sage Publications.

Robbins, L. (1963). "The Robbins Report, Higher Education Report of the Committee Appointed by the Prime Minister Under the Chairmanship of Lord Robbins. London: Her Majesty's Stationery Office." Downloaded 10th January 2013. www.educationengland.org.uk/documents/robbins/.

Ross, A. (2003). *No Collar: The Humane Workplace and its Hidden Costs*, New York: Basic Books.

Saldana, J. (2003). "Dramatizing Data: A Primer." *Qualitative Inquiry*, 9: 218–236.

———. (2011). *Ethnotheatre: Research from Page to Stage (Qualitative Inquiry & Social Justice)*. New York: Left Coast Press.

Sikes, P. (2000). "Truth and Lies Revisited." *British Educational Research Journal*, 26 (2): 257–270.

———. (2006). "Working in a 'New' University: In the Shadow of the Research Assessment Exercise?" *Studies in Higher Education*, 31 (5): 555–568.

Sparkes, A. C. (2002). *Telling Tales in Sport and Physical Activity: A Qualitative Journey*. Leeds: Human Kinetics.

———. (2013). "Qualitative Research in Sport, Exercise and Health in the Era of Neoliberalism, Audit and New Public Management: Understanding the Conditions for the (im)possibilities of a New Paradigm Dialogue." *Qualitative Research in Sport, Exercise and Health*, 5 (3): 440–459. doi: 10.1080/2159676X.2013.796493.

Symonds, A. (1991). "Gender Issues and Horney Theory." *American Journal of Psychoanalysis*, 51 (3): 301–312.

Tedlock, B. (2000). "Ethnography and ethnographic representation." In *The Handbook of Qualitative Research*, edited by N. Denzin and Y. Lincoln, 455–486. Thousand Oaks, CA: Sage.

Ursell, G. (2000). "Television Production: Issues of Exploitation, Commodification and Subjectivity in UK Television Markets." *Media, Culture & Society*, 22: 805–825.

Washburn, J. (2003). *University, Inc. The Corporate Corruption of Higher Education*. New York: Basic Books.

27 Rhetorics of Interruption

Navigating Sexism in the Academy

Elise Verzosa Hurley, Amanda Wray, and
Erica Cirillo-McCarthy

A researcher was discouraged from going up early for tenure because she took family medical leave. She was told that only "superstars" went up early, and multiple faculty encouraged the researcher to slow down the time clock to tenure even though she has a strong record of publication, service, and teaching.

A pre-tenure faculty member was approached by a male tenured colleague to "jokingly" offer advice about her appearance, noting that women with her ethnic background should never color their hair. While the comment was not intended to be malicious, this seemingly innocent interaction underscores the way in which her body was gendered, racialized, and assumed to be open to commentary.

A fixed-term lecturer at an elite institution often hears her male colleagues bring attention to men's "minority" status in the writing program and in writing studies as a field, comments which ignore the gender inequity currently present at her institution's administration and faculty ranks.

Despite the gains higher education has made toward diversity, inclusion, and gender equality, our own embodied experiences as feminists in the academy located in three different institutional contexts suggests that instances such as those encountered in the previous anecdotes remain pervasive. Although the academy is most often conceived of as an enlightened intellectual community, it is also a social institution; thus, it is not impermeable to the social realities that occur beyond its ivory tower walls, realities informed by the prevalence of post-feminist and post-racial rhetoric in an increasingly neoliberal climate. Marian Meyers (2013) points to a "post-feminist" sensibility as waging war on female academics by, among other things, producing a dominant rhetoric of gender parity. Sexism, especially through a neoliberal lens, is considered in terms of individual and overt acts of discrimination, often understood primarily as unequal pay and a biased system of rewards (Aguirre 2000). While academic women do make 21% less than their male counterparts (AAUW 2015), we experience sexism and gender harassment in multiple forms beyond financial disparity. Everyday experiences with sexism accumulate over time to have real consequence on women's health and well-being, not to mention their professional aspirations and ability to succeed.

Feminist scholar Sara Ahmed (2012) calls diversity workers to "describe the effects of inhabiting institutional spaces that do not give [one] residence" (177). In response to this call, our chapter documents ways in which feminist academics navigate and negotiate various sexist, misogynist, patriarchal, and exclusionary practices across academic institutional contexts. Drawing on survey data, we argue for a more robust understanding of interruption as an interventionist rhetorical practice, and we analyze the ways in which feminist academics have used (as well as refrained from using) tactics and strategies of interruption, focusing particularly on its potential not only to disrupt exclusionary discourse but also to transform it. Ultimately, we argue for the value of tactical and strategic interruptions as a means of enacting change in academic professional contexts.

Theoretical Framework

Feminist rhetoric and composition scholar Nedra Reynolds (1998) argues that interruption allows rhetors to "draw attention to their identities as marginalized speakers and writers" while also attending to the politics of exclusion and the ways such politics manifest in everyday discourse (60). Interruption can include speaking louder than or over someone, physically removing one's body away from a situation, and engaging someone in a dialogue or posing critical questions that might interrupt status quo ways of thinking, among other possibilities. Rhetors who use interruption as an interventionist rhetorical move, Reynolds argues, offer one possibility for effecting social change. However, in order for interruption to be efficacious in a given context, one's interruption must be recognized as valid, requiring a reframing of perceptions that typically surround the act of interrupting as rude, uncouth, or ignorant of prevailing social conventions. At the crux of Reynolds's argument, then, is the notion of agency as "not simply finding one's own voice but also about intervening in discourses of the everyday and cultivating rhetorical tactics that make interruption and resistance an important part of any conversation" (59).

While we concur with Reynolds that *consciously* interrupting and intervening in everyday practices of exclusion is necessary and important work, we also want to acknowledge and recognize that agency is inextricable from power and privilege. In the context of everyday interpersonal interactions in the academy, we may often feel as though we *should* consciously interrupt. At the same time, the consequences of interruption may seem too high a price to pay particularly in unexpected confrontations that require us to negotiate power differentials. Thus, we understand agency not as something to be harnessed or attributed to any one individual, but as socially located, shifting, and relational. Carl Herndl and Adela C. Licona (2007) call this "constrained agency" wherein subjects are "differently enabled or constrained to act and speak within a given context" (150). Herndl and Licona argue that agency is leveraged among differentially articulated conditions of power and authority in relation to shifting material contexts and ideological positions, which helps explain why "the same person is sometimes an agent of change, sometimes a figure of established authority, and sometimes an ambiguous, even contradictory, combination of both social functions" (135). Herndl and Licona's theory of constrained agency illuminates why we might feel more comfortable interrupting sexism with our students in the classroom and less comfortable interrupting our colleagues in conversations.

In addition to our understanding of agency as situated and relational, we recognize that sexism and other exclusionary practices are intersectional and occur along multiple matrices of oppression and privilege (Crenshaw 1989, 140). As our research illustrates, feminist academics do not experience sexism and exclusion in the same ways, and whether they *can* or how they *do* interrupt (should they choose to) reflect differential agency related to, among other things, perceived personal and professional risks within a given situation. Labeling, for instance, is just one mechanism for silencing and discouraging interruption (consider stereotypes surrounding the "angry" Black woman, the "dramatic" queer, or the "man-hating" feminist). In addition to perceptions of interruption as socially improper, interruptions by and from different bodies may also garner different degrees of fallout. Moreover, the mere *presence* of some bodies (mostly those of color, differently abled, and/or non-binary) can be perceived as interruptions simply by virtue of being there, without ever engaging in discourse.

As teacher-scholars trained in rhetoric, we also acknowledge the role of *kairos* in how individuals negotiate constrained agency and their intersectional identities in relation to the forms of interruptions they choose to enact. Often defined as the "opportune moment" in which to engage in discourse, a more nuanced definition of *kairos* recognizes that "appropriateness and timing interanimate each other in such a way that it is almost impossible to consider *kairos* outside of the most problematic philosophical and rhetorical realm, the realm of action, the realm of ethics" (Harker 2007, 82). *Kairos* is not just about the right time and the right place but is also about *what happens* when the right time and right occasion arrives. The form interruption takes shapes the ways individuals "move into and out of agentive spaces as the result of the kairotic collocations of multiple relations" (Herndl and Licona 2007, 147). *When* academics choose to interrupt, then, is equally important as *how* they interrupt and *why*.

Methods, Research Participant Demographics, and Contexts of Sexism

Research participants for this study[1] were recruited through a formal call placed on faculty and staff listservs at several universities, regional and national listservs,[2] social media, and interpersonal networking at the 2015 National Women's Studies Association Conference and Feminisms and Rhetorics Conference. We attempted to reach a diverse pool of participants representing teaching and non-teaching staff at all levels and departmental identities within academia, and we secured 355 participants. The 23-question survey included qualitative and quantitative means for learning where and by whom most sexism occurs in the academy. Additionally, we aimed to identify how participants interrupt in order to further understand how it can function as a rhetorical tool for social justice education and anti-oppression. Because covert sexism is regularly overlooked as "harmless," we chose to list behaviors and asked participants to identify how frequently these behaviors[3] happen on a weekly basis. This naming strategy provides more accurate reporting, according to Vicki J. Magley et al. (1999), because it complicates the normalization of gendered and sexist harassment behavior in the work environment. Research participants reflect 38 states and 9 countries outside the U.S. Respondents were predominantly (72%) from public institutions of higher education serving undergraduate and graduate students (58%) with a student population of 5,001 to 30,000 (42%). One to 51 years in academia are represented in this data,[4] with additional demographic information summarized in the following tables:

Not being taken seriously or treated as a professional is cited as the most common (78%) form of sexism experienced. Respondents also felt silenced and/or dismissed in group situations (73%), experienced "jokes" or comments related to perceived gender roles (72%), and lived microaggressions (70%). One of the biggest challenges, as a respondent puts it, is that "[sexism] can be so subtle and yet so pervasive that it's hard to believe it's really happening." In a frequency scale of 1 to 5, participants name supervising faculty/administration as the primary perpetrator of sexism (2.89 mean) with co-workers in their department (2.71 mean) and students (2.62 mean) following closely behind. Respondents are *most* likely to interrupt sexism when encountered in the classroom with students and *least* likely to interrupt with supervising faculty/administration, faculty from other departments, and via listservs/email exchanges. As expected, respondents are most concerned with professional consequences when interrupting the sexism of supervising faculty/administration, with 72% of the participants indicating the two highest levels of concern on a five-point Likert scale. Interrupting sexism in one's home department presents the second highest level of concern for backlash. For many working in academia, the places where they most encounter sexism are also the places where they feel the greatest amount of risk if and when they interrupt.

Table 27.1 Research Participant Demographics by Position

Tenure Track Assistant Professor	20%
Associate Professor	22%
Full and Emeritus Professors	10%
Graduate Students	11%
Non-Tenure Track Full-Time Faculty	16%
Non-Tenure Track Part-Time/Contingent Faculty	6%
Staff	5%
Administration	6%
Unspecified	4%

Table 27.2 Research Participant Demographics by Gender

Female	86%
Gender Queer/Trans	6%
Male	7%
Other	1%

Table 27.3 Research Participant Demographics by Discipline

Arts and Humanities	68.5%
Natural Sciences	7.8%
Social Sciences	8%
Business and Information Technology	5.5%
Education	2.3%
Mathematics	3%
Administrative and Staff	5.5%

Note. Overrepresentation in our data pool includes those who claim English, Composition, and/or Rhetoric as their home discipline (51%). Though we advertised the survey across many university contexts, our own home discipline (Composition and Rhetoric) and academic spaces influenced who saw our call for participants and, more influentially, who completed the survey.

Tactical and Strategic Interruptions: Analyzing Participant Responses

Drawing on Michel De Certeau's (1984) theories concerning everyday practices, we situate our data regarding the ways in which academics interrupt sexism and exclusionary practices within his discussion of tactics and strategies. De Certeau most often links the notion of *kairos* to tactics, which he defines as "the space of the other" and "an art of the weak" (37). Tactics, thus, take advantage of kairotic ruptures and are effective due to the "clever utilization of time, of the opportunities it presents and also of the play that it introduces into foundations of power" (39). Strategies, on the other hand, reflect long-range planning in order to stabilize domains of knowledge and power (36). We argue that in order to dismantle systems of patriarchy and exclusion in the academy, interruptions must take *both* tactical and strategic forms.

Tactical Interruptions

Tactical interruptions to sexism and other exclusionary practices are discussed by nearly all of our research participants, primarily as an immediate, individual reaction that sometimes, but not always, provides results. Four tactical interruptions we discuss here are those that appear most frequently in the survey data: posing critical questions, silence, physical distancing behaviors, and speaking back.

Critical Questioning

Posing critical questions to draw attention to status quo sexist ideologies is the most common interruption tactic, used by 69% of our respondents. Posing critical questions has the potential to bring the issue of sexism to the forefront of the conversation, encouraging all to see and, perhaps, reflect on the sexist act or policy. For example, one respondent wrote that when hearing a colleague state "this must be where all the hot chicks hang out," she asked him why he thought that was an appropriate comment to make. She goes on to point out that the "confrontational" questioning "places the obligation of answering or even naming the sexism on them [the offender]." More significantly, posing critical questions allowed this respondent to "navigate . . . uncomfortable situations without facing consequences" while also "maintain[ing] my dignity." When we consider the deteriorating effect that engaging with sexism has on one's health, finding a way to sustain one's dignity in an undignified situation can be a powerful tactic.

Employing questioning as an interruption tactic allows one to critique a situation without the exhaustive nature of having to explain sexism or patriarchy to those who reproduce exclusionary practices. However, posing critical questions relies on being ready for the occasion on the fly, with critical questions on hand. Sometimes, simply asking *what do you mean by that* invites the offending speaker to reconsider the intentionality of his or her words and to, perhaps, hear what he or she initially spoke in a new way.

Silence

Sixty-one percent of our research participants use silence as a tactic of interruption. Queer studies and other feminist scholarship have explored the ways in which silence factors into imposed invisibility and marginalization of oppressed groups (Hutchinson 1999) as well as an expression and performance that can function as a tool of resistance (Wagner 2012). Margaret Montoya (2000) argues that tactical practices of silence produce centrifugal forces that allow "the languages of outsiders [. . . to] decentralize and destabilize that power and privilege" (268). Silence, thus, creates a "tension" that can interrupt and, over time when *kairotically* employed, may work to dismantle ways of talking that normalize sexist thinking and practices. For example, one researcher responded to a colleague's comment about her "post-baby figure" by maintaining eye contact and a stony silence. As one respondent notes, "Sometimes a silently raised eyebrow is surprisingly effective." For silence to be an effective tactical interruption others must notice it; that is, silence works as an effective interruption when an audible response is expected.

A context of silence, however, can contribute to a sense of hopelessness in that those experiencing sexism may feel alone, unaware that these behaviors are, indeed, sexism and that others are subjected to the same types of harassment. Some participants struggle with silence as an act of resistance because it is culturally read as passive and imposed:

> Silence is a strategy I have used, but [it] leaves me feeling empty. I feel that it may at times be effective in dealing temporarily in a situation but is a Band-Aid. No change occurs when I'm silent. It merely masks that there's an issue.

Another respondent rejected silence as enough interruption, stating, "While I understand that silence and avoidance may also be strategic responses for many in the academy in these situations, a failure to respond would make me feel even more 'less than' than the original comment." Many factors contribute to silence being employed as a tactic of interruption, including the choice to, perhaps, locate a more opportune moment where one's agency is better suited.

Physical Distancing Behaviors

Fifty-nine percent of the survey pool indicated that they physically remove the self from the situation in an effort to interrupt gender-based prejudice, sexism, and sexist ideologies, and 23% stated that by entering into a situation (with or without comment) they interrupt. Some respondents responded to sexism by saying no to feminized work, typically service work, and also through physically removing themselves from the space or conversation. One respondent argues,

> Most of my experiences of sexism deal with feminization of service and the assumption that I'll do the "dirty work" of the department or institution. My best tool for interruption is not saying yes—though that's not always perceived as interruption, just resistance.

We see this rejection of compliance as a form of interruption, for it resists the assumption that faculty, especially pre-tenure faculty, will agree to undervalued service work (e.g., committee work, student advising, mentoring). Academia is littered with stories of women and scholars of color burning themselves out on service work rather than attending to other promotional expectations such as research and publication. All of this leads to the marginalization of service as women's work; therefore, saying no or removing oneself from that labor helps to interrupt the institutionalized discourse of gendered work within a department. More important, withdrawing participation can be considered a means of destabilizing the power dynamics of the situation.

Individually Speaking Back

Speaking back, which can be defined as directly confronting the offending person(s), was practiced by 48% of our respondents, with 38% naming sexism to the individual or group as an additional form of speaking back. Unlike critical questioning, speaking back aims to immediately stop the sexism as it is currently being practiced. Critical questioning often intends to invite self-reflection and a change of opinion, whereas speaking back is more intent on the present, perhaps even wishing to impose silence. Almost all respondents articulated a deep understanding of the risks associated with speaking back, and many cited fear of backlash. For example, one contingent faculty member pointed to the bind of speaking out without leverage: "I felt uncomfortable doing this [speaking out] a lot given my precarious employment position. I wish I could do more about sexism, but I feel that I really have no power here."

Respondents also detailed instances when speaking back transformed not only interactions but also the discourse. When faced with sexism, one respondent explains, "I called it what it was publicly. People listened. There was an apology. It never happened from that individual again. We enjoy a good working relationship now." We acknowledge that the perceived assertiveness needed for the direct approach is more available to some than others and, thus, before speaking back, individuals must take into account the power structures in which they are enmeshed in order to avoid a potentially precarious situation. Another respondent felt that speaking back has the power to resist the stereotype that "new professors (especially women) should just be quiet."

Strategic Interruptions

Because strategies have a "connection with the power that sustains them from within the stronghold of its own 'proper' place or institution" (De Certeau 1984, xx), strategic interruptions can be a useful and kairotic approach to redress institutional inequity. Strategic interruptions employ coalition building and making change at the institutional level, such as diverse hiring practices and effective training on inclusive language. Forms of strategic interruption present in the survey data that we wish to discuss include building coalitions or organizing with others, initiating policy change, written documentation, and social justice–oriented pedagogical practices.

Building Coalitions

Coalitional practices take many forms within the academy, including conducting collaborative research to document oppression and the use of interruption tactics (such as critical questioning) across multiple contexts. We understand "coalition" through the lens of Patricia Hill Collins (1998) and other feminists who advocate for working across differences as a necessary aspect of building alliances. Salary and academic leave adjustments were cited in our data as products of coalition building. A female identified respondent explains: "[A]t my university, a strong coalition of women colleagues studied, challenged, and successfully changed the prevailing systemic sexism in the salary system." Raising awareness about sexism across academic spaces increases visibility, not just of sexism but also of coalition building, which invites others into collaborative action.

Parenting was commonly cited as an incentive for coalition building within the academy. Respondents felt institutional sexism due to the double bind regarding the lack of support mechanisms related to childcare as well as the benevolent sexism many female academics experience in relation to motherhood (Mason, Wolfinger, and Goulden 2013). One respondent feels that "the lack of childcare or lactation space on my campus is continually sexist," and another expressed the institutional challenges of juggling academic work and parenting, noting that she felt unsupported during maternity leave and has to

> nearly daily field comments about how hard it must be to have to work and leave my child, or questions about how I can leave to go do my own scholarship and work and not tend to my child. It's constant.

Another instance of benevolent sexism respondents commonly experienced is the career advice for women not to have children in order to focus on research until after graduate school or after tenure. In fact, a graduate student respondent wrote that "the works demands of a tenure track professor make the profession difficult for women who want to have children. For this reason, I will not pursue a Ph.D." And yet, through coalitions, individuals are able to improve their everyday lives as well as work toward institutional change. As one respondent celebrated:

> I have also chosen to build coalition with other mothers in the department to help combat negative comments like [the ones said by a male colleague]. Since that time, our department has installed a parent and baby room with a changing table and fridge for storing pumped breast milk.

The efficacy of building coalitions, however, is not guaranteed. In building successful coalitions, we must seek diversity. One respondent commented that exclusionary groups, even when they serve the needs of an underrepresented group, may work against coalitional practices. The respondent states, "

> I also think that creating spaces in academia that are exclusive to women (i.e., purposefully keeping men or people who identify as male out) is only doing the same thing to them that has been done to us for too many years. Lead by example, not exclusion.

Moreover, other systemic factors may present obstacles to building coalitions and finding allies, such as when a participant commented that "coalition building has proven impossible in an institution whose policies and practices ensure that most who would be interested in such a coalition don't make it past tenure (whether by choice or not)." Working in an environment rife with sexism, inequality, and exclusion can feel isolating; however, our research indicates that similar experiences are more common than any one individual might think. Finding allies, sharing experiences, and building coalitions across campus may draw greater attention to how the cards are systematically stacked against some academics, paving the way for other forms of strategic interruptions that can lead to action and change.

Initiating Policy Change

A number of respondents emphasized the importance of initiating policy changes as a strategic interruption. In addition to disparities in salary and academic leave, respondents also pointed to insufficient inclusion practices. As one respondent notes, "There is little commitment to changing institutional practices in ways that make the academy more welcoming to minority groups or to women. If women are not succeeding, we do not question what systemic obstacles they may face." Thus, initiatives for diversity and inclusivity at the institutional level are championed by a number of respondents, and initiatives to increase diversity at the institutional level through policies such as hiring practices were of paramount concern. As one respondent writes,

> I teach at a college that was founded by women for women, and which even now that we're co-educational, still serves a majority of women. We have not had a woman president or vice president of academic affairs since becoming co-ed. We still have very few women in positions of real power.

In contrast, a faculty member who "work[s] for a university with a female president and several female deans" asserts that "having more female leadership makes a difference." Changing campus culture requires more than a mandatory annual diversity and sensitivity training session; policy initiatives also hinge upon ongoing commitments to changing practices and actions.

Written Documentation

Since individual calls to attend to sexism and exclusionary practices can often be ignored, dismissed, and/or challenging to prove, research respondents noted formal complaints and written documentation as a useful (though not always necessarily effective) strategy of interruption. For example, in response to repeated instances of a department chairperson's unwillingness to take a faculty member seriously, one respondent noted the importance of "taking a long approach, recording instances to establish a pattern." Formally documenting instances of sexism over time anticipates and circumvents the case that sexism and gender-based prejudice occur as isolated or extreme instances of bad behavior. Another respondent noted that written documentation not only provides a record of what has occurred but can also be helpful in "pointing out sexist language and behavior without being labeled as 'emotional.'" Written documentation makes one's experience of a situation appear less subjective and more concrete, somehow more quantifiable in terms of severity and frequency. Written documentation also enables allies in positions of authority to better advocate for faculty members. Consider, for example, the following response from a male research participant:

> There have been numerous instances where colleagues reported either blatant or microaggressive acts of sexism in the workplace, but as an untenured faculty member who was not present during the act, I felt powerless to act on my colleagues' behalf.

Upon tenure and appointment to department chair, this respondent actively encourages "faculty to document their concerns and bring them to my attention so that I can intervene." This example highlights the shifting nature of agency in relation to changing power dynamics and illustrates the ways in which one's privilege can be used to improve working conditions for others. Another respondent, who states they have not been the target of sexism, is the administrator to whom faculty and students report sexism, and "[s]ince I am fairly empowered to deal with such things, I deal with it, usually directly, in personal conversations." No doubt this respondent embodies certain privileges that make face-to-face, direct interruption something perpetrators of sexism will take seriously. Not all administrators will find this strategy equally effective due to differentially articulated intersections of identity and power; for example, women administrators interrupting in this way might be perceived as "too sensitive."

Although many of our respondents find that documentation practices can be a useful strategy of interruption, documentation alone may not guarantee sufficient change. A research participant notes, for example, that while she filed a formal complaint to her institution's promotion and tenure committee, she fully believes the university "to do nothing and expect[s] the retaliation to continue." Similarly, in response to an overtly sexist departmental environment, one respondent noted that despite forming a coalition of women faculty and graduate students to discuss gender inequality and feminist strategies, "We report to our chair every time an incident is reported to us. Nothing has happened. It's extremely frustrating." In addition to contingent efficacy, initiating formal documentation can also be particularly risky when considering the potential for further interpersonal conflict and departmental backlash. A female participant stated,

> I know the problem [sexism] is ongoing, exists for all the women in my department, and will not change with a comment or interruption—so unless I file a grievance with the union, his behavior is accepted as par for the course.

For pre-tenure faculty and others in tenuous positions, complacency may seem like the only option when weighing out the potential ramifications of interruption.

Social Justice–Oriented Pedagogical Practices

Finally, because agency is differentially articulated as an instructor in the classroom in contrast to the academic workplace at large, numerous respondents viewed social justice–oriented pedagogy as the form of strategic interruption that they most often engage. Broadly, social justice–oriented pedagogy helps make sexism and other forms of oppression more apparent to students in relation to the cultural norms that attempt to excuse, minimize, and make them invisible. This way of teaching is, in essence, a means for "speaking back" to traditional histories, rhetorics, and practices by bringing in new and different voices to the canon, while also teaching students to be informed by multiple perspectives as a step in critical thinking. For example, one respondent recounts an instance from a first-year composition course where the readings included "non-hetereosexual, non-monogamous romantic/sexual relationships . . . [that] led some students to voice their own views on gender and sexuality, some of which were based on sexist cultural assumptions." The respondent invited the author of that particular reading to attend class where

> we pointed out the sexist assumptions that these beliefs were based on, which it seemed led students to at least reexamine their inherited beliefs, if not alter them. This event didn't seem to have any negative consequences; many students expressed that they enjoyed that particular class meeting more than most.

In this particular example, the respondent used this particular moment of cognitive dissonance experienced by students not to accuse them of being "wrong" or "misguided" but as an avenue for thoughtfully considering other perspectives.

While we have described the ways in which interruption can function as both tactical and strategic approaches to intervening in sexism, we also acknowledge that these terms are fluid, especially with regard to social justice–oriented pedagogy. An instructor who chooses to interrupt sexist comments and assumptions in the classroom certainly engages in tactical interruption; however, when intentionally and regularly incorporated in the curriculum across the university, the interruption can also function strategically. Both tactical and strategic pedagogical interruptions can create more opportunities for questioning the status quo in ways that allow our students to learn to be better ambassadors of social change.

Everyday Means for Facilitating Institutional Change

When we began this research, we did not anticipate the explicit and egregious sexism in the academy. We assumed that covert sexism would dominate responses or that sexism would be mostly embedded systemically as opposed to being carried out so commonly in everyday situations. Additionally, our data illustrate the pervasiveness of heteronormativity present in academia, reproduced by all genders across administrative, faculty, and staff positions. We sought to understand the potential value of interruption—the situations in which they manifest and how they are enacted. Sometimes interruption does not take grandiose and dramatic forms but is often quite mundane. As a respondent notes, "I don't have young ones, but I do bring my older kids to campus often just to try to interrupt the very family-unfriendly space/structure. Well, and also I don't have reliable childcare." As our chapter illustrates, rhetorics of interruption hold great potential in fighting sexism, exclusion, and inequity, whether that interruption takes the form of individual, often quotidian tactical actions, or occurs in concert with multivocal, multidirectional strategic interruptions. Interruption, in its variety of forms and possible locations, offers academics who encounter sexism potential ways to enact change on what and whom the academy values by making sexism more visible and vilified.

Notes

1 The University of North Carolina Asheville Institutional Review Board approved this survey study August, 2015; survey opened October 19 and closed November 22, 2015.
2 Including the Writing Program Administrators, International Oral History Association, and Council for Programs on Technical and Scientific Communication listservs.
3 Meta-sexism (the questioning and doubting of experiences), "jokes" or comments (including those not intended to be malicious regarding physical appearance), being dismissed and/or silenced in group situations, not being taken seriously or treated as a professional, microaggressions (such as assumption that men are in charge and women get the coffee), and labeling (such as "darling" or "Mrs." instead of "Dr.").
4 Forty percent have worked in academia fewer than 10 years, 35% between 10 and 20 years, and 16% more than 20 years.

References

Aguirre, A. Jr. (2000). *Women and Minority Faculty in the Academic Workplace*. San Francisco, CA: Jossey-Bass.
Ahmed, Sara. (2012). *On Being Included: Racism and Diversity in Institutional Life*. Durham, NC: Duke University Press.
American Association of University Women. (Fall 2015). *The Simple Truth About the Pay Gap*. www.aauw.org/files/2015/09/The-Simple-Truth-Fall-2015.pdf.
Collins, Patricia Hill. (1998). *Fighting Words: Black Women and the Search for Justice*. Minneapolis: University of Missouri Press.
Crenshaw, Kimberlé W. (1989). "Demarginalizing the Intersection of Race and Sex: A Black Feminist Critique of Antidiscrimination Doctrine, Feminist Theory and Antiracist Politics." *University of Chicago Legal Forum*, 140: 139–167.
De Certeau, Michel. (1984). *The Practice of Everyday Life*. Berkeley: University of California Press.
Harker, Michael. (September 2007). "Ethics of Argument: Rereading Kairos and Making Sense in a Timely Fashion." *College Composition and Communication*, 59 (1): 77–97.
Herndl, Carl G., and Adela C. Licona. (2007). "Shifting Agency: Agency, Kairos, and the Possibilities of Social Action." In *Communicative Practices in Workplaces and the Professions: Cultural Perspectives on the Regulation of Discourse and Organizations*, edited by Mark Zachry and Charlotte Thralls, 133–153. Amityville: Baywood Publishing.

Hutchinson, Darren Lenard. (1999). "Claiming and Speaking Who We Are: Black Gays and Lesbians, Racial Politics, and the Million Man March." In *Black Men on Race, Gender, and Sexuality: A Critical Reader*, edited by Devon Carbado, 28–45. New York: New York University Press.

Magley, Vicki J., Charles L. Hulin, Louise F. Fitzgerald, and Mary DeNardo. (1999). "Outcomes of Self-Labeling Sexual Harassment." *Journal of Applied Psychology*, 84: 390–402.

Mason, Mary Ann, Nicholas Wolfinger, and Marc Goulden. (2013). *Do Babies Matter? Gender and Family in the Ivory Tower*. New Brunswick, NJ: Rutgers University Press.

Meyers, Marian. (2013). "The War on Academic Women: Reflections on Postfeminism in the Neoliberal Academy." *Journal of Communication Inquiry*, 37 (4): 274–283.

Montoya, Margaret. (2000). "Silence and Silencing: Their Centripetal and Centrifugal Forces in Legal Communication, Pedagogy and Discourse." *Michigan Journal of Race and Law*, 5: 847–912.

Reynolds, Nedra. (1998). "Interrupting Our Way to Agency: Feminist Cultural Studies and Composition." In *Feminism and Composition Studies: In Other Words*, edited by Susan C. Jarratt and Lynn Worsham, 58–73. New York: The Modern Language Association of America.

Wagner, Roi. (2012). "Silence as Resistance Before the Subject, or Could the Subaltern Remain Silent." *Theory, Culture & Society*, 29 (6): 99–124.

28 Overcoming the Department Bully

Women, Men, and Collaboration

Karla S. McCain

I started my career as an assistant professor at exactly the kind of small liberal arts college I wanted, and I was so excited about teaching my own classes and mentoring undergraduate students in my research lab. I didn't meet Professor X until I had already accepted the position at the college because he had been abroad for January term during my interview. I was eager to meet him when I arrived on campus because the areas of chemistry we teach are closely related. It was clear from that first meeting that he cultivated an eccentric and curmudgeonly persona, but his behavior to me at that time was not unpleasant or unprofessional. Having moved directly from my Ph.D. program with no teaching experience beyond being a lab TA, I struggled my first couple of years to feel comfortable in the classroom and develop as a teacher. I was very intimidated by lecturing to my large general chemistry class of about 60 students and desperately needed to develop confidence in the classroom. I suffered with a bad case of imposter syndrome. This is unfounded belief that you are not as smart and qualified as your colleagues and causes a deep fear that you will be exposed as such to them (Clance and Imes 1978). Imposter syndrome is a common experience for women in academic science, and it was in this state that I first began to experience problems with Professor X.

Cumulative advantage and disadvantage refers to the process by which small differences in treatment can add to significant differences over time both positively or negatively (Merton 1948; Merton 1968; Rossiter 1993; Valian 1999). One can think about it as similar to the way compound interest works to either help grow a significant nest egg from small contributions or plunge one deeply in debt from relatively small loans which are never paid back. A computer simulation of a hypothetical corporation with eight levels of employees had an initial population with equal numbers of men and women at the bottom level and only a 1% bias toward promoting men. They found that after many iterations the top level was only 35% women (Martell, Lane, and Emrich 1996). Cumulative advantage was initially developed by Merton (1968) to explain why in scientific collaborations the most famous and established partner received the most credit. He argued that not only were eminent scientists given more credit for collaborative or multiple, independent discoveries, but also that their work was also more likely to be noticed and communicated broadly. This, in turn, increased their self-esteem and encouraged them to tackle riskier, but more important, experiments which sowed the seeds for their next accolade. Later work applied this logic to the opposite effect experienced by women in science (Rossiter 1993, Long 1990), where small disadvantages snowball into larger career difficulties. Success builds on itself, but so does failure. I will use this framework to describe not only how my experience with gender-based bullying almost derailed my career, but also how overcoming it continues to reap benefits for me.

My department has a research requirement for majors, and each student is required to present at our departmental seminar at least once before they graduate. Despite my rocky start in the classroom, I felt much more confident about research and was really pleased at the pace I was obtaining preliminary results. I had enough data after my second summer of research to submit my first publication and received positive feedback about my work when I presented it to colleagues at other institutions. That context made it all the more disorienting to me when Professor X started aggressively questioning my research students during seminar and dismissing my overall conclusions. First and most importantly, I was incredibly concerned about my students and how they would feel about such a public attack because they may not have realized that they were being used as proxies for me. I also worried about the effect of this aggressive questioning on the opinions of others in my department. Like many small chemistry departments, I was the only person of my specialty in the department, and I knew that I had to effectively communicate the science I was doing to people with very different backgrounds. Would they think that Professor X, whose specialty is closest to mine, was correct in his assessment of my work? As he publicly attacked my scientific research, I experienced accumulated disadvantage in several ways. First, it compromised my ability to recruit potential research students who observed the aggressive questioning of my current students. Second, it undermined the perception of my technical expertise with my other colleagues because they saw someone who was similarly trained evaluate my work so viscously. Finally, the attacks made me seriously doubt my own competence and ability to practice science independently. This questioning fed the doubt I had about my abilities and intensified my imposter syndrome.

Department meetings were very tense my first couple of years at the college for a multitude of reasons, and it took me quite a while to understand all of the politics that contributed to that atmosphere. I was afraid to say much, but I was sometimes shocked at how resistant to change Professor X was, even on issues that seemed trivial to me. As I tried to contribute productively to discussions in my department, things only became worse. While he was grumpy with everyone, I was the only one he personally attacked in the meetings with accusations about my character and abilities. He accused me repeatedly of behaving in mean and uncaring ways to my students. One time, he stood up dramatically from the table and went to the chalkboard to show through a derivation that an equation I used in a lab question was patently wrong, when in reality we had just started with two different assumptions. Even though I intellectually knew that things he accused me of were not true, the contempt they contained hurt and increased my feelings of unworthiness. I felt as though he must have figured out how much I did not yet know and that I deserved his disrespectful behavior. This berating in front of my other colleagues further contributed to my accumulated disadvantage regarding my standing in the department and my ability to see myself as a competent professional. While none of my other colleagues came to my defense publicly, they were supportive in one-on-one settings. The toxic level of fear in our department at that time made it hard for anyone to take a courageous stand against the bully.

I was particularly unprepared for his behavior because my prior experiences in science and academia had been so positive. I had been a very successful student in college and had an incredibly supportive advisor in graduate school who was an excellent mentor. During graduate school, I developed an interest in women in science and read voraciously about the topic. I recognized the concern about increased service work for women from my own experience and wondered about how issues related to integrating work and family life might affect me in the future. I was fascinated by Virginia Valian's (1999) description of the implicit bias that results from the mismatch between our gender schemas for women and the schemas we have for scientists and professionals. Valian argues that because our collective hypotheses or schema for women emphasize being "nurturant, expressive, communal, and concerned about others" (13), while the schema for men emphasizes being "independent, autonomous action (agentic, in short), assertive, instrumental, and task-oriented" (13). The schema for a scientist overlaps significantly more with our schema for men. Men are evaluated more positively as scientists because their masculinity reinforces the qualities we associate with being a scientist. On the other hand, women are evaluated more negatively as scientists because their femininity is discordant with the qualities we associate with being a scientist. The fact that implicit bias operates in everyone and offers explanations for institutionalized gendered differences in career outcomes without an obvious sexist villain fit with my experience. I believed that I lived in a time when explicit bias and sexism only existed in biographies of women from generations far removed from mine. For example, Sue V. Rosser (2004) surveyed women who had received an National Science Foundation (NSF) award intended to provide opportunities for women in science and encourage them to pursue research careers. She found that less than 5% of her respondents reported that overt discrimination and harassment were the most significant challenges women face when planning their careers. From this vantage point, I did not recognize that what was happening to me was because of my gender; I thought it was just something wrong with me as a scientist and a teacher. I worried that I was not going to earn tenure or learn to be effective in the classroom because I lacked the innate ability to do so. Not having confidence in my abilities made improving my teaching much slower and more difficult. While he never sought me out to harass me, seeing Professor X in the building unexpectedly made me very anxious because it made me remember and relive the awful episodes I had experienced with him in the past.

While I was not the first women hired in my department, I was the only one left by the end of my third year as a faculty member. One left for a promotion into administration at another institution and the other left because she did not receive a favorable decision in her third-year review. Because the two women were no longer a part of the department for very different reasons, I never framed the phenomena as the inability of my department to retain women. It was not until a new woman joined my department during my sixth year that I began to see how Professor X repeated the same patterns with her as he had with me. I also knew how talented my new colleague was and how his behavior to her was not at all commensurate with her job performance. The realization that my problems with Professor X were because of my gender, and not my abilities or performance, was a transformative revelation and hugely freeing for me. As a scientist, one of the ways I thought about it was that my new colleague was like a control experiment. Her considerable teaching experience and NSF grant did not make up for the fact that she was a woman to Professor X. Understanding that I was experiencing explicit sexism, and having the support and commiseration of a colleague who shared the experience, was the first step I took to addressing the problem and overcoming it. This insight helped to stop the cycle of accumulating disadvantage.

While having a woman colleague provided a lot of emotional support, two untenured women did not have the political power to change the behavior of Professor X who was the most senior member in the department by about 20 years, and by this point, also chair. Two things precipitated the next step. First, I was granted tenure which gave me the security and confidence to better advocate for myself. Second, the worst meeting in the history of our department happened during the spring workshop following my eighth year on faculty. Professor X's behavior was extreme enough that day to motivate the other men in my department to acknowledge that the situation had to be addressed. Because men outnumber women in science, especially as rank increases, sympathetic male allies often play an important positive role in women's careers. Many women, including myself, have supportive relationships with male mentors who positively support and promote their career (Rosser 2012). Another example of the positive influence of male allies is a shared desire for institutional policies which make it easier to be an active, involved parent (Etzkowitz, Kemelgor, and Uzzi 2000). This is particularly true for younger men who desire to be significantly involved in parenting. I also have come to believe that male allies can be helpful in addressing explicit sexism.

It happened that the following fall semester, Professor X was on sabbatical. Our department used the weekly department meeting time that semester to almost exclusively talk about what had been happening between Professor X and the women faculty and how to function better as a department. It is important to understand that this was hard work for all of us and required a very high level of trust. Our meetings were at 3:00 p.m. on Fridays and were a difficult emotional place to begin the weekend. While everyone was always civil and I trusted that each person cared about me and wanted to move forward productively, there was still frequent frustration and occasional tears.

We worked without much of a formal agenda at the beginning, but with a sincere desire on everyone's part to make our department function better. My woman colleague and I spent a lot of time early in the process describing our experiences and convincing them that they were different from their experiences. The fact that Professor X was generally viewed as eccentric or as a curmudgeon provided a cover which made his more insidious bullying behavior difficult to identify. It was easy to assume that we as women were too sensitive and just overreacting to his gruff persona. There were times when it felt as though we had reminded our colleagues of our experiences over and over again, but eventually we made progress. It was particularly hard to get our colleagues to acknowledge that his behavior was both instigating and wrong; they initially wanted to frame it as just the result of some quirky personality difference. One of the ways in which institutionalized sexism works is to minimize complaints of sexism from women by invoking a stereotype that they are overly emotional and catastrophize their experiences. This was also my experience when I had tried in the past to bring concerns to administrators above the level of my department because my descriptions of his behavior were difficult to believe as unembellished without witnessing the events.

A second line of discussion was an analysis of the communication patterns which had led to outbursts in the past. One key conclusion was that conflict was imminent when our meetings moved from being discussions where everyone contributed reasonably equally to debates where every other comment was from Professor X. A second strategy he employed was to use debate techniques to trap women in their words instead of engaging in the real content of the disagreement. Frequently, he used a strategy of taking a comment made or a position advocated for to its ridiculous extreme. The example I can remember best happened during a discussion about the general chemistry lab manual. I advocated for students calculating standard deviations if we were going to do error analysis instead of the easier to calculate, but statistically meaningless, quantity that was currently in the lab manual. His outburst at me for that suggestion included the accusation that I wanted students to calculate linear regressions by hand—an incredibly involved and tedious set of calculations. The logical fallacy he employed was that if I was advocating for more rigorous statistical approach in this case, then I must want the most rigorous statistical approach in all cases.

Especially as our semester of discussions came to a close, the topic turned to what strategies we could use to avoid these types of problematic communication patterns at future meetings. First, our new chair committed to intentionally calling for formal votes where a majority carried the decision instead of relying on complete consensus as our department had in the past. While consensus decision making can be helpful in building support for new policies or change, it provides the perfect venue for a bully to derail all new ideas by providing him with de facto veto power. We also discussed ways of ensuring that our discussion and debate avoided the problematic patterns we had identified which included having a staff member take minutes and having an audio or video recording of the meetings. The bottom line was always that someone other than a woman was going to need to both notice and challenge his behavior when it crossed the line. In the past, if a woman objected to his behavior, it was not sufficient to stop it; Professor X just intensified his outburst. This is not a conclusion that I find very appealing because it comes dangerously close to implying that women are weak and in need of protection from men. However, I think that the situation was not simply that we as women needed protection from a sexist bully, but that our department as a community of teachers and scholars was suffering in ways that diminished everyone's dignity and humanity.

As the semester drew to a close, it was clear that we had made significant progress and built stronger relationships. This began a more virtuous cycle of accumulating advantage by increasing the social capital I had in the department. Social capital is "the web of contacts and relationships that provide information, validation, and encouragement" (Etzkowitz, Kemelgor, and Uzzi 2000, 117). It is important for building influence and progressing in one's career because social capital brings access to resources and opportunities. However, I still worried about what would happen when Professor X returned from sabbatical in the spring and whether or not my colleagues would be willing to step up and confront him about his behavior.

While nothing controversial happened in the following semester, we had planned a one-week workshop during the summer to reenvision and revise the curriculum for general chemistry lab. While this project had been increasingly necessary for several years to improve student experience and address retention, the adoption by majority vote of a new textbook with a different sequencing made it no longer possible to postpone it. Our chair had an excellent plan to structure the conversation on the basis of a method presented at a conference, and I was hopeful but apprehensive as the week began. About halfway through the first morning, a bad conversation pattern started with Professor X, drawing me into a back-and-forth debate by using his extreme positions strategy. Immediately, the two other tenured men in my department called for a short break in our morning session. And that was all it took to change the dynamics in my department for good. When the session restarted, Professor X no longer engaged in personal attacks or tried to exercise veto power to derail change. In fact, he was almost completely silent. To his credit, our chair sought Professor X's feedback or assent when decisions were made, but he never substantively responded.

I was in such shock the rest of the week as we made excellent progress on our work without outbursts or interference. Initially, I was worried that the change in his behavior would not last, but it did. It has taken me a lot of reflection to come to an understanding of what happened that day. Despite all of the after-school specials about how bullies who want to steal your lunch money back down when confronted, I did not think it would really happen. Although an observer that day would have thought it looked easy to confront him, without the long and difficult work we had done in the fall to better understand each other, that day would never have come. Professor X retired a few years later, but it was a bit anti-climactic when it finally happened. The climate in the department had already improved so much because of all the work we had done to improve our communication and affirm our commitment to no longer tolerate bullying behavior.

In the years since this happened, my department has built upon this work of intentionally addressing communication and trust to become, in my somewhat biased opinion, the most functional and successful department on our campus. We have successfully advocated for and hired two new expansion lines and a new hybrid faculty/staff position, introduced innovative, new curricula in several courses, had significant success in obtaining external research funding, and seen our numbers of majors/minors rise. While the women in my department felt his harassment most acutely and personally, a sexist bully is bad for everyone. He almost completely prevented women from contributing their human capital for the good of the department, but he made it more difficult for everyone else to as well. This is very consistent with literature that argues that environments that are transparent and supportive are good for everyone, but especially for women and other marginalized groups (Valian 1999). An accumulation of advantage was experienced both by me personally but and by my department more broadly. Our greater ability to work together for the good of students increased our standing in the eyes of the administration which helped us secure more resources. More resources helped us grow and attract students, creating a positive cycle.

More personally, this experience caused me to grow immeasurably in ways which contribute regularly to my career success and continue to help me accumulate advantage. The realization of this growth happened relatively quickly after the department confronted Professor X. I suddenly had the freedom to no longer censor myself out of fear from contributing to my department and the campus more broadly. Doing the work of better understanding how he was able to push my buttons has fortified me to recognize and resist when others are trying to do so. I know to always try to weigh comments about my competence and performance against the evidence I have about my level of effort and achievement and to consider the possible motives of the commenter. Knowing that I was able to overcome the harassment by Professor X has empowered me to deal effectively with many different types of people. Not only has my experience made me more cognizant and compassionate toward colleagues in similar situations, but also it has given me the confidence to proactively offer help and support. I have increased my engagement with gender issues on campus by leading reading groups and helping to advocate for better policies for women and others with less institutional power. Because it is a significant hope of mine that fewer women in the future have experiences like this, I believe there are other ways to access this self-knowledge and power. However, figuring out the ways that I learned from this experience and being grateful for that growth helps me maintain as sense of agency and reject victimhood because I can see how my actions contributed to improving my department and that the experience made me stronger and more confident.

Over the last few years, I have begun to more seriously think about a career path in administration and have moved into a half-time administrative position at my institution. One of the things that attracts me to that path is the desire to help ensure all new faculty are given the mentoring and support they need to succeed and that they are evaluated in ways which are fair and transparent, minimizing both implicit and explicit bias. While administrators have a more explicit role to play in ensuring institutional policy and federal law are followed, situations like Professor X are considerably more complicated. His behavior would likely not be classified as illegal under Title IX, just very unprofessional. It is very important for women who find themselves in these situations which are legally ambiguous at best to cultivate many kinds of relationships in order to build social capital.

While an initial reaction to sexist bullying can be to withdrawal in order to avoid any more negative reactions from people, distancing yourself from potential allies is harmful in the long run. I needed relationships for emotional support, but I also needed mentors to help me grow as a teacher, collaborators for research projects, and colleagues with similar interests for institutional service. These relationships increased my social capital by offering encouragement, giving important feedback on my teaching, providing me access to unique research samples, and conferring important institutional knowledge and history. These relationships afforded me opportunities to demonstrate what I was capable of effectively contributing to our institution, and they also allowed me to see that I had qualities which were valued there. However, I do think administrators can and should take action to promote a healthy, transparent culture at their institution and hold deans and chairs responsible for overseeing strong, functional departments and most importantly providing them with the training to be able to do so. Not only is this the right thing to do from a fairness and equity perspective, but it also helps our institutions to better fulfill their missions.

References

Clance, Pauline Rose, and S. Imes. (1978). "The Imposter Phenomenon in High Achieving Women: Dynamic and Therapeutic Intervention." *Psychotherapy: Theory, Research, and Practice*, 15 (3): 241–247.

Etzkowitz, Henry, Carol Kemelgor, and Brian Uzzi. (2000). *Athena Unbound: The Advancement of Women in Science and Technology*. Cambridge: Cambridge University Press.

Long, Scott, J. (1990). "The Origins of Sex Difference in Science." *Social Forces*, 68 (4): 1297–1316.

Martell, Richard F., David, M. Lane and Cynthia Emrich. (1996). "Male-Female Differences: A Computer Simulation." *American Psychologist*, 51: 157–158.

Merton, Robert K. (1948). "The Self-Fulfilling Prophecy." *The Antioch Review*, 8 (2): 193–210.

———. (1968). "The Matthew Effect in Science: The Reward and Communication Systems of Science Are Considered." *Science*, 159 (3810): 56–63.

Rosser, Sue V. (2004). *The Science Glass Ceiling: Academic Women Scientists and the Struggle to Succeed.* New York: Routledge.

———. (2012). *Breaking into the Lab: Engineering Progress for Women in Science.* New York: New York University Press.

Rossiter, Margaret W. (1993). "The Matthew Matilda Effect in Science." *Social Studies of Science*, 23 (2): 325–341.

Valian, Virginia. (1999). *Why So Slow? The Advancement of Women.* Cambridge, MA: MIT Press.

29 Reembodying the Positionality of MiddleMAN Administrators in Higher Education

Bre Garrett, Aurora Matzke, and Sherry Rankins-Robertson

In December of 2015, Hillary Clinton, a democratic candidate for U.S. president, returned to her podium a few minutes late following a five-minute break. The debate briefly continued without her, until she walked onstage, apologized for her tardiness, and took her place among the candidates. Instead of remaining focused on the debate, media outlets soon bombarded the public with bathroom commentary—Was she stuck in line? Was the bathroom farther away? Did she need to "poop," or could she have incontinence issues as an aging mother? *The New York Times*, *Huffington Post*, and *Slate* all joined the chorus in the days that followed. Overall, the commentary displayed a range of misogyny and sexism, illustrating the extent to which female leaders are always, already identified by embodiment.

Hillary Clinton's bathroom break made national headlines and became a topic worthy of sound bites, posts, tweets, and shares, because, as a woman, her body and bodily motions are socially inextricable from her intellectual contributions and policies. Namely, the news threads demonstrated that women's bodies create enough curiosity and disparity from "the norm" of U.S. leadership standards to constitute news. *Huffington Post* feminist blogger, Soraya Chemaly[1] (2015) offered a critical response to the conversation in "Women: The Blog." Documenting the audience's reaction to Clinton's tardiness, Chemaly highlights, "Women, the laughter [at the debate] acknowledged, live in the interstitial spaces of a world shaped by and for men." To stretch Chemaly's analysis, women live in a world shaped by and for the individual subject: able-bodied, normative, masculine, and independent. Masculine ideals such as strength, endurance, stamina, and power construct a very narrow platform for leadership performance, which not only limits available skill but also eludes other available rhetorical moves and strategies. As a result, leadership characteristics and ethos often rely on a normative design of bodies, erasing core and necessary values of interdependence, collaboration, and difference.

The media response to Clinton's tardiness, to the female body as a subject overwhelming all other discourse, is not isolated to one bathroom break. In many public displays that signal female bodily difference, such "othering" of the body is often culturally perceived as aberration or weakness. When referring to Hillary Clinton, and other women in male-centric positions of power, one often hears "woman" first as a primary mark of embodied identity. In Clinton's case, if she had won the race, she may have been labeled as the "first woman president." The term "woman" often carries cultural connotations that offer a range of meaning and positions the dichotomy of terminology embedded within any one role: princess, trophy wife, angel, mom, darling, or nana and then to the far extreme of whore, old lady, crone, nag, monster-in-law, or bitch—to name a very limited number—all containing implications regarding the ways the body is present and/or used.

A body must bend and twist to facilitate practice or action; a body must, at times, engage with new technologies, materials, and discourses—and with multiple different audiences and stakeholders. In positions of leadership, bodies must be able to access public delivery space and sustain behaviors culturally and socially valued as masculine and ableist. Entrance to public space is not synonymous with agency and participation. Noted by Elizabeth Grosz[2] (1994), "The body . . . is the very condition of our access to and conception of space" (91). As administrators marked by our physical, corporeal bodies, we must work to understand the systematic management of bodies. We must understand that for many with which we work, we are women first and administrators second. What does it mean to be a woman administrator? What are the spatial limitations—the conceptions of space that others have created for us? As administrators, we must reclaim embodied space to speak for ourselves and advocate for others. Such moves are not without consequences and require risk and vulnerability, characteristics that make professional interactions more living and livable.

Despite equality gains, historically women's cultural value has been located in their bodies, as mothers, as females, as domestic counterparts. Female bodies have linked women to subordination and struggle. As Debra Hawhee[3] (2004) explains, the view of a normative body as masculine and fit crystallized in the western rhetorical tradition via ancient Greece and has traveled across the western canon. The body as a sign carries with it a historicity of being a place of virtue—an instrument of visible, audible, spatial, and kinesthetic delivery, evaluated or read in relation to *normative ethics*, or principles and rules that set up standards of good and evil, self and other, normal and abnormal (Shildrick 2002).[4] The 20th century in particular marked a concentrated time in which women theorists attempted to rediscover the physical body as a location of politics. Struggling against social and cultural inscriptions on feminine bodies, some women sought to distance themselves entirely from their bodies. In other cases, women attempted to reclaim the body in a politicized practice characterized by Gayatri Spivak[5] (1987) as "strategic essentialism," praising the female body, female sexuality and, in some cases, even motherhood as preferred and empowering cultural positions. Working as female (and feminist—note these are not synonymic terms) leaders in higher education, we situate ourselves with this history in order to point out that we are still, as ever, hyper-defined by our perceived gender.

By asking questions about bodily place and positionality, we come to explore the rhetorical capabilities of our own bodies, and from this space of interpersonal agency, we can renegotiate the role of *middleman*, or an agent who serves as the mediatory between the faculty and students we serve and the administration to which we report. For us, embodied leadership is about knowing how to enter and access particular rhetorical moves when access is not automatic, and then implement and locate alternative routes. Rearranging space and shifting context, extemporaneously, is not something that feels common to most because, culturally and educationally, most of us have not been educated in what Petra Kuppers[6] calls "somatic engagement," or working with the full capacities of one's body in interpersonal and interdependent situations. Bodies are sites of rhetorical activity in that a situated body performs as a site for invention and delivery.

Drawing on the intersectional methodologies of feminist epistemologies, disability studies, and multimodal composing, this chapter emphasizes the importance of instantiated embodied difference, opening spaces for reconceived possibilities of how feminist administrators in higher education recognize and make use of rhetorical affordance(s). In rhetorical studies and disability studies, affordance is a term that refers to the possibility of use, exploring how media, technology, modality, or body offers or enables particular actions. In opening certain capabilities, a question of affordance also warrants a grappling with availabilities and constraints or limitations. Affordances are never neutral or bound solely to the objects/tools that they characterize. Rather, as Cynthia Selfe[7] (2010) explains, cultural practices and norms allocate affordances according to what becomes normative, "appropriate" use.

Like many women, the authors have come to know their environments through negotiating a multiplicity of identities and differences. And while we have navigated the discovery of who we are as educators, we are continually negotiating (and sometimes justifying) our identities as women in administrative positions—and dually—as pre-tenured assistant professors. Administrative roles accentuate embodiment. To echo and adapt the words of Kristie Fleckenstein[8] (2003), "we carry the weight of our physical lives into our *leadership* lives" (46). The work of any administrator fluctuates among a number of different positionalities, duties, and roles, which makes the work function more like a performance, consisting of both deliberate and extemporaneous acts. Dancing among teaching, researching, assessing, mentoring, administering, and designing curricula, women administrators in higher education may find themselves at the disposal of strict schedules, impromptu meetings, and daily urgencies that can feel, at times, quite discombobulating—particularly in relation to increased anxiety and stress, unattended relationships, and perpetual insomnia.

We are three women who are diverse in our leadership styles, at different institutions that span from the east coast to the west coast; we work at a range of institutions—liberal arts, regional state university, and metropolitan—each functioning in "middle management" roles. We have found these roles to be fraught with sexist interactions and exchanges, where our identities as women precede, if not at times supersede, our professional selves. Our bodies, and the ways they are perceived, speak for us. And in order to investigate collective action as a response to sexist practices, we continue to question the difference it makes to foreground bodies as rhetorical sites. Specifically, we seek to understand how the interactions, reactions, and actions (moves we identify as instances of *embodied delivery*) regarding our bodies affect the various trajectories of our respective leadership positions. In addition to embodiment theories, we also question what might we understand and/or take away from our collected experiences.

Braided throughout our chapter, we insert snapshots of labor narratives from our three administrative positions: a co-director of a writing program at a small, private liberal arts university; a writing program director at a mid-size, regional public university; and an associate vice chancellor at a metropolitan university who is the former writing program administrator. The narratives act as sounding boards from which we reexamine the question "How might collective action in response to sexist language and practices across institutions influence and inform women as administrators?" Our different responses offer lessons learned about feminist administration from sexist encounters—no matter how seemingly small or localized the act. Through the narratives, we document both interpersonal experiences of sexism and institutional/structural forms of sexism.

The narrative snapshots enter almost as intrusions, without introduction or resolution, as that is how we most often experience them. For readers, this may feel jarring and lacking context. We incorporate the stories as enactments of what Sharon Crowley[9] (1999), citing Susan Bordo, describes as "the micropractices of everyday life" (358). We continue to perform the work of a middleman or, as we have identified, middleMAN, and identify what this work looks like, the level of reflexivity, and the reconfiguration of actions as the result of our interactions continues to change. We continue to collectively and collaboratively address these as public issues.

As the fairly new writing program administrator (WPA) on campus, I was invited to speak directly with an upper administrator regarding the state of developmental writing in relation to our program. When I arrived to his office, he greeted me, as we had a working relationship, and said, "You know what's really interesting about you?"

Of course, I inquired.

"People aren't really sure what they're getting when they see you and then you are . . . well, you're you."

I responded, "I'm not sure I'm following you."

So he attempted to elaborate: "Well, you know, you come in, in your little suit and all, and then you're . . . well, you're you." Of course, I was following him, but I took the bait.

"I'm not sure that I understand what it is that you're saying."

Perhaps in his attempt to compliment me, he tried again: "Well, you know, you're all dolled up, looking polished and professional, and then you're so 'you.' You know, direct and straightforward." Slowly I took my seat at the table, in my little suit, and commenced business about our developmental writing program, being the only person I knew how to be . . . me.

Simply defined, a middleman administrator is an intermediary. Neither an ordinary worker nor one of the "Powers That Be," middlemen administrators exist in-between the people and the power. She or he is the voice that must negotiate as well as represent a multiplicity of different standpoints. Responsible for the success of everyday operations, middlemen are often in the unenviable position of having quite a bit of responsibility with little ability to make direct change. Consequently, they often find themselves "in the middle" of interactions across campus, frequently checking in with superiors or with the office/entity that approves decisions/actions. And, indeed, those in the higher leadership positions are, most frequently, men—not only in these positions but also in the positions to which the middlemen report; however, when women serve as the middleMAN, she must embody characteristics often attributed to and associated with masculine performance. As discussed in Martha West and John Curtis's[10] 2006 study, "AAUP Faculty Gender Equity Indicators," women still lag behind significantly in percentages of women faculty roles, leadership positions, and faculty ranking, even though an equal number of women seek out and hold doctorate degrees in the U.S.; the study looked at "1,445 colleges and universities" and found that "half of Ph.D. degrees were earned by women," whereas only "26% of women held tenure-track faculty positions" and of those only "19% held the rank of full professor" (4–7). Many contributing factors calculate in this imbalance, as can be found in Canan Bilen-Green, Karen Froelich, and Sarah Jacobson's (2008)[11] showing that "women are even more scarce on the administrative career ladder" (3). Their study of 221 doctoral granting institutions showed that "13.5% of schools had a female president while 23.5% had a female provost" (5). As women in academia gain leadership positions, many of these roles will initially be low-power positions: work which, in some cases, as our experience exemplifies, may come without official administrative status or support staff, while often requiring the time of two or three employees. And, perhaps unavoidably, these positions may exacerbate sexist interactions. Each author is a middleMAN, working with curricular design, assessment, teacher training, and student support services for, arguably, one of the largest student populations on each of our campuses. Our daily campus interactions include moments of silencing, interruption, belittlement, and misunderstanding. How we respond—how we are *able* to respond—necessitates strategies of what we have come to call embodied delivery, or actions that foreground bodily presence, interdependence, and the temporality of ability.

Erasing embodied positionality from leadership practice reinforces the ever-impinging "view from nowhere" that perpetuates the myth of universal or common bodies—and normative abilities. Writing in 2002, Sharon Crowley[12] observed,

> That all parties to discursive transactions are embodied remains unmentioned in either rhetorical theory or composition studies because both fields still cling to liberal-humanist models of the speaking subject—a sovereign, controlling disembodied and individual voice that deploys language in order to effect some predetermined change in an audience.

(178)

Crowley's account introduces an interesting dilemma in the relationship between bodies and rhetoric, between bodies and composing—not that bodies do not have a place or function in communication, but the place of bodies, she writes, "remains unmentioned" ("Body Studies"). To strip embodiment from a composing situation, from a rhetor, projects forward a generalizable or universal style and process that, seemingly, *anybody* can complete. To remove bodies covers over critical differences, a cultural and political move that silences bodies of color, bodies of other ethnicities, bodies with disabilities, and bodies gendered differently than masculine (Royster 1996; Glenn 2004; Lewiecki-Wilson and Brueggemann 2007). Those unable to complete conventional processes and embody dominant leadership or administrative styles are marked according to labels that represent deviation from norm: basic writer, female writer, learning disabled writer.

I was eating lunch in the cafeteria with a new colleague. Joking about the fast pace of the first couple of weeks, my colleague smiled and called out to someone behind me. The man came over and was introduced to me as someone whose title suggested a good deal of power at my new institution. My colleague mentioned that I was "the new hire." Smiling, and while still standing next to me, the visitor pulled a chair directly next to me and then while standing he placed his left, booted foot in the center of the chair. The conversation continued for several minutes, the visitor flexing his hips with his crotch facing me, as he asked me questions. My colleague looked disturbed. The visitor soon left, as my answers became single-syllable responses and I began to eat with my head down. When we were alone, my colleague said, "I'm so sorry! I don't know what came over him. He's a really nice guy."

Gendered interactions that blatantly emulate sexual behavior such as body thrusting further objectify—and in some cases threaten—not only female bodies but also all bodies involved. Aside from highly unprofessional gesturing, such acts—however engaged under the guise of fun— anoint power positions and reinscribe female bodies as physical, carnal means for male gaze and pleasure. Women in the public sphere, across history, have recognized the clinging connection between embodied communication and access to public ethos, or the credibility from which one speaks. In their "Introduction" to *Available Means: An Anthology of Women's Rhetoric*, Joy Ritchie and Kate Ronald[13] (2001) argue that "Women have discovered different means of persuasion, often based in contexts other than those Aristotle might have imagined: the kitchen, parlor, and nursery; the garden; the church; the body" (xxi). Much feminist effort has focused attention to counter disembodiment and "the erasure of corporeality" (Shildrick 2002),[14] as well as to open theoretical possibilities for understanding diverse, rather than universal, conceptions of subjectivity (1). Grosz[15] (1994) urges, "what is at stake is the activity and agency, the mobility and social space, accorded to women," as well as "other kinds of bodies and subjectivities" that deviate from idealized norms (19). Working against the very construct of any normative way of being, Brenda Brueggemann and her collaborators[16] (2001) disrupt normative ideologies of embodiment: they argue that bodies are "temporarily" situated in terms of ability, for ability is prone to, at any time, abrupt shifts, ranging from life-altering debilitations to short-term adjustments to chronic conditions (consider any sudden and unexpected illness or bodily positionality that interferes with typical movement, behaviors, schedules, or plans). Consequently, we add to the value-ridden middleman equation (woman/man) a more comprehensive intersectionality that acknowledges the leadership of women of color, transgender women, women from working-class backgrounds, pregnant women, women from multilingual backgrounds, disabled women, and women from non-Judeo-Christian faith systems and histories.

As female and feminist leaders, we turn attention to bodies in order to jar connotations of *commonplace* that may suggest sameness or shared experience. However common to have or be a body, bodies differ in color, size, shape, ability, behaviors, preferences, desires, and styles. Not *all* bodies have equal access to positions of power or to the domain of public leadership. While we each have experienced similar instances of sexism and sexist behaviors due to our leadership positions, we, by no means, argue that our bodies or embodied positionalities are "the same." However, the three of us share the common experience—identification based on embodiment—that allows us to make meaning across distance and community, a strategy that has allowed for interstitial moments of meaning making, and through this chapter we attempt to extend that community through space and time.

Fresh out of graduate programs—with extensive teaching and some administrative experience—all three of us accepted administrative, tenure track positions as WPAs at our current institutions. The three of us met, in the summer of 2012, as we sweated through the desert heat of Albuquerque, New Mexico, at the Council of Writing Program Administrators (CWPA) annual workshop intended for new WPAs. In her two short weeks in her new position, one of the authors had already encountered a significant barrier who was actively working to maintain the old and familiar ways of the program, despite the need (and request by the hiring committee) for significant, programmatic change. She spoke to Shirley Rose, one of the workshop leaders, while the other two of us listened. After Dr. Rose departed, the three of us sat down and began to brainstorm options to moving around the barrier and discuss the emotional response of the troubled WPA who wondered if she'd made the "right" choice to come in as a pre-tenured administrator.

That day, we began to cultivate a long-term relationship that has resulted in weekly calls, sporadic texts, long Skype conversations that find us amid our evening rituals whether that has been with wine in hand, cooking dinner, or nursing a baby, and late night sessions to resolve and dissolve disruption, often in dealing with disruptors, of progress. Oftentimes, these calls and videoconference sessions occur next to our spouses, who sometimes begin eating dinner without us or hold the baby as she screams for her mother. The normative expectation as role of wife and mother remain and often are sacrificed; each of us has faced personal challenges in our home and professional partnerships because as female administrators much more is demanded of us—when often our male counterparts have the luxury of society's meta-narrative (Lyotard 1979)[17] that "he's doing his job." Domestic responsibilities more often fall to the female, regardless of whether she also works outside of the home. For example, business meetings that run late or extend to happy hour, where important decision-making continues, rarely take into consideration parents who must retrieve children, make dinner, and prepare for end-of-the-day home life. Professional expectations remain inextricable from bodily positionality, particularly in relation to reproduction and motherhood.

*Each year, I meet with my mentoring committee to review and discuss my annual progress toward tenure and promotion. As an untenured faculty member, the mentoring group provides me with invaluable advice—suggestions about what to do differently, how to unburden my heavy service load, and much appreciated praises on my accomplishments. The committee members take extra time to write a report that summarizes the sessions. In one report, sent to both my department chair and me, a member of my mentoring committee drew attention to the fact that I was pregnant and requested a self-narrative that would account for the pending baby/work balance. "How will she be able to maintain the level of progress that she has thus far demonstrated?" he questioned. I felt outrage that he included such a statement in an official report that provided a traceable narrative for my tenure file. This was a public document—and a materialization of the feminist adage: the personal is political. I requested that committee member remove any reference to my pregnancy and work/home balance. I never stated what I had been internally shouting and eventually shared with my co-authors: Such a statement would **never** be included in a man's review file.*

Some feminist theorists and performance studies theorists refer to this bodily back-and-forth, in-and-out relationship as a feedback loop, visually depicted as a Möbius or figure-eight shape (Grosz 1994; Fleckenstein 2003).[18] The feedback loop imparts a certain communicative relationship that invokes bodies as sites of interaction and agents of interpretation. In reflecting and collaborating together across a three-year period, a time that coincided with our new administrative appointments, we made deliberate efforts to collaborate, to write together, and to exchange occasional reality checks concerning our daily, lived experiences as feminist leaders.

We created a model of interdependence in which we have relied on one another and each other's experiences to respond to the middleMAN position as a woman. As rhetorical strategy that makes use of multitude of bodily experience, we've built a mini-coalition with a necessary layer of reflection.

We have intertwined not only our daily lives, but also we come together at conferences where we met and present each year; we seek out other venues to present and publish our shared experiences. Responses to these shared experiences have warranted such remarks, from not only each other but also those who respond to us in forums and emails, as "Are you serious?" "Do you think that's legal?" "Oh, I'm *so* sorry that happened." In our careful attention to our jobs, and the relatively new landscapes we still find ourselves in, we have established that we can offer one another significant help. It isn't that we don't know how to do our *jobs*. Rather, we understand that we have the opportunity to forge an interdependency that resists the understanding of our*selves* that we saw locking into spaces of our new (academic) homes—our bodies speak to our new communities, and not only are we often surprised by what they are saying, but also we are, at times, struggling to understand or change the conversation. Collectively, we understand that we need to bring attention to the personal by foregrounding the person. Yet what may have been intimate details of our persons were now on the proverbial tables of our jobs, and there are times that we still aren't sure what they are doing there.

I was going over the daily tasks with our office manager in the department office. When we were finished, she scrunched up her face and said, "Y'know, if you want to change classrooms, I'm totally OK with doing that for you." I was confused.

"Change classrooms? Why would I want to change classrooms?"

"Well, your classes are all the way on the other side of campus."

"Sure, but I have several hours to get there. I was under the impression it was very inconvenient and difficult to change rooms."

"Uh, it is. But, y'know, you're pregnant." What followed was a half an hour conversation where I was informed that the classroom-switching request had already escalated past the dean, and several instructors had agreed to move their students for me, so that I "didn't have to walk so far." I apologized to everyone involved. To this day, I don't know who requested the room switch, but it was not me nor with my authority to accommodate my body.

While some may perceive this action taken on her behalf as one of "kindness" or "consideration," the arrangements were taken fully in response to projections of assumed difficulties that she had neither expressed nor needed. Specifically, as a leader in the department, this underlying sexism threatens her authority to those who, most of which reported to her, were asked to accommodate her through "othering" her on the basis of her body.

We have helped one another by listening deeply. We cultivate response and process strategies from across our experiences that we are then able to turn into values, or transferrable practices, for leadership. Collectively, at intermittent occasions, unplanned calls, early morning texts, on-the-way-to-work phone chats, we reimagine possibilities for wider spaces of participation. We identify the realm of consequences—the concrete outcomes of potential actions. We must also measure the weight of silence and question whether we are, through silence, participating in oppressive work environments. We labor with one another to define our bodies as sites for creative invention and delivery. We learn how to take moments of disembodiment and to forge emergent, on-the-spot, collaborative invention that moves beyond the bounds of any one situation or activity.

Together, by deconstructing the ways we are disembodied, we imagine a storehouse of potential responses to sexist actions and interactions.

A body's physicality and ability become heightened as one moves through spaces and makes contact with others—as one encounters instances in which access is not automatic: limitations, roadblocks, and unexpected detours. Bodies may remain unnoticed in times of smooth travel. Nevertheless, at any given moment, bodies solicit—even demand—attention: the sudden need to go to the restroom, a moment of forgetfulness, illness, hunger, fatigue.

We carry our physical lives into our leadership lives. Embodied leadership requires us to emphasize the corporeal nature of our interactions—the visual, tangible, audible, taking up space, and moving through space bodies perform. These roles remind us that bodies are rhetorical materials intricately involved in actions, even if the physical is not explicitly identified or even acknowledged. Bodies perform as rhetorical topoi, sites of invention and delivery, sites arranged by and arranging of time and space, sites of memory. And, as we have argued when placed in administrative contexts with other bodies, women's bodies are constantly on display, as kairotic spaces of performance and indulgence.

I walked along a pathway with one of the program instructors giving a general account of a meeting where it was brought to my attention that a campus constituent felt my expectations in certain areas were too high. I turned to the instructor, "How are you doing? How does this workload feel?"

The instructor looked shocked by the question. "Honestly? It's a lot, and I worry I'm going to disappoint you, but I know you're with me one hundred percent."

"That's right," I said, "I am. And if anything, I don't want to disappoint you, because tomorrow, I'll need you to be with me."

The instructor smiled as she headed to class, and I continued walking to my next meeting.

In conversation with the authors of this book collection, we seek recommendations for how to change ideologies. The following questions provide a critical checkpoint: what do we do with the display? How do we respond when we are positioned? And, how do our collective actions in response to sexist practices and language move across institutions to inform our strategies for feminist leadership? In this chapter, we argue for (1) displaying the positioning, which may be used as ethos-building fodder, (2) acknowledging, through self-reflection, shared experience and scholarship, the corporeality of the female middleMAN administrator, that makes concrete the embodied delivery necessary to define bodies as rhetorical topoi, and (3) finding creative power through contact with difference and dissonance, as we reinvent patriarchal assumptions of time, logic, self, and community.

We work from a premise that bodies have affordances, and certain bodily affordances allow for communicative choices and abilities. As we share, as we grow together, we build a repository of embodied movements—of dialogue and response, of physical action and reaction—that we are able to harness and modify for local, kairotic intervention. Knowing that we are not alone when we confront these practices, we respond with patience and clarity. When we are confronted with inappropriate behaviors, questions, and personal comments, we ask questions in order to "other" what may have been normative speech—it is not because we do not know the answers to the questions we ask but to call attention to the unacceptable. If we are unable to address an incident in real time, we contact one another and devise responses on the basis of the exigent circumstances. Consequently, in our conversations, presentations, and publications, we work to give space, time, and attention to the embodied realities of our professional lives that encompass the residual of our personal lives. If anything, this approach has highlighted that, aside from blatant instances of sexism, there is very little uniformity in the types of responses that will be effective in our individual communities.

Yet, despite the continued differences, we do offer embodied delivery, as a result of the microlevel, cross-institutional mentoring we provide for one another, three concrete, strategic actions that have resulted in positive gains with stakeholders across our institutions:

1. **Kairotic Interventions:** Building on Margaret Price's[19] (2011) notion of kairotic space, "less formal, often unnoticed, areas of academe where knowledge is produced and power is exchanged," we seek out relationship-building opportunities with constituents above, alongside, and below our middleMAN areas, so that relational truths might trump sexist ones.
2. **Attention to Embodied Time:** We understand, accept, and even, in some instances, encourage more flexible approaches to normative time frames, schedules, and the use of time in meeting spaces, to call attention to, and account for the bodies with which we work.
3. **Feminist Leadership Collaboration:** Together, we hypothesize scenarios and responses that give us the ability to positively intervene, so that we are not caught underprepared when sexism occurs. We often share scenarios regarding working with others, sharing power roles with others, inviting others to participate, working across position levels, and engaging multiple perspectives, to name a few.

We place these three interweaving action plans at the close of the piece, so that the reader might come to them with our embodied histories in mind. Instead of the generalizable advice new female administrators often hear, "Go to Human Resources," "Wait until tenure," "Find a new institution," (all responses that we have received by friends, colleagues, or mentors), we offer the different capacities of our bodies, our localities, so that we might learn more about ourselves, in the processes, and then contribute positively back to our homes, work environments, disciplines, and higher education for female administrators. Interdependency and reciprocity, we are convinced, will transform how we position ourselves, and how we interact with others.

Notes

1 Chemaly, "Biology Doesn't Write Laws: Hillary Clinton's Bathroom Break Wasn't as Trivial as Some Might Like to Think."
2 Grosz, *Volatile Bodies: Towards a Corporeal Feminism*, 91.
3 Hawhee, *Bodily Arts: Rhetoric and Athletics in Ancient Greece*.
4 Shildrick, *Embodying the Monster: Encounters with the Vulnerable Self*.
5 Spivak, *In Other Words: Essays in Cultural Politics*.
6 Kuppers, Olimpias, Performance Research Projects. Kuppers curates workshop enactments that combine movement, touch, and sound in order to create moments of spontaneous, fluid action.
7 Selfe, "Interview with Cynthia Selfe," by Brian Bailie.
8 Fleckenstein, *Embodied Literacies*.
9 Crowley, "Afterword: The Material of Rhetoric."
10 West and Curtis, "AAUP Faculty Gender Equity Indicators."
11 Bilen-Green, Froelich, and Jacobson, "The Prevalence of Women in Academic Leadership Positions, and Potential Impact on Prevalence of Women in the Professorial Ranks."
12 Crowley, "Body Studies in Rhetoric and Composition."
13 Ritchie and Ronald, "Introduction."
14 Shildrick, *Embodying the Monster: Encounters with the Vulnerable Self*, 1.
15 Grosz, *Volatile Bodies: Towards a Corporeal Feminism*, 19.
16 Brueggemann et al. "Becoming Visible: Lessons in Disability."
17 Lyotard, *The Postmodern Condition: A Report on Knowledge*.
18 Grosz, *Volatile Bodies: Towards a Corporeal Feminism*; Fleckenstein, *Embodied Literacies: Imageword and a Poetics of Teaching*.
19 Price, *Mad at School: Rhetorics of Mental Disability and Academic Life*.

References

Bilen-Green, Canan, Karen A. Froelich, and Sarah W. Jacobson. (2008). "The Prevalence of Women in Academic Leadership Positions, and Potential Impact on Prevalence of Women in the Professorial Ranks." WEPAN Conference Proceedings.

Brueggemann, Brenda Jo, et al. (2001). "Becoming Visible: Lessons in Disability." *College Composition and Communication*, 53: 368–398.

Chemaly, Soraya. (December 25, 2015). "Biology Doesn't Write Laws: Hillary Clinton's Bathroom Break Wasn't as Trivial as Some Might Like to Think." *Huffington Post* "Women: The Blog". www.huffington post.com/soraya-chemaly/biology-doesnt-write-laws_b_8874638.html.

Crowley, Sharon. (1999). "Afterword: The Material of Rhetoric." In *Rhetorical Bodies*, edited by Jack Selzer and Sharon Crowley, 357–379. Madison: University of Wisconsin.

———. (2002). "Body Studies in Rhetoric and Composition." In *Rhetoric and Composition as Intellectual Work*, edited by Gary A. Olson, 177–187. Carbondale, IL: Southern Illinois University Press.

Fleckenstein, Kristie S. (2003). *Embodied Literacies: Imageword and a Poetics of Teaching*. Carbondale, IL: Southern Illinois University Press.

Glenn, Cheryl. (2004). *Unspoken: A Rhetoric of Silence*. Urbana: Southern Illinois University Press.

Grosz, Elizabeth. (1994). *Volatile Bodies: Towards a Corporeal Feminism*. Bloomington: Indiana University Press.

Hawhee, Debra. (2004). *Bodily Arts: Rhetoric and Athletics in Ancient Greece*. Austin: University of Texas.

Kuppers, Petra. (2011). *Somatic Engagement*. Oakland: Chainlinks.

Lewiecki-Wilson, Cynthia and Brenda Jo Bruggemann, eds. (2007). *Disability and the Teaching of Writing*. Boston, MA: Bedford/St. Martin's.

Lyotard, Jean-Francois. (1979). *The Postmodern Condition: A Report on Knowledge*. Translated by Geoff Bennington and Brian Massumi. Minneapolis: University of Minnesota Press.

Price, Margaret. (2011). *Mad at School: Rhetorics of Mental Disability and Academic Life*. Pittsburg: University of Michigan Press.

Ritchie, Joy and Kate Ronald. (2001). "Introduction." In *Available Means: Anthology of Women's Rhetoric(s)*, edited by Joy Ritchie and Kate Ronald, xv–xxx. Pittsburgh: University of Pittsburgh Press.

Royster, Jacqueline Jones. (1996). "When the First Voice You Hear Is Not Your Own." *College Composition and Communication*, 47 (1): 29–40.

Selfe, Cynthia. (2010). "Interview with Cynthia Selfe." By Brian Bailie. *Composition Forum*, 21.

Shildrick, Margrit. (2002). *Embodying the Monster: Encounters with the Vulnerable Self*. London: Sage Publications.

Spivak, Gayatri Chakravorty. (1987). *In Other Words: Essays in Cultural Politics*. New York: Methuen.

West, Martha S., and John W. Curtis. (2006). *AAUP Faculty Gender Equity Indicators*. Washington, DC: American Association of University Professors.

30 We Are All Needed

Feminist Rhetorical Strategies for Building Trust among Colleagues

Sara Hillin

Attending graduate school in English in the late 1990s and early 2000s, my peers and I were made to realize that in no uncertain terms, we were not *owed* full-time work, and when and if we did land that coveted faculty position, there were myriad others behind us, just as qualified, who for possibly duplicitous reasons did not make the cut. This acknowledgment is not necessarily feminist in itself, *but* it has shaped how I, as writing director at a small liberal arts college, prioritize concerns from my colleagues within my department. This chapter addresses the beneficial uses of feminist rhetorical strategies—invitational rhetoric, eavesdropping, rhetorical listening, and silence—in the context of a leadership position. In academe, for the most part, decisions are made through negotiating and thesis driven argumentation, and this technique is perpetuated as the norm, almost without question. As Barbara Tomlinson (2010) states, "Reading, writing, and argument are social practices sedimented with ideologies of legitimacy, propriety, and fairness so powerful and pervasive that we presuppose their value rather than examining their effects" (104). We do not tend to question the well-worn sanctity of the classically arranged argument, or even an ad hominem attack here and there—these are rife in the ivory tower. However, feminist rhetorical tactics account for most of my successful political maneuvering in the academy, and I find that through them I get much work done and am able to push certain needed conversations to the next level.

Contextualizing Writing Program Administration as a (Feminist) Rhetorical Situation

Scholarship related to the labor of composition is exceedingly relevant to feminist leadership in academe, as it implores us to consider, in depth, the contexts in which *all* levels of faculty work and participate in university governance, even though such activities may not be written into their contracts. Marc Bosquet (2008) has been particularly outspoken on the deplorable conditions under which contingent faculty often work, offering a particularly salient set of questions about the uneasy oversight wielded by many in writing program administrator (WPA) positions: "How does the WPA's right to establish curriculum and set policies square with the teachers' right to autonomy over their work? Who defines teaching that doesn't 'work out'? Why should it be the WPA and not other teachers?" (181). And, indeed, part of the struggle for a feminist administrator is to find that balance, collaboratively, between setting rigid standards for curricula, outcomes, syllabi, and classroom practice, and letting these instructors find their own ways and develop teaching identities through inevitable trial and error.

Jill Gladstein and Dara Rossman Regaignon (2012) render in their work *Writing Program Administration at Small Liberal Arts Colleges* the many "leadership configurations" for WPA roles in institutions such as mine, and one in particular bears relevance to my situation "The *Solo WPA/WCD* configuration," they write, "conjures up the image of the WPA who serves as 'all things writing' on his or her campus" (51). Though Gladstein and Rossman Regaignon reason that this leadership configuration can be seen as "necessarily overburdened and isolated," I have also experienced the flip side of this paradigm, in which I am allowed "leeway to design and implement initiatives in the hybrid space between the curriculum and student-centered domains" (52). This work is done through careful rhetorical strategizing, as multiple groups have a stake in how my plans are implemented and assessed. I characterize my work as writing director as a constant response to exigencies—faculty workload concerns, opportunities for curriculum development, faculty development needs, advocacy for non-tenure track faculty—that lead to rhetorical situations. I am, as all academic leaders are, continually in a position to use rhetoric "to produce action or change in the world," as a "mode of altering reality," and as a "mediator of change" (Bitzer 1968, 3–4). I have found that rhetorical strategies typically cast as feminist have been the most effective in achieving these goals.

Eileen Schell (2003) adds some wisdom on such matters firmly entrenched in feminist ethos. She explains that as we are well aware, those who teach composition are largely "part time and tenure-track faculty, many of whom are women . . . who are positioned in low-paying, low-ranking positions within the hierarchy of the increasingly corporatized American academy" (38). Schell (2001), in her work exploring connections between Marxist and materialist theories in feminist composition studies, makes an observation that likely resonates with many of us in leadership positions: "The working conditions of contingent faculty in higher education create widespread ill effects for all concerned" (4). The unsettling truth is that any of us in administration in departments that employ workers in these capacities is complicit in the perpetuation of these ranks, regardless of how hard we may work to negate the worst aspects of these inequities.

The largest single contingent within our department, non-tenure track full-time faculty, is largely made up of women faculty—such is the trend nationally in writing programs. Theresa Enos (1996) summarizes the nature of this set up in her *Gender Roles and Faculty Lives in Rhetoric and Composition*, explaining that

> Rhetoric and Composition studies as a whole is devalued, in part because it is "women's work" . . . lower division writing courses in colleges and universities are staffed primarily by women who receive low pay, low prestige, and lessened job security in comparison to their male counterparts.
>
> (vii)

Enos adeptly encapsulates a problem that has its roots in an insidious and fairly endemic type of sexism that has pervaded English departments for decades. Such conditions are brutal enough to have spawned the term "academically battered woman" (ix), and though no one person in any department can undo the past and continuing wrongs fostered by patriarchal hierarchies and power plays, feminist leaders who operate from a standpoint of empathy, an "ethic of care" even, can choose to use rhetorical means to make life a bit better for their colleagues staffing lower division courses.

Rhetorical Listening in Feminist Academic Leadership

For a woman writing director, the choice in facing the inevitable promotion to this position presents two possible paths: run like hell on principle, because I see the injustices and my own inability to solve each and every one, or accept the leadership challenge with the knowledge that not all battles can be won, and forge trust among colleagues at every level through sincere and honest rhetorical means. Most of those in my department might already know that I consider myself a feminist. Many of my publications concern feminist and women's discourses, and I do my best to speak up for our untenured and non-tenure track faculty. I routinely use what I consider to be feminist rhetorical techniques to move conversations forward or stop what I see as bad ideas from coming to fruition. Surprisingly, however, I have never had a sense of being seen as the stereotypical "angry" feminist. Still, the specter of this stereotype is one that I guard against—once I am labeled as such, my audience will stop hearing me.

Barbara Tomlinson (2010) explains that political and academic discourse "abounds with a recurring set of formulaic claims that feminist scholars (and feminists in general) are angry, unreasoning, shrill, humorless, ugly, man-hating, perverse, and peculiar" (101). "One never," she writes, "encounters the feminist's argument for the first time because it comes already discredited" (102). The trope of the angry feminist is most certainly embedded in academe—and although I do not want the label, I do feel angered by situations, which seem to represent institutionalized sexism, and so where is the middle ground? Is it possible to have a credible presence as an angry feminist without being *the* "angry feminist"? I am interested in questioning hierarchies and seeking to resolve what can be resolved through feminist rhetorical strategies, one of which is rhetorical listening.

Scholar Krista Ratcliffe (1995) seeks to redefine rhetoric itself as an act of listening. "Because agency is situated within webs of controlling ideologies, each of which generates and is generated by its own discourse conventions," she comments, "we must continually remember that while we are listening to discourses, we are also listening *within* them" (67). She also hints at a conception of standpoint theory that is relevant to feminist academic leadership, stating that "within the logic of listening in the world, standpoints emerge as . . . overlapping subject positions" where "rhetorical identification is based not only on common ways of life but also on respect for ways of lives that we will never live" (71). Ratcliffe's theory's relevance to my chapter is that I am sometimes in a position to listen to *and* consequently speak for people whose positions are different from my own, and yet if I am denied the possibility of credibly displaying empathy for them, my own rhetoric, and the possibility of persuading others to take their issues into consideration, will not work.

Rhetorical listening has served me well in administration—faculty know their concerns are noted and that I will, if possible, act on them in whatever way I can. I try to imagine all these discursive events as potentially productive on my end, employing rhetorical listening as articulated by Ratcliffe (1999), who defines this practice as "a trope for interpretive invention, one that emerges from a space within the *logos* where listeners may employ their agency . . . to situate themselves openly in relation to all kinds of discourse, whether written, oral, or imagistic" (204). Rhetorical listening involves an element particularly relevant to academic leadership, which is the listener's "willingness to promote an *understanding* of self and other that informs our culture's politics and ethics" (204). This strategy necessarily draws on the listener's ability to empathize with the speaker and to realize that affecting positive change involves correctly reading into both the problem and determine all possible solutions.

When women do land sought-after tenure track positions, we work to balance the triumvirate of teaching, scholarship, and service, navigating the masculinist hierarchies but often without raising concerns about our own or others' place in the academy. Later on in positions of leadership, it is vital that we recall our experiences in that vulnerable space and use that empathy in mentoring incoming junior faculty. As a leader who has some responsibility for supporting the career paths of our department's tenure track faculty, most of whom are women, I know that though I cannot change what the university has set in stone concerning standards for teaching, scholarship, and service, I can guide these scholar teachers through the rocky years of pre-tenure life. The authors of "For Slow Scholarship: A Feminist Politics of Resistance through Collective Action in the Neoliberal University" (Mountz et al. 2015) echo my sentiments concerning the mentoring of junior faculty, stating that an admirable goal is to "slow scholarship down as part of challenging the growing inequities in higher education" (1240). This goal is a complement to Bosquet's (2009) concern that higher education "has become a form of speed-up and competition, and people have accepted the idea that they should spend their lives competing in a labor market that's rigged almost entirely for the benefit of capital" (114). Research, after all, should essentially be about contributing to a new or ongoing conversation, rather than purely functioning as a means to an end: fodder for a tenure dossier produced hurriedly and under duress.

Advocating for slowing things down in regard to the accelerated pressure to produce scholarship constantly takes a physical and psychic toll, and advocating a slower approach "from a feminist ethics of care, then, cultivates collective challenges to such elitist exclusions" and "is about making the university a place where many people—professors and student, from multiple places of privilege or marginalization—can collectively and collaboratively thrive" (Mountz et al. 2015, 1240). Though I have in no way made a dent in the general university requirement that one must publish in order to receive tenure, I have, in collaboration with my chair, worked to draft departmental guidelines for the recommended volume of production in that area and what counts for us as scholarship. This effort has, I believe, brought comfort to our tenure track faculty who deserve, at the very least, some reasonable guidelines in writing.

Productive Rhetorical Silence as a Part of Feminist Academic Leadership

Silence is an additional rhetorical technique described as feminist by scholar Cheryl Glenn, and it is one particularly necessary and useful for feminist administrators, who spend much time playing the waiting game. Glenn (2002) comments that we all "inhabit silence," and neither speech nor silence is more successful, informative, revealing, or concealing than the other; rhetorical success depends upon the rhetorical situation." Silence, she tells us, is "purposeful silence" when it is "self-selected" and it can be "productive." And it can be used particularly as "rhetorical listening that leads to understanding" (263–264). Though I am a quiet and even typically silent person by nature, I have sensed that colleagues take note when I am initially silent on a particular issue, and they realize I am considering options before weighing in.

Massive shifts in our core curriculum, three years in the making, left our second semester composition course as an option for many majors rather than a requirement, as it had been. Due to my untenured status at the time during which the core was revised, I was unable to be a part of that conversation, save an email or two to the chair touting the value of our 1302 course. Thus, I was relatively silent but spent all that time considering the impact of that fairly devastating decision on our students and faculty, as well as what solutions there might be to buffer the loss. Predictably, this change has resulted in a loss of course sections over the last two years, which affects the salaries of our non-tenure track faculty. Now, however, as a tenured program director, I am able to come out of that silence to work with faculty to revamp our 1302, offering some sections as Writing Across the Curriculum (WAC)-based options for students. Rallying for change prior to now would have been unfeasible. Recently, I facilitated a meeting regarding our 1302 course, how it has been articulated, and how we *could* reasonably make changes within the scope of our student learning outcomes and how those compare with similar regional universities, but, again, using invitational rhetoric, I did not *suggest* changes, respecting instead the views of both the faculty who would like to do something more innovative and those who prefer to adhere to the traditional curriculum.

Invitational Rhetoric and Advocacy

In my approach to leadership in this position, I do not adopt feminist rhetorical techniques in some arbitrary way because I find feminist pedagogy and theory appealing and they inform my scholarship (which they do), but rather because I genuinely believe I have been able to use these strategies, in different capacities and on different occasions, to the advantage of others who do not share my level of privilege. Some of these strategies, such as invitational rhetoric, come more naturally to me, while others, such as using influence on the basis of where I see myself in the larger power structure, I use more consciously and are a bit more outside my comfort zone.

Sonja Foss and Cindy Griffin (1995) explain in "A Proposal for an Invitational Rhetoric" that regardless of the definition of feminism we might work from, all feminists are "united by a set of basic principles," and these are "equality, immanent value, and self-determination" (3). Invitational rhetoric, the authors propose, "constitutes an invitation to the audience to enter the rhetor's world and see it as the rhetor does" (4). In most of my successful attempts to affect change for the benefit of my colleagues, such as recently acquiring funding for six adjunct and non-tenure track faculty to travel to the Conference on College Composition and Communication, I have asked administrators to consider the proposals from my vantage point—in this case, I invited others to consider the possibility that knowledge gained at the conference by these six faculty (most of whom had never attended an academic conference before) would then be dispersed to the rest of the department, leading to the faculty's increased sense of agency over their own well-informed classroom practices. It was agreed that our department would cover registration and mileage for two faculty, and the dean's office would cover those expenses for six. Faculty did, indeed, take notes and come back eager to share their insights from the conference with the rest of our composition cohort.

What I have found in using invitational rhetoric is that it often works best when I know an idea of mine will at first be met with opposition. For example, four years ago I decided that I did not want to chair a search committee that might without intervention perpetuate the hiring of more non-tenure track faculty members who would be, like several of our current faculty, laboring under heavy teaching loads with less job security than tenure track faculty. I suspected that such a plan might be in the works. We were given one line officially, but in the back of my mind was the fact that several faculty had left in the past few years, leaving vacant lines that had been untouched. Knowing that tenure lines do not simply magically open up, but also that we had a few unfilled vacancies left by composition faculty, I suggested to the committee that we hire two tenure track rhetoric and composition faculty rather than one, and eventually, after opinions from both the committee and other department members were solicited, my department chair, fully on board with what I suggested, moved forward with me on the plan and requested the dean's consideration on the matter.

To my delight, the proposal was accepted, and we were able to hire two tenure track rhetoric faculty and at least forestall the hiring of non-tenure track faculty at a less equitable salary. This was only a tiny victory. For here's the rub: do we still have non-tenure track faculty in our department who deserve more compensation for the hard work they do? Absolutely. Did the move I made solve this dilemma? No. *But*, what I attempted to do was illustrate that the work of composition teaching is worthy of staffing our large department with more than one expert in the area, and so far it seems this belief has come to fruition in gratifying ways: our new rhetoric and composition faculty provide guidance and faculty development and are a part of important conversations that affect the working lives of our non-tenure track faculty. Their ability to enrich the department in these ways was a large part of my justification for requesting the second hire. The invitational rhetoric I initially employed respected the positions of those making the ultimate decisions, but it also invited them to consider the many benefits our department would accrue with more faculty who could expand our course offerings and boost the increasingly popular writing minor and rhetoric component of our degree plan.

French Feminist Thought and Academe: Leading as the "Other"

I should note that my thinking on feminist academic leadership has been cultivated by feminist theory in a variety of areas, particularly French feminist thought. I begin with Helene

Cixous (1976) and Simone de Beauvoir (1949) because both of these theorists offer commentary addressing the tradition of sexism that is embedded not only in ideology but also in language itself: both of these affect life in academe and, in turn, academic leadership. De Beauvoir asks, in *The Second Sex*,

> Why is it that women do not dispute male sovereignty? No subject will readily volunteer to become the object . . . it is not the Other who, in defining himself as the Other, establishes the One. . . . Whence comes this submission in the case of woman?

(4)

Women are, of course, employed in mass numbers in academe, but they do not have the same long-standing tradition of serving in "high" positions such as program directors, chairs, deans, provosts, and so forth. They/we are still "the other." We have been defined as such through centuries-old machinations that have generated gendered power structures and hierarchies that seek to exclude, demean, and expel those who do not perform a set of increasingly time consuming, possibly ill defined, and diverse tasks.

"Publish or perish" is alive and well. So what tensions does this situation create when women are awarded such a coveted position as program director, department head, or dean? Helene Cixous's (1991) words from "Coming to Writing" seem poignantly relevant here—though not specifically related to a life in academe (though the references to boundaries and walls do seem apt), she does touch on the idea of woman occupying an invisible, inarticulate space, one in which she has to adopt a new language to carve out her right to speak. "'Being,'" she writes,

> was reserved for those full, well-defined, scornful people who occupied the world with their assurance . . . were at home everywhere I 'was'-n't except as an infraction, intruder, little scrap from elsewhere, always on the alert. The untroubled ones.

(p. 16)

Feminist academic leaders occupy this exact type of space—uneasy, on the alert, trying to reconcile our notion of the best of what the academic life *can* be for us, our colleagues, and our students, with what it really is, as opposed to the "untroubled" elite who take up administrative positions of increasing power with apparent ease, doling out decisions that affect faculty for good or ill.

Our Shifting Positions: How Do We "Stay Feminist"?

When we become tenured, we often find ourselves, as a result of personnel shifts, unexpectedly in a position of power, perhaps in the form of serving as a program director or a department chair. In my case, this happened quick as a flash, with no formal interview—five months after being tenured I was asked if I would serve as writing director, and I accepted the challenge, as I was the only Rhet/Comp Ph.D. in the department. When these shifts happen, we are called to confront the same masculinist agendas, hierarchies, and attitudes that existed in our periphery only a short while ago as we muddled through six hard years of work, hoping for the security of tenure. In our new positions, whether long term or interim, feminist leaders must work to establish our good will toward those whom we serve. Our own roots can be a powerful ally in impelling us to act on our colleagues' behalf. A reflection from Eileen Schell (2003) can act as a starting point in supporting the claim that even though our own titles, access, and labor dynamics may change, our own connections with an invariably contingent past must remain strong if we wish to foster trust with our colleagues—their struggles mirror our own, no matter how far in the past they might be:

As an adjunct and a graduate student, I had ample opportunity to observe how graduate students' and adjuncts' teaching and interactions with students and their personal lives were affected by low pay, short-term contracts, inadequate office space, and lack of insurance.

(33)

Truth be told, were it not for a few serendipitous circumstances, I would likely still be patching together adjunct positions to do what I love: teach writing. This knowledge is one tool that allows me to take stock whenever possible of my colleagues' and students' needs. In my writing pedagogy course, I inform students about listservs such as Writing Program Administrators Listserv (WPA-L) and movements such as the National Adjunct Walkout Day, not to deter them from the teaching profession, but rather to encourage them to rhetorically eavesdrop on the labor issues that plague our profession.

Eavesdropping on Professional Conversations to Empower and Implement Change

Although I act as the sole WPA on campus, I involve faculty collaboratively in planning faculty development, circulating questionnaires about topics they feel are most urgent; I meet weekly with our group of graduate students to go over assignment design; I make sure everyone has an office; and I do what I can to reward the monumental efforts displayed by non-tenure track faculty in the areas of scholarship and service. It is encouraging to see that this very issue has been mentioned in a broader and timely discussion of non-tenure track faculty on the WPA-L, where Seth Kahn (2016) rightly observed that "the myth that NTT [Non-Tenure Track] don't and don't want to do research is deeply destructive, and anything that enables us to say 'Adjuncts don't do research' is a bad thing'" (May 29). But more importantly, I listen constantly and "eavesdrop," which is a strategy suggested by Krista Ratcliffe. Ratcliffe (2000) defines rhetorical eavesdropping as an "ethical rhetorical tactic" and positions it as a means to learn from others with true situated knowledge (graduate assistants, adjuncts, non-tenure track and tenure track faculty). Rhetorical eavesdropping is essentially the following: "Standing outside, in an uncomfortable spot, on the border of knowing and not knowing, granting others the inside position, listening to learn" (90).

The ideal outcome of rhetorical eavesdropping for a feminist academic leader, insofar as I have experienced it, is to use what I hear to address and possibly even solve a common frustration before it bubbles over into a smoldering widespread discontentment. Eavesdropping for the past 18 years on the WPA-L discussion list has equipped me with endless anecdotal evidence to use in response to discussions on everything from assignment design to formal evaluations of instructor teaching effectiveness. And I believe it is imperative that a feminist academic leader eavesdrop on these places where professional conversations happen and harsh realities are brought to light without the veneer of self-censorship in a peer reviewed publication.

Recently, a colleague visited with me about a troublesome situation with students who continually sought black-and-white responses to questions in his composition course. I had heard the same refrain before from other colleagues, but this time, as a result of both eavesdropping and more direct discussion, I decided to act. I provided all composition faculty with a copy of Perry and Magolda's taxonomy (from Erika Lindemann's 2001 *A Rhetoric for Writing Teachers*) which explains that students learn in a variety of contexts, ranging from absolute knowing to independent knowing. I added a note explaining what this taxonomy meant in terms of our own reasoning/researching/writing skills in relation to those of our novice writer students, and also how I thought it might help them in their classes. This act showed my colleagues that I eavesdrop rhetorically and act with their best interests in mind and will provide, to the best of my ability, a sound explanation for any pedagogical suggestions.

Trust and Care Work: Foundations for Feminist Academic Leadership

My job as a feminist academic leader is rooted in establishing and maintaining trust. Revisiting Carol Gilligan's work on the ethics of care, as well as scholarship on feminist standpoint theory, has helped me to untangle my complex relationship with this administrative post. Care, in Gilligan's paradigm, "retains its connection to the 'feminine'" (Tong 1998, 81), and she believes that "women tend to espouse an ethics of care that stresses relationships and responsibilities, whereas men tend to espouse an ethics of justice that stresses rules and rights" (80). Women's discussions of morality also make them "center discussions of morality around people's wants, needs, interests, and aspirations" (85). Although I do acknowledge and balk somewhat at the stark essentialism guiding Gilligan's assertions, I cannot also help but notice that in my approach to this leadership position, and in the rhetorical choices I make in it, I too am guided mostly by what I believe others want and need, because I recognize that every single departmental member is essential.

Dynamic shifts in personnel, enrollment, and the attitudes and actions of those in upper administration toward faculty in different ranks will inevitably put the feminist leader in the uncomfortable position of negotiating to achieve decisions that affect colleagues. Sometimes these might land that leader and their colleagues in a kind of lose/lose situation. "When no option exists that can be construed as being in the best interest of everyone," writes Gilligan (1977, 496), "when responsibilities conflict and decision entails the sacrifice of somebody's needs, then the woman confronts the seemingly impossible task of choosing the victim." Academe is rife with such cruelties—search committees in which qualified candidates are excluded in the quest for one new hire, rising class caps that support a surge in enrollment but alter working conditions for faculty, and the list goes on. In situations where I have had a hand in a decision that affected my colleagues, I have remained open and transparent about the process and the outcome. But there remains in all of these situations an uneasiness about the matrices of power in academe that seem to inevitably victimize someone.

Conclusion: Feminist Leadership Invites Everyone into the Conversation

A standpoint, Kristen Intemann (2010) explains, is "said to be *achieved* through a critical, conscious reflection on the ways in which power structures and resulting social locations influence knowledge production" (785). Perhaps a great advantage to feminist academic leaders is that no matter how high we climb in the ivory tower, we still retain a bit of that otherness which compels us to acknowledge these inequities and the ways in which we can act to improve the working lives of fellow faculty and staff. While we go about our day-to-day tasks, we also cultivate an evolving standpoint that considers the lives, desires, and needs of those around us, and how those are affected by sexism inherent in the academy. And although complete empathy may not be impossible, as "social position shapes and limits what we can know because it influences the kinds of experiences one has (784)," we must still work hard to bring the voices of marginalized faculty into the important conversations that impact their working conditions. Sometimes we need to step back and allow our contingent and non-tenure track faculty colleagues acts as leaders as well, respecting their roots in the community and the institution (Maisto 2012, 193). The use of feminist rhetorical strategies, as well as a constant and careful reflection on how our own understanding of ethical dilemmas weighs on our duties as leaders, can bolster our ability to do needed work within gendered systems of oppression.

References

Beauvoir, Simone de. (1949, 1989). *The Second Sex*. New York: Vintage Books.
Bitzer, Lloyd. (1968). "The Rhetorical Situation." *Philosophy and Rhetoric*, 1 (1): 1–14.

Bosquet, Marc. (2008). *How the University Works: Higher Education and the Low-Wage Nation*. New York: New York University Press.

Bosquet, Marc. (2009). "Higher Exploitation: An Interview with Marc Bosquet." *Minnesota Review*, 71–72: 101–122.

Cixous, Helene. (1991). "Coming to Writing." In *"Coming to Writing" and Other Essays* edited by Deboah Jenson, 1–58. Cambridge: Harvard University Press.

Enos, Theresa. (1996). *Gender Roles and Faculty Lives in Rhetoric and Composition*. Carbondale, IL: Southern Illinois University Press.

Foss, Sonja and Cindy Griffin. (1995). "Beyond Persuasion: A Proposal for Invitational Rhetoric." *Communication Monographs*, 62: 2–18.

Gilligan, Carol. (1977). "In a Different Voice: Women's Conceptions of Self and Morality." *Harvard Educational Review*, 47 (4): 481–517.

Gladstein, Jill and Dara Rossman Ragaignon. (2012). *Writing Program Administration at Small Liberal Arts Colleges*. Anderson: Parlor Press.

Glenn, Cheryl. (2002). "Silence: A Rhetorical Art for Resisting Discipline(s)." *Journal of Advanced Composition*, 22 (2): 261–291.

Intemann, Kristen. (2010). "25 Years of Standpoint Feminism and Standpoint Theory: Where Are We Now?" *Hypatia*, 25 (4): 778–794.

Kahn, Seth. (May 29, 2016). "Re: CCCC Statement on NTT Writing Faculty." Message to Writing Program Administrators Listserv [WPA-L].

Maisto, Maria. (2012). "Taking Heart, Taking Part: New Faculty Majority and the Praxis of Contingent Faculty Activism." In *Embracing Non-Tenure Track Faculty: Changing Campuses for the New Faculty Majority*, edited by Adrianna Kezar, 190–204. New York: Routledge.

Mountz, Alison, Anne Bonds, Becky Mansfield, Jenna Loyd, Jennifer Hyndman, Margaret Walton-Roberts, Ranu Basu, Risa Whitson, Roberta Hawkins, Trina Hamilton, and Winifred Curran. (2015). "For Slow Scholarship: A Feminist Politics of Resistance Through Collective Action in the Neoliberal University." *ACME: An International E-Journal for Critical Geographies*, 14 (4): 1235–1259.

Ratcliffe, Krista. (1995). "Listening to Cassandra: A Materialist-Feminist Expose of the Necessary Relations Between Rhetoric and Hermeneutics." *Studies in the Literary Imagination*, 28 (2): 63–77.

———. (1999). "Rhetorical Listening: A Trope for Interpretive Invention and a 'Code of Cross-Cultural Conduct.'" *College Composition and Communication*, 51 (2): 195–224.

———. (2000). "Eavesdropping as Rhetorical Tactic: History, Whiteness, and Rhetoric." *Journal of Advanced Composition*, 20 (1): 87–119.

Schell, Eileen. (2003). "Materialist Feminism and Composition Studies: The Practice of Critique and Activism in an Age of Globalization." In *Fractured Feminisms*, edited by Laura Gray-Rosendale and Gil Harotoonian, 31–43. New York: SUNY Press.

Schell, Eileen and Patricia Lambert Stock. (2001). "Introduction: Working Contingent Faculty in[to] Higher Education." In *Moving a Mountain: Transforming the Role of Contingent Faculty in Composition Studies*, edited by Eileen Schell and Patricia Lambert Stock, 1–44. New York: NCTE Press.

Tomlinson, Barbara. (2010). "Transforming the Terms of Reading: Ideologies of Argument and the 'Trope of the Angry Feminist' in Contemporary US Political and Academic Discourse." *Journal of American Studies*, 44 (1): 101–116.

Tong, Rosemarie Putnam. (1998). *Feminist Thought: A More Comprehensive Introduction*. Boulder: Westview Press.

31 | The Bullying We Don't Talk About

Women Bullying Women in the Academy

Fran Sepler

Malia James was a junior faculty member at a large public university. Serious and thoughtful, she strived to be fully involved in the life of her academic department. Being a philosopher, she had an awareness of challenges for women philosophers, both from her participation in professional groups where the challenges were widely discussed, but also through her experiences as a student, often finding it difficult to get the mentoring and professional support that seemed more accessible to her male colleagues. She was, therefore, thrilled to land in her current department which was reputed to be progressive and was strikingly diverse. There were many accomplished women philosophers, the dean of the school among them.

It was, therefore, jarring to James when, in the midst of her second year on the faculty, she found herself struggling to understand what was happening to her. Janice Wayford, a scholar of some renown and known particularly for her ardent advocacy for women in the field, seemed to be manifesting a profound dislike for James—a dislike that threatened to derail James's career if James couldn't figure it out.

At first, Wayford had been doting, inviting James to coffee, offering advice, even telling her which of the men in the department were "friendly," and which not. As time passed, the invitations diminished and James's invitations to Wayford were rejected, often with a comment that as a second-year professor, James shouldn't really have the time to be "visiting." In department meetings, James noticed that Wayford seemed inattentive when James spoke and even interrupted her a few times. Most recently, James heard from a colleague that Wayford had made a comment deriding James for publishing in "lesser" journals and other sideways comments that weren't overtly critical but undermining. Most seriously, the department chair had recently asked James to meet to discuss some issues raised by students in her "Foundations" class. He told her that the students had suggested she was poorly prepared for several classes and that they were worried about acquiring a fundamental grasp of core information. He suggested she approach Wayford for some advice and assistance in assuring her teaching was "qualifying." The next day, one of her students approached her and told James she felt bad being part of the group that complained to the chair but stated they had been pressured by Wayford to do so.

If the stereotype were accurate, the bully would be the bombastic academic blowhard who neither listens nor cares to engage his female colleagues. The bully would be loud and caustic, pompous and rude, and while being his target would be painful, at least one could take refuge in the company of other women. Women, after all, are collaborative and relational. If only the stereotype were accurate.

In my years of practice as a consultant, investigator and coach, little has surprised me more than the prevalence and aftermath of what I have come to call the "quiet" bully. Quiet bullying is bullying behind closed doors. It involves the small "p" politics of vilification. It is largely, but not exclusively, the province of women, and in academia it is particularly ferocious. It is also a pernicious manifestation of early gender policing—pressure to conform to gender stereotyping. In an ironic way, it is actually a result of girls and women being expected to be relationally skilled.

Gender Socialization and Relational Aggression

Although every woman has a distinctive experience in gender socialization, the stereotype that girls are collaborative and relational is hard to escape.[1] When I visit elementary schools, I see arguing girls told to "work it out," "offer apologies," and "play nice," while warring boys are separated. When we gather the children together and ask them to tell us what they are best at, or what they like best about themselves, the girls are likely to tell you they are nice, or that they have many friends, that they are generous or caring. The boys will instead tell you about something they are good at. The myth of a natural, almost genetic, relational capacity strength is hardwired into women's identity at an early age. If being better at something gets a boy recognition from peers, having lots of friends does the same thing for girls. When boys compete, they strive for mastery. They will physically challenge each other, seek to "win" every game, and roll through rotating roles of dominance. They do so routinely and joyfully, and the loser of any competition knows that they will have the opportunity to be the winner when the next game is played. Boys are taught that it is normal and positive to compete and disagree. For girls, competition is more covert. Being "aggressive" is viewed askance and outside the expectation that girls will be empathetic, supportive, and collaborative. Girls are, nevertheless, fiercely competitive. To be the best, they have to have more and better relationships. When girls compete, they strive for intimacy (Arher and Cote 2005). Who can be the most liked? Talk to a middle school girl socialized this way and she will tell you instantly the relative status and relationship strength of her network or tribe. She will happily describe who is a best friend and who is on the outs—who is having a problem with whom and why that conflict exists. Unlike the boys who live to fight another battle, girls who "lose" may find themselves shunned, badmouthed, or worse, cutting into their very core self-esteem.

Early on, systems of relational reward and punishment pave the path for girls to acquire social currency. Girls learn to build intimacy with other girls by carefully gathering relational "points." They do so by cultivating some while whispering, telling secrets and making fun of others (Bosson 2006). While on its face this appears to be precisely the opposite of what is relational, triangulation is a powerful tool. If I can persuade you to, along with me, dislike a third person, the strength of our relationship grows and the strength of the third party's drops. The most successful at living this gendered reality create carefully cultivated and interlocking networks of friends, making sure to be the lynchpin of the relationships and doling out reward and punishment to those who strengthen or weaken the relational ties. These are the seeds of the proverbial "mean girls" of adolescence.

The mean girls have learned that conforming to gender stereotypes is important. "Aggression" by girls is tied to the implicitly sexist but very real prospect of "unlikeability." Overt acts to attempt mastery by "being better than" or being aggressive place girls squarely in competition with boys. Gender policing punishes this territory crossing by taking away their relational currency. The mean girls learn that being mean needs to be strategic. Mean girls learn that relational aggression is a powerful tool to keep themselves in control of their destiny while never appearing to challenge male power. Schools are gendered places, and gender roles are often heavily reinforced. The result is female aggression against females (female to female bullying), an ironic reinforcement of the very oppressive gender roles the aggressor has been subject to herself:

> When women use bullying as a way of interacting with other women, they become complicit in reproducing systems that oppress women, further marginalizing themselves and other females. Each act of bullying marks targets (i.e., women) as deserving of abuse and disrespect.
>
> (Lutkin-Sandvik and Dickenson 2012)

The female bullies, or the mean girls, become artful at what Kaj Björkqvist describes as "**indirect aggression**" (Björkqvist and Lagerspetz 1992), hostile behavior that is carried out in order to harm an opponent without "outing" or being identified as the aggressor. Crick and Grotpeter describe "**relational aggression**" as behavior, either over or covert that is intended to harm others via damage to relationships or group inclusion (Crick and Grotpeter 1995). These are the tools of the quiet bully. They seize on the target's identity-driven need to be in a relationship to feel successful and then betray that need to up their own stock. Then the mean girls go to work.

Woman-on-Woman Bullying in the American Workplace

A 2009 survey of 1,000 American workers released by the San Francisco–based Employment Law Alliance found that 45% of respondents had been bullied at work and that 40% of the reported bullies were women. They reported that female bullies directed their hostilities toward other women 80% of the time—up 9% since 2007. Male bullies, by contrast, were generally equal opportunity tormentors.

A 2011 survey of 1,000 working women by the American Management Association found that 95% of them believed they were undermined by another woman at some point in their careers. Quiet bullies use a variety of predictable forms of relational and social aggression. The most common are

- Planting false or partially false narratives about targets;
- Damning with faint praise—offering a compliment, and quickly dialing it back with a statement of deficit;
- Using others to lodge complaints about the target;
- Demonstrating apparent care and concern to build trust and then taking advantage of trust to embarrass or humiliate the target by sharing information provided under the guise of "friendship" or mentoring;
- Gaslighting; telling a target that the target has made an error or insulting the target, then denying that they have done or said what they did or said;
- Refusal to engage, avoiding, or shunning;
- Moving the goalposts: stating objectives or benchmarks only to have them change when the target reaches them;
- Shunning or ostracizing the target;
- Recommending that others complain about the target.

Simply by virtue of identifying the most common tactics of quiet bullies, one can discern that unlike the physically intimidating "loud bully," the behavior is often covert, easily denied, and strikes as often indirectly as directly.

One of the most trying qualities of quiet bullies, having mastered the "rules of the game" in relational warfare, is that they tend to be very, very good at managing their relationships with their own superiors. Just as the "mean girls" carefully calculate how to keep their currency high by strategically engaging and alienating with others, the quiet bully has a keen sense that being liked and respected by their superiors is key to maintaining their powerful hold on others (Keashly 2012).

Layla Mason was the head of finance for a mid-sized university. Her office was viewed as one of the most high-performing administrative departments on campus and Mason a respected senior leader. One thing that the president of the university system found most impressive about Mason was the engagement and loyalty of her staff. Beyond consistently meeting deadlines, their printed products were always world class and unassailable. Mason had the confidence of the administration so profoundly that when the University System's flagship campus had a scandal in its finance department, Mason was tapped to lead that department out of its crisis. While on this temporary assignment, she learned that two of her key staff had been terminated for misconduct, and that Maya Kimball, the interim leader (who would be returning to her position as a direct report of Mason), had been the one to work with internal investigators and human resources to bring about the terminations. Mason wrote a letter of praise to Kimball with copies to the President's Cabinet. She praised Kimball's ethics and courage and expressed gratitude for Kimball's "firm hand on the wheel" while Mason had been called to service elsewhere.

Upon her return to campus, Mason met with the head of human resources for a "debrief" in which she quickly expressed frustration with her understanding that that Kimball was not supposed to make "major personnel changes" in Mason's absence. Further, she asked the HR director if the investigation had considered prior "bad blood" between Kimball and the terminated employees. Behind closed doors with Kimball for the first time, Mason asked Kimball if she would be able to continue as a "mere employee" after "enjoying the fruits of power" over her co-workers and suggested a realignment of Kimball's duties to involve more independent work and fewer collaborative assignments.

Within a month, under the guise of "reorienting," Mason held one-on-one meetings with all of her direct reports and their direct reports, a rather unusual depth for Mason's communications. After one of these meetings, Roger Gray, a colleague of Kimball's, asked her to join him outside the office for coffee. He told her that he, and several of his direct reports, had been asked very pointed questions about Kimball, her leadership and her style. He told her that he didn't know what was going on, but that his instincts were that she should be speaking to her union representative. Kimball decided not to do so but did speak with a counselor from the EAP program about her increasing level of anxiety, her sense that she was under investigation, and her feelings of helplessness. The counselor suggested she take a "mental health day," which Kimball did. When she returned, she learned that there had been a hastily called "all hands meeting" to discuss a proposed reorganization. While no names were attached, an organizational chart had been circulated that had Kimball's current position reporting to a now-peer. Kimball made an appointment to speak with Mason. When she arrived at Mason's office, she found both the Department's HR representative and her union representative waiting for her. She learned she was being placed on a Performance Improvement Plan for her poor relationships and lack of candor regarding prior conflicts with the terminated employees.

The special betrayal of the woman-bullied woman can't be understated. For if the aggression is relational, the consequences cut directly into the target's own sense of competence and identity. Being shunned or denigrated undermines the target's sense of identity as powerfully as it bolsters the aggressor. The target is not harmed just by the bullying behavior but also by the larger institution's response to their coping or adapting to the situation. This, the "death spiral" of workplace victimization, is not unlike that manifested in protected class harassment, but the key difference is that protected class harassment is illegal, and there are remedies available within and outside the institution. In the case of workplace bullying, and especially same-gender bullying, the target may not even have a name for what is happening (Crothers and Lipinski 2009).

The Adaptive, Maladaptive Spiral of Workplace Bullying

In the death spiral, the target of bullying begins to feel stress of a high magnitude when in the workplace or even when away from the workplace but contemplating returning to the workplace. The stress may at first be manageable but, as time goes on, it becomes intrusive. Wired to avoid pain, the human brain works to keep the target away from the source of the stress. The target may awaken to somatic symptoms or intense anxiety, making a call-in an easy choice (O'Donnell and MacIntosh 2010). The target may self-sabotage, failing to fill the gas tank on a Sunday night and finding themselves on the road's shoulder on Monday morning. This phenomena—**absenting**—

may not be as overt as actually calling in sick. It might take the form of avoiding certain parts of the workplace that trigger anxieties—avoiding meetings, no longer joining colleagues for informal gatherings—or it may be digital absenting; focusing only on cyberspace and having limited human contact in the real world. This very primitive survival tactic has limited utility. Absence is generally not acceptable in a work environment and certainly not in the academic workplace where service and teaching are part of the evaluative criterion. Too much, or too visible, absenting will generally result in negative feedback, which will compel the target to acknowledge that they must change their tactic to respond to increasing feelings of anger, anxiety, fear, shame, or depression.

If absenting is not an option, **adaptation** is. The most common form of adaptation is attitudinal (Cortina 2001). Needing to be at work, one not need be vulnerable more than absolutely necessary. By adjusting her attitude, the target can arm herself emotionally, rebel against the work climate, and create at least a veneer of emotional and psychological insulation. Common forms of attitudinal adaptation include becoming sullen and withdrawn, creating alliances with other unhappy persons in the workplace, and becoming combative or engaging in passive aggressive behavior. This type of adaptation is the reason the term "death spiral" is applicable to target responses to women-on-women bullying. In order to survive the very environment in which the bullying is happening, the target now looks unstable, incompetent, or both. This is precisely the moment the bully has been planning for. Unable to seek help for fear of reprisal, the target has now begun to "look like" a problem employee. As the target adapts and behaves in unlikeable ways, and even destructive ways in the workplace, her colleagues will flee from her. The bully continues, on the other hand, to "look like" a reasonable person. Soon enough, the target will begin to manifest performance problems such as missed deadlines, canceled classes, research errors, and failed submissions. The spiral has completed.

Ironically, it is often just when the bottom of the spiral has been reached that the target decides that she has no choice but to complain—to a dean, a provost, a chair, or an HR department that has been dealing with the manifestations of this individual's dysfunction. The likelihood that the complaint will be received neutrally or impartially is, therefore, limited. Rather, there may be an assumption that the reason the complaint is being made is to protect the target from the consequences of their own poor performance, attitude, and attendance. Often the agents of the college or university will give low credence to the target on the basis of perceived instability. Thus, the target is often doubly stigmatized—first by the bullying conduct itself, and second by institutional bias borne of adaptive behavior.

Bullying is often intersectional. People of color report being bullied far more than White people (Namie 2014). LGBTQ people report being bullied more than gender-conforming or heterosexual people (Career Builder, Inc. 2014). Unlike explicit or overt bullying which might trigger a claim under anti-discrimination policies (to the extent such policies exist: LGBTQ people are not protected from discrimination in the workplace in some states. Some states offer protection from discrimination only on the basis of sexual orientation and not gender identity, and others offer protections only to public sector employees.). Covert bullying will rarely reach the standard required to suggest the conduct is discriminatory harassment. Rather, it will layer on top of institutional and individual discrimination and marginalization, causing the person who is not a member of the dominant culture to stagger under dual duress and likely destabilize more quickly (Berlingeiri 2015).

Solutions Are Elusive

The plight of the woman-bullied woman points out the powerful need for deliberately constructed networks of allies in academic institutions. When one is covertly bullied, it is often impossible to turn to near colleagues for help; either they have been co-opted by the bully or are fearful of becoming the bully's next target. Rather, the support and help must come from those with sufficient social and intellectual distance to offer the target credence and the opportunity to be heard. For those fortunate enough to work in a large university, an Ombuds office is often the repository of these complaints and, therefore, can observe patterns over time (Hollis 2016). When this is possible, the simple act of validating the target might be enough to embolden her seeking help through more formal channels. For those without access to an Ombuds, the isolation of the bullying can be withering. Women-focused organizations meant to support and empower women sometimes are reluctant to recognize woman-to-woman abuse or bullying and deflect the target (Chestler 2001). Well-meaning administrators sometimes diminish complaining targets as experiencing stereotypical infighting rather than recognizing the intensity and impact of bullying.

It is an unfortunate reality that most woman-to-woman bullying goes largely unreported and persists until the target either voluntarily leaves the situation or is denied tenure or terminated for cause. Organizations interested in giving serious attention to the prevalence of this type of bullying would be well served to ensure thorough exit interviews with departing staff and faculty members and to watch for high levels of attrition in particular departments. From an investigative standpoint, interviewing previous employees and faculty members is often the only way to establish that patterns of destructive behavior are taking place.

Having investigated claims of bullying over 30 years, one of the most stunning patterns I find is that women who bully other women, particularly women in high-ranking positions, are often dumbfounded to learn that their staff or department has complained and provided ample testimony to support a claim of bullying. Recently, a woman executive whose 14 staff members had unanimously described her as "abusive," "toxic," "manipulative," and "ruthless" arrived at her interview with no idea that she had been the subject of complaints. As I began to ask her general questions about her approach to leadership, she cut me off and told me, "Just talk to my people. They think I'm a terrific leader." Had this been the first time I had seen such a complete "blind side," I would have been stunned, but it was at least the twentieth time, and I was no longer surprised. As with other cases, her own superiors insisted that she had been spoken to or coached in the past about her behavior. This suggests that women who bully women may not get early feedback that is appropriate in form or content. It is quite possible that those who manage women who treat other women abusively downplay or underestimate the damage that relational aggression can cause and treat the behavior more as a "style" issue than an issue of abusive conduct (Neuman 2012). This suggests that education on the dynamics of relational aggression for organizational leaders is critical. They must view "quiet" bullying as seriously as they view the screamer or the thrower and provide strong feedback at the first sign of a problem. If a bullying person knows her career is at stake, she may take a greater interest in making behavioral changes than if she is merely told that she has a "style issue." If the problem is recognized early, organizations can undertake a process of "action learning" in which 360-degree feedback and other non-punitive methods are used to bring the concerns out of the bullying person's blind spot and into the light (Crawshaw 2010).

Ultimately, the prevention of bullying anywhere in an academic institution is about attending to the larger culture and the development of faculty and faculty leadership. Bullying thrives in cultures where covert exercise of power is rewarded rather than rejected. It thrives where internal competition is stoked in lieu of a collaborative environment. It grows when conflict is shoved under the rug and candor is considered risky. These cultural attributes are part of the overall climate of some academic institutions and can change only when there is a long-term leadership commitment to do so. While policies for reporting and addressing workplace bullying might provide some relief for the courageous few who wish to report it, a far greater commitment to individual dignity and overall civility might make a particular institution unattractive to someone who prefers to operate the way that covert bullies do.

Strategies for Targets

Early Intervention: The best, and sometimes the only, time to stop a bully without using a formal reporting system is prior to entering the "death spiral." This means that survival is dependent upon trusting one's own instincts that something is "not right" in the way one is being treated. In instances in which a person perceives he or she is being targeted, sabotaged, or manipulated, it is important that he or she documents carefully what has happened in order to be sure to preserve the facts. The process of writing out an incident can also clarify for the target what to say in a conversation with a support person or the source of the bullying. The documentation should include the following:

- What exactly happened?
- What information were you given?
- What were your expectations?
- How did the situation differ from what you expected?
- How did you react?
- How did this affect you, and how is it currently affecting you?
- Was anyone else involved? How? (Adapted from McCulloch 2010)

A target can choose to act on only one or two incidents by providing feedback to the perceived bad actor. In this case, the conversation should focus on *perceptions* and *outcomes.* Starting with facts (this is what happened), moving to perceptions (here is the way it seemed to me), and then to outcome (this is how it has affected me) can begin a productive dialogue. This strategy is, however, not recommended if the behavior has been going on for a long time or the target is "in the spiral" and having psychological, physical, or emotional pain.

When the Problem Is Ongoing: Once a target is "in the spiral," and attendance, performance, or attitudinal shifts are beginning to occur, it is essential that he or she seeks assistance from others. Armed with good documentation, a target can seek help with coping from a counselor, can seek intervention from a personnel officer or manager, can seek support from his or her social network, or seek advice from mentors or peers. The goal of seeking support and help is to:

- Keep in perspective that the problem is real and that the target is not to blame,
- Find healthy ways to cope with the real stress and pain of being treated abusively,
- Be affirmed and emotionally validated that the situation is difficult,
- Assess ongoing risk,
- Develop a problem-solving strategy and support for each step. That problem-solving strategy could be
  - Ask for a formal investigation into the conduct (if the institution has anti-bullying protections), with the possibility of sanctions to the bullying party;
  - Seek a facilitated conversation or shuttle mediation with the bullying individual;
  - Find a path to structurally reduce the opportunities for ongoing bullying;
  - Seek a climate assessment that does not name the target as a complainant.

Leaving as a Strategy: As discussed earlier, institutional support is critical to being able to address all bullying, and especially woman-to-woman bullying. An organization that educates widely, responds seriously to concerns, and promotes a culture of respect will retain its talent by working hard to find resolutions to workplace problems. An institution that does not make that commitment will struggle with retention. Ultimately, if one works in an organization that fails to respond, it is important to assess all of one's options. At the end of the spiral is the possibility of a lifelong case of post-traumatic stress disorder and health problems (Birkeland and Einarsen

2010). For this reason, it is critical that leaving always be identified as a potentially life-saving option for someone being bullied. This, of course, is an unjust result, but one which is necessary when an institution has made protecting the bully its priority.

I am confident that higher education is taking bullying far more seriously than in the past. Public institutions in particular are seeking to codify an anti-bullying sentiment in statements of principle or actual policies (see, for instance, Schmidt 2014). Many have instituted complaint processes and resolution options for those who are aggrieved. Much education is needed about woman-on-woman bullying and relational aggression, how it manifests, and how it can disguise itself as a personality conflict or style issue or play into gender stereotypes about women "just not getting along." It is a pernicious and damaging problem that affects women's capacity to succeed in academia.

Note

1   While the binary of "girls" and "boys" is central to this essay, it must be noted that those children whose gender identity does not fall into the binary struggle with these stereotypes in ways beyond the scope of this essay.

Bibliography

Arher, J., and Cote, S. (2005). "Sex Differences in Aggressive Behavior." In *Developmental Origins of Aggression*, edited by R. E. Tremblay, 425–443. New York: Guilford Press.

Berlingeiri, A. (2015). "Workplace Bullying: Exploring an Emerging Framework." *Work, Employment and Society*, 29 (2): 342–353.

Birkeland, M., and S. Einarsen. (2010). "Outcomes of Exposure to Workplace Bullying: A Meta-Analytic Review." *Work and Stress*, 26: 309–332.

Björkqvist, K., K. Lagerspetz, and A. Kaukiainen. (1992). "Do Girls Manipulate and Boys Fight? Developmental Trends in Regard to Direct and Indirect Aggression." *Aggressive Behavior*, 2: 117–127.

Bosson, Je. (2006). "Interpersonal Chemistry Through Negativity: Bonding by Sharing Negative Attitudes About Others." *Personnel Relations*, 13 (2): 135–150.

Career Builder, Inc. (2014). *Career Builder Survey.*

———. (September 18, 2014). *Career Builder Workplace Bullying Survey.*

Chestler, P. (2001). *Womans Inhumanity to Woman.* New York: Nations Books.

Cortina, Le. (2001). "Incivility in the Workplace: Incidence and Impact." *Journal of Occupational Health Psychology*, 6 (1): 64–80.

Crawshaw, L. (2010). "Coaching Abrasive Leaders: Using Action Research to Reduce Suffering and Increase Productivity in Organizations." *International Journal of Coaching in Organizations*, 29 (8), 50–77.

Crick, N. E., and J. Grotpeter. (June 1995). "Relational Aggression, Gender, and Social-Psychological Adjustment." *Child Development*, 710–722.

Crothers, L., J. Lipinski, and M. C. Minutolo. (2009). "Cliques, Rumors, and Gossip by the Water Cooler: Female Bullying in the Workplace." *The Psychologist Manager Journal*, 12: 97–110.

Hollis, L. (2016). "Canary in the Mine: Ombuds Office as First Alert for Workpalce Bullying on Campus." *Journal of the International Ombudsman Association*, 9: 23–31.

Keashly, L. (2012). "Workplace Bullying and Gender: It's Complicated." In *Gender and the Dysfunctional Workplace*, edited by Suzy Fox and Terri R. Lituchy, 78–95. Northampton, MA: S. F. Edward Elgar Publishing.

Lutkin-Sandvik, P., and E. Dickenson. (2012). "Priming, Painting, Peeling and Polishing: Constructing and Deconstructing the Woman Bullying Woman Identify at Work." In *Gender and the Dysfunctional Workplace*, edited by S. F., 61–77. Northampton, MA: Edward Elgar Publishing.

McCulloch, B. (2010). "Dealing with Bullying Behavior in the Workplace: What Works? A Practitioners View." *Journal of the American Ombuds Association*, 3 (2):39–51.

Namie, G. (2014). *Survey of Workplace Bullying.* Benecia, CA: Workpalce Bullying Institute.

Neuman, J. H. (2012). "Gender and Sex Differences in the Form of Workplace Aggression." In *Gender and the Dysfunctional Workplace*, edited by Suzy Fox and Terri R. Lituchy, 14–29. Northhampton, MA: Edwin Elgar Publishing.

O'Donnell, S., and J. A. MacIntosh. (2010). "A Theoretical Understanding of Sickness Absence Among Women Who Have Experienced Workplace Bullying." *Qualitative Health Research* 20 (4): 439–452.

Schmidt, P. (April 7, 2014). "University of Massachusetts Mounts Assault on Workplace Bullying." *The Chronicle of Higher Education.*

32 Infographic

TYPES OF SEXISM | 01

	STRUCTURAL	INTERPERSONAL
HOSTILE	Sexual assault, sexual harassment or gender-based harassment, workplace hostility, bullying	Microaggressions Gaslighting
BENEVOLENT	Expectations of service, invisible labor, assessment, assumptions about needs, demands for proof	Chivalry Paternalism

02 MICROAGGRESSIONS

Microaggressions that are often unconsciously delivered in subtle snubs or dismissive looks, gestures, and tones.

These exchanges are so pervasive and automatic in daily conversations and interactions that they are often dismissed and glossed over as being innocent and innocuous.

Figure 32.1 The Surviving Sexism Infographic

03 OTHER COMMON BEHAVIORS

INTERSECTIONAL
ASYMMETRIES

TOKENISM

GASLIGHTING

 The Talk   Women warning other women about men instead of addressing the harasser in a larger context

04 STRATEGIES

Structural

IDEOLOGICAL

Address systemic power

Emphasize diversity

Question leadership models

Cultivate awareness of Title IX requirements

Develop shared and stated values

MATERIAL

Family leave

Tenure clock stopping

Transparent pay and promotion guidelines, tenure

Clear guidelines around accommodating 'off-site' teaching (online activities to replace f2f work)

Clear and transparent policies around student supervision (especially for off-site activities like field trips)

Policies around "exit interviews" to identify

 &

Interpersonal

Raise consciousness

Question the script

Be a feminist killjoy

Listen to people

Take bullying seriously

Understand experiences as complex

Don't offer alternate explanations

Give credit

Mentoring/reciprocity/ongoing and sustainable

Support structures (online, at the conference, mentoring, bibliography)

Needs assessment surveys

Undergraduate and adjunct mentoring

Develop shared and stated values

Make visible the labor of mentoring (letters of support for promotion, etc.)

Networking/coalition building

The included information was drawn from our chapter contributors.

powered by

Piktochart
make information beautiful

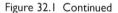

Figure 32.1 Continued

Contributors

Jen Almjeld is an Associate Professor of Writing, Rhetoric and Technical Communication at James Madison University, teaching courses in gender, media theory, and composition. Her publications appear in *Computers and Composition, Kairos,* and *Girlhood Studies.* She also directs the Girlhood Remixed camp for tween girls interested in multimodal composition.

Kristine L. Blair is Dean of the College of Liberal Arts and Social Sciences at Youngstown State University and former Professor of English at Bowling Green State University, where she taught courses in digital rhetoric and scholarly publication in the Rhetoric and Writing Doctoral Program. Blair currently serves as editor of both the international print journal *Computers and Composition* and its separate companion journal *Computers and Composition Online.*

Laurie Ann Britt-Smith is Director of the Center for Writing at the College of the Holy Cross and former Associate Professor of English at the University of Detroit Mercy. In addition to her work in writing studies, she is interested in and has published work on rhetorics of social justice and the intersections of identity, public discourse, and spirituality.

Marilyn J. Bugenhagen, Ph.D. serves as a Faculty Associate in Concordia University–Wisconsin's organizational leadership graduate program. Her higher education experience includes Academic Affairs Associate Vice President, tenured graduate faculty, and Director of Student Services. Her research interests look at the quality of relationship in leader and organizational behavior.

Erica Cirillo-McCarthy currently teaches in the Program in Writing and Rhetoric at Stanford University. Her research interests include writing center and composition pedagogy, multimodal composition, spatial and visual rhetorics, and institutional critique. She has published her research in *Academic Exchange Quarterly* and the *Journal of Global Literacies, Technologies, and Emerging Pedagogies.*

Kirsti Cole is an Associate Professor of Rhetoric, Composition, and Literature at Minnesota State University. She is the faculty chair of the Teaching Writing Graduate Certificate and Masters of Communication and Composition programs. She has published articles in *Feminist Media Studies, College English, Harlot,* and *thirdspace,* and her collection *Feminist Challenges or Feminist Rhetorics?* was published in 2014. Her work ranges the intersections of writing studies, social media, and gendered rhetorics.

E-K. Daufin, Ph.D. (Ph.D. The Ohio State University) is a Professor of Communications at Alabama State University. Her research focuses on White supremacy, patriarchy and capitalism, and weight stigma as social justice issues in the media, higher education culture. She co-authored a *Journalism & Communication Monograph* on women in communication higher education titled *Junior Scholars in Search of Equity for Women and Minorities.* (As a junior scholar at the time, she was unable to get the senior scholars to change the regrettable "women and minorities" part. They said she should have tried harder.) Dr. Daufin also authored a *Journalism Educator* article on a first-of-its-kind national survey titled "Minority Journalism Higher Education Professionals' Job Satisfaction." She is also a Spoken Word social change activist, dancer, musician, National HAES (Health At Every Size) and media and weight expert.

Susan Diab is a visual artist and founder-member of APEC Studios, Hove, UK, whose work is widely exhibited. A Senior Lecturer in Fine Art Critical Practice at the University of Brighton, she created the groundbreaking and unique Fine Art Placement Scheme, earning her a Teaching Excellence Award in 2013. www.susandiab.com

John Draeger is Associate Professor of Philosophy and Director of Scholarship of Teaching and Learning at SUNY Buffalo State. He teaches courses in the history of moral and political philosophy, contemporary ethical issues, and philosophy of law. He divides his scholarly energies between work in social philosophy (e.g., moral critiques of racism, sexism, and homophobia) and work in Scholarship of Teaching and Learning (e.g., metacognition, higher-order thinking, general education, and academic rigor).

Nathan R. Durdella is an Associate Professor in the Department of Educational Leadership and Policy Studies at California State University, Northridge (CSUN), where he teaches graduate-level courses in action research, academic planning, and qualitative research methods and focuses his research on student-faculty interaction, college student transitions, and qualitative dissertation methodology.

Saba Fatima is an Assistant Professor of Philosophy at Southern Illinois University Edwardsville. She has published on social and political issues faced by Muslims in *Social Theory and Practice*, *Hypatia*, and *Social Philosophy Today*. Her research interests include virtue ethics, non-ideal theory, social and political within prescriptive Islam, Muslim/Muslim-American issues within a framework of feminist and race theory.

Bre Garrett is an Assistant Professor of English and Director of the Composition Program at the University of West Florida. She has published on multimodal composing, first-year composition pedagogy, and embodied rhetorics. She is currently researching embodied composing and accessible curricular design. Additionally, she is conducting institutional research on student writing as part of a grant award.

Salma Ghanem is Professor and Dean of the College of Communication at DePaul University. She earned a Ph.D. in journalism from the University of Texas at Austin. Her background blends the theoretical and applied aspects of the field of communication in the areas of leadership and political and intercultural/international communication.

Hawa Ghaus-Kelley, Ed.D., is a Professor at National University, Horizons University and at California State University, Northridge (CSUN), in the Department of Secondary Education, where she teaches graduate-level courses in research methods, action research, and directed comprehensive studies in the Masters in Education Program. She is also the Coordinator for Student Teaching and Performance Assessment for California Teachers. She was a women's rights advocate in her previous profession. Her current research focuses on women's leadership styles and behaviors in academia.

Carol L. Glasser is an Assistant Professor of Sociology at Minnesota State University, Mankato, where she also serves as the Director of the Kessel Peace Institute. Her research examines social movements, critical animal studies, and gender inequality. When she is not researching or writing, she is committed to helping create a more just world through volunteering, advocacy, and activism with various movements advocating for social justice.

Mary Louise Gomez is Professor of Teacher Education at the University of Wisconsin–Madison. She teaches courses for undergraduates concerning social justice and courses for graduate students that focus on life history and narrative. She serves on the editorial boards of *Teaching and Teacher Education* and *Research in the Teaching of English*.

Rochelle Gregory is an English Instructor and Honors Coordinator at North Central Texas College in Corinth, Texas, where she teaches first-year composition and technical writing while overseeing the college's Honors program. She also serves as an Associate Editor of the *KB Journal*.

Anna Grigoryan recently completed an Ed.D. in educational technologies from Pepperdine University's Graduate School of Education and Psychology. She has taught English composition and English for academic purposes at various post-secondary institutions in Kazakhstan, Turkey, Brazil, the U.S., and the United Arab Emirates. Her research focuses on the affordances of digital technologies in instructor feedback and faculty professional development.

Holly Hassel is Professor of English and Gender, Sexuality and Women's Studies at the University of Wisconsin–Marathon County. She has co-authored the introductory women's and gender studies textbook *Threshold Concepts in Women's and Gender Studies* with Christie Launius. She is currently editor of the journal *Teaching English in the Two-Year College*.

Jennifer Heinert is an Associate Professor of English and the Director of the Virtual Teaching and Learning Center at University of Wisconsin Colleges where she teaches writing, literature, and gender and women's studies courses. Her research interests include gender and labor, scholarship of teaching and learning, pedagogies, and multicultural American literature.

Heather Hill-Vásquez is Professor of English and past Director of Women's and Gender Studies at the University of Detroit Mercy. Her recent presentations and publications have focused on *The Hunger Games*, *To Kill a Mockingbird*, a late medieval Nativity Play, Chaucer's Wife of Bath, and phenomenology and women's pain.

Sara Hillin holds a PhD in Rhetoric from Texas Woman's University. She has been a full time faculty member in English at Lamar University in Beaumont, Texas, since 2006. Her research interests include composition theory and practice, feminist pedagogy, and 20th century women's rhetorics.

Ashley Hinck is an Assistant Professor in the Communication Arts Department at the Xavier University. Hinck's research examines fan-based citizenship performances as new civic practices emerging from networked media. Hinck's research has appeared in *Communication Theory*, *Argumentation & Advocacy*, *Transformative Works & Cultures*, and the *Cinema Journal Teaching Dossier*.

Shelly Schaefer Hinck is a Professor in the Communication and Dramatic Arts Department at Central Michigan University. Her research interests include civic engagement, political debates, service-learning, and leadership. Her work has appeared in *Argumentation & Advocacy*, *Scholarship of Teaching and Learning*, *Sex Roles*, and the *American Behavioral Scientist*.

Diane M. Hodge is a Professor of Social Work and the Director of the School of Social Work at Radford University. She has taught courses on social work practice, theory, and feminist-focused electives for 20 years. Her research interests include women's health and mental health, social work practice issues, and teaching methods for online education.

Elise Verzosa Hurley is an Assistant Professor of Rhetoric, Composition, and Technical Communication at Illinois State University. Her research and teaching interests include visual/spatial rhetorics, professional/technical communication, multimodal composition, and community engagement pedagogies. Her scholarship has appeared in *Technical Communication Quarterly, Kairos: A Journal of Rhetoric, Technology, and Pedagogy, Rhetoric Review*, and other edited collections.

Yuko Itatsu, Ph.D., is an Associate Professor in the College of Arts and Sciences at the University of Tokyo. Originally from Japan, she earned a Ph.D. in history from the University of Southern California as a Fulbright Scholar. Her research interests include American pop culture and innovation in global higher education.

Laura Jennings is an Associate Professor of Sociology at the University of South Carolina Upstate. Her research interests include intersecting inequalities of race, social class, gender, and body size. She teaches courses on these topics as well as social statistics and sociology of the family.

Sara Kitsch is a doctoral candidate in the Department of Communication at Texas A&M University. Her research concentrates on rhetoric of women in politics and gender construction in commemorative spaces. Kitsch's recent focus is the First Lady and how discursive performance of the role embodies a particular type of citizenship.

Melissa M. Kozma is Senior Lecturer in Philosophy and Gender, Sexuality, and Women's Studies at the University of Wisconsin, Barron County. Dr. Kozma's research and teaching focus on feminist philosophy, ethics, social theory, and political philosophy as well as race, public policy, and social justice.

Yvette Lapayese is a Professor and Associate Chair of the Department of Specialized Programs in Urban Education at Loyola Marymount University. Her areas of expertise include feminist theories and epistemologies, critical social theories, and critical media literacy. She has published in *Race Ethnicity and Education, Journal of Latinos and Education, Perspectives on Urban Education, and Gender & Education*. Her book *Mother-Scholar: (Re)imagining K-12 Education* was published in 2012.

Ann-Marie Lopez is an Assistant Professor of English at McMurry University in Abilene, Texas, where she teaches First-Year Composition, literature, and film courses. She also develops the curriculum for and teaches the Developmental Composition courses for the University.

Heather Maldonado, Ph.D., serves as the Assistant Dean of University College and Director of Academic Standards for SUNY Buffalo State. Her higher education experience includes professional staff appointments in student affairs and academic affairs, adjunct faculty status, and various positions within shared governance on campus and in the state system. Her scholarship focuses on issues related to gender in higher education.

Katie Manthey is an Assistant Professor of English and Director of the Writing Center at Salem College. Her research and teaching centers on cultural rhetorics, dress studies, fat studies, and civic engagement. She is a body positive activist and moderates the website *Dress Profesh*. Her work has appeared in *Peitho, Jezebel,* and *The Journal of Global Literacies, Technologies, and Emerging Pedagogies.*

Aurora Matzke is an Assistant Professor of English and Writing Program Co-Director at Biola University in La Mirada, California. Working in the areas of feminist rhetorics, open access education programs, and general education reform, Aurora is presently pursuing research on the demonstration of love in public rhetorics.

Karla S. McCain is a Professor of Chemistry and the Director of Accreditation and Assessment at Austin College. She also serves as the Director of the Gender Studies Program, teaches an interdisciplinary course about women and science, and regularly gives presentations about the under-representation of women in STEM.

Meg McGuire is an Assistant Professor of English at the University of Delaware, where she teaches courses in digital media, technical and professional writing, and environmental rhetoric.

Lisa Meloncon is an Associate Professor of Technical Communication at the University of South Florida where she also directs the undergraduate writing program. Her teaching and research focuses on the rhetoric of health and medicine and programmatic and professionalization dimensions of technical and professional communication.

Kristen R. Moore is an Assistant Professor at Texas Tech University. Her research focuses on public forms of technical communication, with a particular focus on planning projects as sites of social (in)justice. She teaches courses on field research, institutional and public policy, and public rhetoric. Her scholarship has been published in a range of edited collections and journals, including *JTWC, JBTC, Programmatic Perspectives,* and *Learning, Media & Technology.*

Jessica Moriarty is a Principal Lecturer at the University of Brighton, where she is course leader on the Creative Writing M.A. and English Literature and Creative Writing B.A. Her research is on autoethnography, writing and community, and writing as craft.

Molly Niesen is Assistant Professor of Communication Studies at Eastern Illinois University. Dr. Niesen's teaching and research interests focus on media, advertising, policy, history, consumer activism, and political economy.

Safiya Umoja Noble is Assistant Professor of Information Studies in the Graduate School of Education and Information Studies at UCLA. Dr. Noble's teaching and research interests focus on culture and technology issues surrounding Internet applications. Dr. Noble is the mother of one boy and bonus mother of a young adult stepdaughter.

Krystia Nora is an Assistant Professor of English at California University of Pennsylvania teaching First-Year Composition courses, the English Capstone, and more. She chairs her department's assessment and composition committees and has published in *Writing on the Edge* and *The CEA Forum.* She is also co-editor of the EAPSU Journal.

Kathryn Northcut is an Associate Professor in Technical Communication at the Missouri University of Science & Technology in Rolla, Missouri. Her scholarship is typically in the areas of visual technical communication and technical communication pedagogy. She is co-editor of *Designing Texts: Teaching Visual Communication,* Baywood, 2013, with Eva R. Brumberger.

Cassandra Phillips is the Writing Program Administrator and an English faculty member at the University of Wisconsin Colleges. She teaches developmental, first-year, and advanced writing. Her research includes gender and labor, writing program administration, student learning, and writing pedagogy.

Christine Quail is Associate Professor of Communication Studies and Multimedia at McMaster University. Dr. Quail's teaching and research interests focus on critical and cultural studies of television, gender, media culture, and political economy. She is the mother of two girls.

Sherry Rankins-Robertson is Associate Vice Chancellor for Academic Affairs at the University of Arkansas at Little Rock (UALR). She joined the UALR in July of 2012 as the Writing Program Administrator in the Department of Rhetoric and Writing. She is currently working on a collaborative edited collection titled *Applications for the Framework for Success in Postsecondary Writing: Scholarship, Theories, and Practice* with Nicholas Behm and Duane Roen. Additionally, she and Joe Lockard are editing a collection titled *Prison Pedagogy*.

Michelle Rodino-Colocino is Associate Professor of Film, Video and Media Studies and Women's, Gender, and Sexuality Studies at Penn State. Dr. Rodino-Colocino's teaching and research interests focus on feminist and critical-cultural studies of media, labor, and activism. She is the mother of one girl.

Diane Rodriguez-Kiino, Ph.D., is an Assistant Professor of Higher Education Leadership at California Lutheran University. In 2014–2015, she taught courses on American higher education as a Fulbright Scholar in Japan. She holds a Ph.D. in education policy with an emphasis on international intercultural education from the University of Southern California.

Heather Rosenfeld is a geography Ph.D. student at the University of Wisconsin–Madison. Her research interests include human and non-human relations, alternative economies, technology and environmental justice, and feminism in the academy. She is currently working on a dissertation on farm animal sanctuaries. Comics sneak into most of her research, teaching, and activism.

Eileen E. Schell is Director of the Composition and Cultural Rhetoric Doctoral Program, Associate Professor of Writing and Rhetoric, and Faculty Affiliate in Women's and Gender Studies at Syracuse University. She currently holds the L. Douglas and Laura J. Meredith Teaching Professorship (2015–2018), the highest teaching honor at Syracuse University. She regularly teaches undergraduate and graduate writing, rhetoric, and creative non-fiction courses. Schell is the author of five books and co-edited collections, including *Gypsy Academics and Mother-Teachers: Gender, Contingent Labor, and Writing Instruction* (Heinemann, 1997) and *Rural Literacies* (Southern Illinois University Press, 2007), co-authored with Kim Donehower and Charlotte Hogg.

Jeanine Weekes Schroer is an Assistant Professor of Philosophy at the University of Minnesota Duluth. Dr. Schroer's teaching and research concern race and racism and feminist ethics and social theory as well as the function of slurs and nonsense in political discourse. In her spare time, she codes in Python and plays with chickens.

Fran Sepler is the President of Sepler & Associates and is best known for her pioneering work in harassment prevention and workplace investigations. She has developed techniques and protocol used by organizations throughout the United States to investigate complaints of workplace misconduct and is the author of "Finding the Facts: What Every Workplace Investigator Needs to Know," published in 2008.

Missy Skurzewski-Servant earned a B.A. in exercise science from Ripon College, a M.S. in kinesiology from UW–Milwaukee, and a Ph.D. in leadership studies from Marian University. Currently the Dean of General Education and Business at Mid-State Technical College, she previously spent nine years as an administrator and professor at the University of Wisconsin–Sheboygan.

Patricia Sullivan directs the graduate program in Rhetoric and Composition at Purdue University, where her recent teaching includes methodology, games and user studies, institutional rhetoric, professional writing theory, and modern rhetoric.

Yuko Takahashi is the Eleventh President of Tsuda College in Tokyo, where she has served as a Professor of English since 1997. In 2013–2014, she served as a Fulbright Scholar at Wellesley College in Massachusetts. She holds a Ph.D. from the University of Kansas and is a widely published author on women and education.

Nicole A. Williams is a faculty member at Bridgewater State University, where she teaches courses in First Year Composition and the Writing and Writing Studies Program. Her research interests include motherhood in academia and pedagogy in the composition classroom.

Amanda Wray is an Assistant Professor of English at the University of North Carolina, Asheville, where she teaches rhetoric, writing, and feminist studies. Her research focuses on anti-oppression rhetorics, contemplative studies, community-engaged pedagogies, writing in the workplace, and oral history.

Lizabeth Zack is an Associate Professor of Sociology at the University of South Carolina Upstate. She teaches courses on social movements, political sociology, and urban sociology. Her research examines political activism in the United States and the Middle East, including current work on environmental activist campaigns in Jordan.

Index

· Lightning Source UK Ltd.
 Milton Keynes UK
 UKOW05f0518251117
313316UK00003B/45/P